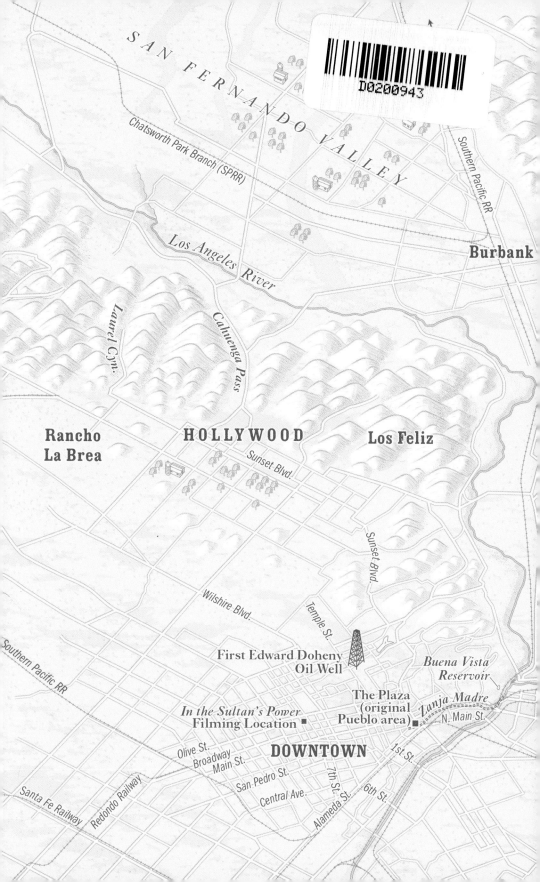

SAN FERNANDO VALLEY

Chatsworth Park Branch (SPRR)

Los Angeles River

Southern Pacific RR

**Burbank**

Laurel Cyn.

Cahuenga Pass

**Rancho La Brea**

**H O L L Y W O O D**

**Los Feliz**

Sunset Blvd.

Sunset Blvd.

Wilshire Blvd.

Temple St.

Southern Pacific RR

**First Edward Doheny Oil Well**

*Buena Vista Reservoir*

*In the Sultan's Power*
Filming Location ■

**The Plaza
(original
Pueblo area)** ▪

*Zanja Madre*

N. Main St.

Olive St.

Broadway

Main St.

**DOWNTOWN**

1st St.

San Pedro St.

7th St.

6th St.

Santa Fe Railway

Redondo Railway

Central Ave.

Alameda St.

D0200943

# THE
# Mirage Factory

## ALSO BY GARY KRIST

*Empire of Sin*

*City of Scoundrels*

*The White Cascade*

*Extravagance*

*Chaos Theory*

*Bad Chemistry*

*Bone by Bone*

*The Garden State*

# THE
# Mirage Factory

## ILLUSION, IMAGINATION, AND THE
## INVENTION OF LOS ANGELES

## Gary Krist

CROWN
NEW YORK

Library of Congress Cataloging-in-Publication Data is available upon request.

ISBN 978-0-451-49638-6
Ebook ISBN 978-0-451-49640-9

Printed in the United States of America

Book design by Elina Nudelman
Jacket design by Elena Giavaldi
Jacket photographs: (left) From the Fletcher photograph collection, courtesy of
the California History Room, California State Library, Sacramento, California;
(right) USC Libraries. California Historical Society Colletion, 1860–1960

10 9 8 7 6 5 4 3 2 1

First Edition

FOR ELIZABETH

# CONTENTS

# THE
# Mirage Factory

# AUTHOR'S NOTE

*The Mirage Factory* is a work of nonfiction, adhering strictly to the historical record and incorporating no invented dialogue or other undocumented re-creations. Unless otherwise attributed, anything between quotation marks is either actual dialogue (as reported by a witness or in a newspaper) or else a citation from a memoir, book, letter, police report, court transcript, or other document, as cited in the endnotes. In some quotations I have, for clarity's sake, corrected the original spelling, syntax, word order, or punctuation.

# Prologue

*Los Angeles, the Invented City*

# An Echo of Dynamite

The gatehouse blew shortly after one a.m.—a powerful blast that ricocheted off the wall of mountains to the west and resounded across the dark, lonely valley. Another sound followed a moment later. It was less violent but more ominous: the low, rolling, slowly deepening roar of rushing water.

Someone had bombed the Los Angeles Aqueduct. A case of stolen dynamite, fitted out with a blasting cap and a makeshift fuse, had exploded under the Alabama Gatehouse, located about 210 miles north of the city, near the remote town of Lone Pine in the Owens Valley. One of the building's five spillgates—thick metal doors designed to release excess water from the aqueduct after heavy storms—had been ripped apart, allowing two hundred cubic feet of water per second to pour uselessly down a spillway and out across the parched valley floor. By the time the aqueduct's flow could be shut off at another gate some twenty miles north of the breach, over one hundred million gallons would be wasted—in one of the driest corners of the country, in the middle of one of the worst droughts in years.

By the time Detective Jim Bilyeu of the Inyo County Sheriff's Department arrived on the scene, a small crowd of Lone Pine residents had gathered near the still-smoking gatehouse. Some were actually applauding the destruction, pounding each other on the back in celebration. Hostility toward the aqueduct—and toward the distant, insatiably thirsty city that had built it—was widespread across the sparsely populated Owens Valley in 1976, and many locals felt that the L.A. Department of Water and Power (LADWP) had been dealt a well-deserved blow. "If I ever find out who bombed the gates," one man allegedly remarked, "I'll buy him a steak dinner."

This resentment was not new. Ever since the city built the aqueduct in the early 1900s, tensions between Los Angeles and the Owens Valley had been high. Many in the valley felt that the city had stolen their water, acquiring property and water use rights under false pretenses and then greedily drawing off the flow of the Owens River, allowing L.A. to flourish while the local economy languished. This valley—despite being a "Land of Little Rain," as a local writer had famously called it—was at one time an aspiring agricultural region. In the decades around the turn of the century, plentiful water from the Owens River, which gathered the runoff of forty mountain streams in the nearby high Sierra Nevada and channeled it through the otherwise arid region, had sustained livestock and irrigated fields all up and down the hundred-mile-long valley. At its southern end, the river had even broadened out into a large, shallow lake, where local residents could go boating and migrating waterfowl could cavort among the swaying reeds.

Then in 1913, the aqueduct had come, and most of that water had been taken away to nurture the growth of far-off Los Angeles. The people of the Owens Valley had rebelled. Several times during the drought-stricken 1920s, they had responded with dynamite, bombing the aqueduct at various points along its 233-mile path. Relations between city and valley remained poisonous for years. Eventually, though, the parties came to a compromise, declaring an uneasy truce, and the bombings stopped.

Now, decades later, the LADWP was trying to wring yet more water from the valley. To meet the city's needs during this latest drought, they had begun intensive pumping of the valley's groundwater basin, threatening to destroy what was left of the region's vegetation and turning the lower Owens River into nothing more than a dry ditch, winding down the valley to a barren alkaline plain that had once been a lake. No wonder, then, that those people standing around the ruined gatehouse were applauding the bombers. As one valley resident later admitted, "We'd all thought about doing something like that—but they actually hauled off and did it. So we . . . clinked beer bottles in their honor."

Not that this latter-day echo of the 1920s bombing campaign caused Los Angeles much harm. A series of reservoirs much closer to the city held enough water in reserve to ensure that Angelenos suffered no shortages or interruptions in their service. Within a few days of the sabotage, the shattered spillgate was already repaired and the aqueduct was flowing again. County and federal authorities lost no time in ferreting out the perpetrators: two young locals who, after a few beers, had decided that they were fed up with the city's water-grabbing and decided to do something about it. For the bombing of the Alabama Gatehouse, they were eventually indicted, tried, and sentenced to minor jail terms. After doing their time, they were allowed to fade into obscurity.

It was a pattern that had developed over many years: Los Angeles siphoning off resources, industry, and population from elsewhere to satisfy its insatiable desire for growth. The city's leaders had turned this process into something of an art form, getting what was needed to prosper by whatever means necessary. Water was only one of the city's requirements, and the stagnation of the Owens Valley only one of the consequences of this voracity.

The Owens Valley, meanwhile, just grew drier, and—as it had for decades—the great megalopolis to the south just grew bigger and thirstier.

# Implausible City

It struck me as an odd thing that here, alone of all the cities in America, there was no plausible answer to the question, "Why did a town spring up here and why has it gr          ?"

—Morris Markey, journalist and California historian

LOS ANGELES, CALIFORNIA
1900–1930

It was no sensible place to build a great city. This corner of southern California—often bone dry, lacking a natural harbor, and isolated from the rest of the country by expansive deserts and rugged mountain ranges—offered few of the inducements to settlement and growth found near major cities in other places. The Spaniards, who first explored the region in 1542, declined to put down roots here for over two centuries; even then, in the 1700s, they sent mainly soldiers and Franciscan friars to establish missions and convert the local Indians to Christianity. When the Mexicans took over in 1821, they settled the area a little more heavily but still regarded it as a province, a hinterland, a backwater without the water.

Only after the Mexican War of 1846–48, when southern California became American, did anyone really start to postulate a grand metropolis in this desert, centered on a narrow, unreliable waterway known optimistically as the Los Angeles River. Only Americans, it seems, could dream of something so unlikely, so contrary to simple common sense. Of necessity, the place would have to be forced, like an amaryllis out of season. A certain amount of contrivance, or even trickery, would be required to bring resources, population, and industry to a place that lacked them all. But eventually the implausible became actual. By the end of the 1920s, the world city of Los Angeles, California, was a reality—an urban giant grown up in a place where no city should rightly be.

This book is the story of that extraordinary transformation. It begins in 1900, when Los Angeles was still a largely agricultural town of some 100,000 residents (and one that the National Irrigation Congress regarded as having "no future" as anything larger). The explosive growth that followed over the next three decades had nothing natural or inevitable about it. Each step in the city's evolution had to be conceived, engineered, and then sold to an often-skeptical public. And as with any evolutionary process, not all visions of the city's future survived this test. Some would die quickly and fruitlessly; others would prove unsustainable over the long term, pushed aside by the interests of richer and more powerful elements in the population. But a few would leave an outsize mark on the city, taking root and giving rise to a metropolis unlike any other in the world. The pivotal period from 1900 to 1930 would witness, most notably, the realization of one of the largest and most controversial public works projects in history, second in magnitude only to the Panama Canal at the time; the invention of an entirely new form of entertainment—and of a new kind of industry to produce and sell it; and the flowering of a seductive urban ethos—arguably the birth of the whole idea of a "lifestyle"—based on utopian notions of leisure, physical wellness, and spiritual fulfillment. This combination of urban growth factors was unique, and it proved to be uniquely effective. By 1930, for better or worse, Los Angeles emerged as a major city of over 1.2 million people, and one with a distinctive identity: as an obscenely wasteful but alluring garden in the desert, as the focus of the entire world's movie dreams (and often its moral censure), and as the heliocentric mecca of spiritual seekers across the country. Every city can be regarded as an artificial construct, an audacious projection of human will, imagination, and vanity onto the natural landscape; but none was more artificial—or more audacious—than this one.

Single individuals do not build cities, but three L.A. icons—an engineer, an artist, and an evangelist—both embodied and, to a unique extent, drove the three major engines of the city's rise from provincial player to world-class star. William Mulholland (the engineer) was L.A.'s fabled water czar, whose wildly ambitious vision of a 233-mile aqueduct brought water to the desert and allowed the city to grow far beyond its natural capacity to support urban life. David Wark Griffith (the artist) was the seminal film director of the silent era, the man who almost single-handedly transformed the motion picture from a vaudeville-house novelty into a major creative (and fabulously lucrative) industry, important enough to help build a city. And Aimee Semple McPherson (the evangelist) was the charismatic faith healer and pioneering radio preacher who, courting both scandal and fanatical devotion, founded her own religion and cemented southern California's reputation as a national hub for seekers of unorthodox spirituality and self-realization.

In this marginal and unfinished corner of the country, each of these three innovators discovered a kind of tabula rasa, an environment offering enough physical and mental space to permit their ideas to develop and ultimately flourish. Far from the entrenched attitudes and rigid power hierarchies of the hidebound East, each was free to create a distinctive vision of the city's future and do the hard creative work to give it concrete form.

The images they conjured up—of a blossoming city in the desert, of a thriving factory of celluloid dreamworks, of a community of seekers finding personal salvation under God's good sunshine—all had elements of the swindle about them, like mirages whose heady promises could evaporate on closer inspection. Each was tested by strong countercurrents of opposition, as scandals and accusations of corruption and malfeasance erupted continually to threaten their chances of realization. But the images proved resilient. More important, they succeeded in bringing the Los Angeles we know into being: people were enticed by the images; they came to live and work here; the city grew.

In the end, Mulholland, Griffith, and McPherson all paid a price for their ambitions. Each self-destructed in the late 1920s in spectacular fashion, finally succumbing to shifting tides of popular morality and technological change. All three found themselves humiliated and reviled as a fickle public turned against them. But while these individuals fell, the city they had worked to build barely registered their loss, entering the 1930s as the largest and fastest-growing U.S. city west of the Mississippi.

Few people could have imagined it all back at the turn of the century, when the dusty town of Los Angeles seemed destined to remain the thirty-sixth largest in the nation, behind places like Indianapolis, Toledo, and even Fall River, Massachusetts. What made the difference for L.A. was a combination of many different acts of imagination and engineering, supported by a great deal of sometimes deceptive advertising. But these efforts, large and small, gave the city what it needed to thrive: a source of water to sustain it, an industry to support its growth, and an ethos to bring it fame and notoriety. And in the process, this improbable place—the grand metropolis that never should have been—moved inexorably from the margins to the center of American life and consciousness.

# CHAPTER ONE
# A Thirsty Place

*William Mulholland in the field*

It began, appropriately enough, with a deception: the two middle-aged men who left Los Angeles on the morning of September 18, 1904, claimed to be going on vacation. Traveling via Mojave, they planned to rent a mule-pulled buckboard wagon (furnished, according to tradition, with "a demijohn of whiskey") and set out across the lonely, arid stretches between the city and the Sierra Nevada mountains to the north. Along the way, they'd bivouac beside the primitive wagon road every night and dine by firelight on bacon and canned baked beans, talking and drinking under a vast, star-scattered desert sky.

But this was in reality no innocent holiday excursion. The two men were indeed old friends, but they were on a serious mission, bound for a distant, little-known valley just to the east of the towering Sierra. And their purpose—which, for various reasons, had to be kept secret—was to ensure the future of the small but aspiring young city they had come from. The whiskey would be their sole concession to pleasure.

William Mulholland and Frederick Eaton were looking for water. Mulholland, as superintendent of what was then called the Los Angeles Water Department, needed it badly. Eaton, a lifelong Angeleno with a keen eye for business opportunities, knew where it could be found. Eaton had in fact been trying to sell his friend on this potential water source for over a decade. He'd first mentioned it back in 1892, shortly after discovering the Owens River on a business trip, but Mulholland had laughed at him. At the time, the city's fifty thousand residents drew far more water than they needed from the Los Angeles River, and the idea of importing more of it from some obscure desert valley clear across the state seemed absurd—"on the face of it, as likely as the city of Washington tapping the Ohio River," as one engineer put it. But now, twelve years later, Mulholland was decidedly more receptive to the idea. With L.A.'s population exceeding 150,000 and local water supplies running dangerously low, he was desperate enough to consider even absurdities.

After several days of rough desert travel, the two men steered their mules up a gradually rising stage road, between two barren, rock-strewn mountain ridges, and descended into the secluded geological depression known as the Owens Valley. Here Mulholland finally set eyes on the water his friend had been talking about for so long: a broad, shallow lake fed by a strong, steadily flowing river far more abundant than any waterway in the Los Angeles region. For Mulholland, it was a revelation. This was water enough to support a city ten times the current size of Los Angeles. The lake itself, lacking any outlet, was too alkaline to be tapped, but the water in that river was pristine, originating in the pure mountain streams that drained the snow-rich Sierra just to the west. And the Owens River stood at some four thousand feet above sea level, far higher than Los Angeles itself, meaning that its water could theoretically be brought to the city by means of gravity alone.

No detailed records survive to document exactly what Mulholland and Eaton said or did on this history-making buckboard trip to the Owens Valley. But it *is* known that Mulholland spent much of the journey taking notes on the terrain and recording elevations with a primitive barometer. These measurements would enable him to calculate an approximate route for that water over the miles of mountains and deserts that stood between it and the city that needed it.

The project taking shape in Mulholland's mind on that September day would require nothing less than the re-engineering of a large swath of southern California geography. But he was convinced that it was feasible. Unlikely as it sounded, William Mulholland knew he could essentially move the Owens River almost 250 miles south to Los Angeles. If only he'd be allowed to do it.

~

For a future great city-builder, William Mulholland had stemmed from some fairly unpromising roots. The second son of lower-middle-class Irish parents, he was born on September 11, 1855, in Belfast, where his father was stationed as a guard for the British Mail Service. When the boy was five, not long after the end of the Great Famine, the family returned to their native Dublin. Though hardly destitute, the Mulhollands did not have an easy life, and it became no easier after Willie's mother died just two years later. His father soon remarried, and while his stepmother was by all reports an affectionate parent, she promptly bore several children of her own to occupy her time. Willie and his brother Hugh (just eleven months his junior and almost like a twin) were largely left alone and soon became known in the neighborhood as "a pair of Dublin jackeens"—Irish slang for undisciplined reprobates who roamed the city streets when they should have been in school. One day, after a sound thrashing from his father for bad grades, Willie ran away from home and went to sea. Eventually he joined the British Merchant Marine, signing on with the crew of a three-masted merchantman called the *Gleniffer*. He was fifteen years old by then, and his education—the formal part of it, at least—was finished.

Over the next four years, Mulholland made no fewer than nineteen Atlantic crossings on the *Gleniffer*, to ports all over North America and the Caribbean, gradually rising to the position of navigating officer. He realized, however, that a life on the sea "would get me nowhere in a material way." So on June 9, 1874—while berthed in New York harbor—he disembarked from the *Gleniffer* for the last time, determined to make a life for himself in America. He headed west to Michigan and worked for a summer on a Great Lakes freighter and the following winter in a Manistee lumber camp (where, as he later wrote, "it was doubtless the 'salt-horse'"—a kind of salt-cured beef regularly fed to the lumber crews—". . . [that] gave me such a taste for water"). But the young man was too restless to stay for long. After a serious logging accident that nearly cost him a leg and allegedly pushed him to the brink of suicide, he bolted to Cincinnati. In Ohio he took up with an itinerant handyman and spent the better part of the next year traveling around the countryside, picking up minor repair jobs here and there.

By the fall of 1875, Mulholland was ready to settle down for a while. Reconnecting with his brother Hugh, who had followed his older sibling to America, he next made his way to Pittsburgh, where the boys' uncle, Richard Deakers, owned a prosperous dry goods business. Here

Mulholland worked for over a year as a clerk in his uncle's store. And although he later admitted being ashamed of this rather tame episode in his life, it proved to be an important recovery period for him, reviving his taste for life after the recent bout of depression. Always a voracious reader despite his lack of education ("Damn a man who doesn't read books," he often said), he found himself eager to satisfy a growing interest in history, current events, and, as he later put it, "all phases of experience except girls—I was never known as a lady's man."

One subject that piqued his interest was California. While in Pittsburgh, he read a book by Charles Nordhoff called *California: For Health, Pleasure, and Residence* and was intrigued by its depiction of an unspoiled place of healthy sunshine, open spaces, and unlimited opportunity. The Deakers family was likewise intrigued, especially since several of the children had contracted tuberculosis and needed to escape the cold, damp Pittsburgh winters. Sometime in late 1876, Richard Deakers decided to sell his business and move the family west to the more salubrious climate of Los Angeles. Willie and Hugh lacked the means to buy a ticket but would hardly let this be an impediment to coming along. When the Deakers family sailed out of New York harbor aboard the *Crescent City* on December 9, 1876, their sea-savvy young cousins sneaked onto the ship as stowaways.

They nearly got away with it. Willie and Hugh concealed themselves belowdecks by day and slept in a lifeboat by night. But sometime shortly before the ship reached Panama, the boys were glimpsed by one of their younger cousins, little Annie Deakers, who shouted, "There's Cousin Hugh and Cousin Willie!" A nearby bosun overheard and captured the boys. They were put to work for the rest of the journey and then unceremoniously expelled at Colón. While the Deakers family went ahead by rail to Panama's Pacific coast, Willie and Hugh, unable to pay the steep twenty-five-dollar fare to cross the isthmus, were forced to walk. It was a distance of some forty-seven miles, through dense, swampy, mosquito-infested jungle. Sometime during the journey, an insect laid its eggs in one of Willie's toes, which swelled bigger and bigger until Hugh had to cut it open with a knife to drain it.

By the time the brothers reached Balboa, the Deakers family had

sailed on without them. Undaunted, Willie and Hugh found work aboard
a Peruvian ship bound for Acapulco, where they signed on with another
ship to San Francisco. Once in California, they bought two horses and
headed south via the San Joaquin Valley. Mulholland was impressed with
what he saw and, despite the hard journey and his straitened circumstances, felt buoyantly hopeful about the future. "I was tremendously
interested in the whole country," he later wrote. "Everything was new,
deeply interesting. The world was my oyster, and I was just opening it."

Sometime in January or February 1877, they finally reached L.A.,
and Mulholland got his first glimpse of the town that was to become his
life's project. Apparently it was love at first sight. "Los Angeles was a
place after my own heart," he would later say. "It was the most attractive
town I had ever seen." The years of restless wandering were over. William Mulholland had found—some five thousand miles from home—
the place he wanted to be.

~

Appealing as the town might have seemed in the eyes of a penniless,
twenty-one-year-old Irish immigrant, Los Angeles in 1877 was hardly a
garden spot of bucolic charm. With a population of some nine thousand
souls, it still retained the unkempt contours of a southwestern frontier
settlement, where sheep and chickens rambled along the unpaved roads
and the tranquillity of warm evenings could be shattered by eruptions of
Old West–style lawlessness. The town's per capita murder rate was as-
tonishingly high, and just six years earlier, nineteen Chinese immigrants
had been brutally lynched right in the center of town by an irate mob—
with few serious legal consequences for the perpetrators.

Even then, however, Los Angeles had higher aspirations. Less than
a century had passed since the first forty-four Spanish settlers—the so-
called *pobladores*, most of them of mixed African and Native American
ancestry—had arrived here from Sinaloa, a thousand miles to the south.
It had been just forty years since the pueblo they established had become part of the United States. But already Los Angeles had its eye on
the future. The town had got its first long-distance rail connection just
months before Mulholland's arrival, when the Southern Pacific Railroad

completed its line from San Francisco. Eager to grow the population, local boosters were soon honing their sales pitches to convince well-off easterners and midwesterners to come via the rail connection and settle here. These promoters, soon to be organized as the Los Angeles Chamber of Commerce and led by the tireless and inventive Indiana-born Quaker Frank Wiggins, drew heavily on the romanticized legend of southern California's Spanish mission past. They depicted L.A. and environs as a kind of "semi-tropical" paradise—"The American Italy," or "a Mediterranean land without the marshes or malaria." This desirable place was not just pleasant but healthful as well. According to one doctor, the local climate could relieve or cure any number of chronic ailments, from insomnia, cirrhosis of the liver, and tuberculosis to constipation, "functional female disturbances," and the organic ills of advanced age.

As pleasant as the place may have been, one still needed money to survive here, and Mulholland at first had difficulty finding his way. After going months without securing a job in the town he found so attractive, he was already contemplating leaving it. He said goodbye to his brother and the Deakers family and began walking from L.A. to the harbor in San Pedro to sign on for another stint at sea. On the way, he encountered a man drilling a well near Compton and offered to help him. By evening, the man had seen enough of Mulholland's initiative to offer him a job as a well-digger. The young Irishman accepted, and the fateful match between water and William Mulholland was made.

He would not remain a laborer for long. Mulholland was blessed with a keen problem-solving mind and a work ethic that kept him "constantly in motion." And his intellectual curiosity was still boundless. One day on the well-digging job, his drilling crew unearthed some fossils about six hundred feet below the surface. Mulholland was fascinated. "These things fired my imagination," he later wrote. "I wanted to know how they got there, so I got ahold of Joseph LeConte's [*Elements of Geology*]. Right there I decided to become an engineer." He began to devote his nightly reading to technical subjects, gradually transforming himself into an entirely self-taught hydraulic engineer.

In the spring of 1878, Mulholland joined the privately held L.A. City Water Company (LAWC) as a ditch-tender. This was not easy work

("Sometimes I had to jump into the water to clean out those ditches," he recalled. "It was no gingerbread job!"), but Mulholland somehow still had energy enough to continue his evening studies. His principal goal was to understand the hydrology of his adopted home and in particular the idiosyncrasies of the rather temperamental waterway that made life there possible. "The river was the greatest attraction [for me]," he would later write. "It was a beautiful, limpid little stream with willows on its banks. I always loved the Los Angeles River." Ever since the early, pre-American pueblo days, the settlement had relied on water from the river for virtually everything. A large diversion canal—called the Zanja Madre, or Mother Ditch—brought water from the river to a small reservoir in the Elysian Hills, near the current site of Dodger Stadium. From there it was distributed via a series of smaller ditches to the central plaza area and various other corners of the town. The Americans had preserved this arrangement after taking over the territory in 1848, improving the system of *zanjas* (mispronounced as "zankies" by the Anglo newcomers) with a few more modern distribution elements. But even by the time Mulholland arrived on the scene, the system was still relatively primitive, consisting of just three miles of wooden pipe and another mile of iron pipe to supplement the original few thousand feet of open ditches.

Hoping to relieve itself of the burden of maintaining water service, Los Angeles had in 1868 granted a thirty-year lease on the system to the LAWC, which would supply the town with water as a profit-making endeavor for its shareholders. This arrangement was convenient for the city, but it had its drawbacks. With an eye forever on the bottom line, the water company was often reluctant to make expensive improvements and repairs, and residents were constantly complaining about poor water pressure, erratic outages, and even, on occasion, little fish swimming in the stuff that came out of their faucets. Making do with a payroll of only a dozen employees, the company also had trouble keeping pace with the rapid growth in the area's population. This problem became especially acute in the mid-1880s, when a second long-distance railroad line (the Atchison, Topeka and Santa Fe Railway) reached Los Angeles. This new competition for the Southern Pacific line set off a fare war that reduced the cost of a Chicago-to-L.A. train ticket from $125 to $15 to, at one point, a single dollar. The resulting influx quintupled the population by the end of the decade, dramatically increasing the demand for water service.

Fortunately for the LAWC, it had taken on a workhorse like Mulholland. Tall, powerfully built, and sporting a prominent push-broom mustache, he was both physically and mentally formidable. And he could be notoriously short-tempered when anything interfered with his work. Shortly after joining the company in 1878, the twenty-three-year-old "deputy *zanjero*" was down in a ditch, furiously digging mud and stones, when company president William Perry rode past. The executive stopped to ask the young man's name, but Mulholland didn't recognize him. "It's none of your goddamned business," he barked, and continued digging. Perry rode away without comment. Later, another workman let Mulholland know that he had just cursed out the man who paid his wages. Thinking that he would surely be fired, Mulholland headed downtown to the company's office to collect his pay before being given his notice. But the clerk had pleasant news: rather than firing him for insubordination, Perry had been so impressed by Mulholland's single-minded diligence that he'd promoted him to foreman. Apparently Perry recognized what many people in Los Angeles would learn in the years to come: the value of a man possessed.

In 1880, after two years of labor keeping the *zanjas* free of debris and contamination (most annoyingly from laundresses who persisted in washing their clothes in the open ditches), Mulholland was promoted again. He was given responsibility for expanding and modernizing the city's one reservoir, the Buena Vista. From a rough shack on the Los Angeles River, he was able to move to a somewhat nicer shack in Elysian Park, near the reservoir. But the best advantage of the new job was that it brought him into closer contact with the LAWC's senior staff—in particular, with Fred Eaton, then serving as the company's superintendent.

In many ways, the two men could not have been more different. Eaton, scion of one of the first Anglo families to settle in the area (his father had helped found the patrician enclave of Pasadena), was something of a grandee—polished, outgoing, and refined. Mulholland was still very much the blunt, gruff Irish laborer who preferred solitude to sociability. Yet the two became good friends. Though almost the same age, Eaton, the more formally educated engineer, took the role of Mulholland's mentor. The two men would frequently be at odds over the ensuing years, but the memory of their early friendship would always temper their animosity, even when they found themselves openly feuding.

~

In early 1885, Fred Eaton left the water company for a job as the Los Angeles city surveyor and engineer. W. J. Kelley, described as "more of an office man than an engineer," was chosen as Eaton's successor, while Mulholland went on to oversee some key construction projects. Here again he excelled at his task. And when Kelley died of a heart attack just a little over a year after taking the job, it seemed only natural that William Mulholland should replace him as superintendent. Mulholland would hold the title for more than four decades.

It proved to be the perfect match of man and mission. Mulholland hated politics, bureaucracy, and interference from know-nothing officials—"Just let me alone and I'll deliver what you need" was a typical sentiment—and he soon had a reputation at the water company for getting things done, no matter the obstacles. Once, in late December 1888, a flash flood swept tons of stone, brush, and timber into the main conduit of the city's water system at Crystal Springs, nearly plugging up one three-thousand-foot tunnel. Called from his bed on the morning of Christmas Eve, Mulholland spent the next four days working around the clock with his men to clear the obstruction. "I never had my shoes off from Tuesday until Friday night," he told reporters. For his role in saving the city's water supply during the holiday, he was awarded a commemorative watch, though one gets the sense that this kind of grueling physical effort was William Mulholland's idea of fun.

Though he did take time out in 1890 to get married—to a woman named Lillie Ferguson, whom he met while overseeing a pipe-laying project on her father's farm—there was never any doubt that the L.A. water system was his one true passion in life. And by the 1890s, he knew its ins and outs better than anyone in the world. This became clear when, at a meeting of the city's engineering board, no schematic diagram of the pumping and distribution system was immediately available. According to company lore, Mulholland merely called for a street map and proceeded to sketch out the entire system from memory. No one believed this possible, but when his sketch was later compared to the official diagram, the board discovered that Mulholland's map was accurate in virtually every particular, right down to the exact location of every gate-valve and fire hydrant in the city.

~

In 1898 the LAWC's thirty-year lease ended, and the city—under its new mayor, Fred Eaton—moved to take control of the waterworks. This proved to be more difficult than anyone had anticipated. The company initially valued its system at $3 million; the city was offering $1.19 million. It took several years of arbitration for both sides to agree on a price of $2 million. But on February 6, 1902 (after Eaton left the mayor's office), Los Angeles took full possession of its own water system—and of William Mulholland. "When the city bought the works," he would later say, "they bought me with it." Retained as superintendent, he merely kept doing the job he'd already been doing for over fifteen years.

The transition to municipal ownership had come none too soon. By 1902, the city's population had already catapulted well past the 100,000 mark. Despite Mulholland's best efforts, the system had suffered from a lack of capital investment under the LAWC and was now, according to him, "at least ten years behind the actual needs of the city." Once the city took over, the superintendent embarked on a thorough renovation of the entire waterworks, building new reservoirs, overhauling the Buena Vista pumping station, installing water meters, and laying new pipe. All of this was done, moreover, at a slight profit to the city, despite a 10 percent cut in the rates individuals paid for water service.

But these efforts were still not enough. In 1903 Los Angeles entered its tenth straight year of drought. The flow of the Los Angeles River had fallen every year since 1893, and water levels were sinking precipitously in wells from Anaheim to the San Fernando Valley. The Christmas season of 1903, according to one veteran rainfall diarist, was the "driest I have ever known."

And it only got worse over the next months. The newspaper headlines were bleak: "CROP REPORTS NOT ENCOURAGING"; "CONDITION OF SOIL PREVENTS PLOWING"; "DRY WEATHER STILL PREVAILS WITH LITTLE HOPE OF RAIN." Some locals even began to attribute the persistent water famine to divine retribution. "It is because we are so wicked," one longtime resident told a reporter. "The Bible declares that the rains and the blessings they bring are 'for those who obey the law.' We do not obey the law; we break it."

By July 1904, the situation was near crisis. Cattle were dying of starvation in nearby Antelope Valley; entire lakes in the mountains around the city were drying up into mudflats. Writing his annual report on the state of the Los Angeles River, Mulholland seemed grimly determined: "The time has come when we shall have to supplement [the river's] flow from some other source."

That was when he and Fred Eaton took their little camping trip to the Owens Valley. And what he saw there seemed like an answer to a prayer: a water source that could eliminate the threat of future droughts and ensure L.A.'s growth for decades to come. There was just one problem. The residents of the Owens Valley had their own plans for that water, and they weren't going to give up on them without a fight.

# CHAPTER TWO
# Alternate Realities

*Owens Lake in the Owens Valley, before losing its water*

**N**ot all dreams of the future are grandiose, and those of the people of the Owens Valley were humble enough. Most just wanted to make a living growing crops and raising cattle in the place they had chosen as home. And for a time, it looked as if the federal government might even be willing to help them.

In 1900 the entire population of Inyo County—the county that encompasses the Owens Valley and part of Death Valley—amounted to something under five thousand. That number consisted mostly of small-holding farmers and ranchers, along with a few miners who worked the waning silver mines in the mountains to the east. Until 1834, when explorer Joseph Walker "discovered" it, the valley had been known only to native Paiutes and their ancestors, and the succeeding seventy years had seen little in the way of settlement and development. With the Owens River running straight down the center of the narrow valley, farmers and ranchers had an abundant source of water on their doorsteps. But without the capital to build elaborate irrigation systems, agricultural activity had remained modest. Beautiful as it was, the valley was a tough place to eke out a living, and lacking any outside assistance, it seemed destined to remain so.

But then the federal government showed up, with deep pockets and an overweening desire to make something useful out of the Great American Desert. In 1902 Congress passed the Newlands Reclamation Act, designed, as one historian has put it, to "develop marginal land for cultivation through irrigation, enabling thousands of people back East to leave crowded city slums and regain pride of place." Under the auspices of the newly created Reclamation Service, engineer Jacob Clausen was dispatched to the Owens Valley in the summer of 1903 to assess its suitability for an irrigation project. Clausen's report was highly favorable, so his boss—Joseph Lippincott, the agency's supervising engineer for

California—recommended that all remaining public lands in the valley be withdrawn from settlement and set aside for a possible large-scale federal project.

Owens Valley locals were naturally enthusiastic at the prospect of Uncle Sam stepping in to help with the development of their little corner of the world. The proposed project, a series of "high-line canals" running along the foothills of the surrounding mountains, would enable farmers and ranchers all up and down the valley to tap into the bounty of Sierra runoff. At the government's request, many gladly surrendered to the Reclamation Service their claims on potential water storage sites. The future of the Owens Valley was suddenly looking very bright. "Every detail of the undertaking was favorable," one local newspaper owner wrote, "and the people of Inyo, while noting the slowness of definite announcement or action [on the government's part], entertained no doubt of the good faith of the work being done."

That slowness was due, at least in part, to the ambitions of the striving young city 250 miles to the south. As it happened, supervising engineer Lippincott was a friend and former employee of none other than ex-mayor of L.A. Frederick Eaton. In the summer of 1904, Eaton had joined Lippincott and his family on a fishing trip to Yosemite. At some point during the trip, they descended from the Sierra to the town of Bishop in the Owens Valley to replenish their camping supplies. There they met engineer Clausen, who was conducting studies in the area related to the proposed irrigation project. Exactly what was discussed at this rendezvous (during which Clausen led the camping party on a small tour of the valley) would remain a matter of much controversy in the years ahead. But it seems certain that Lippincott and Clausen discussed the Reclamation Service's plans for the region, and that Eaton, with his long-standing desire to procure Owens River water for Los Angeles, heard much that alarmed him. Within days of Eaton's return from the Yosemite trip, he met with William Mulholland and convinced him to make their clandestine, whiskey-sodden buckboard journey to the valley. His message to Mulholland was clear: if Los Angeles didn't act quickly to secure that water, the National Reclamation Service would tie it up for its own purposes.

Mulholland understood the urgency of the matter. After their return from the Owens Valley, he met behind closed doors with the city's board of water commissioners and laid out his case for an aqueduct project as the only feasible answer to the city's looming water crisis. The board gave the plan its blessing and agreed to keep it secret even from the mayor and the city council. In the meantime, Eaton revealed L.A.'s interest in the Owens River to his friend Lippincott, who in turn notified his superior in Washington, D.C.—Frederick Haynes Newell, chief engineer of the Reclamation Service.

For Newell, this news presented a conundrum. The city's aqueduct plan and the federal government's irrigation project were mutually exclusive, at least as currently conceived. But since the Reclamation Service's mission was based on utilitarian principles ("the greatest good to the greatest number" was its unofficial motto), Newell agreed to come to Los Angeles and at least hear what Mulholland had in mind. On November 22, 1904, in yet another backroom colloquy, Newell and Lippincott met with Mulholland, Eaton, and city attorney William Mathews to discuss the aqueduct plan. Convinced of the city's dire need for more water, Newell was sympathetic and agreed to put the federal irrigation project on hold, at least until the L.A. officials could develop a full-fledged proposal. To this end, he even agreed to turn over to Mulholland a copy of engineer Clausen's detailed report on the hydrography and topography of the valley, including important data on stream measurements for the Owens River.

Here Newell was treading shaky ethical ground, and he knew it. Clausen's surveys, after all, had been performed at the federal government's expense, and ostensibly for the benefit of the residents of the Owens Valley. Stepping aside now to give Los Angeles a first shot at the Owens River water, moreover, could cause acute embarrassment to the Reclamation Service once the news became public. But Newell did believe that L.A.'s aqueduct would better serve that "greatest good to the greatest number," so he agreed to give the city a chance to make it work, with one proviso: he insisted that the project be entirely a public one, with no private or corporate interest involved in any way.

This was fine with Mulholland, whose experience with the LAWC had soured his taste for public/private ventures. He promptly went to work, using Clausen's surveys and his own measurements and field observations to draw up a detailed plan for his grandiose scheme. "When my shirt got dirty, I came in for a change," he would later write, "but otherwise I kept to the theme." Transporting water over hundreds of miles of rough terrain would require an enormously complex system of culverts, canals, tunnels, and storage reservoirs, but there was no engineering problem involved that couldn't be solved, given enough time and money.

On that latter issue, money, Mulholland had some work to do as well. The superintendent estimated that the aqueduct would cost upward of $20 million to build—a huge sum in 1904 dollars (over half a billion dollars today), and one that would force the city deeply into debt. The electorate would have to vote for a series of hefty bond issues that would likely meet with heated opposition. Mulholland knew that he had to impress upon the citizenry the absolute necessity of some kind of big-budget solution to the city's water woes—and he had to do it without specifying exactly what he had in mind, since any leak of his plan would set off waves of land speculation along the entire route of the proposed aqueduct, raising costs prohibitively. "Los Angeles should grapple with its great water problem now," he said in a statement to the newspapers in December. "Years of work will be necessary to provide for the future. . . . [T]here is no occasion for panic at the present time, but it is high time to begin to work out our future salvation, for, if we are to become a great metropolis, we shall need much more water than we now have."

Los Angeles could and would become that great metropolis—"the Chicago of the Southwest," as the *Times* had already begun to call it—but it was going to cost money. Lots of it.

~

No one was sure exactly who the man was who showed up in the Owens Valley in March 1905, asking around about property and water rights. He was obviously a prosperous type, with well-tailored clothes and a smooth, polished manner. But he was evasive about his purpose in the valley. To some, he implied that he was a cattleman looking to buy land and livestock for a ranch. But here he was now, in the land office in Independence, claiming to be on government business. He said he had a letter from Joseph Lippincott of the Reclamation Service, authorizing him to check on a few right-of-way applications. He also had several government maps in his possession, which he made a point of showing to various people in the valley. Surely he must work for the Reclamation Service; yet he never did say as much.

The man was former L.A. mayor Frederick Eaton, and the ambiguity surrounding his intentions served his purposes well. He was actually in the Owens Valley to buy property options and water rights as an agent for Mulholland and the L.A. Water Department. If local residents assumed Eaton was here on behalf of the much-desired federal irrigation project, and if they were therefore willing to sell him whatever rights and holdings he wanted for an attractive price . . . well, so be it. Presenting himself as a Reclamation Service agent wasn't exactly a lie—Lippincott really *had* sent him to the land office to check applications—but it wasn't quite accurate either. It was simply a case of *caveat venditor*: let the seller beware.

Eaton was, first and foremost, a businessman, and so he also had his own interests in mind. Until city money could be officially appropriated for the land and water rights, he was buying on his own private account, the understanding with Mulholland and the water commissioners being that he would eventually transfer the options to the city at cost. But Eaton wasn't above trying to derive a little financial benefit for himself in the process. One property in particular interested him—the so-called Rickey Ranch, located in the Long Valley area above the town of Bishop. In addition to being fine cattle territory, it was also the logical location for a reservoir to be built in connection with the aqueduct project. Eaton's plan was to buy the ranch and its cattle and then turn over the water rights and half of the property to the water department, keeping the rest for himself. He would set himself up as a cattle rancher for a few years, and if the city of Los Angeles eventually needed some of his land for a reservoir . . . well, he would be willing to sell it to them, for the right price. On his March trip, he approached Thomas Rickey as a would-be rancher—again, not exactly a lie, but not quite accurate either. Later that same month, after much haggling, he convinced Rickey to sell him an option to buy the ranch for $450,000, with only one hundred dollars up front to seal the deal.

Meanwhile the wheels were turning down south in Los Angeles, as Mulholland's grand plan moved—steadily yet stealthily—through the approval process. In early May 1905, L.A.'s current mayor, Owen McAleer, made a secret trip to the Owens Valley with members of the water board to see the project sites and examine Eaton's optioned properties. (Eaton passed the gentlemen off to locals as either fellow cattlemen or park developers, depending on the audience.) The L.A. officials liked what they saw and, upon their return to the city, quickly approved Mulholland's formal proposal for the aqueduct, at a projected cost of $23 million. The commissioners also voted unanimously to buy the options Eaton had been purchasing for months. Eaton generously let them go at his own cost, but as planned, he got to keep half the Rickey Ranch land and all of the Rickey Ranch cattle. Combined with his hefty $100,000 commission for acting as the city's agent in the deals, this made for a lucrative piece of business. Such were the rewards of a former mayor securing his city's future.

All of this happened none too soon, because rumors about L.A.'s plans, despite Mulholland's best efforts, were gradually leaking out to the public. By late spring, several of the newspapers had gotten wind of the secret. City officials swore their editors to silence until midsummer, when all of the option deals would be finalized, but that didn't prevent the newsmen from dropping the occasional hint in their pages. ("WHERE IS MAYOR MCALEER HIDING?" asked the *L.A. Times* when the mayor and water commissioners made their secret trip up north. "GONE A FISHING, IS IT FOR WATER?") Certain Owens Valley residents were also becoming suspicious. In mid-July two employees in the General Land Office in Independence wrote their superior in Washington about a certain "prominent business man of Los Angeles." The man was buying up land and water rights with such abandon that he now practically controlled the entire flow of the Owens River. "It was generally understood that [these rights] were to be used for the benefit of the government project," they wrote. But now the people of the valley were beginning to suspect that the man "has secured this large supply of water in order to take it to Southern California."

Unfortunately, these perfectly accurate misgivings had come too late. Two weeks after that letter was sent, Mulholland was able to report to the water board that "the last spike is driven. The options are all secured." The very next morning—violating by a day the agreed-upon news embargo—the *L.A. Times* broke the story to its unsuspecting readers: "TITANIC PROJECT TO GIVE CITY A RIVER" ran the page-one headline. "MAGNIFICENT STREAM TO BE CONVEYED DOWN TO THE SOUTHLAND IN CONDUIT TWO HUNDRED AND FORTY MILES LONG—STUPENDOUS DEAL CLOSED."

The fate of the struggling young metropolis had just changed dramatically. Nature itself would be reconfigured for the benefit of the City of Angels. And the man who would make it all happen—at least to hear the newspapers tell it—was water department chief William Mulholland.

~

Over the next week, the other L.A. newspapers hustled into print their own multipage paeans to the proposed aqueduct and the men who had conceived it. "WATER SUPPLY FOR 2,000,000 PEOPLE," the *L.A. Examiner* marveled on its front page. The *Herald* was equally dazzled: "The scale of expansion in Los Angeles now conforms to that of the greater cities of the United States. We are building not only for a surprising present but for a stupendous future." The benefits of the aqueduct, according to the paper, would accrue even before the first drop of water reached the city. "The work of constructing the greater water system will stimulate business activity in Los Angeles. It will create an increased demand for labor here. . . . And the result will be that the exodus from the east toward the western wonder will swell in volume to greater proportions than ever before."

"Los Angeles, the Metropolis of the Great Southwest" was the new motto being pushed by city boosters. Yes, the image of a flowering Mediterranean paradise was still key to the sales pitch—"Gardens instead of desert," as the *Record* put it—but now there was an element of hustling, bustling modernity in the mix: "Workshops, factories, stores, great and small," the paper promised. "A metropolis in *fact*, surrounded by a flourishing country capable of supporting millions."

No publication was more enthusiastic than the *Times*, under its already-legendary publisher, Harrison Gray Otis, a rabidly conservative

Civil War veteran who considered editorial objectivity a weakness. Calling the aqueduct plan "the most important movement for the development of Los Angeles in all the city's history," the paper grew downright evangelical in its embrace of a project that would turn Los Angeles into the Promised Land. "Great is Water!" the lead editorial declaimed. "The mountains may crumble, but water makes old things become new, water brings life where there was death. Los Angeles has found something better than a gold mine. . . . Let all the people say 'Amen!'"

The reference to a gold mine was telling. For decades, Los Angeles had lived in the shadow of its cousin to the north—San Francisco, a city that owed its prominence in large part to the Gold Rush that began in 1848. As a result of that lucky strike, so much wealth and population had flowed to San Francisco and the rest of the Bay Area that it soon dominated the affairs of the entire state. For a time in the 1850s, southern California, tired of its interests always being ignored in the state capital, had even wanted to secede and set itself up as a separate state. Mulholland's aqueduct promised to finally change that balance of power. Granted, San Francisco, with a 1905 population of around 400,000, was still far larger than Los Angeles (which, according to Mulholland's somewhat optimistic estimate, now stood at 185,000), but that didn't stop an Angeleno from dreaming.

The aqueduct would also upend a more pressing urban competition: that between Los Angeles and its proximate rival, San Diego. Until the 1880s, it was widely believed that San Diego, as the only southern California city with a deepwater harbor to compare with San Francisco Bay, would naturally grow up to be the region's giant. But after furious struggles in the 1880s and '90s to attract better railroad connections and to improve its shallow, unprotected port at San Pedro, Los Angeles had pulled ahead in the growth sweepstakes. And now, with the prospect of a virtually unlimited water source at the city's disposal, the question was all but settled. The Great Metropolis of the Southwest was destined to be Los Angeles, not San Diego. And the price of this grand dream of the future was only $23 million.

Of course, the other dream of the future, that of the people of Owens Valley, was now shattered. As news of the big announcement reached them, the farmers and ranchers became furious. At a hastily organized meeting in Bishop, a large and vociferous crowd named a citizens committee to officially register their protest against the city's plans. Angry letters were fired off, not just to the Reclamation Service but to President Theodore Roosevelt as well. Some of these were reasoned and temperate, like the one written by Inyo County district attorney William Dehy. "If the Government's reclamation project for this valley is abandoned," Dehy warned the president, "in order that the City of Los Angeles may add to its wealth and population, it will mean the depopulation and devastation of the whole Owens River Valley." Other letters were more spirited. A Mrs. Lesta V. Parker wrote to TR complaining about "a man named Eaton and a few more equaly [*sic*] low, sneaking, rich men [who] wanted to get controlling interest of the water. . . . Now, as President of the U.S., do you think that is right?"

To judge by these and other letters, much of the ire in the valley was aimed at J. B. Lippincott—soon dubbed "Judas B. Lippincott" in the *Inyo Register.* Many people were incensed in particular by an article in the *L.A. Times* that heaped high praise on the engineer for helping Los Angeles secure the valley's water. "Without Mr. Lippincott's interest and cooperation," the article asserted, "it is declared that the plan never would have gone through." And certainly Lippincott's behavior in the whole affair had been unprofessional at best and treacherous at worst. That March the engineer had signed a private contract to do freelance work for the city of Los Angeles, while still ostensibly a federal employee working on a project with competing interests. And more egregiously, he had allowed Fred Eaton to secure land and water rights under false pretenses, by sending Eaton—a former mayor of Los Angeles!—to the Independence land office on official Reclamation Service business. Lippincott later insisted that his motives had been pure; he was away on emergency business at the time, he said, and needed a trained engineer to check on those right-of-way applications. But choosing Eaton to do this job was tantamount to sending a fox to inspect the local henhouse. A subsequent investigation by the Department of the Interior all but confirmed the breach of ethics. "After considering the whole matter," the investigator wrote in his final report, "I can arrive at no other conclusion than that Supervising Engineer Lippincott's action in the matter is indefensible, and for the good of the Reclamation Service he should be separated from it."

As for Fred Eaton, who by now had become a fixture in the Owens Valley, he was suddenly revealed to locals as a conniving spy rather than a generous and free-spending future neighbor. Caught by surprise when the *Times* story broke in July, he was forced to flee the valley and hide out in San Francisco rather than face an angry mob. "I used to be the best fellow in the world among those people, but now they think I am the Prince of Devils," he complained. "They say I sold them out . . . [and] that when I go back for my cattle, they will drown me in the river."

None of this was helped by the condescending tone the L.A. papers adopted when reporting Eaton's exploits in the valley. The *Herald* chuckled over the naïveté of locals who were selling the ex-mayor their properties, thinking they had a sucker on their hands: "To the ranchers, Eaton appeared to be land mad, and it is said they whispered among themselves that he had been eating loco weed fixed up as a salad." The *Times* declared itself amused by "the deceptions that these simple folk worked upon themselves, fancying all the time that the joke was on Eaton." Little wonder that these "simple folk" were now up in arms. Their hopes for new prosperity, however modest, had evaporated literally overnight. And the principal engineers of this disappearing mirage were a triumvirate of "Los Angeles scoundrels": Lippincott, Eaton, and William Mulholland. In the eyes of many in the Owens Valley, there was only one way of looking at the situation. Los Angeles, in the person of these three men, was stealing the water that was rightfully theirs.

~

Unanimity is not a common phenomenon in any urban population—not even in a small city with one big, obvious need—and it wasn't long before the city's initial near-universal approval of Mulholland's great plan began to erode. As people took a closer look at the project, the way it had been secured, and (most important) the amount of money it would cost, objections large and small started to emerge. The *L.A. Examiner*, a Hearst newspaper, began to argue against the project, especially after Mulholland, the water board, and a compliant city council started pushing aggressively to fast-track a $1.5 million bond issue to get the project started immediately. "PEOPLE WANT ALL THE FACTS BEFORE VOTING WATER BONDS" ran one typical headline. "TAXPAYERS DEMAND MORE LIGHT BE-FORE APPROVING PROJECT." Some complaints about the plan were valid, but others were obviously trumped up: that the Owens River water was too alkaline to be potable; that it was swarming with "typhoid germs"; and that plenty of water could be obtained far more cheaply from alternative sources in nearby Ventura County.

Mulholland dismissed all of these objections. "If there are any people in Los Angeles who think we have gone into this proposition like a lot of schoolboys, with a whoop and a hurrah," the superintendent told reporters, "they should come in here and look over a few of the maps we have made during the last year. . . . [These] objections are from persons who have been nursing propositions for years to unload on the city, and who are sore [now] because their deals have been turned down."

Self-interest did apparently propel much of the criticism. Private power companies, for instance, opposed the aqueduct plan because it would allow the city to produce its own hydroelectricity, reducing the demand for their own product; labor unions disliked the idea of the project being built entirely with nonunionized day laborers. Other critics were legitimately worried at the stunning cost of the aqueduct. They wondered aloud whether Mulholland had been exaggerating the gravity of the city's water crisis in order to frighten taxpayers into voting for his aqueduct, no matter what the cost. This concern had been fed by a story, broken by the *L.A. Record* the previous summer, that large amounts of water were being flushed through the sewer system and out to sea, perhaps intentionally, to lower the reservoirs and thus magnify the perception of a crisis. Mulholland had quickly isolated the cause of the water runoff—faulty valves were allowing reservoir water to leak into the storm sewers—and fixed the problem. But this wasn't enough to prevent conspiracy theorists from drawing their own conclusions (which eventually made their way into the highly fictionalized account of L.A.'s water story in the 1974 film *Chinatown*).

But on August 24—only two weeks before the city was to vote on the $1.5 million bond issue—Hearst's *Examiner* published an exposé of behind-the-scenes chicanery that would be far more difficult for city officials to explain away. According to the paper's investigations, a syndicate of prominent L.A. businessmen had for months been buying up property in the San Fernando Valley, northwest of the city, near the proposed southern terminus of the aqueduct. On March 23, 1905, just one day after the approval of Mulholland's plan by the city's water board, the syndicate had exercised an option to purchase the Porter Ranch—a huge tract of semiarid land encompassing a significant portion of the valley's total acreage. This was damning enough, but there was even worse to come. It soon became public that the partners of the syndicate included not only Harrison Gray Otis and Edwin T. Earl (publishers, respectively, of the *L.A. Times* and *L.A. Express*, two newspapers conspicuous in their full-throated support of the plan), but also one Moses H. Sherman, a member of that very same board of water commissioners that had approved the aqueduct plan behind closed doors.

Could all of this be merely coincidental? The editor of the *Examiner* didn't think so, and many other critics of the plan agreed. To them, it seemed obvious that the syndicate had acted on insider information—provided, presumably, by Commissioner Sherman. They had used it to snap up cheap marginal land before news of the aqueduct became public (news that, of course, would increase the value of those holdings astronomically). And while there was no evidence that Mulholland himself benefited from, or was in any way influenced by, the syndicate's designs, one thing was clear: some very rich men in Los Angeles were going to get even richer as a result of the new bounty of Owens River water.

As it turned out, the vast majority of L.A. residents were unfazed by the *Examiner*'s last-minute revelations. Such was the personal prestige of William Mulholland, now affectionately known as "the Chief," that the voters chose to disregard the cost, the engineering challenges, and the evidence of profiteering involved in the project. When the first bond issue came up for a vote on September 7, 1905, it passed by a stunning 14-to-1 margin. And ten months later, the second, much larger bond issue passed as well, by a nearly as impressive vote of 10 to 1. By this time, of course, the Reclamation Service had officially abandoned its irrigation plans in the Owens Valley. And it had done so with the blessing of Theodore Roosevelt himself. "It is a hundred or a thousandfold more important to state," the president concluded, quoting a California senator, "that this [water] is more valuable to the people as a whole if used by the city than if used by the people of the Owens Valley." One can only imagine Mrs. Lesta V. Parker's reaction to *that*.

"The chance to acquire such a supply [of water] is the greatest opportunity ever presented to Los Angeles," a jubilant Mulholland told an audience of eager Angelenos once the fate of his plan seemed assured. This was hardly an exaggeration. Yes, it would require a monumental—and expensive—multiyear effort, but the water czar was determined to do whatever had to be done to let the city of Los Angeles become great.

The situation looked a bit different from that of the Owens Valley. Back when the aqueduct plan was first announced, the blithely propagandistic *L.A. Times* had pronounced the residents of Inyo County satisfied with their end of the deal. "Everybody in the valley has money," the paper averred, "and everyone is happy."

But the editor of the *Inyo Register* had a different perspective: "The government held Owens Valley while Los Angeles skinned it."

# CHAPTER THREE
# Stories in Light and Shadow

*David Wark Griffith*

oward the end of 1907, just as Mulholland and his crews were gearing up to begin construction of the aqueduct, two men showed up in Los Angeles with some strange luggage in tow. Their names were Francis Boggs and Thomas Persons, and together they constituted an entire traveling film crew from the Selig Polyscope Company of Chicago, one of the first motion picture studios in the country. Boggs, the director, and Persons, the cameraman, had come to finish work on a movie—an adaptation of the Dumas classic *The Count of Monte Cristo*—and were looking for outdoor locations to shoot a few key scenes. As it happened, the harsh midwestern winter had set in too early that year for them to complete the film's exteriors in Illinois, so they had got permission to take their camera and other equipment west to southern California, where the winters were mild and pleasant. Since money was tight in the barely nascent business of moviemaking, the film's cast could not come along. So Boggs intended to hire local talent to play the characters originated by actors in Chicago. Motion pictures were still such a new and makeshift medium that audiences, he figured, would never notice the difference.

In downtown Los Angeles, they found a handsome if somewhat disheveled young man—a sometime actor who supplemented his income by selling fake jewelry on Main Street—and took him to a beach outside the city. Here they filmed the famous scene of Edmond Dantès emerging from the waves after his escape from the island prison of the Château d'If. Boggs had a few technical problems to deal with during the shoot. For one, the jewelry hawker's false beard had a tendency to wash off in the Pacific surf, requiring expensive retakes. But eventually the director and Persons got what they needed. After finishing a few more scenes at various locations up and down the coast, they wrapped up work, shipped the film back to Chicago to be developed and edited, and then left town.

A year and a half later, on the morning of May 6, 1909, a former stage actor named Hobart Bosworth was sitting in his office at the Institute of Dramatic Arts, a small acting school on South Broadway that he had opened the previous January. Now forty-one years old, Bosworth had been a well-known thespian, but a lifelong struggle with tuberculosis had ruined his once rich and resonant voice. He had been forced to quit his job with the local Belasco theater company and resort to teaching the skills he'd once practiced. But although his name was still respected in L.A. theatrical circles, the school he'd founded was, by his own admission, "not a tremendous financial success," and he found himself chronically strapped for cash.

On this pleasant Thursday morning, Bosworth received a visit from "a quiet gentleman in fashionable clothes" who identified himself as James L. McGee, business manager of the Selig Polyscope Company. McGee and director Francis Boggs were in town to make some motion pictures. (The owner of the company, Colonel William N. Selig, had apparently been pleased with the results of the Monte Cristo film released the previous year.) Would Mr. Bosworth be interested in performing the lead role in one of them?

Bosworth, a rather proud Shakespearean specialist who claimed to be a descendant of Miles Standish, found the question outrageous. "I was shocked," he later wrote, "and insulted and hurt by turns." He told McGee that he barely knew what a motion picture was, having seen only one—a film of the Jeffries-Sharkey boxing match of 1899. He had not been tempted to see any others, let alone act in one. Indeed, Bosworth felt sure that his old New York theatrical manager "would turn over in his grave were he to feel that I had debased my art so completely."

But McGee was persistent. No one, he insisted, would ever know that Bosworth had taken the job. The picture would be shown only in little Main Street nickelodeons, where his friends would never set foot; Bosworth's name would never be used in association with the production. And then McGee mentioned what the actor would be paid: $125, for two days of work.

"Alas, my code of ethics fell before the onslaught of Capital," Bosworth admitted. "The prostitution of art began then. I was the first to fall."

When Bosworth showed up on Saturday morning for the first day of filming, his spirits sank. The Selig "studio"—on Olive between 7th and 8th Streets in downtown Los Angeles—was nothing more than an open-air wooden platform, set up in a vacant lot next to a Chinese laundry. The stage was littered with carpets and debris, but director Boggs, to whom Bosworth was now introduced, told him not to worry: "Never mind the floor, we will only cut to your knees; the rest won't show." Boggs then let him look at the film's "continuity notes"—essentially a handful of scrawled pages describing the action of each scene to be shot—which the director had apparently written up the night before. The film, which was to be called *In the Sultan's Power*, involved a dashing American traveler who rescues a young Frenchwoman from the seraglio of a diabolical Turkish nobleman. Bosworth was to play Jack Thornton, the hero who outwits the sultan and wins the heart of the helpless heroine.

When filming began, Bosworth was amazed at the chaos of the process. "All was hurried, makeshift, and in a measure confused," he later recalled. "I, who had spent so many years before audiences . . . had to emote before a black box with the thick end of a beer bottle, as it looked, for the lens." His only audience, besides director Boggs, was the cameraman—"a careless chap who chewed gum, looked at everything but us, the actors, [and] chiefly cocked his eye at the sun to see if there was apt to be any light change in the scene." All of this, moreover, had to be done while wet laundry flapped on drying racks next door and amid the cacophonous outbursts of the Chinese workers hanging it.

Accustomed as he was to "the traditions of the leisurely legitimate stage," Bosworth could hardly believe the speed with which everything was accomplished on a movie set. Scenes were mounted with a bare minimum of rehearsal, whereas he was used to rehearsing for weeks before a performance. And they were shot all out of sequence, depending on the light and the location, with no regard for where they would appear in the finished narrative. "I watched the development of this story, each little scene telling its part, with open-mouthed astonishment," he said. But after filming a few final scenes on Sunday afternoon (at the still-unfinished Hotel Wentworth in Pasadena), the production was complete in the promised two days of work. Boggs, Persons, McGee, and the rest of the company moved on to make another film in the northern part of the state while Bosworth went back to his acting school.

The next day Bosworth made little of the episode in his journal. "All Saturday and yesterday," he wrote, "I acted as leading man before a kinetoscope, a strange but not unpleasant experience, and I look forward to seeing myself act when the films are given here. I was paid $125 for two days' work, my climax in day's earnings."

That bland entry notwithstanding, Bosworth had actually just made cinema history. *In the Sultan's Power* is now regarded as one of the first narrative films to be shot entirely in the Los Angeles metropolitan area. It would not be the last.

~

To anyone living in Los Angeles in the first decade of the twentieth century, the idea that motion pictures would be crucial to the city's future (or to any city's future) would have been laughable. The "flickers" had been around for barely ten years, and were still mostly seen as little more than a gimcrack novelty. Sometime in the early 1890s, inventor Thomas Edison—combining a number of innovations developed by early pioneers like Coleman Sellers, Eadweard Muybridge, and Etienne Jules Moray—had created what he called a Kinetoscope. Essentially a peephole viewer box displaying a short scene on a continuous loop of 35-mm film, the Kinetoscope was introduced with great fanfare at the 1893 Chicago World's Fair. Audiences were intrigued, so Edison began producing the machines in quantity and selling them to penny arcades around the country. But since only one paying customer at a time could view the ninety-second films, the commercial potential of the invention seemed limited.

Developments in film projection in 1895 and 1896, however, changed the financial calculus of movie exhibition. Once films could be projected onto a large screen, more people could view them at the same time, meaning that more pennies (and eventually nickels) could be collected faster. Movies were soon being shown after live acts at vaudeville shows, or as part of multipicture programs at arcades and storefront theaters. The films were simple at first, depicting either actual events (the arrival of a train at a railroad station; President McKinley strolling in his garden) or brief, often comic situations (a woman's skirts blown up by a stiff wind; a man sneezing). But what they lacked in sophistication they made up for in novelty and immediacy. When early audiences watched Edison's eighteen-second-long *The Execution of Mary, Queen of Scots*—whose director, Alfred Clark, used a dummy and a stop-camera trick to simulate the monarch's beheading—they could thrill to an experience more visceral than any they could have in a live stage production.

Even so, movies would likely have faded as just another nine-day-wonder had it not been for another innovation: the introduction of a prolonged narrative line, with multiple scenes leading one to the next. The French were the pioneers with this idea. In the early years of the twentieth century, George Méliès, a professional magician, made a series of films that combined whimsical animation and playful visual trickery to create actual extended storylines. Movies like *A Trip to the Moon* of 1902 (which includes the iconic scene of a space capsule crashing into the eye of the moon) proved that an audience's interest could be sustained for far longer than the sixty or ninety seconds of a typical early Kinetoscope. Learning from this example, Edison director Edwin S. Porter made *The Great Train Robbery* (1903), a twelve-minute western that would prove to be a milestone in American filmmaking. Porter employed a number of innovations in the film—most notably camera panning, to follow the action, and parallel editing, cutting between scenes that occur simultaneously but in different places. The result was a dynamic feat of early visual storytelling, complete with trigger-happy desperadoes, a quickly assembled posse of outraged citizens, and a climactic chase scene on horseback. It came as a revelation to American audiences of the time, who responded by making it one of the first true box office hits.

This success did not go unnoticed. Soon other moviemakers were following Porter's lead, adopting his freer, more flexible style of editing to create stories that filled an entire reel (eight to twelve minutes) of film. Audiences couldn't get enough of them. Entrepreneurs began opening more and more small theaters (dubbed "nickelodeons" because of the five-cent admission price) devoted exclusively to motion picture exhibition. And when theater owners found that they could change their programs daily—or even twice daily—and still fill their seats, the demand for new films grew explosively. Movie production companies sprang up in major cities like New York, Chicago, and Philadelphia. And since there would be no motion picture copyright law until 1912, they could all steal ideas and stories from one another with impunity.

All of this activity was still happening under the radar of most Americans, for whom the phrase "theatrical entertainment" meant performances of stage plays and musicals by live actors. Movies remained a pastime of the inner-city working class—often immigrants who couldn't afford a ticket to the legitimate theater and for whom silent films presented no language barrier. As such they were regarded as a somewhat disreputable phenomenon. So-called respectable people didn't go to see them, and movies soon became the target of sanctimonious reformers eager to point out the moral and even medical harm they caused, especially to impressionable children susceptible to the movies' alleged glorification of sex, crime, and violence. Even stage actors and playwrights—not very high on the respectability scale themselves—were reluctant to enter the new field, applying for work at film studios only when financial desperation set in.

One such holdout was David Wark Griffith, a frustrated thespian who, like Hobart Bosworth, had never dreamed of taking a job in anything so disgraceful as a movie. Born on January 22, 1875, on a farm called Lofty Green in Crestwood, Kentucky, he grew up under the lingering shadow of the Civil War, which had all but ruined his once-prominent slave-holding family. His father—Jacob Griffith, a.k.a. "Thundering Jake"—had fought as a colonel for the Confederacy and had never quite gotten over the family's lost glory. By the time David was born, the great house on the estate had burned down, and the Griffiths (descendants, according to Jacob, of a line of Welsh warrior kings) were forced to eke out a living in one of the outbuildings on their much-mortgaged property. "Here," as Griffith was later to lament, "was whelped the wolf pup of want and hunger that was to shadow me all my life."

When Thundering Jake died a few months after David's tenth birthday, he left the family with a raft of debts that forced his widow to sell the Lofty Green property and to move the family out—first to a farm owned by her eldest son, and eventually into the nearby city of Louisville. Here the self-styled country boy got his first taste of big-city amusements. Having grown up in a place where entertainment consisted mostly of "listening to whittling oldsters by the horse trough," he was fascinated by the variety of concerts, dramatic performances, and vaudeville shows on offer in Louisville. When he was seventeen years old and out of school, he decided he wanted to make a life in the theater. His mother disapproved. The Griffith ancestors had doubtless committed "variously assorted villainies" in their day, she told him, "but none is on record as having fallen so low as to become an actor." Her son, however, would not be discouraged, and he soon landed a part with a traveling theater company called the Twilight Revellers. Their first tour ended ignobly, with the entire company attempting—unsuccessfully—to sneak away from their boardinghouse in the dead of night to avoid paying their bill, but young David was hooked. "I was forced to beat my way back to Louisville," he later recalled. "But now . . . now . . . *I was an actor.*"

It was not the last time he would find himself stranded in a strange town at the end of an aborted road tour. Throughout his late teens and early twenties, "Lawrence" Griffith (as he styled himself in the playbills) acted in many different roles, ranging from a spear-carrying extra in a Sarah Bernhardt production to a star turn as Alessandro in the play *Ramona*, but rarely for very long and never to any great acclaim. Although his travels took him from Minneapolis to Portland to Los Angeles to Chicago to Atlantic City, with extended stays in San Francisco and New York, the work was hardly steady; between gigs he was often forced to take odd jobs—picking hops, shoveling coal, or working on lumber freighters—to keep body and soul together. Still, he persisted: "Success was always just around the corner," he wrote, "and hope put a glow over the dingiest lodging house."

While doing repertory with a company based at the Grand Opera House in San Francisco, he met a young actress named Linda Arvidson. Given the gamines Griffith would later be obsessed with as a director (Mary Pickford, Lillian Gish, and others), the grave-faced and womanly Arvidson would hardly seem to have been his type. But Griffith—who, with his prominent aquiline nose and gangly physique, always regarded himself as homely—found himself drawn to her, and she to him. A romance developed, and although the two were often parted because of their peripatetic way of life, their bond remained strong.

Then, in April 1906, the great San Francisco earthquake and fire forced a deepening of their relationship. Griffith was acting in Minneapolis at the time, but Arvidson was still working in the stricken city. She sent him a telegram reassuring him that she was safe but hinting that an escape from the chaos would not be unwelcome. He took the hint and arranged for them to rendezvous in Boston in early May. There, on May 14, 1906, they were married in the Old North Church (of Paul Revere fame).

It may have taken an earthquake to precipitate his wedding, but Griffith was in any case ready for a life change. Now thirty-one years old, he had spent more than a decade on the road, sleeping in flophouse dormitories and railroad coaches, trying to make a living as an actor with only middling success. He was ready to settle down and make a serious effort to write for a living—something he'd been contemplating for years. He and Arvidson moved into a small sublet apartment on West 56th Street in Manhattan, where (with no theater work likely until the fall) she busied herself setting up a household while he tried to finish a play he'd been working on in the lulls between acting jobs. The writing went well, and it wasn't long before the play—a romance called *A Fool and a Girl*—was ready to send out into the world. On Christmas Eve 1906, Griffith came home from a day of pounding the pavements for work, looking tired but with a strange smile on his face. He slipped something under Arvidson's plate at the dinner table, where they were about to sit down to a modest holiday meal of hamburgers with gravy. She lifted her plate to find a bank check. A producer had bought *A Fool and a Girl*, for an advance against royalties of seven hundred dollars.

This advance was a remarkable windfall, around seventeen thousand dollars in today's currency. It also heralded a period of success for the neophyte writer during which he also sold a short story (to *Cosmopolitan*) and a long poem (to *Leslie's Weekly*). But the good fortune didn't last. When *A Fool and a Girl* opened in Washington, D.C., critics savaged it, and it closed after a short run. A second play—*War*, a grand drama about the American Revolution that even Griffith's wife called "pretentious"— found no buyers. Nor did he sell any more poems or stories. By early 1908, unable to find work as either an actor or a writer, he found himself again shadowed by that "Old Wolf" of want and hunger. One January day he ran into two fellow actors at an automat called Three-Cent John's on 42nd Street and told them of his woes. One of them suggested he try his luck at the new motion picture studios, but Griffith demurred. "I'll lose standing as an actor with theater people if they see me in a movie," he said.

"None of them has seen us yet and it hasn't hurt us," his friend replied. "The money is worth going after."

"Do you think I'd stand a chance?"

"Well, there's no harm trying. You might even sell them a scenario."

This latter possibility was more appealing to Griffith. Back in 1898, while doing summer stock in Chicago, he had seen his first motion picture and didn't like it at all. "I found it silly, tiresome, inexcusably tedious," he reported. "It was in no way worthwhile and I consider the time wasted." He conceded, however, that the line at the box office was impressive. Certain he could write a better story than the ones he had seen, he now cobbled together a reworking of Sardou's play *La Tosca*. This he took up to the Edison Studio in the Bronx, where Edwin Porter (director of *The Great Train Robbery*) was head of production. No one was interested in his scenario, but one of Porter's staff directors, J. Searle Dawly, offered him a job as an actor in the movie he was just casting. Reluctantly, Griffith accepted.

The story of the film, *Rescued from an Eagle's Nest*, was simple enough: A baby playing outside its mountain cabin home is grabbed by a passing eagle (actually a stuffed crowlike bird manipulated by wires) and carried off to a cliffside aerie. After suitable histrionics from the child's parents and assorted neighbors, a heroic mountaineer played by Griffith steps in to effect the rescue. Lowered by ropes to the ledge on which the eagle has stowed the child, he wrestles with the bird, beats it to death, then grabs the captive and climbs back to safety, restoring the child to its mother amid much joyful celebration. The film took four days to make—some of it shot in the Bronx studio and the rest shot on the Palisades cliffs just outside Fort Lee, New Jersey—and, as promised, it was easy money. But apparently Dawly was unimpressed by his new recruit; no more work followed from the Edison Studio.

Undaunted, Griffith decided to try his luck with Edison's principal competitor: the American Mutoscope and Biograph Company (later known just as Biograph), headquartered in a large townhouse at 11 East

14th Street in Manhattan. Again he came armed with scenarios, but again the person in charge, George McCutcheon, the company director, thought he'd be more useful in front of the camera. Feeling desperate by now, Griffith accepted McCutcheon's offer of an acting job, hoping it would just be a stopgap until the Broadway season started again in the fall. But he would never act on a theater stage again.

~~

When Griffith started acting for Biograph in the spring of 1908, there were about nine principal film studios active in the United States. Thanks to the tight control Edison exercised over patent rights, all but one of them had to pay license fees to use Edison's movie cameras and other equipment. The exception was Biograph, founded by William Laurie Dickson, Edison's former assistant—and the man largely responsible for developing the technologies his boss later claimed as his own. After leaving the Edison Studio in 1895, Dickson had invented a new peep show machine called a Mutoscope to compete with Edison's Kinetoscope. He'd also come up with a motion picture camera and a projector that would not infringe on the Edison patents. But since Biograph films required exhibitors to buy or rent all of that special equipment, the studio began losing ground to Edison and the "Edison licensees." One of Biograph's financial backers, worried about its investment, sent in an executive, Jeremiah J. Kennedy, to evaluate the business and, if necessary, liquidate the company's assets.

Rather than dismantle the company, however, Kennedy decided to rejuvenate it. Realizing that the battle against the Edison group was hopelessly one-sided, he entered into negotiations with the other studios' lawyers to work out some kind of compromise. The result was the Motion Picture Patents Company (MPPC), formed in late 1908 as a combine of Edison, the Edison licensee studios, and Biograph. Unofficially dubbed the Film Trust, the MPPC would for a time hold a virtual monopoly on American motion picture production. And although the trust's stranglehold would eventually be challenged by a number of upstart studios (known as "the independents"), Biograph's viability as a film studio was, at least temporarily, assured.

Meanwhile Kennedy, along with Biograph's second-in-command,

Henry Marvin, also hoped to improve the quality of the products that the studio put out every week. For some years now, virtually all Biograph films had been directed by George McCutcheon, an older man whose ill health was making it difficult for him to keep up with the rapid pace of production required in the industry's early days. McCutcheon's son Wallace briefly took over the reins as principal director, but he had other ambitions (he yearned for a stage career in musical comedy) and chafed at the demanding job. By mid-1908, Henry Marvin was making inquiries after a capable director who could help Wallace McCutcheon crank out the studio's target of two films per week.

Enter the actor still calling himself "Lawrence" Griffith. Now thirty-three, he was old enough to take on the responsibilities of director, which at this point in the industry's development mainly involved rehearsing the actors and keeping them in line on the set; all other functions—like choosing camera angles and lighting schemes—were performed by the cameraman. Griffith, moreover, had proven himself a reliable and energetic worker, and he even seemed to evince some genuine creativity, having by this point sold several film synopses to the Biograph story department. Arthur Marvin, brother of Henry and one of the studio's two cameramen, suggested to his brother that Griffith might be a good prospect as a second-string director.

But unlike countless actors in Hollywood history to come, Griffith wasn't sure he really wanted to direct. Contrary to his expectations, he was enjoying this interlude as a motion picture actor. "It's not so bad, you know," he told his wife after two days of work on a Biograph western, "five dollars for simply riding a horse in the wilds of Fort Lee on a cool spring day." He suggested that she herself offer her acting services at the 14th Street studio (though as "Linda Arvidson" and not "Mrs. Griffith," since he thought Biograph might be reluctant to hire a married pair). So when Marvin approached him with the directing offer, Griffith hesitated. "I am working regularly [as an actor] for McCutcheon now," he said. "If I try directing he will not like it, and if I fall down he won't give me any more parts."

Marvin assured him that a trial project as director would not jeopardize his standing as an actor with the company, no matter how it turned out. He then handed Griffith a story synopsis entitled *The Adventures of Dollie.* According to studio gossip the project was a "lemon," but the story was no more ridiculous or simplistic than most film scenarios of the day. It was an adventure tale about a young child spirited away by gypsies, hidden in a barrel, and then sent floating down a river and over a small waterfall, before being joyfully rescued by her father. From this rudimentary material, Griffith was to produce a one-reel movie.

Shortly before the start of filming, Griffith wisely consulted with the most experienced movie man he knew: Billy Bitzer, Biograph's principal cameraman, who had been shooting for the studio since the early Mutoscope days in the 1890s. Griffith showed up at Bitzer's apartment one evening after dinner and asked for help translating the bare bones of the *Dollie* story into an effective visual narrative. Bitzer, a rather pudgy, cigar-chewing problem-solver, grabbed a nearby laundry cardboard and wrote down all the parts of the story that would have to be dramatized, putting each under one of five categories: "Heart Interest, Drama, Danger, Comedy, and Rescue." Griffith never mentioned this episode in his autobiography, but it's hard not to think of it as a seminal moment in cinema history. Bitzer was outlining for the future Father of Film the five basic elements of visual storytelling that would inform every movie he was to make. And although Griffith, as a would-be playwright, must have had at least an instinctive grasp of dramaturgy, this explicit lesson from a seasoned pro (if such a thing could exist in an industry barely a decade old) was undoubtedly formative. According to Bitzer, when Griffith left that night, he exuded an air of self-confidence that would stay with him through the hard years of creativity ahead.

It was Arthur Marvin, not Bitzer, who was assigned to be the cameraman for the *Dollie* film, but he and Griffith worked well enough together. (Just promise him a bottle of beer, Bitzer advised Griffith, and you'll get Marvin to do whatever you want him to.) Over the two days of photography—June 18 and 19, 1908, on location in Sound Beach, Connecticut—Griffith and Marvin filmed twelve scenes, each consisting of a single medium shot, taken from a fixed camera location. Linda Arvidson, whom no one knew was the director's wife, was cast as the mother, while the father was played by Arthur Johnson, a tall handsome actor Griffith had waylaid on the street for the project just a few days before filming. The resulting movie cost sixty-five dollars to make, and although it was nothing revolutionary, the Biograph executives were satisfied. By the time the film opened at Keith and Proctor's Theatre on Union Square in mid-July, they had already allowed Griffith to make several others. And much to their (and Griffith's) relief, the audience seemed to like his first effort. "Not a snore was to be heard," Linda Arvidson reported, "[so] we concluded we'd had a successful opening night."

But Griffith's success with *Dollie* turned out to be more than just another new director passing muster. Exhibitors may have seen nothing special in the film, but their customers did—audience demand for the film was exceptionally strong. Before the summer was out, Biograph had sold twenty-five prints of *The Adventures of Dollie*, surpassing the previous house record of fifteen. The films Griffith had made in the interim went on to succeed as well. Biograph was so pleased that by late July, Griffith was directing all of the studio's films. On August 17 he signed his first one-year contract with the company, assuring him a base salary of fifty dollars per week, with a royalty of one-twentieth of a cent on every foot of film sold to the exchanges.

What followed was a year and a half of unprecedented creative experimentation, as Griffith—working mainly with Bitzer as his cameraman—produced a series of short films that essentially defined a new mode of artistic expression. It was a period "without parallel in the emergence of any art form," according to film historian Arthur Knight. "Griffith took the raw elements of movie-making as they had evolved up to that time and, single-handedly, wrought from them a medium more intimate than theater, more vivid than literature, more affecting than poetry."

The innovations began almost immediately. By the time Griffith was beginning his eighth assignment as director—*For the Love of Gold*, a nine-minute film shot in that first summer of 1908—he was already bridling at the standard method of rendering every scene in his story as a single shot taken from a single camera location. Eager to show the reactions of some cardplayers during a game, he asked Bitzer to move the camera closer to the actors partway through the scene, so that the audience could more clearly discern their faces. The resulting scene thus consisted of two shots: the standard medium shot of the actors as they would be seen on a stage, and a cut to a three-quarter shot. This cut, he felt, would allow the audience to see for themselves what the characters were thinking, without resorting to the thought bubbles or intertitles used by other directors in similar situations. This was not, as Griffith was later to claim, the first use of a close-up in the movies. Bitzer himself would eventually point out that Edison's 1894 Kinetoscope *Fred Ott's Sneeze* was entirely shot in close-up. But Griffith's close-up was, in a way, even more revolutionary. As film historian Robert M. Henderson has written, "Now Griffith was able to express thought visually. He had also destroyed for all time the idea that a shot and a scene were synonymous. The shot was now the basic film unit, and a scene . . . might consist of an unlimited number of shots."

In *The Fatal Hour*, his next film, Griffith introduced what would become one of his signature techniques: cross-cutting, or parallel editing, to create a sense of mounting suspense. Near the end of the film, a female detective is tied up in a criminal's hideout with a loaded gun aimed directly at her head, set to go off when an attached clock strikes midnight. Griffith builds toward a climax by cutting between this scene and a shot of the woman's rescuers racing toward the hideout in a horse-drawn carriage. The two scenes converge at the end, when the rescuers arrive and free the detective just before the gun goes off. Of course, the audience knows in advance that this has to be the outcome, but Griffith's technique works nonetheless, pushing the action to an unbearable height of tension. (Griffith would go even further in his 1909 film *The Lonely Villa*, in which he cross-cut not two but three different elements—a threatened mother and children cringing in a locked room, the criminals who are trying to break down the door, and a husband rushing wildly to the villa to save his family.)

Here again, Griffith didn't invent cross-cutting—Edwin Porter had used a cruder version of the technique in *The Great Train Robbery* five years earlier. But Griffith refined it and expanded its use, adding it to a toolbox of dramatic effects that was growing by the week as he and Bitzer experimented ever more boldly on set. Vignette shots, fade-outs, jump cuts, reverse shots—all began as ideas to try out and, if effective, to keep in mind for the next movie. Combined with some creative new lighting and makeup techniques, they evolved into a powerful and endlessly adaptable language of visual storytelling: "a coherent, basic screen grammar," as Griffith biographer Richard Schickel has called it. No longer were movies just imitations of stage plays, filmed from the equivalent of a prime seat in the orchestra; Griffith was freeing the medium from those static conventions. Thus did "Lawrence" Griffith, the failed actor and playwright, finally find success—by creating an art form in which he could excel. He accepted his new path at the time of his second contract renewal, in 1910, by signing his real name to his work for the first time. From then on, he was David Wark Griffith, the film director.

Of course, while Griffith now saw motion pictures as an art form, his bosses emphatically saw them as a commercial product, and they met each of his innovations with resistance. Of an early example of parallel editing in a Griffith film, one studio executive griped: "How can you tell a story jumping about like that? The people won't know what it's about." Griffith argued that this was exactly how Dickens told a story in a novel, switching from one character and scene to another. The moody lighting in another film likewise rankled the denizens of the front office. Film stock was too expensive to squander on such experiments, they said. And besides, people wanted to see what was going on! But Griffith was confident enough at this point to stand his ground.

When his "experiments" opened in the nickelodeons, he was invariably vindicated. Audiences *did* understand what he was doing, and they responded by coming to see Biograph pictures in great numbers. Theater owners started featuring regular "Biograph Days," certain that a full program of the studio's films could fill their houses to capacity. People began writing fan letters to the studio, praising the typical Biograph for "the finish, the roundness, and the completeness of the story." As one early moviegoer recalled, "Even we children sensed that Biograph features were 'different.'"

Meanwhile audiences also began taking note of individual actors and actresses. In these early years, film studios were reluctant to publicize the names of their featured players, fearing that individual billing might empower them to ask for more money. But that didn't stop moviegoers from identifying their favorites as "the Biograph Girl," or "The Lone Indian," or "the Curly-Haired Girl." And many of the actors Griffith was assembling for his company would prove to be enduringly popular in the years to come. One of Griffith's early lead players—the mellifluously named Florence Lawrence, the original Biograph Girl—was such a box office draw that one of the independent studios eventually poached her. They enticed her with a big raise and a promise of prominent on-screen billing, in the process creating the first bona-fide "movie star."

Henry Walthall, a popular stage actor (who, incidentally, had appeared with Griffith in *Rescued from an Eagle's Nest*), soon joined the ensemble, becoming a Biograph stalwart and ultimately one of the best-known and most accomplished actors of the silent era. Another future big name was Mack Sennett (actually Michael Sinnott), "a big bear-like figure [with] gorilla arms" whom Griffith took on to play the occasional goon or galoot. Sennett proved to be far smarter and more ambitious than he looked. He was soon engineering "chance meetings" with Griffith after their workdays, during which the two would walk the streets for hours, discussing the new art form. Griffith was, according to Sennett, "my day school, my adult education program, my university." Eventually Griffith let him direct some of the studio's comic films— never a Griffith strong point—which often featured another celebrity-to-be, actress Mabel Normand. Under Griffith the Sennett-Normand team gained experience they would parlay into the great Keystone comedies of the 1910s.

Perhaps the most significant addition to the Biograph troupe was a petite, golden-haired teenager who appeared at the 14th Street studio in the spring of 1909 and asked to see the man in charge. Accounts of this momentous first meeting differ, but all (including her own) agree that the diminutive young woman's haughty confidence both amused and intrigued the director. "In rapid fire," Griffith recalled, "she informed me that she was a regular actress and had been the last season with [Broadway impresario] Mr. David Belasco, but would condescend to work for a short period in the movies"—assuming, of course, that he could meet her salary demand of twenty-five dollars per week. Her name was Gladys Smith, she told Griffith, but she appeared professionally under the name Belasco had given her: Mary Pickford.

Whether or not Griffith met her presumption with presumption of his own ("You're too little and too fat, but I may give you a chance," he said, according to Pickford), he did agree to her salary terms. Taking her back to a dressing room, he personally applied her makeup—making her look like Pancho Villa, she later complained—and gave her a screen test. The always-obtuse Biograph executives didn't like the results, complaining that her head was too big for her body, but Griffith knew better. He took her on and gave her principal roles almost from the start. And thus the greatest female silent film star was born.

⁓

By the end of 1909—after eighteen months of sixteen-hour days and seven-day weeks that had yielded more than two hundred films—Griffith was ready for a change of venue. The past year and a half with Biograph and his cameraman Bitzer had been a period of intensive creativity. Biograph films were now the gold standard of movie production, sought out by the exchanges and imitated by moviemakers throughout the industry. Though the American middle class was still scornful of the whole idea of movies (and suspicious of their moral effects), Griffith had done much to improve the reputation of the upstart industry. Even the notoriously stodgy *New York Times* had begun to take notice. On October 10 the newspaper printed its very first movie review, of Griffith's *Pippa Passes*, based on a Robert Browning poem and starring Mary Pickford. The film's success, according to the *Times* critic, clearly signaled a new taste among moviegoers for "highbrow effects." In fact, he teased, we might soon see audiences demanding Kant's *Prolegomena to Metaphysics*, "with the *Kritik of Pure Reason* for a curtain raiser."

The condescension of the Gray Lady notwithstanding, Griffith knew by now that he was on to something with enormous potential, both financial and artistic, if only he had the freedom to work as expansively as he wanted to. The studio on 14th Street was proving too small and inflexible, and although he'd been doing more and more shooting outdoors on location—in places like Fort Lee, Atlantic Highlands, and Cuddebackville, New York—these locales were often unusable because of the weather. Griffith hated the New York winters in any case ("perhaps because he was a Southerner," according to Bitzer), and so he began lobbying the front office to allow him to take the company to California for the season. He had been hearing about the success of filmmakers shooting in Los Angeles, and he felt "he could guarantee [that] Biograph would benefit from the sunny weather and picturesque settings." To his surprise, the new president of the studio, R. H. Hammer, agreed. In mid-January 1910, halfway through the filming of a movie called *The Newlyweds*, Griffith was allowed to select a group of some thirty actors and crew as his traveling company and head cross-country. He, Hammer, and Linda Arvidson (whom he now had to admit was his wife) traveled in style on the Twentieth Century Limited, while the rest made their way by the less grandiose Black Diamond Express and California Limited trains, via Chicago.

Four days later, on January 20, 1910, they all reconvened at the Alexandria Hotel in Los Angeles, ready to get to work. Their arrival went largely unnoticed in the now-bustling town, but it was, in retrospect, big news. Biograph had come west, and the epicenter of the nascent movie industry had come with it.

# CHAPTER FOUR

# On Location

*Hollywood, circa 1905*

When Griffith and his Biograph crew arrived in Los Angeles on January 20, 1910, they were not the first moviemakers to take up an extended residence in the city that would become the industry's capital. Francis Boggs of Selig—who had left town after the completion of *In the Sultan's Power*—had returned in September 1909 to set up a permanent Selig studio at 1845 Alessandro Avenue, in the part of the city then known as Edendale (around today's Silver Lake and Echo Park). Hobart Bosworth, having weathered another "lung breakdown" in the interim, was more than delighted to accept Boggs's offer to become the studio's leading man, at the same "gorgeous salary" he had received for his debut four months earlier. He immediately got back to work with Boggs, playing the part of Virgilias in a costume drama called *The Roman*.

Two months later, in November 1909, an independent outfit called the New York Motion Picture Company, started by two former bookies, Charles Baumann and Adam Kessel, set up shop in an abandoned grocery store down the street from Selig and began producing movies under the moniker Bison. They had allegedly come west after a fracas on the streets of New York with some "Edison bulls"—that is, the intimidating detectives hired by the trust to prevent unauthorized use of his patented camera and film stock. Much has been made of this episode, and some Hollywood historians cite the geographical distance from Edison's enforcers as the main reason so many moviemakers came to Los Angeles. But a good number of the companies that arrived in these early years—Lubin, Essanay, Méliès, and Vitagraph all came shortly after Griffith and his crew—were fully licensed members of the trust, with no need to escape the long arm of the law. And certainly the city's physical suitability for filmmaking was compelling enough. As Hobart Bosworth pointed out, "We could make Westerns here all the year, sea pictures all the year, pictures of mountains, plains, desert, bungalows, palms, and eucalypti. . . . No fog, little rain (too little), the most benign climate—all within sixty miles."

Even urban street scenes were easily shot in the Los Angeles of 1910, since the city's downtown was by now densely built up. Manhattan it wasn't, but new ten- and twelve-story Beaux Arts buildings were filling the grid below the former pueblo at a rapid pace. The city also came equipped with the warren-like streets and alleys of Chinatown (much used in early crime dramas), a lingering Mexican atmosphere around the old plaza, and a number of elegant hotel lobbies that could double as the finest interiors of New York or Boston. And if a scene called for a suburban or rural setting, it was easy enough for a film crew to climb aboard one of the ubiquitous Red Car streetcars of the Pacific Electric Railway or Yellow Cars of the Los Angeles Railway and be out in the boondocks in a matter of minutes.

Most Angelenos had yet to take much notice of the new industry growing up in their midst. Although Los Angeles was the site of the very first dedicated movie house in the country—the Electric Theatre, converted from an old arcade in 1902 by entrepreneur Thomas Tally—this town full of culturally conservative midwestern transplants hardly saw itself as a future movie capital. Some residents actively sought to discourage the industry's development, as witnessed by the numerous "NO JEWS, ACTORS, OR DOGS" signs that soon appeared in the windows of boardinghouses. According to one early screenwriter, a committee calling itself the Conscientious Citizens had even managed to gather ten thousand signatures on a petition for the city to expel the disreputable movie people.

As for Hollywood itself, it was still a quiet suburb of mostly fruit orchards, punctuated by the occasional flower-draped cottage—"a lazy little village," as Cecil B. DeMille would soon describe it, "in its shining pink stucco dress, dreaming peacefully at the foot of gentle green hills." Incorporated in 1903 as a dry Christian community, it would vote to annex itself to Los Angeles in 1910 to gain access to the water brought by Mulholland's aqueduct, still under construction. And although it was already connected to downtown by one of the Red Car lines, which ran down the center of what would become Hollywood Boulevard, the town was still unaware of the central role it would play in the future of the motion picture arts and sciences. Not until October 1911 would the first movie studio come to Hollywood proper, when two Englishmen, William and David Horsely, began making movies under the name Nestor in a decrepit roadhouse off Sunset Boulevard. But the Horselys were to be the vanguard of a horde. Within months of Nestor's arrival, more than a dozen other companies were plying their trade in and around the sleepy town in the foothills of the Santa Monica Mountains.

Meanwhile, about seven miles southeast, the man who was to make Hollywood a household name was getting busy. Griffith had rented a downtown loft on Main Street and an open lot at the corner of Grand Avenue and Washington Street. To call the latter a studio would be generous. According to Mary Pickford, "Our stage consisted of an acre of ground, fenced in, and a large wooden platform, hung with cotton shades that were pulled on wires overhead. On a windy day our clothes and curtains on the set would flap loudly in the breeze. . . . Dressing rooms being a non-existent luxury, we donned our costumes every morning at the hotel." The lot was situated between a lumberyard and a baseball park and lined on one side with telegraph poles, on which small boys would sometimes perch during filming sessions, "watching the proceedings and throwing us friendly salutations, which didn't always help along the action," as Linda Arvidson wrote. Rehearsals were conducted in the Main Street loft, where "a kitchen table and three chairs were all there was of furniture," Pickford remembered. "Mr. Griffith occupied one of the chairs, the others being reserved for the elderly members of the cast. The rest of us sat on the floor."

No wonder Griffith filmed as much as he could on location. His first movie in Los Angeles, a romance called *The Thread of Destiny*, was shot mostly at the atmospheric San Gabriel Mission, northeast of the city. Then came *In Old California*, filmed in Hollywood (and traditionally regarded as the first film made entirely within its borders), followed by an adaptation of Tennyson, *The Unchanging Sea*, shot on the beach in a still remarkably wild-looking Santa Monica. The crew encountered their fair share of adversity in these early days. While filming *In Old California*, for instance, some starchy guests at the nearby Hollywood Inn became upset by Marion Leonard's emotive performance before the camera. "They resented the love-making," Linda Arvidson recalled, "and began making derogatory comments about movie actors. . . . [O]ne 'lady,' becoming particularly incensed, shouted loudly, 'Well, I wouldn't dress up like a fool like that woman and act like her, no, not for all the money in the world.'"

A week or so later, work on *The Two Brothers* (filmed at the San Juan Capistrano Mission) was delayed by three days of rain—in sunny California!—fraying everyone's nerves and leaving Griffith with an enormous hotel bill that would rankle the studio bosses back east. And when the weather finally cleared enough to film, the cast was physically attacked by a group of the mission's Mexican-American parishioners, who threw rocks during the shooting of a holy procession. (They regarded the faux ceremony as disrespectful and sacrilegious.)

Such incidents aside, Griffith did find working in Los Angeles liberating. Although he and his troupe would return east for the next three summers (before relocating to Los Angeles more permanently in late 1912), it was in California that he would do his most important and expansive work. Far from the eyes of his meddling bosses in New York, he could ignore their long-distance directives and make the kind of motion pictures he wanted to—"California pictures," as they came to be called, full of open spaces and new ideas. Of course, the movies had to continue making money for the shareholders, but in the early 1910s, as Mack Sennett noted, "Anything on film made money. The only requirement was that it be reasonably new."

In 1912, after a long-fought lawsuit brought against them under the Sherman Anti-Trust Act, Edison and the Motion Picture Patents Company lost their stranglehold on movie production technology, meaning that the independents could now operate without fear of the trust and its stifling license requirements. The number of companies making movies exploded. As Griffith himself later wrote, "Now the combine was broken. Anybody could make pictures. New talent, new brains jumped in." And they jumped in by the score. New directors like Thomas Ince, Allan Dwan, and Cecil B. DeMille came west to try their hand in what was already a $40 million industry, with an estimated weekly audience of 45 million people. That was an awful lot of five-cent admissions to work with, and they made many things possible. As Hobart Bosworth said, "The vast waves of nickels that were piling upon our beach gave

us the where-with-all [*sic*] for experimentation." L.A. movie production
soon became a creative free-for-all, and since it was happening way out
west, filmmakers could get away with almost anything. "All was fish that
came to our net," Bosworth admitted. "Nobody, in those days, thought
of plagiarism or rights. We took material wherever we could get it. . . .
Nobody cared. We were despised movie people."

By 1913, more than forty different companies were making movies
in Los Angeles, adding $20 million to the local economy. Residents,
suddenly aware that the influx of movie people might actually have an
upside, were becoming accustomed to encountering costumed actors
on the streetcars, or turning a corner to find an Old West shootout in
progress before a camera. As early screenwriter Francis Marion recalled,
"During the noon hour you were apt to see Bluebeard and all his wives
cozily eating ham sandwiches and hardboiled eggs [in the parks], while
the Apostle John sat under a pepper tree with his arm around a bathing
beauty."

But although many people were suddenly making movies all over Los
Angeles, no one doubted who was the true artist of the form. " 'D.W.' was
the master that every young director watched, studied, and imitated,"
director Henry King would later recall. Early Hollywood memoirs are
full of paeans to the man already being called "The Belasco of Motion
Pictures." Allan Dwan—a director who, like so many of the silent filmmakers, had stumbled into the business by accident, having been hired
as a scenario writer while he was installing lights in Essanay's Chicago
studio—regarded Griffith as the standard to shoot for. "I watched everything he did, and then I'd do it, in one form or another. I'd try to do
it better. And I'd try to invent something that *he'd* see."

Even Hobart Bosworth—now writing, acting in, and directing films
for Selig—cited Griffith, along with the late Francis Boggs, as his principal role model. (In one of the more bizarre incidents in early Hollywood history, Boggs was shot and killed in October 1911 by a mentally
disturbed gardener at the Selig studio in Edendale; the shooter, who
used a pistol stolen from Bosworth's office, also seriously wounded Colonel Selig himself before being wrestled to the ground by other employees.) According to Bosworth, "Every scene I made I wondered how HE,
D.W., would make it, and [I] tried to make it as I thought he would like it

done. I think he influenced all of us directors in just that way, but I don't think that even he, with his great grasp of his medium, knew much more about [it] than we did."

This was true. Griffith was still improvising as he went along, like everyone else in town. Working without an art director, without a special effects department, without even a script, he and Bitzer continued to refine and experiment with the techniques they had developed in New York, honing an increasingly agile and expressive style of visual story-telling. To compare two Griffith films, *The Lonedale Operator* of 1911 and *A Girl and Her Trust* of 1912, is to see how rapidly he was making progress. The movies tell essentially the same story: a young female te-legrapher in a remote railroad station holds off some burglars while her rescuers race to the scene in a freight train. But the latter film is far more polished and accomplished. It employs faster, smoother cross-cutting to build suspense, and the story is tweaked to a higher level of drama. The later movie also contains arguably the first example in the Griffith opus of a tracking shot. (A camera mounted on a moving automobile filmed the locomotive from the side as it sped through the landscape.) Released exactly one year apart, the two films seem to belong to different eras of filmmaking. To view them consecutively is to witness, in the space of thirty minutes, the maturing of an art form before one's very eyes.

Meanwhile Griffith and his troupe were also making strides in per-formance technique. Griffith would allegedly do anything to get what he wanted from his actors. He would shout, cajole, play on competing actors' jealousies, swing an actress around in an impromptu waltz, or act out the entire scene himself. Sometimes he let his actors work things out for themselves; other times he would direct their every expression and gesture, "from the lifting of an eyelid to the correct way to scream." Re-hearsals could go on for hours. "Mr. Griffith would move around us like a referee in a ring," Lillian Gish recalled, "circling, bending, walking up to an actor, staring over his great beak of a nose, then turning away. By the time that we had run through the story several times, he had viewed the action from every conceivable camera angle. Then he would begin to concentrate on characterization." He was constantly urging his players toward a more naturalistic acting style than was prevalent on the stage of this era. "Not so much, not so much," he would yell at an overemoting actor. "Less, less—simple, simple, *true*. Don't act it, feel it; feel it, don't act it." Once he even told Miriam Cooper that her mother had died, to get her crying in just the right way.

Lillian Gish, who would come to be more closely associated with the Griffith opus than any other person except Bitzer, was a new addition to the Biograph troupe. Lillian, her mother, and her sister Dorothy came to the New York studio one day in June 1912, looking for their friend Gladys Smith, a.k.a. Mary Pickford. (They had all shared an apartment back when the girls were child actresses on the stage.) Griffith chanced upon them in the foyer and was instantly intrigued. He brought the girls in to test for his next picture, *An Unseen Enemy*, and proceeded to gauge their believability as wildly frightened children by chasing them around the studio, firing a pistol in the air. The sisters thought he had gone mad, but after a while he put the gun away and smiled. "That will make a wonderful scene," he said, suddenly calm. "You have expressive bodies. I can use you. Do you want to work for me?" They did.

There were many other comings and goings at Biograph during the early Los Angeles years. Griffith inspired extraordinary loyalty in his actors, but some did leave, lured away by independent producers with promises of big salaries and high-profile projects. Mary Pickford had quit in December 1910 to join IMP (and to elope with Biograph leading man Owen Moore), though she returned to the Griffith fold in 1912 for a few more movies. Mack Sennett left in the summer of 1912, taking Mabel Normand with him, to start Keystone and begin making cinema history of his own. But there were always new actors eager to take their place: Donald Crisp, Blanche Sweet, Mae Marsh, Lionel Barrymore. (Also leaving the troupe at this time was Linda Arvidson, who found a love letter her husband had written to one of his other actresses. The two would remain estranged for years before finally getting a divorce in 1936.)

By 1912, Griffith's ambitions had grown beyond what could be portrayed in a one-reel movie. He wanted to focus on more serious subject matter—in particular, on historical epics and literary classics. And he wanted to explore these stories in greater depth than was possible in ten or twelve minutes of film. Directors in Europe were already making feature-length movies (i.e., those consisting of four or more reels), but the conventional wisdom among the establishment American studios was that audiences wouldn't sit through a one- or two-hour film, and that exhibitors wouldn't show them. But now some of the more forward-thinking independents were putting out films of two reels or even more. Griffith was determined to follow suit, despite the nattering from the front office in New York. He had tried this before, first in 1910, with a two-part Civil War drama under the titles *His Trust* and *His Trust Fulfilled*. Griffith had wanted both reels to be shown consecutively on a single program, but Biograph refused. He tried again in 1911 with *Enoch Arden*, a two-reel adaptation of another Tennyson poem. Again, Biograph released the reels separately, as Part One and Part Two, to be shown on consecutive nights. This time, though, audiences rebelled, demanding to see both parts of *Enoch Arden* in one evening. Biograph ultimately allowed exhibitors to show the parts together, but they insisted that Griffith go back to the tried-and-true single-reel format.

After much wrangling, in late 1912 Griffith secured Biograph's permission to make a limited number of two-reelers, but each of these longer projects had to be preapproved by Henry Marvin and the other executives. Griffith played by the rules in 1913, producing several two-reelers, but was soon yearning to go even longer. He started filming a much more ambitious project without preapproval. *Judith of Bethulia* was a biblical epic that he thought might compete with similar features coming over from Europe, including a recent four-reel *Queen Elizabeth* from France and an eight-reel *Quo Vadis* from Italy. For the set, he built an entire walled city over a twelve-square-mile lot in the wilds of the San Fernando Valley, creating budget overruns that incensed the New York office. Ultimately, Biograph sent accountant Johannes Epping to L.A. to police their wayward director's extravagance. But once Epping saw what Griffith had in mind, he was converted from adversary to advocate, and let Griffith have whatever money he needed.

The film Griffith brought back to New York in July 1913 was almost six reels long and had cost more than double his original estimate of sixteen thousand dollars. Henry Marvin was furious. Summoning the director to the front office for a dressing-down, he flatly told Griffith that he would no longer be directing Biograph films but would merely be supervising the work of other (presumably more controllable) directors. J. J. Kennedy was only a little more forgiving. He told Griffith that he would be allowed to edit *Judith* to a more reasonable length of four reels, or about an hour long, but unless the director made a solemn promise to keep his future films to one reel, he would have to go someplace else to make them. "If you stay with Biograph," Kennedy told him, "it will be to make the same kind of short pictures that you have in the past."

"I thought I knew an exit cue when I heard one," Griffith would later write, "and here it came." Other studios, hearing rumors about the trouble at Biograph, approached him with proposals. Adolph Zukor, partner in a company that would eventually become the all-powerful Paramount, offered Griffith fifty thousand dollars a year to direct for him. Griffith was worried about Zukor's reputation for maintaining tight control over all projects and so turned him down. More appealing was an offer from Harry Aitken, the head of a new film-distribution company called Mutual. Aitken proposed taking Griffith on as an independent producer, with all of the creative freedom that title implied. The salary offered was only three hundred per week, but Griffith would be given some stock in the new company as well as a percentage in the films he would make for the production arm of the company (called Reliance-Majestic). He would also have the right to make two entirely independent productions per year.

This last provision apparently sealed the deal. It was artistic freedom that Griffith wanted more than anything—the freedom to create on as grand a canvas as he could conceive. And he wanted Bitzer to do it with him. "We are just grinding out sausages, Billy," Griffith told his longtime cameraman, "and will continue to do so as long as we remain here [at Biograph]. After five years, I think I have a right to my own vision, without being overruled by a lot of dunderheads in the front office." And so, on September 29, 1913, Griffith's break with Biograph was announced in the *New York Dramatic Mirror*. After five years and some 457 films, D. W. Griffith was leaving the studio he had saved from bankruptcy. And he was taking Bitzer and the bulk of his best actors with him.

He also took a big idea with him. "We were going [back] to California," Bitzer later wrote. "Mr. Griffith knew what he wanted to do—a big Civil War epic *in twelve reels*." It would turn out to be history-making in more ways than one. The film Griffith had in mind would be the biggest, most elaborate gamble that he, or anyone else in the film industry, had ever taken.

# CHAPTER FIVE
# "A River Now Is Here"

*The first flow of water down the cascade spillway at the opening
of the Los Angeles Aqueduct*

On the afternoon of November 5, 1913, some thirty to forty thousand people—nearly one-tenth of the current population of Los Angeles—gathered at the foot of Newhall Pass, a rugged, still sparsely populated spot at the northwestern corner of the San Fernando Valley. They had come to witness what the *L.A. Times* called "the biggest and most heartfelt celebration ever held in Los Angeles": the opening of the long-awaited aqueduct. The governor of California, the state's two senators, the mayors of San Diego, San Francisco, and Los Angeles, and a personal envoy from President Woodrow Wilson would all be there to mark the day. But even among such an august group, the guest of honor would of course be William Mulholland, the man responsible for giving Los Angeles the abundant new source of water it desperately needed. For this tremendous accomplishment, Mulholland was being called "the Goethals of the West" (a reference to the engineer in charge of the almost-completed Panama Canal). His name was even being bruited about as the next mayor of Los Angeles—though when asked to run, he responded with the famous demurral, "I would rather give birth to a porcupine backward." No, campaigning for public office was never on Mulholland's to-do list. But today—even though his wife lay ailing with uterine cancer in the hospital—he was at least willing to accept the city's encomiums for the great work he had undertaken in its name.

It had been, needless to say, a monumental effort—and one immortalized (since this *was* Los Angeles) in a motion picture documentary newly released by Harry Aitken's Mutual Film Corporation. Since 1906, when surveying for the project had begun, Mulholland and his crews had been hard at the task. Even creating the infrastructure necessary to begin construction had been an elaborate enterprise. No paved road existed from the town of Mojave north to the Owens Valley, so an agreement had to be reached with the Southern Pacific Railroad to build a train line to Lone Pine, in order to transport men and machinery to the various points along the route where work would begin. There had been hydroelectric power plants to construct to provide electricity for the building effort, along with numerous commissaries, hospitals, and housing for the workers. The city had even erected its own cement factory. "I'm going into this as a man in the army goes to war," Mulholland said at the outset. "It will take the life out of me."

The project did resemble nothing so much as a military campaign. In command was a real-life general—Adna R. Chaffee, a Civil War veteran who now served as chairman of the board of public works. Under the aging Chaffee's authority, Mulholland, the field general in the campaign, divided his army of engineers, tunnel workers, dredge drivers, and day laborers into eleven divisions, each responsible for one segment of the aqueduct route. Over 500 miles of roads and trails, 377 miles of telephone and telegraph wires, 218 miles of power transmission lines, and 2,300 buildings and tent houses had to be constructed to supply the aqueduct's fifty-seven separate work camps. The preparation effort alone was so protracted and expensive that Mulholland was able to amuse himself one day by putting a tremendous scare into the L.A. Chamber of Commerce. When invited to give the group a progress report in December 1908, and digging of the actual conduit had barely started, the Chief's assessment was grim: "Well, we have spent about $3 million all told, I guess, and there is perhaps nine hundred feet of aqueduct built. Figuring all our expenses, it has cost us about $3,300 a foot."

After the predictable gasps from the audience—at that rate, the thing would cost the city billions!—Mulholland relented. "But by this time next year," he continued, "I'll have fifty miles completed at a cost of under $30 a foot, if you'll [just] let me alone."

The city's businessmen and politicians did let him alone, at least in the early years of construction, and he made excellent progress. Aside from the commissary service, the medical department, and one small construction project, all of which were contracted out to private enterprises, the building effort was a totally public, municipal endeavor. That meant that the city itself took responsibility for hiring workers, buying equipment, creating its own power, and manufacturing its own building materials. The rationale for this was simple: Mulholland was convinced that he could get the job done quicker and more cheaply than anyone else could.

He proved to be absolutely right. Of course, he delegated work to trusted and familiar lieutenants—among them his friend Joseph Lippincott (who served as assistant chief engineer), Ezra F. Scattergood (in charge of hydroelectric power), William B. Mathews (who handled the inevitable lawsuits generated by the project), and the eleven individual division heads. But it was the Chief himself who handled the bulk of the planning and execution. Working without extensive notes and improvising engineering solutions when necessary—not unlike D. W. Griffith on his sets—Mulholland took a hands-on approach to the whole project, spending huge amounts of time out in the field, away from his home and family. ("Father?" his young daughter once quipped. "You mean that man who sometimes eats dinner with us?") For years on end he traveled up and down the aqueduct route, both on horseback and by automobile, sketching out a schematic in the sand here, bawling out a slow-moving digging crew there. Mulholland's tongue, by one account, "could scrape barnacles off a ship bottom," but he nonetheless inspired intense loyalty among his subordinates—mainly because he was willing to work longer and harder than any of them. "I took a vacation once," he would remark late in life. "I spent an afternoon at Long Beach. [But] I was bored to death from loafing and came back to work the next morning." Although this was an exaggeration (the Chief took a camping trip to the Sierra every July, according to his granddaughter), the sentiment behind it was genuine. Mulholland's work was his life, and when one's work was the fourth-largest engineering project in American history to date, it didn't leave time for much else.

~

By early 1909, construction of the aqueduct was in full swing. At the height of activity close to four thousand men were simultaneously at work on the project. Some of these were trained engineers and expert mule- and equipment-drivers, but the vast majority were rough-hewn, transient day laborers, working eight-to-ten-hour shifts with hand tools in the hot desert sun. The crews laying the railroad line were mostly

Mexicans, while the aqueduct builders were an assortment of Greeks, Bulgarians, Serbs, Slavs, Italians, and other southern and eastern European immigrants. Although there was occasional tension between the Mexican railroad gangs and the "white" aqueduct crews, one thing they all seemed to share was a nearly insatiable thirst. At any given time, according to one foreman on the twenty-four-hour-a-day tunnel-digging effort, he had "one crew drunk, one crew sobering up, and one crew working."

On paydays, some of the little towns along the route—like Mojave, now being called "the wickedest town in the West"—could degenerate into around-the-clock bacchanalias. Many are the reports of Boschian scenes of brawling, drunkenness, gambling, and prostitution in aqueduct towns. "I saw lights on in every saloon, dance hall, and gambling room," worker Erwin Widney recalled, describing his arrival in Mojave at four-thirty one morning in July 1908. "Men [were] passing in and out, some voluntarily, some propelled, some head first, some feet first." When a shot rang out from a saloon called the Bucket of Blood, he saw "a wild scramble as men and women poured from the doors and windows."

And it wasn't only Mojave. One morning some weeks later, Widney noted the aftermath of a similar payday spree around the saloon in Little Lake. "At a rough estimate, I will say that 75 to 100 men lay prone in the morning heat all around the place," he remembered, "[some] as close as a few yards and [some] as far away as a quarter of a mile." City officials eventually got a bill through the state legislature outlawing saloons within a four-mile radius of the aqueduct. But human ingenuity being what it is, the problem of rampant drunkenness remained.

Even so, work on the aqueduct proceeded rapidly. One particular challenge, the boring of a five-mile tunnel near Lake Elizabeth, through the Sierra Pelona Mountains, saw speed records being broken every week. Under a bonus system devised by Mulholland and Lippincott, underground workers were paid an extra forty cents for every foot of tunnel excavated beyond the day's benchmark goal. Workers responded by digging like mole rats, eventually finishing the tunnel a remarkable 450 days ahead of schedule and $500,000 under budget.

At another potential trouble spot—in the Jawbone Division near

Cinco, where the aqueduct had to pass through a formidable territory of jagged mountains and plunging canyons—Mulholland also achieved impressive success. Early in the planning process, a team of inspecting engineers had expressed concern about the terrain. "That is very rough and difficult country for canal digging," one of them remarked to Mulholland.

"It is rough on top, but we are not going to dig on top," the Chief allegedly responded, explaining that the water would be channeled underground where possible. "When you buy a piece of pork, you don't have to eat the bristles."

In places where the bristles couldn't be avoided, Mulholland had innovative solutions. To bring the water across some of the deeper canyons of the Jawbone Division, where underground conduits or elevated crossings would be impractical, he employed sag or pressure pipes (often incorrectly called inverted siphons). Sag pipes use a simple principle of physics to induce water to run uphill: as long as the upstream end of the pipe is higher than the downstream end, water flowing into the upper end will run out the lower end, no matter how many ups and downs in between. Sag pipes had been known since Roman times, but never had they been used for such great changes in altitude. Some of the pipes needed were up to ten feet in diameter, so even transporting the huge sections of pipe to Jawbone Canyon was a massive undertaking. Mulholland at first tried a newfangled solution, hauling them with the recently invented gas- or steam-powered tractors known as caterpillars. But the terrain and weather conditions proved to be too much for the machines; the Chief eventually had to replace them with reliable, low-tech mules— thirteen hundred of them, pulling the twenty-six-ton sections of pipe in teams of fifty-two animals for each.

This combination of up-to-the-minute technology and old-fashioned human (and equine) sweat was typical of the entire aqueduct effort. On the one hand, Mulholland brought to his task the full weight of modern ideas and new inventions—like the revolutionary hydraulic sluicing technique he used to build reservoirs, an innovation later adopted widely by other engineers. He also invented a new kind of mechanical dredger for use in the Alabama Hills, a machine he loved "as though it were his baby," and that his men dubbed "Big Bill" in his honor. But ultimately the Chief was banking on the sheer hard work of the men with picks and shovels to bring the project to completion on schedule. "We'll pull her through on time, never fear," he told a reporter in 1909, "if the men in the ditch can have their swing."

The work was going so well that Mulholland's project soon became a victim of its own success. By May 1910, the construction crews were so far ahead of schedule that expenditures were outpacing the flow of funding from scheduled bond sales, and Mulholland found himself running out of ready money. At the same time, fluctuations in the New York bond market caused the city's bonding firm there to turn conservative, and they stopped buying aqueduct bonds entirely for several months. Mulholland and Mathews hurried east to negotiate a compromise but came back empty-handed. On May 20, unable to pay his men, Mulholland was forced to initiate massive layoffs, reducing his workforce from its recent high of 3,900 to just 1,100. For several months, work at many points along the 233-mile project ground to a virtual halt. (Only the vital Elizabeth Tunnel crew were maintained at full staff.) The immediate crisis had passed by August, when the New Yorkers resumed buying bonds, but Mulholland found he had difficulty rehiring laborers, many of whom had naturally moved on to other opportunities elsewhere. It would be some months before the construction effort could be revved up to full speed again.

But Mulholland's woes were just beginning. For some time now, aqueduct workers had been dissatisfied with the quality of the food being served in the project's commissaries. The contractor engaged to feed the whole workforce—Daniel "Joe" Desmond, who had made a name for himself providing emergency food service for victims of the 1906 San Francisco earthquake—was having trouble providing ample, wholesome meals for twenty-five cents each, the limit he could charge. Meat and vegetables spoiled quickly in the desert heat, and bread had a tendency to take on extra protein in the form of weevils. After violent food riots erupted at several construction camps, Desmond renegotiated his contract so that he could charge an extra nickel per meal, promising better food for the money. But the price hike pleased no one, especially when Desmond's meals did not improve significantly.

This dissatisfaction, combined with lingering grievances over the recent layoffs and other cutbacks, provided fertile ground for union organizers from the Western Federation of Miners. The WFM had been trying to organize the aqueduct workers since the beginning of the project, but thanks to the paucity of excavation work elsewhere and the popularity of policies like the bonus system, they hadn't made much headway. Now they found a more receptive audience among the disgruntled workers. In November 1910, they called for a strike of tunnelers, and about seven hundred heeded the call, shutting down the Elizabeth Tunnel effort and severely curtailing work at other tunnels up and down the line. "Preferring loafing to working," the rabidly antilabor *L.A. Times* sneered, "several hundred laborers . . . on the aqueduct have quit their jobs, giving as a reason that they would not pay the increased price of mess in the camps."

It was something of a miracle that there hadn't been trouble before this. Throughout its history, Los Angeles had been known as one of the least union-friendly places in the country. The city's business community, led by *Times* owner Harrison Gray Otis and other members of the powerful Merchant and Manufacturers Association, had waged a fierce battle against organized labor for decades, seeing the open shop as the only way for their upstart metropolis to compete economically against San Francisco. Because of their staunch opposition, not to mention the seemingly endless supply of new workers flooding into the rapidly growing city, unions had difficulty getting a foothold in L.A.'s nascent industries. As a result, wages were notoriously low—up to 40 percent lower than those in San Francisco. As one latter-day observer put it, no other American city "presented so able an array of militant, uncompromising opponents of unionism and as fervent a championship of the open shop."

By 1910, this conflict had come to a head. A series of strikes by brewery and metal working employees had prompted the city to pass an antipicketing ordinance in July, leading to the arrest of hundreds of demonstrating workers. Resentment built up through the rest of the summer until, at one a.m. on the morning of October 1, an explosion ripped through Ink Alley, a passage between the stereotyping and press rooms of the *L.A. Times* building on First and Broadway. Although the bomb was likely intended to be more symbolic than deadly—aimed at the most visible enemy of labor in town, Harrison Gray Otis—it managed to ignite the tons of flammable newspaper ink being stored in the alley. Within minutes, the entire building was aflame, with more than one hundred employees inside. By morning twenty people were dead, and the *Times* building had been reduced to a smoldering skeleton.

It was, as the *Times* insisted in the boldest of bold type, "THE CRIME OF THE CENTURY," and everyone in Los Angeles had a theory as to who was responsible. Otis blamed the unions, the unions blamed a gas leak, and some conspiracy theorists even blamed Otis, charging that he blew up his own building to stoke antilabor sentiment. Given the old man's reputation for vindictiveness, this last notion was perhaps not inconceivable, but few people seriously entertained it. Most authorities were convinced that organized labor was behind the blast. A nationwide investigation—led by the most famous detective in the country, William Burns of the Pinkerton Agency—was launched to find the culprits.

The strike on the aqueduct, coming just one month after the *L.A. Times* bombing, was both symptomatic of and a contribution to the general atmosphere of discord and mutual suspicion in the city. When Mulholland remained adamant in his refusal to raise wages to bring the strike to an end, the unions vowed to up the stakes by taking political action. "As there seems no possible way to settle this strike with the city officials," the unions told the mayor and city council in January 1911, "the aqueduct employees will have to . . . make the taxpayers aware of the facts in the present situation."

Thus did Mulholland's aqueduct become a political football in the famously contentious L.A. mayoral election of 1911. Amid more strikes and the sensational arrest of two labor leaders—John and James McNamara—for complicity in the *L.A. Times* bombing, local unions joined forces with the Socialist Party to put up a candidate for mayor in the October election. That candidate, prominent labor lawyer Job Harriman, made the aqueduct a central issue in his campaign. Mocking the man he called "Saint Mulholland," Harriman rehashed all of the old accusations about fake water shortages and behind-the-scenes connivance, characterizing the aqueduct as a boondoggle for rich land speculators paid for by the unsuspecting citizens of Los Angeles. Mulholland answered every charge as best he could, citing rainfall statistics and water consumption figures, but, as in many elections, the issue under contention was merely an avatar for the real conflict: the struggle between labor and capital.

In October Harriman won a plurality of votes, forcing a runoff between him and incumbent mayor George Alexander in December (the first L.A. election, incidentally, in which women were allowed to cast a ballot). For a time, it looked as if the Socialist candidate might actually win—at what cost to the aqueduct effort, no one knew. But then, just five days before the election, a development in the *L.A. Times* bombing case all but ruined Harriman's chances. The McNamaras, whom many thought were being framed for the crime, changed their plea from not guilty to guilty—apparently on the advice of their principal lawyer, Clarence Darrow, to avoid a possible death sentence. Job Harriman, who had campaigned on the McNamaras' cause and had even assisted on Darrow's defense team, found himself swept aside in the resulting swell of antiunion feeling. When Election Day arrived on December 6, he lost to Mayor Alexander by a landslide, in a turn of events that was to set back the labor movement in Los Angeles for a generation.

For Mulholland, this outcome came as an enormous relief. But Harriman's accusations against him still rankled, so the Chief requested that the city council launch an official public investigation into every aspect of the aqueduct effort, from its conception through its current state of near-completion. The impulse was noble, perhaps, but Mulholland's confidence that any such probe would entirely vindicate him and his associates proved naïve. In the highly politicized atmosphere of Los Angeles in that election year, the five-person "People's Investigating Board" conducted an inquiry that was clearly propelled by antiaqueduct sentiment. In August 1912, running low on funds and hobbled by the resignation of two members who claimed that the inquiry was hopelessly biased, the board closed its proceedings and issued a report. It was predictably negative in tone, going so far as to recommend that the city take legal action against Fred Eaton for his high-handed dealings in the Owens Valley. But even this hostile board found nothing criminal to bring against Mulholland and the other aqueduct officials. In what must be one of the most extraordinary statements ever made in a report of this kind, they wrote that although their investigations had found no evidence of graft, some would likely have turned up if the board had been given enough time, since "a knowledge of human nature indicates that men would have been found who had succumbed to temptation."

The board did turn up some examples of poor judgment and engineering expediencies that would later come back to haunt Mulholland. And the report did contain enough blistering criticism—justified or not—to help Socialist-backed candidate Henry H. Rose win the next mayoral election in 1913. But even Rose eventually became an enthusiastic Mulholland supporter. After taking a comprehensive ten-day tour of the aqueduct, the newly elected mayor came back with nothing but praise. As far as he could tell, Rose announced to reporters, "criticism of the aqueduct is captious." The water it carried was pure and sweet (hardly "poison," as one Socialist-leaning paper had charged), and he'd found no evidence of poor construction, inefficiency, or corruption. And although the damning board report was eventually published, at great expense, in an enormous, folio-size tome, few (besides, perhaps, the screenwriter of the movie *Chinatown*) gave it much credence in later years. The whole process was, according to one official city historian, "an outstanding example of waste of money and effort on the part of a few men to create confusion and distrust."

⌒

Meanwhile work on the aqueduct rapidly approached completion. By early 1913, the Elizabeth Tunnel was already long finished, and the last touches were being put on the Jawbone Division sag pipes. In February, while work was still being done on the aqueduct's lower portions, Mulholland and a group of officials held a small ceremony at the intake north of Independence, opening the gates and diverting water from the Owens River into the brand-new conduit. From here, the water would run down the valley to Haiwee, where it would take several months to fill a reservoir before being released in May to continue the journey south. Trouble with an experimental rock pressure tunnel at Sand Canyon forced the official opening ceremony to be postponed, but by September, Mulholland was able to make his final end-to-end inspection of the great work and declare it sound. "The big job is finished," the Chief announced in October. "Nothing remains now but to shoot off a few firecrackers, turn on the water, and tackle the next big job."

On the bright, sunny afternoon of November 5, 1913, it was finally time to shoot off those firecrackers. To greet the arrival of the Owens River water at Newhall Pass (where the water would make its last descent from the mountains into a reservoir in the San Fernando Valley), people had been gathering since before dawn, coming on foot, by automobile, or on one of six special trains run by the Southern Pacific from downtown. By the time Mulholland and the other dignitaries appeared on the scene at noon, thousands of spectators—many carrying little drinking cups to get a first taste of the water in their future—swarmed over the sere, scrub-covered hillsides, while the fifty-piece Catalina Military Band played festive music in the open air. The recent controversies were forgotten as Angelenos celebrated what was by any measure a stunning accomplishment: a six-year, state-of-the-art engineering project, completed on time and well within its $23.5 million budget.

The future assured by that project was even more worthy of celebration. As the *L.A. Examiner* boasted, "The completion of the Owens River Aqueduct marks another step forward for Los Angeles in the fulfillment of its destiny as not only one of the great, but one of the greatest cities in the world." The *Times* was, as usual, even more extravagant: "A mighty river has been brought from out [of] the mountain wilderness, across the desert swept by winds of heat, and all of its vast energy utilized to generate electric power for the factories and foundries, the mills and smelters and refineries that have come and will come. . . . [The aqueduct] brings assurance of metropolitan grandeur and future prosperity such as but few cities of the world can hope to attain."

At 12:10, when the principals had taken their places on the dais at the foot of the still-dry cascade spillway, the ceremony began. The band played a rendition of "America," after which Rep. William D. Stevens welcomed the crowd and soprano Ellen Beach Yaw sang a specially composed ode entitled "Hail the Water." Then came the speeches, heavy with rhetoric about the city's future greatness. As the *Examiner* described it: "Throughout the ceremony, Mulholland was lionized; at every mention of his name, the great audience cheered with unbounded enthusiasm."

Shortly after one o'clock, Mulholland himself got up to speak, to an ovation that lasted several minutes before it could be quieted. For a man who once admitted that he would "rather skin dead dogs than make speeches," this would not normally be a moment he'd relish, especially since his wife Lillian, having undergone an operation for uterine cancer just days before, was at that moment recovering in a hospital bed. But Mulholland was keenly aware of the symbolism of this ceremony, in which he, as chief engineer, would officially turn over to the mayor of Los Angeles the aqueduct he'd built. The man known for plain speaking therefore allowed himself to wax poetic: "This is a great event, fraught with the greatest importance to the future prosperity of this city," he began. "I have been already overwhelmed and honored. What greater honor can any man ask than to have the confidence of his neighbors? You have given me an opportunity to create a great public enterprise and I am here to render my account to you."

Turning almost biblical in his diction, he continued, "The aqueduct is completed and it is good. No one knows better than I how much we needed the water. We have the fertile lands and the climate. Only water was needed to make of this region a tremendously rich and productive empire, and now we have it. . . . On this crude platform is an altar to consecrate the delivery of this valuable water supply and dedicate to you and to posterity forever a magnificent body of water."

After more applause and the presentation of a silver loving cup from the city, Mulholland pulled a lanyard that unfettered a giant American flag over the platform. As the flag unfurled, cannons boomed and aerial bombs exploded in the air over the valley. This was the signal for the men at the gates high on the hillside—all of them key engineers—to begin turning the great wheels that would release the water into the spillway.

"The water came," the *Times* reported. "In a wall reaching from side to side, and about two feet high, it rolled over the top of the cascade and surged downward. Its front was almost a straight line, a rushing wall of water with all below it dry and dusty. . . . Soon the entire cascade was a roaring, rushing waterfall growing larger every minute."

Now Mulholland uttered the exhortation he would forever after be famous for. "There it is," he shouted, gesturing toward the gush of water. "Take it!"

The crowd erupted again. This water, after all, would nurture their city for decades to come. To symbolize this fact, a child—a baby named Merle Eva Moselle—was brought forward to drink the first bottle of the precious liquid, skimmed from the aqueduct's flow. But there was too much disorder for many people to notice. Hundreds pressed around the edges of the spillway, trying to feel its chill spray on their overheated faces. One man in a feathered Tyrolean hat leaned over the edge and wondered aloud how fast the water was flowing toward the new San Fernando Reservoir some ways down the valley. As he bent over, the hat blew off his head and fell into the rushing water. Mulholland, who was passing by at that moment, leaned in and told the man—with a typical engineer's precision—"You'll find it [i.e., the hat] at the dam in seven minutes."

And so, as the Catalina band played "The Star-Spangled Banner" to close the ceremony, Los Angeles could finally feel confident that the greatest obstacle to its growth had been removed. There would be more celebrations to come—a grand Industrial Parade in the city the next day, followed by another ceremony at the newly completed Exposition Park south of downtown. There would be more band music, more receptions, more gaseous speeches comparing Los Angeles to ancient Rome and the other great cities of history. But there would also be plenty of work left for Mulholland and his subordinates. There were still supplemental reservoirs to plan, hydroelectric plants to build, and a distribution system that would bring the new water from the San Fernando Valley to every far-flung corner of the growing metropolis. (The first Owens River water would not reach the taps of most L.A. consumers until April 1915.)

It would be a long time, in other words, before Mulholland could rest. The Chief was, by his own admission, worn out by his labors of the past five years, but the "magnificent heritage" he had promised the people of his city still required much stewardship and problem-solving. Seeds of future trouble could even be discerned amid the pomp of that November day, in the conspicuous absence of one major player in the Los Angeles water story—Frederick Eaton. Mulholland had given his former mentor ample credit in his speech. "I am only sorry," he'd said, "that the man whom I consider the father of the aqueduct is not here, former mayor Eaton. To him all honor is due; we only put together the bricks and mortar."

But the reason Eaton wasn't present was that he and Mulholland had been feuding for some years now. Disappointed that he hadn't made quite the killing he'd expected when he first proposed the aqueduct, Eaton had been playing hardball with Mulholland over a possible reservoir on his ranch property in the Long Valley section of the Owens Valley. The original plan had been to build a small reservoir and dam here, and Eaton had ceded the city the land to do so. But now Mulholland felt that he needed to build a taller, 140-foot dam on the site to create a reservoir large enough, and located far enough north, to ensure an adequate supply of water both to the growing city and to the Owens Valley ranchers in times of drought. Eaton was willing to sell him the additional rights and property he needed to build the bigger dam—for the cool sum of one million dollars. Mulholland thought this price preposterous, and the two men, both known for their stubbornness, had been dickering ever since, neither one willing to budge. "I'll buy Long Valley three years after Eaton is dead," Mulholland allegedly groused in private, despite his public praise for the man. And so, despite having the rights for a smaller dam at Long Valley, the city built no dam at all for several decades.

For the moment, however, Mulholland could afford this standoff. There was currently plenty of water for everyone, not least the Owens Valley farmers and ranchers. Thanks to a series of relatively wet years, combined with new infrastructure created during the aqueduct construction project, valley residents had been faring well in the years since the aqueduct plans were first announced, and their relations with the city had normalized since the stormy days of 1905. But with the L.A. population increasing by leaps and bounds (adding an estimated 100,000 new residents every two years), the surfeit of water would not last long. What's more, Eaton's intransigence would eventually force Mulholland to build a series of smaller reservoirs closer to the city to ensure enough supply for all contingencies—which would have its own dire consequences in the years to come.

But for now, optimism in Los Angeles was high. As soprano Ellen Beach Yaw sang at the ceremony that day:

*Lift your voice in gratitude,*
*A river now is here,*
*Whose glorious waters, flowing free,*
*A paradise will rear.*

# CHAPTER SIX
# The Birth of an Industry

*Henry Walthall and Lillian Gish in a scene from* The Birth of a Nation

One day in the spring of 1914, at his capacious new studio compound near the confluence of Sunset and Hollywood Boulevards, D. W. Griffith pulled Lillian Gish aside during a lull in filming and whispered to her, "After the others leave tonight, please stay."

It was clearly an order, not a request, and Gish had a feeling she knew what this secret meeting was going to be about. Several days earlier, during a tête-à-tête lunch with the director at the White Kitchen restaurant, she had noticed Griffith's pockets overflowing with handwritten notes and other papers—a sure sign that he was working on a new film idea. "My curiosity was aroused," Gish recalled, "but it would have been presumptuous of me to ask about them. With Mr. Griffith one did not ask; one only answered."

That evening, after the rest of the actors and crew left for the day, Griffith met with a small group of his most loyal players from the Biograph years—Henry Walthall, Bobby Harron, Mae Marsh, Miriam Cooper, Elmer Clifton, and a few others in addition to Gish—and told them what he had in mind.

"I've bought a book by Thomas Dixon, called *The Clansman*," Griffith said. "I'm going to use it to tell the truth about the War Between the States. It hasn't been told accurately in history books."

Griffith then summarized the plot, a story of two families—the Stonemans from the North and the Camerons from the South—split apart by the horrors of war but reunited after the end of Reconstruction. The film would be the biggest, most ambitious motion picture ever attempted. He swore all of the actors to secrecy about his plan, lest his competitors hear about it and try to put out their own Civil War epic before him. "I know I can trust you," he said finally, then dismissed them for the night.

Griffith had reason to be cautious. Now that he had established his reputation as the premier film director in the country, his ideas were being copied by directors good and bad throughout the industry. According to one story, director Allan Dwan once sent a spy to work on a Griffith film and report back everything he had seen. Griffith, moreover, felt that he had already been cheated of credit for one film milestone: to punish him for making his four-reel epic *Judith of Bethulia*, Biograph had held the picture in its vaults for almost a year before releasing it in March 1913. In that time several even longer productions, including Thomas Ince's *The Battle of Gettysburg*, Cecil B. DeMille's *The Squaw Man*, and Hobart Bosworth's *The Sea Wolf*, had been released, precluding any Griffith claim as the pioneer of the American feature-length film. He was determined not to let the same thing happen in his quest to create an epic of three hours or more.

And Harry Aitken was willing to give his new director the opportunity to do so. Aitken and his brother Roy, like many of the early studio heads, had entered the film industry as exhibitors. In 1905 the two Wisconsin farm boys had made a hundred-dollar investment in a string of nickelodeons in Chicago, which proved a great success. Eventually they realized there was money to be made in the production and distribution ends of the business as well. In 1911 they formed the Majestic Film Company (mainly to produce shorts featuring Mary Pickford and her husband Owen Moore) and then, sometime later, the Reliance Film Company, for which they contracted many of the biggest stars in the business. By 1912, when their distributing arm, Mutual, acquired thirty-one different film exchanges around the country, the Aitkens had become one of the biggest players in the fast-growing industry, with majority and minority interests in several other film companies as well. Since the big money on Wall Street was still skeptical of this new business, however—"People with capital don't have faith in the future of movies," Roy complained to his brother in 1914—the financing of their various film endeavors was always precarious. Harry Aitken was also more interested in growth first, consolidation of gains later, which ensured that the brothers were always stretched thin, making deals and borrowing money from private investors whenever and wherever they could.

As a result, they had taken Griffith on with some firm provisos. Although the director would be allowed to pursue his pet projects, he would also be responsible for maintaining Majestic's regular output of two films per week in order to supply the insatiable demand of the Aitkens' film exchange. Some of these projects would be filmed by other directors under Griffith's supervision, but some he'd have to direct himself. Griffith assured them that this was possible, since he would work furiously on the preproduction of his Civil War epic on his own time—in the evenings and at other in-between times when work on the bread-and-butter films was stopped. He warned that the project he had in mind would be expensive but assured the brothers that they would not regret the investment. "This Clansman picture," he told them, "will be worth a hundred of the other movies."

But even Harry Aitken's staunch belief in the project was jolted when Griffith started talking actual numbers. The film, Griffith said, would cost $40,000 to produce. Meanwhile Thomas Dixon was asking another $25,000 cash for the rights to his novel. That made a total of $65,000, when—to the Aitkens' knowledge, at least—few other American films had ever cost more than a fraction of that sum.

"Gentlemen," Harry Aitken said at a meeting with Griffith and Thomas Dixon, "$65,000 is a very big sum to raise for one picture. But I suppose it could be done. . . . This industry won't stand still, even for us. We've got to look toward the future and anticipate great things."

It was a remarkable leap of faith on Aitken's part—and one that the Majestic board of directors were less sanguine about making. At a specially convened meeting several days later, the directors rejected the project as too risky and advised Aitken to stick to films of four reels or fewer. Aitken was unfazed. He and his brother resolved to make the film anyway, planning to raise the money for Griffith via a syndicate of private investors who would each buy a percentage interest in the film project and receive in exchange a pro rata portion of the profits, if and when they arrived. But here, too, the Aitkens encountered trouble. Almost all of their prospects shied away from even a small investment in something as unlikely as a ten- to twelve-reel film. Harry ultimately had to borrow the money as a straightforward loan, meaning that if the film failed, he personally was on the line for the money. He did, however, convince Dixon to accept a cut of the film instead of requiring an outright purchase of the rights. Dixon received $2,000 as an advance and a

25 percent interest in the film's returns (a "concession" that would eventually prove to be the most lucrative business deal the author ever made).

However shaky the financial arrangements, Griffith finally had the green light to make the picture of his dreams: "the story of the South," as he called it, "[which] had been absorbed into the very fiber of my being." According to Bitzer, the prospect of work on this new project "changed D. W. Griffith's personality entirely." Gone were the days when he was content to grind out films like sausages. "His attitude on beginning [*The Clansman*] was all eagerness. He acted like here we have something worthwhile." True, Griffith would have to churn out a few potboilers by day to keep the studio's cash flow moving, but by night he could finally start producing what he considered true art. "You get that old camera of yours to photograph this right, Billy," he told his longtime cameraman. "We'll give them pictures that will blow off the tops of their heads."

~

While Griffith was busy planning high art at his new Sunset Boulevard headquarters, other directors around town were making strides with more overtly commercial cinematic products. By 1914, movies were being made all over Los Angeles and environs, but a few creators stood out as the principal rivals to Griffith's eminence. Thomas Ince, who had come west in 1911, about a year after the first Biograph winter season in Los Angeles, was now royally ensconced in an elaborate studio compound called Inceville in the Santa Ynez Canyon, near Santa Monica. A former stage actor who, like Griffith, had been driven to the movies "by the specter of the wolf" (i.e., poverty), he had been sent to Los Angeles by Baumann and Kessel's New York Motion Picture Corporation to shoot westerns under the moniker Bison. At a time when about one-quarter of all films produced in the United States were westerns, Bison pictures—particularly those starring Thomas Hart, Ince's old roommate from their theater days—stood out, not only for their lean, unsentimental sense of drama but also for their fastidious realism. In order to ensure authenticity, Ince hired the company of the 101 Ranch Wild West Show as extras. His films also typically featured a culminating tour de force that became known as the "Ince Punch"—a spectacular scene involving a special-effects-laden earthquake, flood, or volcanic eruption to bring the film to a rousing finish.

Ince's most important contribution to film history would be as a pioneer of studio specialization. "A director could no longer be the jack-of-all-trades," Ince later recalled about these adolescent years of the industry. Instead, a studio needed to employ "men and women who were especially qualified along certain lines to take charge of its various departments." The Ince studio became an early model for the huge, highly regimented studios of the industry's Golden Age in the 1930s and '40s, when large staffs of experts handled specific production tasks for multiple films at once. This system allowed Inceville to turn out a steady stream of reliable, high-quality movies, like a factory with a never-flagging assembly line. The model proved to be so successful, in fact, that Ince could give up directing entirely by mid-1913 and instead act as a creative producer, putting his personal stamp on the work of a large stable of filmmakers working under his supervision.

Mack Sennett—the Griffith protégé turned competitor—followed a path similar to Ince's, though via the comedy rather than the western. Having left Biograph in 1912 to found the Keystone Studios (also under the auspices of Baumann and Kessel), he started fast, directing an astonishing 140 one-reel comedies in the studio's first year. The results often suffered from the haste; Sennett's comedies could be crude, vulgar, shoddily assembled affairs. But they never dragged. "It's got to move" was the director's signature aesthetic principle, and move the movies did. Chaotic, single-minded, and always very fast, they put a premium on lampooning respectability of all kinds. (He'd even parody a Griffith film if he thought it would generate a laugh.) Eventually Sennett allowed his stars to direct their own pictures, while he, like Ince, acted as creative producer—taking meetings while bathing in the giant bathtub installed in his watchtower office above the studio's lot. Although the Keystone films often took the lowest road of physical slapstick, what saved them was Sennett's inspired troupe of comic actors, including Ford Sterling, usually the chief Keystone Kop, avuncular Chester Conklin, googly-eyed Ben Turpin, and the charming and versatile Mabel Normand (with whom Sennett carried on a universally acknowledged "secret" affair).

Two other Keystone actors would rise to become huge stars of the silent era. Roscoe "Fatty" Arbuckle was a rotund, baby-faced comedian who delighted audiences with a combination of surprising agility and uncanny grace. (According to actress Louise Brooks, dancing with Arbuckle was "like floating in the arms of a huge donut.") He soon became one of the highest-paid actors in the business, not to mention a major box office draw. But the true giant to emerge from the Sennett troupe was a young English music-hall comedian named Charles Chaplin. According to one story, Sennett and Mabel Normand had first seen his act in the fall of 1912 in New York, where he was performing with a group called Karno's Speechless Comedians. By the following spring, Sennett had decided he needed a new performer to give Ford Sterling a little competition, so he wrote Karno a now-legendary telegram (though some say it was Baumann, or Kessel, or even their partner, the ubiquitous Harry Aitken). "IS THERE A MAN NAMED CHAFFIN IN YOUR COMPANY OR SOMETHING LIKE THAT," it ran. "IF SO CAN HE COMMUNICATE WITH KESSEL AND BAUMANN 24 LONGACRE BUILDING BROADWAY NEW YORK."

Despite the garbled name, Chaplin got the message. He was sent out west and hired for the then-princely salary of $150 a week. His first released film didn't garner much attention, but then he devised a new character—pants and shoes too big, coat and derby too small—that proved wildly popular. In an industry known for overnight successes, the Little Tramp's rise was unprecedented in both speed and magnitude. His hit films for Keystone (which included *Tillie's Punctured Romance*, the first American feature-length comedy) soon made him one of the most bankable and well-paid stars in movie history. When he left Keystone at the end of 1914, after just over a year in films, he was taken on at Essanay at $1,250 a week, with a $10,000 signing bonus. Within another year he would join Mutual at $10,000 a week, with a signing bonus of $150,000.

The director who would eventually be seen as Griffith's biggest rival was Cecil B. DeMille, now making movies just two or three miles away, on the other side of Hollywood. Unlike many of the early silent directors, DeMille had come from a fairly wealthy family. His father had been one of David Belasco's business partners, and celebrities ranging from John

Philip Sousa to Annie Oakley had been guests in his childhood home in New York State. After a somewhat brief and undistinguished stint at a military college and then the American Academy of Dramatic Arts, DeMille set out to pursue a career as an actor, playwright, and stage producer, but achieved only middling success.

By 1912, the thirty-year-old DeMille was becoming restless. As the director himself would later tell the story, he was having lunch one day at Claridge's Grill in New York City with his friend and sometime–producing partner Jesse Lasky. Both were bemoaning the fact that show business wasn't really working out for them. "Let's go down to Mexico and join the revolution," DeMille proposed, only half-joking.

"No," Lasky said. "If you want excitement, let's go into pictures."

"All right, let's," his friend replied.

The two allegedly turned over their menus and sketched out a business plan. After lunch (or so the story goes), they walked down 44th Street to the Lamb's Club, where they met actor Dustin Farnum and playwright Edwin Milton Royle. They too seemed amenable to the idea, and right then and there they all decided to form a company to make a movie of Royle's play *The Squaw Man*, with Farnum acting the lead.

Whether or not it all happened so spontaneously, the Lasky Feature Play Company was soon born, with Lasky, DeMille, and Lasky's brother-in-law Samuel Goldfish (he later changed his surname to Goldwyn) as principals in the business. DeMille's family, naturally, was appalled. His brother William, a successful playwright who once immortally referred to movies as "galloping tintypes," wrote Cecil a letter, hoping to discourage the move. "After all," William wrote, "you do come of a cultured family, two of whose members have made honorable names in the field of drama, and I cannot understand how you are willing to identify yourself with a cheap form of amusement . . . which no one will ever allude to as art."

But Cecil would not be dissuaded, and by late December 1913, he— along with a somewhat more experienced co-director, Oscar Apfel— began shooting *The Squaw Man* in a rented, L-shaped barn on the corner of Vine Street and Selma Avenue in Hollywood. ("It was a barn. Unmistakably, it was a barn," DeMille would later write, noting that the landlord continued to stable his horses there.) The area was still rather wild and scrubby, which partially explains why DeMille adopted the uniform that was to become a Hollywood director cliché: riding breeches, high leather boots, and a revolver strapped to his hip (this last for killing rattlesnakes, he said). He also immediately assumed his signature preening arrogance. DeMille always came off, according to his niece Agnes, like a "cock in a barnyard"—an attitude that would seem to be at odds with his utter inexperience in moviemaking at this time.

DeMille proved to be a quick study, and he and Apfel finished filming the six reels of *The Squaw Man* in less than a month. The movie (which was probably more Apfel's work than DeMille's) was a tremendous success, both critically and financially, and DeMille immediately launched into the next one, a western based on Owen Wister's novel *The Virginian*. By the fall of 1914, his and Lasky's little enterprise was making enough money to attract early merger interest from the savvy Adolph Zukor and his Famous Players Film Company. Perhaps even more satisfying to DeMille, his brother William signed up as script supervisor, lured to California (tail tucked neatly between his legs, presumably) by a tantalizing salary offer of two hundred dollars a week. By now Cecil B. DeMille was convinced that he could make movies as well as—and much faster than—the éminence grise down the road. As he wrote to Goldfish in September of that year, "Griffith has now been working for four months on *The Clansman* and is not nearly finished. He is the man we are trying to top and I think we are succeeding."

So there was no shortage of moviemakers in Los Angeles working to get ahead of the reigning master of American film. The movie industry of 1914 was still very much in flux. The dominant names of the early trust years—Edison, Biograph, Kalem—were fading, while new and reconfigured independents jockeyed for position to fill the void. A number of them merged under the soon-to-be-famous name Universal, under Carl Laemmle, to do battle with the older entities. It would still be a few more years before the full emergence of the big studios of Hollywood's Golden Age—Paramount, MGM, Fox, RKO, Warner Brothers, Columbia—but their roots were being planted now, as the fortunes of some players rose and fell. The future of Hollywood (both the place and, as the name was now increasingly being used, the industry) was still uncertain. And much of that future would be determined by what D. W. Griffith did next.

~

Throughout the late spring and early summer of 1914, Griffith worked obsessively on preparations for *The Clansman*. The films he was making "on company time"—*The Battle of the Sexes, The Escape, Home Sweet Home*—were what Bitzer later described as "quickies," cheaply made and quickly distributed four-to-five-reel potboilers that generated a revenue stream to keep everyone's salary paid. But the director's best energies were devoted to his Civil War epic, as he worked with scenario editor Frank E. Woods to hone the storylines and organize the pile of notes and ideas he'd been jotting down at odd moments for months.

He was also making his preliminary casting decisions. The two leads were obvious choices. Henry Walthall—who, like Griffith, was the son of a Confederate colonel—would play Ben Cameron, the so-called "Little Colonel." And the female lead, Elsie Stoneman, the Northern woman who would steal his proud Southern heart, belonged to Lillian Gish, Griffith's current favorite actress (and, many believed, his current mistress). Other stalwarts from the old Biograph troupe would be filling other major roles: Mae Marsh and Miriam Cooper as the Little Colonel's two sisters, Spottiswoode Aitken as their aging father, and Robert Harron and Elmer Clifton as Elsie Stoneman's brothers. The principal black and "mulatto" roles would be played by white actors in blackface (a not-uncommon practice at the time, but one that can't seem anything but ludicrous and offensive to modern sensibilities). The rest of the huge cast included a surprising number of actors and extras who would later be famous as directors in their own right—Raoul Walsh as John Wilkes Booth, Joseph Henabery as Abraham Lincoln, Erich von Stroheim, an extra and one of Griffith's directorial assistants, and John Ford as a hard-riding Ku Klux Klansman. And as a sinister tavern proprietor named White-Arm Joe, Griffith cast a barrel-chested young man recently released from his job as a health aide on Mulholland's now-completed aqueduct project: Elmo Lincoln (actually Linkenhelt), who would eventually rise to celebrity as the cinema's first Tarzan.

Griffith began working with his "set designer" (really just a skilled carpenter named Frank "Huck" Wortman) on a perfect reproduction of a South Carolina town on an empty lot across Sunset Boulevard from the studio. This set was hardly elaborate, but once he began to plan the Civil War scenes, it became clear that Griffith would be sparing no expense in the realization of his magnum opus. The battle sequences he had in mind would dwarf those he had mounted for *Judith of Bethulia*, and he would be hauling cast and crew to locations all around the Los Angeles region—from Big Bear Lake, high in the San Gabriel Mountains, to barren stretches of the Imperial Valley (now bisected by the aqueduct), halfway to Mojave. The Aitken brothers, who hoped Griffith would settle down to more modest projects after he got this big epic out of his system, were understandably nervous. They had advanced the director over half of the $40,000 in the budget, but already he was asking for the rest. "He receives $25,000 credit and immediately asks for more," Harry groused to his brother one day. "Griffith is a brilliant fellow, but we've got to hold him down, Roy, or he'll break us."

By the time rehearsals started in late May, many people on the set had read the book by Thomas Dixon (there was no script to read, since Griffith still worked without a formal scenario), and at least some had misgivings about the project so dear to their chief. The novel, to any objective eyes, was the worst kind of racist screed. Its account of Reconstruction in the South was grotesquely distorted, depicting the freed slaves as lascivious and vengeful, goaded by Northern politicians to run roughshod over their former masters. The heroes of the story were none other than the Ku Klux Klan, who arrive on the scene with great fanfare to liberate the whites from their black oppressors. This was the story Griffith wanted to immortalize on film?

Billy Bitzer, for one, was anything but sanguine. "Personally, I did not share [Griffith's] enthusiasm, having skimmed through the book," he later wrote in a memoir. "I was from Yankee country and to me the K.K.K. was sillier than the Mack Sennett chases. A group of horsemen in white sheets? Preposterous."

Even assistant cameraman Karl Brown, still a teenager at this point, recognized the story for what it was: "Terribly biased, terribly unfair, the usual diatribe of a fire-eating Southerner. . . . It was as bitter a hymn of hate as I had ever encountered." Brown worried that Griffith's skill as a filmmaker would only make matters worse. "I knew Griffith's thoroughness, his dedication, his fanatic intensity of concentration on whatever subject he was handling. He would take every element of this book and make it a thousandfold more terrible than it could possibly be in print. And the result could not fail to be a complete and crushing disaster."

Griffith himself, however, seemed blithely unaware of the controversial nature of his source material. Both the *Clansman* novel and a stage version of the book, after all, had proved quite popular among audiences all over the country. When filming began—on July 4, 1914—he threw himself into his work with a gusto that demonstrated his sense of mission. "This was not just another picture for Griffith," Bitzer recalled. "He was fighting the old war all over again and, like a true Southerner, trying to win it or at least to justify losing it."

But the fact that Griffith was running himself ragged—"the man worked harder than any five people," Blanche Sweet once said of him—didn't mean he wasn't enjoying himself immensely. Dressed in his trademark tailored suit and wide-brimmed straw hat with the crown cut out (he believed that sunlight helped prevent baldness), Griffith shot and reshot scenes until he was satisfied. "I had never seen so much delight in any man's face," Brown wrote of the director in the early days of filming. "Win, lose, or draw, he was having the time of his life, and I can't believe that the thought of success or failure ever entered his mind."

The first scenes he shot were the large battle tableaux, filmed in the San Fernando Valley near today's Universal Studios. Working with an explosives expert and several directorial assistants, he re-created the siege of Petersburg and Sherman's march to the sea, communicating with his subordinates via flags and mirror semaphores to orchestrate huge numbers of men and horses from a great distance. Many accounts have vastly exaggerated the number of extras used in these scenes—one source even put the total at 18,000—but Lillian Gish claimed that there were usually only 300 to 500. They made themselves seem more numerous by crossing the camera's field of vision and then running around, out of sight, to reappear in the scene as a new person. Joseph Henabery described chasing himself in one of the Reconstruction scenes, appearing first as an escaping black character and then, in the same sequence, as one of a group of his white pursuers.

Such tricks aside, the battle scenes could be logistical nightmares. Thanks to Griffith's obsession with realism, they could be dangerous as well, especially where crews had to throw explosives by hand into crowded battlefields. When Griffith wondered aloud what would happen if one of the little bombs actually hit an actor, his expert (nicknamed "Fireworks Wilson") scoffed. "Look, Mr. Griffith," he said. "You're staging a battle, right? You want realism, don't you? Suppose someone *does* get hurt a little. Not much: A foot blown off or something. What you want to do is hustle right on down to where he is and get a good picture of it, and I tell you, sir, it'll *make* your picture!"

Griffith did end up opting for a safer alternative to live explosives for the battle scenes, but in other aspects of production he made no concessions. Whenever he received a complaining telegram from the Aitkens in New York, he would put it aside and burst into song or, on occasion, a two-note *Ha-yah!* that Brown interpreted as a variation on the rebel yell. The Aitkens grew more and more worried about the huge amounts Griffith was spending. "I wake up nights dreaming that hands, hands, hands are always outstretched for money," Roy told his brother one day. Finally, the Aitkens took a train to Los Angeles to personally put a lid on their director's extravagance. Griffith wasted no time in asking them for even more money—but Harry was adamant. "Make the picture with the $40,000 you already have," he said bluntly. "This isn't the only picture we are financing."

At this point, however, Griffith was like a man possessed. After the Aitkens returned east, he set out to raise additional money on his own, selling shares in the film without Harry Aitken's knowledge. Griffith approached every investor he could think of, even his own cameraman. One morning, as per their usual routine, Bitzer came to the Alexandria Hotel to pick up the director in the chauffeur-driven company automobile. While he waited for Griffith to finish exercising (he was an avid shadowboxer and often indulged himself on the set between takes), Bitzer read a telegram the Aitkens had just sent: "WE WILL SEND NO MORE MONEY. FINISH PICTURE IMMEDIATELY."

"Well, Mr. Griffith," Bitzer said, "you better do as they say."

"I will like hell!" Griffith responded. "I'm not inclined to quit now, or any other time." He asked Bitzer if he had any money of his own socked away. Bitzer admitted that he did, whereupon his boss convinced him to drive over to his bank and withdraw four hundred dollars to partially cover the day's payroll. Eventually Griffith would convince Bitzer to invest no less than $7,000 of his savings (over $150,000 in today's currency).

Even that sum wasn't enough to finish the movie as Griffith envisioned it. He tapped many other sources. J. R. Clune, a theater owner, gave $15,000 in exchange for shares in the film and a promise that his downtown auditorium could host the L.A. premiere. A mysterious person known to posterity only as "That Woman" gave $9,000. The movie's costume provider, Robert Goldstein, excused a $7,000 unpaid bill in exchange for a piece of the action. The only person who wanted to invest and was refused was Lillian Gish's mother. She offered the director three hundred dollars, but when he found out that this was the sum total of her entire savings, he refused: "Mrs. Gish, I can't let you do it. You'd be taking too great a risk." ("Had he allowed it, of course," Lillian observed rather tartly years later, "she would have made hundreds of thousands of dollars.")

By the time shooting wrapped up in October, many in the cast and crew were working on credit or deferred payments. Griffith himself was walking around with a hole in his shoe, vowing that he wouldn't buy a new pair "until we start getting money back at the box office." But the great film was finally, and literally, in the can. Now it remained for Griffith to seclude himself for a month or two to edit the miles of footage he'd shot down to a "modest" twelve reels. At the same time, he was also collaborating with conductor Joseph Carl Breil on a musical score and starting work on his next film (an urban melodrama called *The Mother and the Law*), not to mention overseeing a half-dozen films being made for the Aitkens by other directors. No celebration marked the end of the momentous undertaking—wrap parties would belong to a later, more leisurely era of filmmaking—but Griffith knew he had the film he wanted. The production had cost a then-astronomical sum of some $110,000, including an extra $19,000 that Harry Aitken had ultimately been convinced to throw in—with gritted teeth, no doubt. But Griffith was finally ready to give his grand vision to the world.

~

"Well, Roy," Harry Aitken said, "within a matter of fifteen hours we will know what the hard-boiled New York reaction is to our costly *Birth of a Nation*." It was three a.m. on the morning of February 28, 1915— the day Griffith's film was to open for the first time on the East Coast. (The director had changed the title from *The Clansman* to *The Birth of a Nation*, allegedly at Thomas Dixon's suggestion.) This opening matinee would be a preview for the press and other opinion-makers, to be followed by the official public premiere on March 3. The Aitken brothers were understandably nervous. "I did not fall asleep immediately," Roy later admitted. "I couldn't help thinking how much this picture meant to Harry and me."

Not that the early signs hadn't been promising. Once Griffith finally got the film in presentable form, he'd quietly shown two sneak previews on January 1 and 2 at an obscure theater in Riverside, California, sixty miles east of Los Angeles. Only Griffith had attended those showings, wanting some audience reactions to guide last-minute adjustments to the film and its score. The actual L.A. premiere had occurred on February 8 at Clune's Auditorium, hosted there in recompense for the theater owner's investment. The gala event—featuring a forty-piece orchestra and large chorus to accompany the film, as well as female usherettes dressed in Civil War gowns—was a smashing success. The audience went wild at the end of the three-hour extravaganza, "leaping up, cheering and applauding and stamping their feet." According to Joseph Henabery, "They literally tore the place apart." Even the doubters had been forced to revise their opinions. Karl Brown, who had come to the premiere with his parents expecting disaster, experienced something like a spiritual conversion while watching the film. Scene after scene that he thought would surely bomb—that had seemed awkward, unbelievable, or sentimental when he was filming them—turned out to be magnificent in their final form. "I was wrong," he would later admit, taking back all of his earlier criticisms. "What unfolded on that screen was magic itself."

Thomas Dixon, meanwhile, thought so much of the film that he arranged to have it shown for one of his old college friends, who happened to be President Woodrow Wilson. In what was probably the first showing of a narrative motion picture at the White House, Wilson (a Southerner, it must always be remembered) watched the film and apparently approved. What he actually said about it remains in dispute—the White House later denied the quote, and no solid documentary evidence of it has ever been found—but it has gone down in Hollywood lore as a hearty endorsement of both the film's artistic effect and its historical accuracy: "It is like writing history with lightning. And my only regret is that it is all so terribly true."

But the truth of the film, particularly the accuracy of its depiction of African-Americans, had actually been very much in dispute since the beginning. The Los Angeles chapter of the newly formed NAACP had known enough about Thomas Dixon's book to start working against Griffith's film even before it opened at Clune's. Arguing in court that the film was likely to cause riots, they sought an injunction against its exhibition. Although they succeeded in stopping one matinee of the film, the evening shows had gone on—albeit with a heavy police presence. Meanwhile, in the month between the L.A. and New York premieres, the national and New York chapters of the organization had gone to work. They lodged an appeal with the National Board of Censorship, a private industry group whose seal of approval was theoretically—if not actually—required for all films. After viewing the movie at Clune's, the board asked Griffith to make significant cuts to its second half. This he did—though reluctantly, and complaining all the while about what he considered "stupid persecution by ill-minded censors and politicians who were playing to the Negro vote."

That Griffith could be so obtuse may be hard to believe when viewing the film today, but he truly thought he had been fair to African-Americans in the film. According to Griffith, the "bad Negroes" in the film were mostly being manipulated by bad white politicians and carpetbaggers. He had also "balanced" them, in his own mind, by including a number of happy, faithful "good Negroes" in the story. As for using white actors in blackface, this was hardly an uncommon practice in 1915 America, and besides, Griffith claimed, there were very few African-

American actors in Los Angeles, and no money in his budget to bring some from New York.

Even with the board's requested edits, the film shown at the New York premieres was still a reprehensible piece of propaganda, in which black characters sexually assault innocent white women, terrorize their peaceable former masters, and generally abuse their newly won freedom in every way imaginable. In one scene a mixed-race politician strangles a chained dog to death, apparently out of sheer gratuitous cruelty. And yet this racist fantasy proved an enormous success. The Aitken brothers needn't have worried that morning of the New York critics' premiere; it quickly became obvious that the chance they had taken on the engagement—renting the Liberty Theatre, a full-size Broadway house, and charging a full two dollars per ticket to get into it—was going to pay off handsomely. Hundreds of people had to be turned away at the box office, and even then there were standees three deep in the aisle behind the loge seats. And the reaction of the packed house was everything the Aitkens and Griffith could have hoped for. Somehow unperturbed by the film's patent racism, the audience was dazzled by what was clearly a virtuoso epic of unprecedented power. Every technique, every expressive flourish, every camera and lighting innovation that Griffith and Bitzer had developed over the long years at Biograph were here brought together into a masterpiece of visual storytelling.

And the critics were dazzled, too, especially by the sweeping battle scenes and bravura set pieces like the burning of Atlanta. The *New York Times* reviewer was somewhat measured in his praise, calling it merely "an impressive new illustration of the scope of the motion picture camera," but just about every other critic in town was wowed. "Never before has such a whirlwind combination of story, spectacle, and tense drama been unrolled before New Yorkers," wrote the reviewer for the *Sun*. The *Evening Mail* insisted that "the mind falters and the typewriter balks before an attempt to either measure or describe D. W. Griffith's crowning achievement in screen drama." The *Evening Globe* was, if anything, even more hyperbolic: *The Birth of a Nation* was, according to the *Globe*'s critic, "beyond question the most extraordinary picture that has been made—or seen—in America so far."

None of these reviews mentioned anything about a controversy concerning the film's content; the critics, like the film's white audiences, seemed unaware of any unfairness in its depiction of blacks, even when they had to pass through a crowd of black demonstrators to reach the theater. And the reactions were similar nearly everywhere the film opened over the next months. There were actual riots at the Boston and Philadelphia premieres; in Chicago, Mayor Big Bill Thompson tried to ban exhibition of the film, while Hull House activist Jane Addams (who agreed with Big Bill on virtually nothing else) called it "a pernicious caricature of the Negro race." William Monroe Trotter, a newspaper editor who led the protests in Boston, was more specific: "It is a rebel play," he told reporters after being arrested on the night of the film's local premiere, "an incentive to great racial hatred here in Boston. It will make white women afraid of Negroes and will have white men all stirred up on their account." This was a prescient remark, given that *Birth* is widely regarded as being the spark that reignited the modern Ku Klux Klan. But somehow none of this fazed the huge, cheering crowds that greeted the film wherever it played.

Meanwhile the film's incoming grosses were stunning. Griffith and the Aitkens had arranged for twenty different "road shows"—gala openings at large theaters in major urban centers, featuring full orchestras and as much marketing ballyhoo as they could raise. These were expensive propositions, but thanks to high ticket prices and huge crowds, they were soon generating large profits. Other distribution rights were sold to film exchanges, as was the custom at the time, but even those deals were bringing in unprecedented sums. The night of the New York critics' premiere, Harry Aitken got a call from a Boston theater owner who was just getting into the distribution business (having sold his boat salvage company). He made a $50,000 preemptive bid for the New England distribution rights for *Birth*, with a fifty-fifty split on earnings once his expenses were paid. This was an astronomical amount at the time for a single region, so Aitken jumped at the offer. It proved to be a lucrative move for the little-known distributor—a man named Louis B. Mayer, who would use the windfall to launch himself in a much bigger way into the movie business.

So everyone associated with D. W. Griffith was suddenly (and almost literally) rolling in money. Billy Bitzer estimated that his small share in the movie was soon bringing him around $2,800 to $3,500 a week. As for the Aitkens, they were now solvent beyond their wildest hopes. "The worldwide success of *The Birth of a Nation* unloosed a flood of money in our direction," Roy Aitken recalled, "and our heads whirled from our newfound riches."

It wasn't only these individuals whose lives were changed. *The Birth of a Nation*, which earned out its substantial cost in just two months and went on to run continuously for years in many places (reportedly for twelve years straight in certain parts of the South), changed the entire movie industry. As Bitzer would later write, "From the day this picture opened, the movies became big business." The spectacle of 25 million people paying up to two dollars a ticket to see a single film suddenly convinced Wall Street and the big banks that the movies were an industry after all, worthy of serious investment. By June, Harry Aitken was able to tell a *New York Times* reporter, "The once lowly movie . . . has grown in ten years from a few scattered nickelodeons into a combination that ranks fourth or fifth among the great business enterprises of the country."

For D. W. Griffith, this was vindication on a grand scale—both for his faith in himself and for his belief in the possibilities of motion pictures. True, he was still smarting from the criticisms he had received from board censors and the African-American community. For years afterward, in fact, he would make speeches at road show openings around the country, defending the film and complaining bitterly about censorship and other infringements on freedom of expression. He even wrote and published a pamphlet on the topic, entitled "The Rise and Fall of Free Speech in America," which he invited everyone and anyone to reprint and distribute at will for no charge.

But despite his wounded feelings, Griffith was now a figure of national prominence and a money magnet with the freedom to make whatever kind of film he wanted. And although Harry Aitken urged him to temper his ambitions for a while so that they could consolidate their gains, Griffith wouldn't hear of it. On the contrary, he wanted to dream bigger and more ambitiously than ever, and the distance between Los Angeles and the moneymen in New York would allow him to do it. "Moving pictures are still only in their swaddling clothes," he told a reporter for the *New York Times*. "[But] the days of little things in the pictures are gone by forever." His next Big Thing—whatever it might be—would likely be deemed impossible by some. But as he assured the reporter, "I haven't dreamed an impossible thing in seven years—since I started in pictures. That is the beauty of this work. It makes dreams come true."

# CHAPTER SEVEN
# Water and Celluloid

*Santa Monica Boulevard, while still an idea*

It was now the mid-1910s, and serious capital had finally discovered the potential of the Los Angeles mirage factory. It had all happened quickly. That first great mirage—a garden metropolis in the desert, made possible by the building of an aqueduct—had turned into a supremely creditworthy reality. The city was thriving with its new imported water supply; eastern bondholders were receiving their interest payments and real estate developers were laying out new residential developments as fast as the excavators could clear the land. And now a new investment promised even higher profit margins: an *actual* mirage-building machine called Hollywood. This machine could manufacture all kinds of potent visions, from the tantalizingly exotic to the comfortably familiar, and export them to all parts of the country and even the world, at great return to its investors. The twin blessings of water and celluloid were now giving the transforming city the economic and infrastructural backbone of a place with real substance. L.A.'s early detractors—those who had scorned its growth potential because it had "no local forests to burn, no big rivers to dam, no coal to dig"—had been silenced. The city had found its own unique solutions to those disadvantages, and was poised to grow even faster. Having outstripped Denver in population by 1910, Los Angeles now had its sights set on overtaking its longtime regional rival, San Francisco.

L.A.'s new urban credibility, coinciding auspiciously with the manufacturing demands created by the start of the Great War in Europe, was sparking industrialization in other areas as well. The Ford Motor Company opened its first Model T plant here in 1914. Just two years earlier, the Glenn L. Martin Company (a predecessor of the Lockheed Corporation) had been founded in Orange County. One of Martin's employees, Donald W. Douglas, went on to start his own company, Douglas Aircraft, which was later merged into Boeing. Goodyear Tire and Rubber Company came to town in 1919 (citing the city's abundant water supply as the reason for choosing Los Angeles over San Diego or San Francisco); it was soon followed by Firestone, Goodrich, and U.S. Rubber. Admittedly, Los Angeles in the 1910s still lagged behind many older eastern and midwestern cities in industrial output, but this situation was changing rapidly.

Oil was another early success story fueling the city's growth. Geologists had been aware of oil and asphalt deposits around the city for decades, but commercial exploitation remained modest until Edward L. Doheny sank his first well west of downtown in November 1892. Doheny (who was the model—via the Upton Sinclair novel *Oil!*—for the main character in the movie *There Will Be Blood*) went on to drill many more wells over the next years, setting up his own refinery and selling oil to the local railroads, which were in the process of converting their locomotives from coal-powered steam. By 1909, there were an estimated 160 oil wells operating in the area north of Wilshire Boulevard, turning many homeowners into small-time oilmen. Derricks sprouted like mushrooms in their fruit orchards, while mules dragged heavy drilling equipment across their once neatly trimmed lawns. For a time, parts of Santa Monica Boulevard resembled nothing so much as an "oil-workers' shacktown." And although L.A.'s share of the business would not become nationally significant until the discovery of several big oil deposits after the end of the Great War (when local production would zoom to nearly a million barrels a day, an estimated 5 percent of total global production), drilling provided a significant boost to the local economy throughout the 1910s.

L.A.'s reputation as a regional agricultural center had also gone emphatically national, as the new availability of water brought farm and orchard land under more intensive cultivation. Just before construction of the aqueduct had begun, a cooperative of several hundred independent citrus growers had started marketing their products under the single name Sunkist. By 1914, their ad campaigns had been so successful that Americans were eating an average of forty oranges per person annually, an 80 percent increase since 1885. In 1916, hoping to create a new market for their surplus fruit, they more or less "invented" a product called orange juice and somehow convinced the whole nation that it should be an indispensable part of breakfast. Raisin growers in the nearby San Joaquin Valley had similar success with the brand name Sun-Maid, and this became a pattern repeated across a wide range of food items grown in the region. Walnuts and almonds—considered exotic luxuries in 1890, enjoyed perhaps several times a year at holiday gatherings—had by the mid-1910s become daily staples in millions of American households, marketed under umbrella names like Diamond Brand Walnuts and Fancy Brand Almonds. Thanks to growers' ability to create a demand through advertising and then supply it, the region was soon making year-round shipments of produce, including strawberries, olives, celery, and pumpkins—not just to the East and Midwest, but also (via the new Panama Canal) to the markets of London and beyond.

All of this economic growth fueled unprecedented physical growth, as the city's boundaries crept ever farther out into the semiarid plains and mountain valleys. Much of this expansion came through annexation. In the years from 1906 to 1909, the city reached out to its coastline by annexing the port of San Pedro and a narrow corridor of land connecting it to downtown. Hollywood officially became part of the city in 1910, Arroyo Seco joined in 1912, and many other unincorporated places would do likewise in the next decade. In 1915 the city annexed the entire San Fernando Valley—a move that almost tripled its geographical size overnight. Otis and the rest of the land syndicate rejoiced; as part of the city, the valley could now use the water William Mulholland had so obligingly brought to its doorstep, enormously increasing the value of the syndicate's landholdings. Thanks in part to the San Fernando addition—a virtual Louisiana Purchase—the area of L.A. proper would increase from 108 to 415 square miles in the decade from 1915 to 1925.

Much of the sprawl hopped over the still-undeveloped portions west of downtown and took up residence at the beach. The development of seaside resorts like Santa Monica, Manhattan Beach, and Hermosa Beach helped the city make good on its aspirations as a mecca for winter tourists. Perhaps the most interesting seaside community to arise was Venice, or "Venice in America," the brainchild of a man named Albert Kinney, who had made a fortune selling Sweet Caporal cigarettes in the East and used it to realize his idiosyncratic vision on a large tract of sand dunes some seventeen miles west of downtown. Here he built an array of homes, hotels, and amusement halls by the sea, all connected by a series of Venice-style canals serviced by a fleet of gondolas and a staff of gondoliers allegedly imported from the Italian original. Together with other towns being developed up and down the coast, Venice became the most extravagant manifestation of a short-lived beach development boom early in the century. As in many real estate booms, a lot of would-be millionaire investors got burned in the end, when the bottom fell out of the market. But the towns remained after the investors had moved on, adding yet another unique element to L.A.'s evolving identity.

Meanwhile, as the early moviemakers had discovered, downtown Los Angeles had left its pueblo days far behind, sprouting a skyline not too unlike those of New York, Chicago, and other cities east of the Mississippi. "The visitor to the city can at this moment observe skyscrapers in all stages of construction," the *L.A. Times* reported in 1911, noting that "Los Angeles is leading San Francisco, Portland, Seattle, etc., in building activity." More impressive than this vertical growth, however, was the astonishing rate of horizontal growth radiating in all directions, as thousands of new, mostly single-family homes infiltrated the canyons, commandeered the hilltops, and fanned out ever farther across the basins of the metropolitan area. By one 1912 estimate, Los Angeles was building five miles of new streets per month. Many of these were being laid out in theoretical subdivisions months or even years in advance of any actual homebuilding. Savvy developers would erect "SOLD!" signs on lots not actually sold, hoping to create a false sense of urgency among potential buyers. Often these places would be served by projected streetcar lines, carrying hypothetical residents to still-imaginary neighborhoods.

But those conjectural homes did eventually materialize—in most cases, at least—as did the people to live in them. Many were from distant parts of the country and were subject to a certain cultural confusion in their strange new climes. They built homes that were not really appropriate to their adopted surroundings—"New England homes, with high steep roofs to shed snow that did not fall," as historian Carey McWilliams has put it, "with dark interiors that contrasted nightmarishly with the bright out-of-doors, and with deep cellars built for needless furnaces." Swiss chalets and Tudor manses began to dot the hillside chaparral, while squat Queen Annes and many-turreted Victorians sprouted among the rattling palm trees. Other homes were not so out of place, such as the California bungalow, borrowed from the plain, single-story structures of tropical Asia and adapted to a place that (marketing pitches notwithstanding) does sometimes get chilly. The Spanish colonial architecture that became a craze after the Panama-California Exposition of 1915 also fit in well. Those structures, at least, dovetailed conveniently with the Mediterranean image that local boosters were still using to attract settlers: Los Angeles as a romanticized re-creation of California's Mission past, minus the Indians and Spanish-speaking people who had populated it.

The metropolitan landscape was also being reshaped by the new movie money. Highly paid actors, directors, and producers (though most of the big studio owners were still based in the East) began to build elaborate mansions in Beverly Hills and Hollywood, which was quickly losing its pious small-town aura. And thanks to the new abundance of water, these homes could boast that quintessential status symbol: the built-in, often Olympic-size swimming pool. The studios, too, made good use of the Owens Valley bounty. Movie executives like William Selig and Carl Laemmle built private zoos and back lots tricked out with artificial lakes and water tanks, so that even something like the ubiquitous jungle picture could now be shot without leaving the confines of Los Angeles. These were artificial worlds unto themselves, designed to re-create any kind of setting imaginable. As one writer described the lot at Inceville, Thomas Ince's huge studio in the Santa Monica hills: "The tepees sat cheek-by-jowl with a fake Swiss landscape, a Japanese village, a Puritan settlement, mansions and cottages." Anything, in other words, required to create the proper illusion.

L.A.'s illusions—heavily publicized out in the heartland—were by now bringing new migrants to the city by the thousands. Some harbored dreams of making it in Hollywood, but most were just ordinary people attracted by the appealing climate and landscape they saw on their movie screens every week (or else on the colorful labels *qua* advertisements pasted on the crates of oranges and almonds they saw at their local grocers). Whereas the westbound migrants to Los Angeles of earlier decades were generally well-to-do, those who came in the 1910s were decidedly middle-class. These were largely conservative, churchgoing people, disproportionately from the Midwest (leading some self-styled wits to refer to southern California as "the Iowa coast"). The result was a city with, contrary to its later reputation, a distinctly middle-American vibe. "The inhabitants of Los Angeles," journalist Willard Huntington Wright wrote in 1913, "are culled largely from the smaller cities of the Middle West—'leading citizens' from Wichita; honorary pall-bearers from Emmetsburg; Good Templars from Sedalia; honest spinsters from Grundy Center—all commonplace people, many of them with small competencies made from the sale of farm lands or from the life-long savings of small mercantile business." Another condescending observer, Irvin S. Cobb, perhaps summed it up best: "At heart, Los Angeles is a vast cross-section of the Corn Belt set down incongruously in a Maxfield Parrish setting."

⁓

The image of Los Angeles as a clean, safe midwestern town transplanted to the West Coast was one that city boosters had in fact been advertising for decades. In that racist and xenophobic era, the city's lack of diversity was considered a selling point. As Charles Fletcher Lummis had written in an 1895 issue of *The Land of Sunshine* (a magazine that—like Nordhoff's *California*—was actually a Chamber of Commerce marketing device to attract tourists and settlers): "The ignorant, hopelessly un-American type of foreigner which infests and largely controls Eastern cities is almost unknown here." As for the city's Indian and Spanish/ Mexican roots, when they were acknowledged at all, they were presented as a distant enhancement of local color—an appealing topic for tourist entertainments like *Ramona* and *The Mission Play*. The emphasis was always on Los Angeles as an atypical urban bastion of solid "American" (i.e., white, second-generation northern European) values.

But although Los Angeles at this time was indeed a predominantly white place—with over 90 percent of the population being of European descent—it was hardly the advertised "Aryan city of the sun." Its African-American population, which stood at about 7,600 in 1910, was still small but relatively prosperous. Black Angelenos could proudly recall that the majority of the original *pobladores* who established the pueblo of Los Angeles in 1781 were of African ancestry, and that one of the earliest black residents of the city—Bridget "Biddie" Mason—managed to escape slavery here and become a successful business and real estate entrepreneur. L.A.'s reputation as a "safe haven" for African-Americans, free from the more blatant depredations of Jim Crow that plagued other American cities (officially, in the South; unofficially, in the North), had brought many well-off black families to town in the years around the turn of the twentieth century. They established local institutions like the Afro-American Council, the Los Angeles Forum, and chapters of the National Negro Business League and NAACP to preserve this mostly benign racial atmosphere, where blacks could own land and schools were at least nominally integrated. Even so, as the 1910s wore on, the situation for blacks in the city began to deteriorate. In 1912 the so-called Shenk Rule gave local business owners a powerful tool to keep African-Americans from patronizing their establishments—by charging astronomically higher prices to nonwhite customers. The pernicious new law was named after the L.A. city attorney who found that "it was neither extortion [n]or a violation of the Civil Rights Act to charge a Negro more for an article than a white man." This was followed by rumblings of incipient segregation in a court judgment that forced black tenants to vacate office space for white businesses in the downtown Copp Building. Alarm at these ominous developments in part explained the local NAACP's quick mobilization against *The Clansman* in early 1915. And although the city's African-American population would soon be swelled by the first waves of the Great Migration—which after 1920 turned the area around South Central Avenue into one of the great black metropolises of the country—it remained, in the 1910s, a relatively small slice of the overall population.

Asians in Los Angeles faced somewhat different obstacles in these years, as anti-immigration legislation kept their numbers in the city limited. Thanks to repeated extensions of the Chinese Exclusion Act of 1882, made "permanent" in 1904, along with laws that prohibited Asians from owning land, the Chinese population of Los Angeles sank from 7,500 at the turn of the century to just 2,000 in the early 1920s (a disheartening situation that gave rise to the phrase "a Chinaman's chance"). The Japanese population, by contrast, was growing. But since the baseline from which it started was so low (just 152 individuals in the city proper in

1900), even exponential growth brought that number to just over 4,000 by 1910. In 1908 a so-called "Gentlemen's Agreement" with the Japanese government stopped all immigration of unskilled labor from Japan into the United States, which slowed growth considerably, at least in less urban areas. Even so, Japanese made up about 45 percent of the farm labor in California in 1909, and a Little Tokyo neighborhood took root in downtown L.A. to compete with the older Chinatown.

Perhaps the most surprising demographic characteristic was the relative paucity of Mexicans in the city before 1910 or so. Given that southern California was actually a part of Mexico until the middle of the nineteenth century, the shrinkage of the Mexican-born community to just 493 individuals in 1890—and still only 817 by 1900—was astonishing. L.A. went from being a town of over 90 percent Spanish-speakers in 1850 to one of just 10 percent by 1890. The population of Mexican-Americans is more difficult to assess, as the term wasn't typically used until after the Depression, but it was probably much higher. Both populations at this time were concentrated in the barrio adjacent to the old plaza, which was known (to Anglos, at least) as "Sonoratown."

Mexican immigrants began returning to the city in great numbers after 1910, when revolution in Mexico displaced many people and the Great War created labor opportunities in agriculture, railroading, and oil and gas works. At first, most moved to the long-standing downtown barrio, where the establishment of mutual aid societies, political and cultural organizations, Spanish-language newspapers, and other institutions helped the community maintain its integrity amid the encroaching suburbs. But when L.A.'s rapid growth created a need for more space downtown for public and commercial buildings, many of Sonoratown's blocks were razed to make room. Mexicans and other Latinos were forced to move eastward across the Los Angeles River and outward to more far-flung parts of the city. And there—for the time being, at least—the city's Anglo boosters largely ignored them in their quest to promote what they were still calling "the most American city" in the United States.

~

While Los Angeles would not take on the contours of the great multicultural metropolis we know today until the 1920s and beyond, one aspect of the city's later identity was already firmly entrenched by the 1910s: its reputation as a center of unorthodox social thought, spirituality, and healing. Perhaps as a result of the psychological dislocation endemic in a city dominated by newcomers, the temptation to fill the void of disconnectedness with exotic faith and unconventional philosophy seemed irresistible to many who arrived in this land of sunshine and oranges, even those of an otherwise conservative middle-American bent. According to one political leader writing in 1920, the people of Los Angeles were "peculiarly susceptible to sentimental appeal . . . [and] ready to accept any guaranteed panacea for peace on earth and good will toward men." One manifestation of this tendency was a ready embrace of all kinds of cults and quackery, or what Willard Huntington Wright in 1913 called a taste for "faddists and mountebanks—spiritualists, mediums, astrologists, phrenologists, palmists, and all other breeds of esoteric wind-jammers." According to Wright, "Whole buildings [in the city] are devoted to occult and outlandish orders—mazdaznam clubs, yogi sects, homes of truth, cults of cosmic fluidists, astral planers, Emmanuel movers, Rosicrucians, and other boozy transcendentalists."

Often the quackery involved purely physical health-seeking. "A vast amount of therapeutic lore was to be had for nothing in Westlake Park," wrote L.A. novelist Mark Lee Luther. "The elderly men and women, hailing chiefly from the Mississippi watershed, . . . were walking encyclopedias of medical knowledge. They seemed to have experienced all ailments, tried all cures. Allopathy, homeopathy, osteopathy, chiropractic, faith-healing and Christian Science, vegetarianism and unfried food, the *bacillus bulgaricus* [a microorganism in certain kinds of yogurt] and the internal bath [i.e., a colon cleanse] each had its disciples and propagandists."

But the quest for a kind of healing beyond the physical—whether via quasi-religious occult practice or any number of varieties of social utopianism—was even more pronounced in the Los Angeles of the 1910s. It seemed not at all incongruous to many Angelenos when socialist Job Harriman, after his unsuccessful bid for mayor in 1911, chose to withdraw from traditional politics and start an agricultural cooperative *qua* workers' soviet called Llano del Rio. Located in a remote part of the Antelope Valley desert, Llano was hardly a crackpot cult—it resembled nothing so much as the later *kibbutzim* of Israel—but its idealism did tend toward the bizarre. One of the cooperative's mottos was "If you have two loaves of bread, sell one and buy a hyacinth to feed your soul." While the colony experienced some success for a time, its laudable experiment in communal living was doomed by political infighting and the sheer difficulty of producing crops in such an unreliable arid climate.

Other examples of southern California utopianism were decidedly more outré, often centering on a single charismatic personality of greater or lesser eccentricity. The first prophet to make a significant mark in the region was Katherine Tingley, the so-called "Purple Mother" of Theosophy (a system of mystical philosophies emphasizing the search for a direct experience of divinity in life and nature). Tingley came from New York in 1900 to establish the Point Loma Theosophical Community, a.k.a. Lomaland, near San Diego. Using capital raised in the East, she built a forty-building, five-hundred-acre compound in partly Moorish, partly Egyptian style, housing a School of Antiquity, a Theosophical University, a Greek Theater, a Raja Yoga College, and eventually even an opera house in which visiting dignitaries could lecture followers. Dressed in esoteric costumes (purple robes for the women, khaki uniforms for the men), the colony's several hundred residents took time out from their studies to raise chickens, fruit, vegetables, and even silkworms to weave their own silk cloth.

Like anything vaguely threatening to conservative values and the status quo, Lomaland soon found an enemy in Harrison Gray Otis and his *L.A. Times*, which began printing sensational stories about the settlement. These articles—appearing under headlines like "OUTRAGES AT POINT LOMA" and "STARTLING TALES FROM TINGLEY"—described strange orgies and other "gross immoralities," not to mention the enshrinement of a sacred dog (named, rather disappointingly, Spot), who was alleged to be the reincarnation of one of the widow Tingley's dead husbands. Whether there was any truth to these revelations remains unclear, but Mrs. Tingley did sue the newspaper for libel. After many years in the courts, the case was decided in her favor, for which she was awarded some $7,500 in damages.

The success of Lomaland, which attracted Theosophists from around the world, established southern California as a global center for such communities, one of which was soon established in the center of Hollywood itself. Albert Powell Warrington, a retired lawyer from Virginia, appeared on the scene in 1911 and purchased a fifteen-acre hillside lot where, he claimed, the surrounding groves were "magnetically impregnated" with a unique spiritual urge. Warrington—another Theosophist with a taste for Moorish-Egyptian architecture—built on this site a motley collection of buildings, including an Occult Temple, a metaphysical library, and the de rigueur Greek temple, along with a vegetarian cafeteria and an assortment of tabernacles. The community, which he called Krotona, sponsored many fascinating personalities throughout the 1910s. (One of them, the mystic Phil Thompson, founded the new science of stereometry, which somehow made use of a three-dimensional geometric alphabet.) There seems to have been little contact between the Krotona colonists and the nascent moviemaking community, and by 1920 Warrington had decided to move the community to Ojai, in the Topatopa Mountains of Ventura County. But Krotona did leave one lasting legacy in Los Angeles: the Theater Arts Alliance, which spawned the Hollywood Bowl concerts that are still a feature of Hollywood's cultural life today.

L.A.'s hunger for spiritual connectedness also took less esoteric forms. Many of those transplants from parts east, after all, were perfectly satisfied with good old-fashioned Protestant churches like the ones they'd left behind. These were so numerous as to give at least one contemporary observer the impression that "Christianity ranked as the city's leading industry after real estate and motion pictures." But the Los Angeles permutations of even old-fashioned Christianity tended toward the charismatic. It was in downtown L.A. that William J. Seymour, an African-American preacher from Kansas, launched the Azusa Street Revival in 1906. This seminal Pentecostalist meeting attracted a racially and ethnically integrated following that numbered in the thousands and that came to worship at its three services per day, seven days a week, over the space of almost three years. "Full of noisy manifestations, shouts, speaking in tongues, moaning, and singing in tongues," the Azusa Street services drew predictable outrage from Otis and his *Times*. But they are widely regarded as one of the key springboards of the modern Pentecostal movement, which now numbers over 500 million believers worldwide.

The arrival of L.A.'s best-known and most controversial spiritual shepherd, however, was still several years in the future. In 1915 Aimee Semple McPherson—a woman whose potent blending of piety, pageantry, and publicity would speak directly to the city's unique ethos—was still back east, traveling up and down the eastern seaboard, earning her stripes as an evangelist. Not until 1918 would she come west to take the city by storm. In the meantime, Los Angeles would continue to evolve. With a population around the half-million mark in 1915, the city was no longer just a regional capital tucked away in a far corner of the country. Nor, however, was it yet a mature, fully developed metropolis with a stable and recognizable identity. Steering a path somewhere between the inflated aspirations of its marketers and the barbs of its self-styled critics, the "gigantic improvisation" that is modern Los Angeles was gradually finding itself, patching together an identity like any other adolescent—in a process rife with awkwardness, incongruity, and surprising moments of grace.

# CHAPTER EIGHT
# Epic Times

*The elaborate Babylon set for* Intolerance

In the wake of *The Birth of a Nation*'s unprecedented success, everyone in Hollywood was suddenly thinking bigger. "Bigger and better, bigger and better became the constantly chanted watchword[s] of the year," Karl Brown wrote about this heady post-*Birth* time. "Soon the two words became one. Bigger *meant* better, and a sort of gigantism overwhelmed the world, especially the world of motion pictures."

Fueling this lurch toward the titanic, especially for Griffith and the Aitkens, was the abrupt availability of cash—"the sudden cascading of money, money, and yet more money into the studio itself." Much of it was spent immediately. Elaborate new cameras and lighting equipment were bought, while a raft of fresh-faced scenario writers, costume designers, and stage actors (including an athletic young dynamo named Douglas Fairbanks) were brought in from Broadway. There were so many new people milling around the Sunset Boulevard studio that Brown gave up trying to keep track of them. "They were everywhere," the young cameraman marveled, "doing everything from slapstick comedy to Shakespeare."

All of this expansion, moreover, was happening under the auspices of a brand-new company. Harry Aitken, having been ousted from the Mutual board of directors after their refusal to participate in the funding of *Birth*, now had the last laugh as he plowed his huge profits from that film (along with a four-million-dollar investment from Wall Street) into a larger and more ambitious enterprise. Taking the remnants of his Reliance-Majestic production company with him, he engineered a merger with Charles Baumann and Adam Kessel, who controlled the Keystone Studio, to create a tripartite powerhouse boasting the talents of the three premier director-producers in the business: Griffith, Mack Sennett, and Thomas Ince. Called the Triangle Film Company after its three star talents, the company was to make and market a better class of films—"two-dollar pictures," as they came to be known—to attract audiences who would never even think of setting foot in an inner-city nickelodeon.

Griffith, Sennett, and Ince would operate independently, each in his own studio compound around the city. Griffith would continue at the Sunset Boulevard location (to be renamed the Fine Arts Studio), and Sennett would go on at the old Keystone compound in Edendale— though both facilities would be substantially expanded. Ince would have an entirely new studio built for him in Culver City, a rapidly developing area southwest of Hollywood, since filming at his old Inceville location above Santa Monica was too often hindered by brush fires and all-day fogs off the Pacific. Each studio would operate as a separate film production plant, with several movies shooting simultaneously under the supervision of one of the three resident cinematic geniuses.

To feed this three-mawed production machine, Aitken and Baumann pursued as much big-name talent as their overflowing coffers could buy. "We have decided," Baumann wrote to Mack Sennett in June 1915, "to corral both the legitimate and Motion Picture stars, regardless of cost, for the reason of taking the props right from under any other Motion Picture concern in America." Triangle made overtures to the likes of Mary Pickford, Billie Burke (a huge Broadway star at the time, best known now for playing Glinda, the good witch in 1939's *The Wizard of Oz*), and the now-prohibitively expensive Charlie Chaplin. The play for Chaplin was particularly cynical: "This is very important," Baumann insisted in the same letter to Sennett. "We are all of the opinion that if we have to pay [Chaplin] $3,000 a week and *he doesn't even appear in [our] pictures*, we have accomplished a great deal by getting him away from a competing company, thereby leaving no competition in the field for the Keystone films." This ruthless attempt at a Hollywood talent monopoly didn't ultimately succeed, but Triangle snared enough top names to keep all three studios humming night and day.

To handle their prodigious output, Triangle would also be making heavy investments in the distribution and exhibition ends of the business. Aitken planned to set up film exchange offices not just in New York and Los Angeles, but also in San Francisco, Denver, Atlanta, Chicago, New Orleans, Boston, and a host of other cities. This would allow

Triangle to distribute its own films nationwide, rather than selling the rights outright to state- or region-based distributors. As for exhibition, Aitken used some of the *Birth* and Wall Street bounty to assemble a worldwide chain of movie theaters, consisting of over four hundred in the United States and up to two hundred overseas, to show the Triangle pictures. This kind of vertical integration—with production, distribution, and exhibition all under the aegis of a single company—would eventually be deemed illegal, but in the meantime it would help establish Triangle as one of the industry's major players.

Over the next few years, other companies also tried to make the leap to vertically integrated gigantism. In the summer of 1916, Adolph Zukor engineered a merger of his Famous Players studio with the Lasky Feature Play Company and then proceeded to gain control of a major distributor called Paramount. Famous Players/Lasky, a.k.a. Paramount, immediately became the eight-hundred-pound gorilla in the industry. But there were soon plenty of four-hundred- and six-hundred-pound gorillas—besides Triangle and Universal—to give Paramount competition. William Fox, who had turned a 1903 investment in a Brooklyn penny arcade into a thriving chain of movie theaters and a film exchange, moved into production in 1915 as the Fox Film Corporation (eventually 20th Century–Fox). Louis B. Mayer, fresh from his coup in *Birth of a Nation* distribution rights, took on some partners and in 1915 started a production company called Metro Pictures—the first M in what would culminate as MGM, or Metro-Goldwyn-Mayer, some years later. The merger mania got so heated that in the spring of 1916 there were even rumors that Zukor and Aitken might combine to form what surely would have been the U.S. Steel of the movie business.

The movies being put out by these companies were getting bigger, too. At Fox, writer-director Herbert Brenon was filming *A Daughter of the Gods*, an underwater fantasy film of such extravagance that it allegedly cost over a million dollars to produce—the first U.S. film ever to do so. For Famous Players/Lasky, Cecil B. DeMille, who saw the wisdom of the historical epic in the box office receipts of *Birth of a Nation*, was planning *Joan the Woman*; it was to be "the first cinematic spectacle about Joan of Arc," featuring opera superstar Geraldine Farrar and employing the new Handschiegl Process to add color to key scenes (like the burning of Joan at the stake). And Thomas Ince was producing his own superepic: an antiwar film with the grand title *Civilization*. These blockbusters would be sent on the same kind of elaborate road shows Griffith had pioneered with *Birth*, opening in legitimate theaters and in the luxurious new movie palaces—"temples of art," as the trade papers liked to call them—now being built by the likes of Samuel "Roxy" Rothapfel in New York, the Balaban brothers in Chicago, and Sid Grauman right there in Los Angeles.

Of course, no one in L.A. was more grandiose in ambition than D. W. Griffith himself. At dinner one night with the Aitken brothers and actresses Mae Marsh and Miriam Cooper, Griffith announced that he would never make another picture "as insignificant as a four-reeler," and that he had plans for an epic even bigger than *The Birth of a Nation*. He didn't specify exactly what he had in mind, but he did imply that the film would be in some way a response to those who had attacked his treatment of the black characters in *Birth*—attacks that he regarded as a kind of intolerance. "He was smarting from the charges of racial prejudice," Billy Bitzer later confirmed, "[and] was hell-bent to answer his critics with the greatest movie ever made on this theme—intolerance."

But Griffith had a logistics problem. The next film he was set to release—*The Mother and the Law*, an urban melodrama he had shot while editing the early versions of *Birth*—was a minor picture. It was not quite an "insignificant four-reeler," perhaps, but it was certainly no blockbuster. At a test projection of the film for the cast and crew in early 1915, everyone seemed convinced that this should not be the next D. W. Griffith production to reach the public. "We all agreed with him that the film was too small in theme and execution to follow *The Birth*," Lillian Gish later wrote. "Mr. Griffith was in the awkward position of having to surpass himself. Yet he could not afford to discard *The Mother and the Law*."

Instead, Griffith decided to fold his small modern film into a much larger production incorporating four different stories from four different historical settings, all of them relating to his overarching theme of intolerance. Just how much of this grand scheme he revealed to Aitken and the other Triangle principals is unclear, but the cast and crew he assembled were kept almost completely in the dark. Only to his most intimate associates did he even hint at what he had in mind. "I always said I would rebuild Babylon for you," he playfully told Gish one day. "Now I'm going to do it, and make it part of a new story I have planned, showing man's inhumanity to man for the last 2500 years."

Griffith began by renting an extensive tract of land across the street from the Fine Arts Studio on Sunset Boulevard. Here he set Huck Wortman to work in the summer of 1915, laying the foundations for an enormous set depicting the walls of ancient Babylon. Construction would take months to complete, so Griffith used the time to expand the already-complete *Mother and the Law* picture to fit its new role in his larger conception. In the modern story, two young people—called (rather coyly) the Boy and the Dear One, played by Robert Harron and Mae Marsh—are compelled to leave their small town in the wake of a brutally suppressed factory strike. Forced into a marginal existence in the big bad city, convincingly portrayed by downtown Los Angeles, the two soon find themselves in trouble, their woes exacerbated by the efforts of heavy-handed reformers who want to clean up the city's rampant crime and dissipation. The Boy, falsely accused of an underworld murder, is arrested and sentenced to hang, while the couple's newborn baby is taken away from the Dear One by a group of crusading "vestal virgins of Uplift" who unfairly deem her an unfit mother. Clearly a diatribe against what Griffith regarded as the sanctimonious, hypocritical do-gooders who had objected to *The Birth of a Nation*, the film nonetheless didn't satisfy him in its original form. To heighten its polemical and dramatic thrust, he reshot some scenes and added new ones, including one of his signature race-against-the-clock endings, as the Boy is rescued from the gallows by a last-minute pardon from the governor. Hoping to make the prison scenes as vivid and accurate as possible, Griffith even took Bitzer and Karl Brown on a research trip to San Francisco, where they toured the city jail and the San Quentin state prison, with special attention to the latter's death row and execution procedures.

It was during this trip to San Francisco that Griffith saw the architecture of the Panama-Pacific International Exposition, which ran for most of 1915 on the site of what is now the city's Marina District. The director was tremendously impressed by the expo's fanciful, "vaguely Asiatic" buildings (the Palace of Fine Arts is one of its few surviving structures) and decided that whoever had built them would be perfect to realize his vision of ancient Babylon. Many of the painters and sculptors responsible for the fair were still in California, and Griffith wasted no time in hiring them for his production. He put them to work under Huck Wortman to build a set that would make the San Francisco fair's extravagant buildings look sober and spartan.

In the meantime, Griffith wrapped up the additions to *The Mother and the Law* and in September started shooting a new story about the St. Bartholomew Day massacre in sixteenth-century Paris—which he playfully also called *The Mother and the Law*. "It was the same story, only in a different period," Brown mused. "A lot of important people forever picking on a lot of unimportant people." Here the important people were Catholic royals Catherine de Medici and her son, King Charles IX, whom she convinces to kill the kingdom's Huguenots (Calvinist Protestants) because they don't "believe as we do." Exactly what this historical episode had to do with the modern urban melodrama they had just finished shooting—or, for that matter, with the story that would play out against the rising city of Babylon next door—was anybody's guess. But a new Baroque-looking set went up in the shadow of those towering walls, and Griffith began filming. Two months later, another set, this one vaguely Middle Eastern in flavor, went up for another film—also called *The Mother and the Law* and seeming to involve the Passion of Jesus Christ. According to Miriam Cooper, no one could figure out how all of these sets and stories could be intended for the same picture with the same inappropriate title. To keep the different sections straight, the crew began referring to them as F2, F3, F4, etc.—the F standing for "feature" (*The Birth of a Nation* had been F1). "So now if [Griffith] decided to make *The Mother and the Law* twenty times," Brown explained, "we'd simply raise the F number to correspond."

The studio lot began to seem chaotic and almost surreal. Scenario writer Anita Loos, who at this time was working on Douglas Fairbanks adventure films with one of Griffith's underling directors, professed to being confused when actors in different costumes showed up on seemingly inappropriate sets—a sixteenth-century French courtier, say, walking along a street in ancient Judea. Shooting on F5—the Babylon version of *The Mother and the Law*—had not even begun yet, and people were already expressing doubts about whether anything remotely coherent could be made out of the disparate material. "There was so much about the film that didn't hang together," Brown admitted, "that I soon stopped trying to understand any of it."

Through it all, however, Griffith seemed totally at ease, even serene. Working as always without a script, he was developing his concept in rehearsal, trying out new ideas and new business, molding actors and scenes like a sculptor working his clay. To his actors and crew, it seemed as if the project was growing larger and more unmanageable every day. Griffith kept adding new scenes, new sets, new footage—"shooting miles of film that could never be used," according to Joseph Henabery, one of his assistant directors. But Griffith himself never seemed worried. While shooting the prison scenes in the modern story, he'd take time out to read aloud from Oscar Wilde's *The Ballad of Reading Gaol*, to put everyone on the set in the proper mood. While consulting about costumes or the Babylon set with designer Walter "Spec" Hall (the "Spec" was short for "Perspective," Hall's specialty), Griffith would absentmindedly play with coins, pouring them from one hand to the other as he contemplated the look he wanted.

Everyone else at Triangle—especially Harry Aitken and his financiers in New York—became more and more anxious as the weeks went by. According to Brown, "Everybody on the crew was concerned that no actual film was being made of all these shoots." At one point, someone mentioned that they were already well into the second year of shooting on the film—an unprecedented extravagance. Griffith remained unconcerned, exulting in his new license to take as long, and to spend as much, as he wanted. "I don't see why everyone is in such a hurry to get through," he said on the set one day. "We'd only start another one"—that is, another film.

His insouciance was especially remarkable considering how many ways Griffith was being pulled during these months. In addition to directing one of the most elaborate film epics of all time, he was supervising a half-dozen other Triangle productions, even writing the scenario for many of them under the pseudonym Granville Warwick. He was also still traveling to promote the remaining *Birth of a Nation* road shows, making anticensorship speeches at various clubs and community groups, and testifying on film-related issues before Congress and state legislatures around the country.

All of this was in service to Griffith's new identity in the movie world as what Lillian Gish called "the dean of films." In the post-*Birth* era, he was almost universally lauded as a genius—the reigning titan of the brand-new art form. And it seemed that he was beginning to believe it himself. Many of his most ardent admirers admitted that he was becoming somewhat pompous and self-important. Always a bit of a Southern aristocrat (this was when he began to mention the alleged family connection to Welsh royalty), Griffith was now adopting an amused tone of noblesse oblige in his interviews. Many of his utterances to the press began with phrases like: "Of course, it hurts my sense of modesty to admit it, but . . ." When asked by one interviewer to provide a précis of his life, he said, with perfectly calibrated faux humility, "The public cannot care about that topic; [but] you cannot improve on what was written about a real man of note once: 'He was born, he grew a little, he slept a little, he ate a little, he worked a little, he loved a little—and then he died.'" On the set, meanwhile, Griffith was becoming more and more aloof, adopting a remote, God-like detachment from those around him. "There seemed to be an invisible barrier around him," one actor observed. "You couldn't get near him."

To be fair, Griffith was not alone among Hollywood's elite in cultivating a larger-than-life persona for public consumption. The film industry was by now in the business of creating illusions both on and off the screen, assisted by the elaborate apparatus of press agents, publicity departments, trade publications, and fan magazines that had grown up with the industry it served. Many actors and directors were tailoring their life stories to whatever identity seemed most intriguing and/or useful for their ambitions. Erich Stroheim, the son of a Viennese hatmaker, added a "von" before his surname to give himself an instant aura of exiled royalty. Cincinnati-born Theodosia Burr Goodman, whose father was a Jewish tailor from Poland, became Theda Bara (an acronym of "Death Arab"). This new, artificial pedigree—she depicted herself as the Egyptian-born daughter of a French actress and an Italian sculptor—was far better suited to her role as the silent screen's first "exotic" sex symbol.

Sometimes the stories would change from movie to movie or even from publication to publication. Keystone actress Louise Fazenda described her childhood self in one magazine interview as a prim, religious-minded girly girl, "raised in an atmosphere of roasts on Sunday, starched calico dresses that scratched, and missionary meetings." In another magazine, however, she was a ball-playing tomboy who "left the little girls and their dolls and learned to swipe the horse-hide sphere." Whether their fans saw through these constructed identities, or cared much even if they did, is perhaps an irrelevant question. What the fans were buying at the box office with their quarters—and, increasingly, with their dollars—was image, not substance. And by the mid-1910s, Hollywood had already become expert at providing just the kind of fantasies people were willing to pay for.

~

The elephants were becoming obstreperous. The lavishly costumed pachyderms—procured at great expense for just a few minutes of screen time—were supposed to be pushing the Persian attack towers toward the mighty walls of Babylon, but they were instead jostling each other rump to rump, trumpeting madly toward the azure Los Angeles sky. Their handlers couldn't control them, the towers weren't moving, and Griffith—stationed on a filming platform some hundred yards away—was wasting dozens of feet of film waiting for them to get it right.

Finally, assistant director Monte Blue, standing near Griffith, fired one of his revolvers to halt the action. After a few moments, George Siegmann, another assistant director, came running to the filming platform with a report. "It's the elephants, sir," he said. "They won't mix."

Griffith was unruffled. "Find out what's wrong and fix it," he said. "Yes, sir."

It took some time to sort out, but apparently the animal suppliers had sent over elephants of both sexes, and as Karl Brown put it, "the boy elephants saw no point in pushing these silly towers around when there were girl elephants to be courted." Eventually, however, the amorous males were culled from the herd and sent back to the suppliers, leaving the remaining females to push the towers unmolested. Problem solved.

But there were plenty of other problems to take its place. Ever since filming on the Babylon episode of *Intolerance* (a.k.a. *The Mother and the Law*, or F5) had begun in January 1916, Griffith had been facing technical and logistical challenges that dwarfed even those he'd encountered in *The Birth of a Nation.* Whereas in the earlier film he'd had hundreds of extras pretending to be thousands, for this one he really did have thousands. To control them all and coordinate the titanic siege scenes, he had taken on no fewer than fifteen directorial assistants. They were led by the much benighted Monte Blue, who, armed with an assortment of colored banners and two .45s, had to keep them and their scores of charges in sync. The siege scenes, involving an army of Persians assailing an army of Babylonians defending the city from atop its 150-foot walls, were epic in scope, not to mention downright dangerous. Joseph Henabery cites one day on which sixty-seven extras had to be treated in the first aid tent.

For one scene, a horse-drawn chariot had to thunder along at the top of one of those walls, a scene that frightened the life out of everyone involved—except, apparently, Griffith himself. "Let's try it again," he insisted after the first take. "A little faster, if you can."

Set builder Huck Wortman, who hadn't been informed about this scene, ran up to the director at this point, breathless with anxiety. "Mr. Griffith, you can't run horses up there. She ain't built for it! . . . She's liable to collapse on us if we aren't careful!"

But Griffith wouldn't consider changing his plans. "He was leaning casually against a parapet," Brown recalled, "his cheap straw hat shoved back on his head, his mouth slightly open in a grin of purest delight. The man was actually *enjoying* the situation."

Fortunately for those on the walls, after the scene was reshot—at a "runaway, scared-to-death pace" that set the mighty walls to swaying— the director was apparently satisfied. "That was very fine," he said. "Did you get it, Billy?"

According to Brown, Bitzer was so shaken he could barely answer. "Y-y-yes, sir," he said. "I-I s-sure did!"

Once the battle scenes were finished, the great exterior walls of Babylon were dismantled to make room for the biggest set of all—the enormous royal palace court, where the feast of Belshazzar would be filmed. While Wortman and his crews erected that canvas and papier-mâché extravaganza, Griffith took his army of extras south to San Pedro to the closest approximation of the Euphrates River that L.A. had to offer: the Dominguez Slough, a long freshwater pond created by the subsidence of coastal lands. Every day for several weeks, hundreds of Persian soldiers crowded onto the streetcars from downtown, their spears and longbows poking day laborers and shop clerks on their way to work. Nobody in the cast or crew could figure out how the scenes they were shooting now—of chariots racing along the slough—would fit with the battle scenes they'd just shot, let alone with the other far-flung stories they'd been filming for well over a year now. But at this point, they'd given up trying to understand. "Nobody seemed to care," Brown recalled. "After all, it was a Griffith picture, and it was big, very big indeed, and everybody was being paid, so that seemed to satisfy everyone."

Finally, the palace of Belshazzar and its enormous colonnaded courtyard was finished, and it was, according to Lillian Gish, "unlike anything that had ever been constructed for movies." For one thing, the set was about a mile deep and almost two hundred feet high, looming over Sunset Boulevard like a fanciful desert hallucination. And the architecture was opulent to the point of absurdity. As Gish described it, "The court, which was approached by numerous steps, was flanked by two colonnades supporting columns fifty-feet high, each column in turn supporting a great statue of the elephant god erect on its hind legs. Behind the court were towers and ramparts 200 feet high, their crests planted with flowering shrubs and trees to represent the famed hanging gardens. The set was studded with rows of rosettes, rich entablatures, huge torchères, finials, tiled fretwork, and bas-reliefs of winged deities, lions, and bulls."

To photograph this splendid set, Griffith devised one of the most remarkable camera sequences in the history of cinema. His first instinct had been to shoot it from a hot-air balloon suspended 150 feet in the air. But when he and Bitzer tried this, they immediately ran into problems. According to Bitzer: "The trouble was that the basket [under the balloon] rocked, the horizon kept changing, and I began to get seasick. I thought that if my camera did not fall out, I would." So Huck Wortman (allegedly working with an idea proposed by director Allan Dwan) got to work on an alternative. He constructed a 150-foot elevator on an enormous wheeled dolly. This was in turn mounted on train tracks, so the dolly could be moved smoothly forward and backward, with the elevator simultaneously going up or down. A camera on the elevator platform could thus create the visual equivalent of one of today's crane shots, swooping down from a great height while at the same time "zooming in" (years before the commercial manufacture of a true zoom lens) as the dolly was pushed closer to the set.

The sequence Griffith created with this cumbersome bit of machinery was a brilliant tour de force—"technically innovative, confident in manner, bold in its aspirations, sweeping in its effect." Starting a quarter-mile back to take in the full extent of Wortman's set, which was swarming with some five thousand parading extras, the camera moves into the scene at a stately pace, descending and passing through rows of dancers on the great staircase, homing in on the figure of Belshazzar emerging from the palace with his bride. The effect is revelatory, combining grandeur and intimacy in a single shot that instantly expanded the imagistic possibilities of the cinema. As for Griffith's opinion of the scene, he must have realized that he had just made history with the shot, but he didn't let on. His simple reaction was the by-now-familiar verdict: "That was very fine."

Such moments of gratification aside, Griffith was running into increasing difficulties as the Babylonian episode of his film kept growing larger and his once-inexhaustible supply of money began to dry up. Since he kept adding new scenes to exploit his grand Babylonian sets, filming extended through the spring and into the early summer of 1916. The movie had already taken longer to shoot than any other motion picture in history (filming had begun in October 1914), and Harry Aitken—not to mention the entire cast and crew—wondered whether Griffith had any intention of actually finishing the picture. Again, as with *Birth*, Aitken cut off the flow of money from New York; again, as with *Birth*, Griffith responded by selling shares behind Aitken's back to anyone who would invest. To complete the film, he accepted money from Lillian Gish, Mae Marsh, and some fifty others, combined with his own substantial share of the continuing *Birth* receipts. He also bought back a significant percentage of the film from some of its initial backers, who were panicking about Griffith's "criminal folly" as the bills piled up and the months of production passed. This represented an enormous individual investment on Griffith's part, but it was not, to his mind, reckless; he was already telling everyone who would listen that this film would surpass even *Birth* in earning power. But to those closest to him, the risks seemed obvious. "[It] was what he had been doing in one way or another as far back as I could remember," Karl Brown later admitted, "betting everything he had, including his life, on an all-or-nothing gamble."

~

In the summer of 1916, Griffith did wind down the shooting of his epic (notwithstanding some late-addition scenes filmed through that winter, after the New York premiere). Now he had to retreat into the cutting room to turn it all into a single film. It took months, but what he made was a multilayered spectacle unlike anything ever seen in world cinema. "Griffith shuffled all four versions of *The Mother and the Law* together like a pack of cards," Brown would later say, "and called the resulting four-ply story *Intolerance*." Instead of letting each of his four stories proceed in historical order, Griffith edited the film so that the action jumped from one to the other, switching repeatedly from the modern story to the siege of Babylon to the Passion of Christ to the Saint Bartholomew massacre, the jumps signaled only by intertitles or by a repeating short scene of Lillian Gish, as the Eternal Mother, rocking her baby in a cradle. "Each story shows how hatred and intolerance, through the ages, have battled against love and charity," he explained to his audience in an opening title. The end result was a kind of cinematic fugue, with themes developed in one narrative finding echoes and amplifications in the others, playing out across the centuries and continents.

When Griffith first emerged from the editing room, he had a film that ran approximately eight hours. His idea was to run it in theaters in two four-hour parts, shown on successive evenings. The exhibitors wouldn't hear of this and demanded that the film be cut down to a size that could be shown in a single evening. Perhaps feeling uneasy about the size of his own personal investment in the film, Griffith reluctantly complied. He ultimately cut out over half the original footage, but even so, the film as presented was still some twelve or thirteen reels long. (He kept cutting and adding scenes, even after the movie's various premieres.) This put its playing time at well over three hours. What an eight-hour

*Intolerance* would have looked like is one of the great unknowns in the history of cinema.

Even the three-hour *Intolerance*, however, proved controversial. When Griffith screened a prerelease cut for scenario writer Anita Loos, she was appalled by the incessant jumping from story to story, which happens some fifty times in the final version. When the lights finally came up in the projection room, Loos was convinced that Griffith had lost his mind. "I sat a moment in stony silence, which I could only ex-plain to the Great Man by telling him that I had been moved beyond words," she recalled. "Actually, he was so absorbed in his film I doubt he realized my bewilderment."

Others shared her plunging sense of perplexity. After assistant di-rector Joseph Henabery saw the film at its Riverside sneak preview in early August, he likewise could barely speak. "I was utterly confused by the picture," he said. "I was so discouraged and disappointed. . . . Sure, it had wonderful scenes in it, wonderful settings and many wonderful ideas. But to me it was a very disconnected story." According to Hena-bery, Griffith had cut some scenes so short that they were virtually un-intelligible. And like Loos, he found the transitions from story to story disorienting. "He had switched from period to period and he had it all chopped up. He just had too much material."

After the Riverside previews on August 4 and 5 (where, for secrecy's sake, it was billed as *The Downfall of All Nations, or Hatred the Oppres-sor*, directed by an unknown Italian named "Dante Guilio"), Griffith did make some changes—particularly in the titling—before taking it east for the New York premiere. Even then he was still making last-minute changes, wiring back to Hollywood for Henabery to shoot supplemen-tary footage of naked harem women, presumably to spice up the Baby-lonian sections. When the official premiere occurred on September 5, 1916—at the Liberty Theatre on Broadway, where *The Birth of a Nation* had opened—the paste on the latest re-edit of the film could barely have been dry. But Griffith had now simply run out of time. Another elabo-rate rollout had been planned at the Liberty, complete with forty-piece orchestra and chorus performing a Joseph Breul score; there were also costumed theater usherettes and an expensively illustrated program fea-turing production stills and an essay by Griffith on the meaning of the piece. The theater was decked out in the manner of an Assyrian temple, with incense-burners and ornate oriental carpets, and had been fitted with state-of-the-art sound effects machinery and a specially designed lighting system to wash the screen in various colors during the show. According to *Moving Picture World*, no fewer than 135 people were required to put on this lavish production, including seven men responsible just for firing off explosives during the battle scenes. At great expense, Griffith and Aitken were clearly trying to duplicate the excitement of the *Birth* opening just eighteen months earlier.

For a time, it looked as if it might work, and that *Intolerance* would repeat *Birth*'s phenomenal success. The first-night audience cheered at the film's conclusion and gave it a standing ovation. And the reviews, at least some of them, were stellar. *Film Daily* was ecstatic: "Stupendous, tremendous, revolutionary, intense, thrilling, and then you can throw away the old typewriter and give up with the dictionary, because you can't find adjectives enough. Mr. Griffith has put on the screen what is, without question, the most stirring human expression that has ever been presented to the world." The *Los Angeles Times* raved, the *New York Journal* marveled at the achievement, and the *San Francisco Chronicle* compared the film to a Beethoven symphony. The *New York Herald* claimed that it dwarfed even Griffith's previous film: "*The Birth of a Nation* is to *Intolerance* what the old one-reel motion picture is to the present-day feature."

But there were plenty of dissenters as well. The *New York Times* review was deeply mixed. Its reviewer called Griffith "a real wizard of lens and screen," and praised "the stupendous mass of [the film's] panoramas, the grouping and handling of its great masses of players." But the *Times* also faulted the film for its "utter incoherence, the questionable taste of some of the scenes, and the cheap banalities into which it sometimes lapses." Other reviews were downright scathing. According to *The New Republic*, *Intolerance* evinced "no human emotion except visual amazement"; the magazine's critic felt that the film's eagerness to "gorge the senses" was comparable to that of the Barnum and Bailey circus.

Such reactions notwithstanding, audiences throughout the country were at first enthusiastic. The early road shows were nearly all triumphs, attracting *Birth*-like crowds wherever the film opened; for the first four months of its release, *Intolerance* actually outgrossed the earlier block-buster, at least at the Liberty Theatre, and the production's many investors were jubilant.

But then, as Lillian Gish put it, "something went wrong." Attendance dwindled at showings nationwide. A limited engagement in April in Fort Dodge, Iowa, attracted "only fair patronage"; the film closed in Denver after only an eight-day run. To recoup its tremendous costs, *Intolerance* would have had to play to packed houses for many months—as *Birth* had—but the film seemingly had no word-of-mouth and thus no staying power. And with the nation gearing up for entry into the Great War in the spring of 1917, the film's pacifist message struck a discordant note with many moviegoers.

Hollywood legend has exaggerated the extent to which *Intolerance* was a critical and commercial flop. Many critics still regard it as the greatest single motion picture ever made, sound or silent, and it continued to play in second-run neighborhood houses and in return engagements in some larger American cities well into 1918. *Intolerance* was also a huge success in Europe, where it influenced filmmakers, particularly in Russia, for many years to come. But whether it was too "difficult" for American audiences to watch (*Photoplay*'s opinion), too mangled by the excessive cuts forced upon Griffith by his exhibitors (Lillian Gish's opinion), or simply (as Karl Brown thought) a movie with the wrong message at the wrong time, preaching pacifism to a newly bellicose world, the film was a financial failure. Combined with its mixed critical reception, this constituted a major blow to both the ego and the pocketbook of its creator. According to Gish, Griffith would tell stories of wandering through dark theaters where *Intolerance* was playing, "barking his shins on empty seats."

"I don't know where to go or where to turn since my great failure," he told her. "I am going to do a lot of thinking."

As Karl Brown later observed about this period after the release of *Intolerance*: "The picture business was booming. Everybody was making money except Griffith, who was losing it hand over fist." This was almost certainly an exaggeration; according to Griffith biographer Richard Schickel, the losses incurred by the director with this film (which had cost $385,000 to make, not, as rumor had it, over $2 million) were more an "inconvenience" than a ruinous disaster. But many in the film community shared Brown's assessment of the failure's effect on the Great Man: "He had been knocked flat to the canvas," Brown wrote, "and the referee was counting."

It took Griffith the better part of a year to get up from that canvas, distracted as he was by the imminent collapse of Harry Aitken's Triangle Film Corporation (despite the success of *Civilization*, the *Intolerance*-like epic created by Griffith's rival Thomas Ince). Eventually Paramount's Adolph Zukor would swoop in and pick off most of Triangle's distressed assets, and when he did, one of those assets was David Wark Griffith. The director announced the new contract in March 1917, on the day he was boarding a ship bound for England to oversee the London opening of *Intolerance*. While there, he would also start a new film. Commissioned by the British government, the film, to be called *Hearts of the World*, would be another extravagant production, as important in its way as either *Intolerance* or *The Birth of a Nation*. For Griffith, despite the beating he'd just taken, was still very much a major player in the industry he'd helped to found, and his grand visions couldn't be contained for long. Under Zukor's watchful eye, he might have to temper his spending, but not—he hoped—his ambition.

There were signs, however, that Griffith's ideas about where the art of the motion picture was headed might soon face challenges. The war that America was about to enter would end up altering much more than geopolitical boundaries. Sensibilities and attitudes would undergo upheavals as well, as the postwar mood turned against all forms of sentimentality and didacticism. High-toned morality plays like Griffith's—with their Victorian notions about romance and honor—might seem out of step with the taste of audiences looking for a worldlier, more sophisticated take on issues like marriage, morality, and sex. Other directors would respond to this development more readily—in particular Cecil B. DeMille (always much better at discerning the vagaries of popular taste), with agile, more sexually daring films like *The Cheat*, *Male and Female*, and *Old Wives for New*. The temper of the country was changing, and Hollywood was going to have to change with it. It remained to be seen how well Griffith—the Father of Hollywood—could make that transition himself.

# CHAPTER NINE
# One Million Souls to Save

*Aimee Semple McPherson*

In the warm, purpling twilight of December 21, 1918, an overstuffed, road-worn Oldsmobile sedan—its muddy flanks emblazoned with the messages "JESUS IS COMING—GET READY" and "WHERE WILL YOU SPEND ETERNITY?"—drove slowly down Washington Boulevard in Los Angeles. Behind the wheel was a vibrant twenty-eight-year-old evangelist by the name of Aimee Semple McPherson, though virtually everyone she knew preferred to call her Sister. Traveling with her middle-aged mother, her two young children, and a female assistant named Mabel Bingham, Sister had just completed an arduous two-month journey from New York, driving virtually the entire way herself, and she and her passengers were understandably exhausted. But there would be little rest for Sister here, for she had come to Los Angeles with a purpose: to save the city's soul. "Here in the City of Angels," she would later say, "where the power of the Spirit had so wonderfully fallen [in] years previous, we learned that diverse doctrinal differences had gotten the eyes of many off the Lord, and that there was a dearth in the land." Sister was here to remedy that dearth, to put all of those wandering eyes firmly back on the Lord. And if she had actually arrived in town with somewhat more than the "ten dollars and a tambourine" that she later claimed as her only possessions . . . well, that was just her habit of speaking in metaphors—or, rather, in parables. Like so many people in her newly adopted city, Sister McPherson understood that an appealing story can accomplish so much more than the plain, unvarnished facts.

As the Oldsmobile made its way down the palm-lined boulevard, Sister and her entourage were feeling a touch of disappointment. Los Angeles—the city they had been yearning for during the long, hard weeks of their cross-country odyssey—didn't look so different from the other cities they had passed through in their travels. "The streets were not paved with gold," Sister later wrote, "neither were the boulevards lined with angels." But there was little doubt in her mind that she had been right to heed God's call to come west. "I had a feeling that here I would meet my destiny. Here was journey's end."

Sister stopped the car at the address they were looking for: a residence separated from the street by the widest gate she had ever seen. This was the home of Brother and Sister Blake, subscribers to McPherson's monthly evangelical magazine, *Bridal Call*. The Blakes had kindly offered to host Sister and her family for the duration of a revival campaign that she hoped would rekindle the Pentecostal fire in Los Angeles, which had waned in the decade since the glory days of the Azusa Street Revival. McPherson's campaign was scheduled to begin the next day, leaving her no time to recover from the exhausting road trip. But Sister, filled with the urgency of her message about the baptism of the Holy Spirit, never seemed to need much rest. God always seemed to provide the energy she needed.

She sounded the horn of the Oldsmobile, and after a few moments, someone came out of the house to let them in. "As the great gate swung open," she later recalled, ". . . a smiling face greeted us enthusiastically, [and] God spoke to my heart, 'I will open the heart of California to you as wide as this gate.' And bless the Lord, he did!"

~

The long journey that had brought Aimee Semple McPherson to Los Angeles had begun in a remote farmhouse in rural Ontario, not far from the town of Ingersoll, where she was born on October 9, 1890. As she would later tell the story, she had come into this life in response to a prayer: that of her nineteen-year-old mother, Mildred (Minnie) Kennedy. Young Minnie had been forced to give up an active life of service with the Salvation Army for a practical, rather joyless marriage to a farmer almost thirty-five years her senior. She had asked God to give her a daughter who could preach the Gospel in her stead. The answer she received—announced by a ray of sunlight that allegedly broke through a rift in dark clouds as she prayed—was baby Aimee.

Minnie wasted no time in keeping her end of the bargain. When Aimee was just three weeks old, Minnie decided to take the infant to a Salvation Army Jubilee (a worship service) at the local barracks some five miles away—much to the dismay of the child's Aunt Maria. "You'll kill that baby!" the older woman said. "Anyone who does not know how to take better care of a baby than that shouldn't have one!" But Minnie wouldn't be dissuaded. She bundled Aimee up against the cold, unhitched their horse Flossie, and rode the five miles of country road into town. Three weeks later, she made the trip again, this time to formally dedicate the child to Christian service in the "Salvation War." Aimee's father, James—himself a rather lackadaisical Methodist—didn't seem to object, though many others did. The Salvation Army, with its military-style organization and emphatic devotion to relieving misery through "soup and salvation," was not entirely respectable to the sober Protestant establishment of rural Ontario. But baby Aimee seemed to thrive in this atmosphere of uniforms, marches, and pageantry in the name of religion. It was a taste she'd retain for the rest of her life.

Under the careful tutelage of her mother, Aimee became something of an ecclesiastical child prodigy. By the age of five, she could recite virtually any Bible story on request. Other parts of her education were admittedly wanting; when she started school at the local kindergarten, she allegedly knew none of the letters of the alphabet. But thanks to her quick and lively intelligence and good-natured eagerness to please, she soon made up the deficit and became an exemplary student.

Her religious horizons broadened as she grew older. In addition to her Salvation Army work with her mother, she began attending a nearby Methodist church and enrolled in a Sunday school in Ingersoll. Here she became so adept at giving Bible readings that she was soon invited to speak at local churches of many different denominations—Methodist, Presbyterian, and Baptist. Before she had reached her teens, she won a gold medal in a public-speaking contest sponsored by the Women's Christian Temperance Union.

By the time she enrolled in high school at the Ingersoll Collegiate Institute, however, Aimee had also developed some decidedly secular tastes. She had always been attracted to the more festive elements of church life—"the oyster suppers, the strawberry festivals, the Christmas trees, and always the concerts to follow"—and now her success as a public speaker led her to consider a career in the theater. She also began reading novels, attending movies, and going to local dances—all to her mother's stern disapproval. Her worst transgressions arose after she began to learn about Charles Darwin in her high school science classes. As she later admitted, Darwin's theories "had a remarkable effect upon me." She began to doubt the accuracy of the scripture she had been accepting as truth for her entire life. She even began questioning the existence of God. She peppered her mother and father, and even a local preacher, with challenges to their basic religious beliefs. After she expressed her doubts to one of her mother's Salvation Army associates, the appalled Minnie wondered aloud, through bitter tears, how she had failed as a mother.

This incident was enough to give Aimee pause. Headstrong as she was, she still valued her mother's approval. She resolved to at least keep an open mind and heart. One afternoon in December 1907, she and her father were driving home down Main Street in Ingersoll when she saw a sign in a window announcing a Pentecostal mission with meetings every night and all day Sunday. Curious about the meetings—she had heard that "they jump and dance and fall under the power, and do such strange things"—she asked her father whether they could go to one. He agreed, and they arranged to go together the very next night. It was an offhand decision that proved to be one of the most important of Aimee's life.

~

If the rituals of the Salvation Army seemed slightly indecorous to the rock-ribbed conservative Christians of Ingersoll, the goings-on at the town's Pentecostal mission were regarded as downright outlandish. Modern Pentecostalism was a renewal movement that emerged in the United States in the early years of the twentieth century, and its practices were nothing if not flamboyant. Partly a response to a belief that mainstream Protestantism was becoming a compartmentalized, "Sunday-only" phenomenon, Pentecostalism sought a more direct, personal experience of God. This was achieved through what it called "baptism with the Holy Spirit," something that had occurred to the Apostles on the fiftieth day after the resurrection of Christ (thus the name Pentecost, the Greek word for "fiftieth"). Such baptism was a profound religious event—an experience so powerful that recipients were invariably knocked to the ground, where they would be overcome by violent convulsions and begin speaking in tongues. Filled with a conviction that Jesus was "the same yesterday, today, and forever," Pentecostals felt that all gifts of the Holy Spirit as recorded in the New Testament should be central elements of the contemporary church. Thus acts like prophecy, miracle working, and faith healing did not belong only to the distant past; these powers could be manifested in modern times as well. Going hand in hand with these beliefs was a sense of urgency that the end times would soon be upon the earth and that the second coming of Christ could happen at any time. Preparation for this imminent event was a pressing imperative, a twenty-four-hours-a-day, seven-days-a-week project that should take precedence over all other activities in life.

The birth of modern Pentecostalism is generally traced to Topeka, Kansas, in early 1901, when an independent evangelist named Charles Parnham began preaching these doctrines and attracted a small but devoted cadre of followers. The movement spread rapidly after the influential Azusa Street Revival in Los Angeles, initiated in 1906 by Parnham's student, William J. Seymour. Many leaders of the Azusa Street meetings (often called "the cradle of American Pentecostalism") eventually dispersed and organized their own missions throughout the United States and Canada. The Pentecostal Mission in Ingersoll was one of these, associated with the teachings of William Durham, a Chicago-based pastor who had experienced his own spirit-baptism at Azusa Street in March 1907. When Aimee and her father attended the Ingersoll meeting in December of that year, the evangelist in charge was one of Durham's associates: Robert Semple, a Scots-Irishman from Belfast who had been charged with extending the Pentecostal message to southeastern Ontario.

Seventeen-year-old Aimee Kennedy, in her current mood of skepticism and pleasure seeking, would not have seemed the most receptive audience for this message. And in fact her first reactions were dismissive. No one at that first meeting was from the higher echelons of Ingersoll society, and although Aimee was only a farmer's daughter, she "felt just a little bit above the status of those round about me." When a man she knew to be a local milkman was struck by the spirit and fell to the floor, praising the Lord all the while, she couldn't disguise her mirth: "I giggled foolishly," she later recalled, "not understanding it and thinking it very laughable."

But then Robert Semple rose to speak, and Aimee's attitude changed. "I sobered suddenly," she wrote. "He stood some six feet and two inches in stature, had a shock of chestnut-brown curly hair, one lock of which he was continually brushing back from his blue Irish eyes." As soon as he began to preach, she was captivated. "Cold shivers ran up and down my back. I had never heard such a sermon." And when he started speaking of the baptism of the Holy Spirit, something extraordinary happened: "Suddenly, in the midst of his sermon, the evangelist closed his eyes and with radiant face began to speak in a language that was not his own. To me, this Spirit-prompted utterance was like the voice of God thundering into my soul . . . , 'You are a poor, lost, miserable, hell-deserving sinner!'"

This sermon would prove to be a road-to-Damascus experience for Aimee, changing her life forever. Never again would she doubt God's existence or shirk what she knew He required of her. She quit the Christmas play she was to appear in and proceeded to burn her dance slippers, her ragtime sheet music, and her novels. She told Robert Semple of her conversion and began coming to the mission every day, even skipping school in her determination to achieve her own spirit-baptism. Her grades suffered, and her mother heard complaints, not only from the high school principal but from Minnie's Salvation Army associates, who worried that Aimee was throwing in her lot with "rank fanatics." Minnie forbade the girl from skipping school to attend the mission.

Shortly thereafter, Ontario was hit with a powerful blizzard that severed telephone and power lines and closed down roads and the railroad for several days, stranding Aimee in Ingersoll without her parents. She used the time to "tarry for the baptism," praying at the home of one of her Pentecostal "sisters" to bring on the critical personal experience of being filled with the Holy Spirit. Finally, after several days of almost continuous prayer, her striving was rewarded. As she told it: "And then the glory fell. My tightly closed eyes envisioned the Man of Galilee, bleeding, dying, thorn-crowned on Golgotha's Tree. Tears streamed down my face. . . . 'Glory, glory to Jesus!' I repeated over and over."

Falling into convulsions, she began to speak in tongues—the inevitable sign that the baptism had occurred.

Aimee Kennedy had thus been transformed in her faith, and her emotional life was soon to be transformed as well. She had been corresponding with Robert Semple ever since the evangelist left Ingersoll to preach at another mission in Stratford. Now he returned, joyful at the news of Aimee's spirit-baptism. One evening, as they were reading the Bible together, he told her of his aspirations to travel to China to bring the message to the "mighty millions offering a continual challenge to Christianity." Then he shocked her by asking her to marry him and be his helpmeet in this mission. He insisted that they pray together before she gave her answer, but the conclusion was foregone: "I rose and said yes to God and yes to Robert."

They married on August 12, 1908, in an outdoor ceremony presided over by a Salvation Army lieutenant colonel (probably as a sop to the bride's mother). After a brief honeymoon in Toronto, they settled in Stratford, where Robert worked in a boiler factory by day and preached at the mission by night. But the life of a Pentecostal preacher was necessarily nomadic. After a short time in Stratford, they moved to London, Ontario, and then on to Chicago to work and study with William Durham at various missions and camps in the region. During this time Aimee developed a reputation as a tongues-speaker and interpreter, and was herself "ordained" (a procedure that, since Pentecostalism still lacked a centralized authority structure, meant only that she was recognized as someone who had received a divine calling). This status conferred upon her independent credibility as an evangelist, but she still regarded herself as very much her husband's pupil. Robert, she later wrote, "was my theological seminary, my spiritual mentor, and my tender, patient, unfailing lover."

By early 1910, Robert was ready to undertake his long-anticipated mission to China. Unlike missionaries from more established Protestant denominations, the Semples would be making the trip with no guarantees in place: no salary, no housing, no local support network—nothing but a personal conviction that the Lord would provide. Aimee tried to feel confident. After a tearful farewell to Minnie and James Kennedy, the couple set sail in February from St. John, New Brunswick, bound for Hong Kong.

Their sojourn in the East, however, would prove to be disastrous. For a few weeks Robert succeeded in winning Asian souls for Jesus ("Bringing in Chinese," as he called it, singing the phrase to the tune of "Bringing in the Sheaves"), but living conditions were harsh and unsanitary. Aimee, who had learned on the voyage that she was pregnant, came down with malaria shortly after their arrival. Then Robert contracted dysentery, complicated by his own case of malaria. He grew steadily worse until, as Aimee lay sick in another wing of the hospital, he died at one a.m. on August 19—just six weeks after their arrival in Hong Kong—at the age of twenty-nine. One month later, Aimee, age nineteen, gave birth to their daughter. She named her Roberta, after the child's dead father.

"[Then] came hours of terror when I considered my penniless, husbandless future amid the dark, unknown labyrinths of China," she later wrote of this time. The newborn child was a comfort to her, but also a responsibility of frightening proportions. For a time, she considered remaining in China to continue Robert's work (or so she claimed), but when the money for a return ticket arrived from her mother, she made the obvious choice. "My first duty was to take my child to a place of healthful safety," she wrote. "Robert's work was done. Mine was but begun."

On her return, Aimee chose not to go home to Ontario but instead traveled to New York to join her mother. Minnie Kennedy, feeling her own call to religious service, had sometime before decided to leave (at least temporarily) the dreariness of life on the farm with James to take up Salvation Army work in Manhattan. Aimee and the baby moved into Minnie's apartment on 14th Street between Sixth and Seventh Avenues—one block from the Biograph studio building, where D. W. Griffith was just then preparing to take his troupe west to California for their second winter of making movies in Los Angeles. Aimee worked at the Salvation Army Rescue Mission for several weeks while she decided what to do with the rest of her life. Minnie encouraged her to continue this work permanently, but Aimee felt a different calling. "I have a persistent feeling that my only happiness lies in the carrying on of my husband's work of soul-saving campaigns," she told her mother one day.

"But how?"

"I don't know," she replied in frustration.

For the next four years, Aimee floundered. Still grieving for Robert and worrying over Roberta, who proved to be a sickly child, she wandered from her mother's apartment in New York to her father's farm in Ontario to her old haunts in the Pentecostal community of Chicago. Sometime in 1911, when she was back in New York, she met a man named Harold McPherson, a cashier at a fashionable midtown restaurant, who spotted Aimee one day as she was collecting donations for the Salvation Army. He asked to escort her home, and the two soon began dating. McPherson was hardly a Robert Semple; though religious in his way, he was conventional and worldly, and Minnie Kennedy disapproved of him as a bad influence on her widowed daughter. But Aimee understood by now that she and her frail child needed stability and protection in their lives. McPherson proposed to her while on a Fifth Avenue stroll late in 1911, and she (after several weeks of consideration) accepted, but with one major stipulation: "that if at any time in my life [the Lord] should call me back into active ministry, no matter where or when, I must obey God first of all."

Aimee would later depict her marriage to Harold McPherson as a straying from the path of righteousness, a "backsliding" undertaken mainly for the sake of her daughter's health. McPherson was a kind enough man, and he provided her a congenial home with him and his mother in Providence, Rhode Island. Aimee was miserable nonetheless. As she later wrote, "Earthly things—home—comfort. Oh, what did these matter? I was out of His dear will, and my soul refused to be comforted." She became ill and depressed, and not even the birth of another child—a boy named Rolf—could bring her out of her funk. In the winter of 1912, she had to be hospitalized for multiple surgeries (including a hysterectomy) and allegedly nearly died in the recovery room. To Aimee, it seemed as if God were forsaking her, just as she had forsaken Him by turning away from evangelism to marry McPherson.

Finally, as she lay in the hospital, "hover[ing] between life and death," God spoke to her—in a voice so loud, she said, that it startled her: "NOW—WILL—YOU—GO?"

It was the divine summons she had been resisting for so long, to the detriment of her physical and mental health. Now she was ready to answer the call. "With my little remaining strength," she wrote, "I managed to gasp: 'Yes—Lord—I'll—go.'"

In a version of this story Aimee would later tell, her pain was instantly gone when she uttered this promise, and she was up and around within days. In actuality her recovery took weeks. But whatever the delay, she would be true to her word to God. When Harold and his mother objected to her new determination to become a traveling evangelist, she took matters into her own hands. One night in June 1915, when McPherson was out of the house, she quietly bundled up the children, took a taxi to the train station, and bought a ticket for Ontario. Her mother (who had returned to the family farm sometime earlier) had agreed to care for the children while Aimee pursued her evangelism and had even sent money for her train ticket. It was a pattern that would be repeated throughout the two women's lives—Aimee pursuing her calling to preach the Gospel, Minnie providing the logistical and financial support to make it happen.

Harold McPherson, of course, was not pleased to have his family hijacked away in the dead of night. Over the next weeks, he peppered his wayward spouse with letters and telegrams demanding that she come back to Providence to "wash the dishes," "take care of the house," and "act like other women." But Aimee was not like other women. Leaving the children with her parents, she traveled to nearby Kitchener, Ontario, to attend a Pentecostal camp meeting at the beginning of July. From there she accepted invitations to preach elsewhere in the region, including London and Mount Forest. It was in the latter, a farming town of some four thousand people, that Aimee truly came into her own as an evangelist. Finding that she was attracting only a small congregation to her nightly meetings, she decided to try an old Salvation Army trick. She grabbed a chair from the meetinghouse on the town's main road, carried it outside, and set it down in the street. To hear her tell the story: "I mounted the tiny rostrum, lifted my hands high to heaven, closed my eyes, and just stood there lifting my heart to God without speaking a single word aloud. Minutes passed. Nothing happened, but I never moved, never spoke, never lowered my arms. Then a wave of interest and excitement stirred the populace."

People started to gather around her motionless form, curious about this woman apparently pretending to be a statue. When she had quite a crowd around her, she suddenly opened her eyes. "People!" she cried. "Follow me quick!" She jumped off the chair, picked it up, and ran down the street and into the mission. The crowd naturally followed her, and when they were all inside, she told the doorkeeper, "Lock that door! And keep it locked till I get through!"

She preached to that throng for forty minutes that night. Enticed by what they heard, they returned the next night and for many nights to come. And the crowds kept getting larger. As one of her biographers wrote of the incident: "From that August day in 1915 until her death nearly thirty years later, she never again had to work at getting a crowd."

For Aimee, it turned out, was a natural as an evangelist—warm, charismatic, inspiring, endlessly inventive, and, above all, effective. From that day forward, she made scores of converts wherever she preached. Dozens at her meetings were smitten with the baptism of the Holy Spirit, falling to the ground one by one around any crowded hall or auditorium she addressed. Convulsions, tongue-speaking, shouts of Hallelujah! and Praise the Lord! erupted everywhere. She also conducted healing sessions, praying with the sick until, in many cases, they rose and threw aside their crutches and canes, claiming to be cured. Even those who were not spirit-struck or healed by faith were mesmerized by the spectacle. They came back to see her again and again, bringing friends and family with them. Even Harold McPherson—when he finally caught up with his wife to bring her back home—was converted by her strange power. On the night of his arrival in Canada, he stood with his suitcase at the rear of one of her meetings, openmouthed and awestruck. Seeing her preach, he realized immediately that Aimee would not be coming back with him; he would be going with her. That very first night, under her guidance, he was struck with the baptism of the Holy Spirit. He spoke in tongues and resolved on the spot to join her mission to glorify God.

That all of this was being accomplished by a female evangelist—and a young, attractive one at that—only added to the allure. As Aimee knew better than anyone, a woman preacher was a novelty in 1915—"a dress in the pulpit," as she wrote, "[was] something new"—and she faced criticism from conservative clergymen almost from the start. Rather than letting this discourage her, she viewed her gender as an advantage, bringing in the curious who had never seen a female preacher. "If the Lord chose a woman to attract to Himself those who otherwise might not have come," she would say, "who shall question the wisdom of the Lord?"

For the next three years, until the late summer of 1918, Aimee (or Sister, as she now was called by her adoring followers) preached at Pentecostal camps, revivals, and missions wherever she could. For the first year she confined her wanderings to southern Canada, then expanded around New England, using the McPherson home in Providence as a base. But ultimately she decided to range farther afield in her hunt for souls to gather for Jesus. Harold quit his job, the couple sold or stored their furniture and other belongings, and they set out in a new Packard "Gospel Car," staging tent revivals up and down the eastern seaboard. They spent summers up north, at weeks-long events in places like Framingham, Massachusetts, Cape Cod, Philadelphia, and Corona, Queens. But when the weather turned colder, they'd pack up the tent and head south. Minnie would care for the somewhat sickly Roberta at home in Ontario while Aimee and Harold traveled with baby Rolf. They would preach by day, either under the tent or in local churches or halls, and camp by night, turning the reversible front seats of the Gospel Car to provide convenient sleeping quarters by the side of the road. And although the McPhersons were often met by skimpy audiences and skeptical clergy, it wouldn't be long before word would spread and Aimee would start packing in the crowds, converting even the most intransigent doubters.

At one typical meeting, a trustee of the local Baptist church looked on from a rear seat as many of his fellow parishioners succumbed to the influence of the Holy Spirit. "I don't believe that all of this noise and shouting and falling under the power is necessary," he complained when Sister asked him to join her at the altar. "I believe in the Holy Spirit, but not in this shouting and talking in tongues."

Sister coaxed him until he reluctantly came forward to pray with her. It took only a few minutes to produce results. Other believers were "going down one by one," as if knocked over by "heavenly gales that were sweeping from heaven." The trustee seemed unmoved—until, as Sister later recalled, "we heard a great shout, and something struck the floor with a thump.

"Making my way as quickly as possible to the place where this great roaring was coming from, I found its source of origin was none other than the trustee. . . . He shook from head to foot; his heels beat a tattoo upon the floor; he fairly bellowed and roared forth in other tongues as the Spirit gave him utterance, his face filled with joy and glory."

Similar scenes played out wherever she preached—North or South, city or countryside, in an established church or outdoors in a makeshift tent camp. Skeptics were won over, the lame and the sick were healed, and souls by the score were won for Jesus. Meanwhile her fame as an evangelist was blossoming up and down the coast. At first, her reputation spread mainly by word of mouth and personal connections. A snowbird who saw her in West Palm Beach might enlist her to preach the next summer at a hometown church or mission in Connecticut or Maryland, singing her praises to the congregation for months before her arrival. But in June 1917, thanks to the kindness of a small publisher in Savannah, Aimee started publishing *Bridal Call*, a monthly magazine that would "bind her scattered supporters together and keep them informed of the progress of her (God's) work." Two thousand copies of the first edition were printed, but soon she was finding new subscribers everywhere, all of them eager to read articles on salvation, reports on her far-flung revivals, and testimonials of those she had healed or converted. "So plainly the Lord spoke," she would later recall, "giving me articles to write in such bursts of revelation that the tears streamed down my face, while my fingers flew over the typewriter keys." And so her following kept growing.

One of the few souls she lost during these years, in fact, was that of her own husband. Perhaps tiring of his role as second fiddle to his far more charismatic spouse, Harold McPherson began abandoning the crusade for extended periods in the late 1910s. At first, he tried launching his own career as a traveling evangelist. But eventually he gave up trying to save souls and went back to work at a regular secular job. In 1921 he and Aimee would be quietly divorced, and he gradually faded from the life of his wife and the children. In later years, Sister McPherson would rarely even mention the second man who had given her his name.

Aimee soldiered on. Traveling with baby Rolf as her only companion, living day to day on the voluntary donations of those who came to hear her preach, was anything but easy. Often she had to skip meals while on the road; torrential rains leaking through the tent seams would soak her night's bedding and leave her cot ankle deep in muddy water; on one awful occasion in Florida, she had to battle against a raging hurricane all night long, pounding in the tent pegs with a sledgehammer to keep her shelter from blowing away. Finally, on the brink of physical and mental collapse, she telegraphed her mother for help. James Kennedy had died sometime earlier, so Minnie was free to abandon the Ontario farm and race down to Florida with young Roberta in tow. Together again, the four became a kind of three-generation evangelical road show. Minnie took care of the children and acted as her daughter's business manager while Aimee drove the Gospel Car, wrote the monthly magazine, and mesmerized the crowds.

In the autumn of 1918, during a revival in New Rochelle, New York, Aimee fell ill with the Spanish influenza that was sweeping the entire nation in that last year of the Great War in Europe. Her case was not too serious, and despite violent chills and fever, she managed to preach all but one of the services scheduled for the city. But one night when she returned to the dingy little apartment where the family was staying, she found that eight-year-old Roberta had contracted a far more serious case of the disease and was lying near death. Terrified, Aimee sat up all night, praying over the unconscious child until—in a vision as bright and vivid as any she had ever experienced in life—she saw God himself standing above her in the darkened room. According to Aimee, He spoke directly to her heart in a clear, soul-thrilling voice: "Fear not. Your little one shall live and not die. Moreover, I will give you a home in California where your children shall go to school. Yea, the sparrow hath found an house and the swallow a nest for herself where she may lay her young."

It was an opportune directive to come at this time. For months the children, weary of the rigors of travel, had been clamoring for a house of their own. Roberta yearned for a canary, Rolf for a yard full of rose-bushes to play in. Now the Lord was promising to provide exactly what they were asking for, in a climate conducive to everyone's health. And it would be in Los Angeles, the city of clean slates and new beginnings. What could be better? Once Roberta had recovered from the flu—miraculously, of course—they prepared to follow the Lord's instructions. They sold the old Packard, bought a roomier and more roadworthy Oldsmobile, and made arrangements to drive cross-country to their new home-to-be in Los Angeles.

At nine a.m. on October 24, 1918, the Kennedy/McPherson family, accompanied by secretary Mabel Bingham, set out in the packed Oldsmobile from a house on 115th Street in Manhattan, where they had been staying with a Pentecostal associate. They crossed the river on a ferry and proceeded west via the Lincoln Highway toward Philadelphia. For the next two months, they would drive all day, handing out religious tracts and copies of *Bridal Call* to all who would take them. Nights they would spend in the homes of Pentecostal brothers and sisters or just camping by the side of the road. Sister had made arrangements ahead of time to preach a few revivals along the way, in cities like Indianapolis, Tulsa, and Oklahoma City. Many of these places had banned public gatherings because of the ongoing flu epidemic, but the restrictions were miraculously lifted just in time to allow Aimee to speak. And McPherson also engineered countless spontaneous revival meetings. In Claysville, Pennsylvania, for instance, Sister preached to an impromptu gathering of coal miners, and she may even have converted a few Native Americans at Indian reservations en route.

Of course, given the state of western roads in 1918, the travelers experienced their share of nightmares. More than once they had to be pulled from the mud by some local farmer's team of mules; they also had flat tires and several bouts of engine trouble. On one occasion, they drove a precarious mountainside road where they surely would have tumbled over a cliff had it not been for "angels [that] seemed to hold the car to the road even though it was wet and slippery." Somehow they made it through without serious incident.

On that December Saturday when they finally rode through the gates of Brother and Sister Blake's house in beautiful Los Angeles, they knew they had made the right choice in coming all of that way. As God had told her, this was obviously their place to settle. And at her first revival meeting that Sunday, Sister chose an appropriate text to preach on— Joshua 6:16, which reads: "Shout, for the Lord hath given you the city!"

~

For a charismatic evangelist like Sister McPherson, Los Angeles in the late 1910s offered particularly fertile ground. Despite the decade's influx of godless movie people and their trailing entourage of wannabes and hangers-on, the city had remained a magnet for aging health-seekers, middle-class snowbirds, and retirees from the Midwest. These were up-rooted people with a lot of time on their hands, and their search for a sense of community and purpose had already turned the city, in writer John Steven McGroarty's words, into "the most celebrated of all incubators of new creeds, codes of ethics, and philosophies," not to mention "a breeding place and a rendezvous of freak religions." The lost souls for whom Theosophy was too outré and social utopianism too woolly-headed and political were a natural audience for Sister McPherson's message. She knew this better than anyone. "Certainly Los Angeles was ripe for revival," she wrote in one of her memoirs of this period. "This great metropolis appeared to afford perhaps the greatest opportunity for God of any city in America. Thousands of tourists were coming from every state in the Union, many coming to reside. . . . Their other needs had been provided for in the city—homes, amusements, highways, and parks. But, alas, there were few adequately large buildings where they might hear the Word of God in its blessed Pentecostal fullness." The Azusa Street Revival had been a good start, but somehow its momentum had tapered off in the last decade, leaving that "dearth in the land." Now that Sister was on the scene, the city could repair its faith deficit. In a sense, William Mulholland and D. W. Griffith had already seen to the city's physical, economic, and artistic requirements; now Aimee Semple McPherson was here to minister to its spiritual needs.

But all of this would take time. As in Mount Forest and almost every other place she'd ever preached, McPherson had to start modestly in Los Angeles. Her first revival was held at Victoria Hall, a small Pentecostal mission located downtown on the current site of the *L.A. Times* building. Though the auditorium had a capacity of about a thousand, services had been attracting fewer than fifty people—but that was before the arrival of the much-heralded female evangelist from the East. By the end of her first week, Sister McPherson was already bringing in the multitudes, filling every seat in the auditorium and packing the aisles and hallways besides. On weekends, the demand for seats was so great that she was forced to relocate the services to the 3,500-capacity Temple Auditorium on Pershing Square. The city's drifting Pentecostal community, which had become anemic and contentious since the closing of the Azusa Street Revival, was instantly reenergized as word of Sister's gifts spread through the city. Whatever it was that Angelenos were seeking in their spiritual lives, Sister McPherson seemed able to provide it, and they began coming in throngs.

One Sunday evening several weeks after Sister's arrival, a woman in the crowded auditorium rose during a lull in the service and asked to speak. "The Lord shows me that I am to give a lot to Mrs. McPherson," the woman announced. "I have four lots of land and do not need them all. . . . I want to give one of them to Sister to build a bungalow for her babies."

Aimee was astonished. "How did she know I wanted a bungalow?" she asked herself. "We had told that cherished hope to no one."

Then a man stood up in another part of the auditorium. "I want to give the lumber to build Sister's house," he said.

From there it became—as she later put it—a "popcorn meeting. One after another jumped up, offered to donate the dining-room furniture, the living-room rugs, the kitchen linoleum, until practically a completely furnished home had been promised as a gift from those lovely, warm-hearted people." As she later told the story, there were even spontaneous offers of a canary and a collection of rosebushes—the very two things that her children had most longed for.

Three months later, the McPherson family had a house of its own—built almost entirely with volunteer labor and donated construction materials—on a quiet street in Culver City. In Sister's mind, of course, this bungalow was the "swallow's nest" that God had promised her when Roberta lay deathly ill back in New Rochelle—which was why they called it, from then on, "the House that God Built."

For the first time in her adult life, Sister now had something resembling a real, permanent home. Not that she would stay put. Over the next four years, she would use Los Angeles as a kind of base camp, leaving the children at home with her mother while she went out into the wider world, building her following revival by revival. She had always imagined herself as a traveling evangelist, never as a resident preacher with a single church and a congregation of regulars, so this arrangement worked for a time. But Los Angeles would gradually change her mind about that. She saw how her children thrived in the more stable environment of home, school, and church, here in a place where, as she preached, "the glorious One had caused the desert to bloom as a rose, and pools to spring forth in the wilderness, and floods [to flow] in the dry land." She began to conceive a somewhat different image of her future—as the leader of a nationwide or even worldwide ministry, but with a central headquarters in a place her family could call home.

Apparently, God agreed. According to Aimee, he gently but firmly made it known to her that he had brought her to Los Angeles for a particular purpose: "to build a house unto the Lord," right there in the City of Angels. Exactly what form this house might take would remain unclear for several years. But Aimee was certain that God would reveal his plan in good time. Los Angeles was to be her Jerusalem, it seemed, and she was to be God's messenger here. It would prove to be a potent match. In a city full of movie stars, Aimee Semple McPherson was poised to become the biggest celebrity of all.

# CHAPTER TEN
# A Drinking Problem

*Oil derricks at Huntington Beach*

T he only way to stop the growth of Los Angeles," William Mulholland had once said, "is to kill Frank Wiggins." But now in 1920—some ten years after that remark—the maniacally energetic secretary of the L.A. Chamber of Commerce was still very much alive, and his tireless efforts to promote the city were bearing ever-more-abundant fruit. The key to his pitch was the image that he and the other city boosters were selling—of Los Angeles as a "smokeless success," a thriving place of industry and commerce, but with palm trees instead of smokestacks, sunshine instead of smog, and oranges that could be plucked from every open window. This image was designed to appeal to a wide range of would-be transplants, and however accurate or inaccurate it might have been, it was working: "It is no longer a question of whether people are going to Southern California," a Santa Fe Railroad official told city leaders in early 1920, "but whether you will be able to handle them when they get there. They are simply going to go that way in droves. . . . And a large portion are planning to stay."

This was a warning the city needed to hear. For as fast as Los Angeles had expanded in the first two decades of the twentieth century, the pace of its growth was poised to explode in the third. The 1920s were to see a real estate boom like nothing ever experienced in L.A. before or since. The goal of surpassing San Francisco in population had already been achieved by the time of the 1920 census, when L.A. became the tenth-largest city in the country. Now the population was poised to double once again in the years from 1920 to 1925, exceeding the million mark sometime in 1924. About 350 new Angelenos were arriving in the city *every day.* To house them, new residential subdivisions were built by the dozen. The volume of building permits, which in 1919 amounted to some $28 million, would rise to $60 million in 1920, $121 million in 1921, and $200 million in 1922. "Where are the citrus and olive groves, the vineyards and friendly flower gardens that made excursions into the suburbs of Los Angeles the joy of joys?" one longtime resident lamented in 1923. Already nearly half of the population lived outside downtown and the central district, and that percentage would grow rapidly over the next few years, giving the city a suburban, even antiurban, ethos unlike that of most American cities of the day. To call the L.A. of the 1920s "a city without a center . . . a collection of suburbs in search of a city," as historian Carey McWilliams famously did, may be an unfair generalization, but it is not an entirely false one.

One result of this residential dispersal was the birth in Los Angeles of an automobile culture well in advance of other metropolitan areas. Yes, many Angelenos continued to take the Red and Yellow Cars to work every day, but more and more were driving their own Marmons, Nashes, and Pierce-Arrow coupes. By 1920, an estimated 160,000 automobiles were circulating—or often not circulating—on the crowded streets of the city. Weekday traffic in and around downtown got so bad that even the streetcars were habitually running forty-five minutes to an hour late. To combat this congestion, the city council passed an ordinance to ban parking on downtown streets at peak hours. Many motorists defied the law—until the issuance of a thousand parking tickets on the first day of enforcement gently persuaded them otherwise. Suddenly, the streetcars were running on time again. But after local merchants began to complain of a 20 to 50 percent drop in business, the ordinance was quickly repealed—much to the satisfaction of the always pro-business *Los Angeles Times*, which claimed that the ill-conceived experiment proved definitively that "Southern California throb[s] in unison with the purring of its automobiles." Gilbert Woodill, chairman of the local Motor Car Dealers Association, heartily agreed. "The sooner [the authorities] realize that hampering the use of the automobile is hampering the progress of civilization," he announced, "the better off we all will be." And thus was born the still-thriving L.A. tradition of sitting in traffic for a large portion of every day.

As visible as those driving Angelenos were, however, they as yet made up just a fraction of the population. Automobiles were still a luxury item in the early 1920s; most people couldn't afford them, especially as the demographics of new arrivals began to shift—subtly at first—down the socioeconomic scale. Whereas the first great wave of migration to the city in the late 1800s had brought mostly the well-to-do, and the second (in the 1900s and 1910s) had been solidly middle-class, the wave of the 1920s brought the lower middle class—mainly laborers who came to find work in those industries that had found a foothold here in the previous decade. The oil industry, for one, was now booming, thanks to a series of significant discoveries after the end of the Great War. In October 1919, a local farmer named Alphonzo Bell, who had smelled something odd one day while drilling a water well, persuaded Standard Oil to come and sink a few test shafts on his farm in Santa Fe Springs, southeast of downtown. On the night of October 30, Bell was awakened by a huge eruption of mud and gas from the well, followed by the classic gusher of tar-black crude. It took some time for the full extent of the discovery to become clear, but eventually Bell, who had been on the brink of bankruptcy in 1919, earned enough from his oil royalties to buy a huge tract of unde-veloped land west of Beverly Hills, where he founded the now-exclusive residential enclave of Bel-Air.

There were even bigger strikes around this time. Edward Doheny, the godfather of L.A.'s oil industry, had by now sold most of his Cali-fornia interests and was doing business in Mexico and South America. But plenty of larger corporate entities were willing to step in, which they did with great success. In 1920 another significant Standard Oil well blew in at Huntington Beach. The next year Royal Dutch Shell found an even bigger bonanza (it took four days just to cap the powerful gusher) at Signal Hill, a suburb near Long Beach. These lavishly producing oil fields—and the refineries built to process the crude—created thousands of jobs for the new migrants of the 1920s.

These new industrial jobs, supplementing the agricultural jobs cre-ated by the introduction of extensive irrigation to the San Fernando Val-ley, created a demand for labor that the newcomers poured in to meet, despite the low wages dictated by the city's open-shop policies. Many of them were so-called "Americans"—white people of northern European extraction—but now Mexicans, African-Americans, and Japanese were also coming in large numbers, gradually altering the lack of diversity that had been one of the city's cardinal features in the early years. City fathers were still trying to attract those well-heeled white migrants from the East and Midwest; Chamber of Commerce publications even warned that people should not come to Los Angeles unless they "had funds," since unskilled and semiskilled jobs, they claimed, were hard to come by. But the boosters were learning a basic economic truth: you can't have a flourishing agricultural and industrial base without also taking in the workers that make it run. And so, while Chamber spokesmen could still depict the city as "the westernmost outpost of Nordic civilization" with a labor pool "twice as Anglo-Saxon as that existing in New York, Chicago, or any of the other great cities of this country," Los Angeles was slowly but inexorably developing the racial, ethnic, and socioeconomic multiplicity of older and larger metropolitan areas.

It was also developing a few other big-city characteristics. The wealth created by a booming oil industry, a booming movie industry, a booming real estate market, and a thriving port was polishing away the remaining frontier roughness of the old western town, equipping it with some of the glittering civic amenities of cities in the East. In 1919 the Los Angeles Philharmonic was founded by William Andres Clark, Jr., scion of a wealthy copper mining family, and gave its inaugural concert at Trinity Auditorium under the direction of Maestro Walter Henry Rothwell. Soon thereafter a natural depression in the Hollywood hills was turned into a permanent outdoor theater and concert venue known, appropriately enough, as the Hollywood Bowl—an open-air arts center that ultimately would attract some of the world's premier performers.

Los Angeles was also coming into its own as a center of higher education. On May 23, 1919, California Assembly Bill 626 turned a small downtown teaching college, the Los Angeles Normal School, into the southern branch of the University of California, adding an undergraduate program in arts and sciences and laying the foundation for what would eventually be known as UCLA. Meanwhile, two miles southwest of downtown, adjacent to Exposition Park, a new president with the magnificent name of Rufus B. von KleinSmid was turning a former Methodist college into the private University of Southern California, financed with a by-now-familiar formula of individual donations and the lucre of a powerhouse collegiate sports program. With the simultaneous emergence in Pasadena of the California Institute of Technology (or Caltech) from its roots as a vocational school, the Los Angeles region of the 1920s was becoming an educational destination like few others in the country.

But unbridled growth had its downsides. Having a flourishing oil industry so close to the city's core blighted many residential neighborhoods, turning them into forests of creaking derricks littered with tar-blackened storage tanks and heavy equipment. ("It was like drilling for oil at Fifth Avenue and Forty-Second Street in Manhattan," one visiting Texas oilman remarked, exaggerating just a little.) Planners tried to keep other industrialized areas—and the laborers who worked in them—isolated at the outskirts of the city. To this purpose, they created zones like the East Side Industrial District, near the Los Angeles River, and a large swath of industrial suburbs between downtown and the port at San Pedro, around the Central Manufacturing District.

But while the Chamber of Commerce depicted the resulting cityscape as "a land of smokeless, sunlit factories surrounded by residences of contented, efficient workers," the reality was often quite different: residential dead zones and neighboring areas of substandard housing (often self-built) for underpaid, nonunionized blue-collar workers of a type that would never appear in chamber brochures. Like any metropolis of its size, Los Angeles was also now dealing with the big-city ills of crime, drug use, and commercialized vice. In the wake of Prohibition (Los Angeles had voted itself dry in 1917, well in advance of the Eighteenth Amendment), an alliance of machine politicians, gangsters, and vice lords—known unofficially as "the L.A. System"—had grown up in the city, corrupting its police department and poisoning local politics with graft, influence peddling, and occasional outbreaks of gangland violence. According to historian Carey McWilliams, who arrived in L.A. at about this time, the city of the 1920s was becoming very different from the image it was still trying to project in its publicity materials. "The surface was bright and pleasing," he wrote, "but the nether side was often dark and ugly."

~

For William Mulholland, the problems created by rapid urbanization were all secondary to his principal concern. Whether rich or poor, criminal or law-abiding, white, black, Asian, or Mexican—all of these new

Angelenos needed water to drink and bathe in, and the supply situation was rapidly becoming critical again. The city was growing faster than even his most extravagant projections had foreseen. The big question in 1913, when the aqueduct was first completed, had been what to do with all of the surplus water it brought to the city. Now, less than a decade later, the big question was how and where to get more. By 1918—thanks in large part to the annexation of the San Fernando Valley—every gallon of water transported from the Owens Valley was being used at times of peak demand. And that was before the current population explosion increased demand even more. New conservation measures, like the installation of water meters in homes and increased diversions of Owens River surface water, had helped for a time, but it had become clear to Mulholland that the growing city needed new sources of water if it wanted to avoid drastic measures like rationing, especially after a multi-year drought set in around 1920.

He therefore began to look farther afield—deeper into the heart of California to the Mono Basin, north of Owens Valley, and elsewhere. These water grabs, some successful, others not, created tensions with communities all over southern California. "[Los Angeles] stole our water, gas, and power while our eyes were shut to our own opportunities," the mayor of Bakersfield complained at a League of Municipalities banquet in 1920. "Next thing you know, they will want to use the Vernal Falls at Yosemite." The remark was meant ironically, but it wasn't entirely far-fetched. By the early 1920s, Mulholland was even turning his eyes eastward to the superabundant waters of the Colorado River. After a tour of the Boulder Canyon area, he persuaded the board of public service commissioners to begin preliminary surveys for another long aqueduct to bring water to the Los Angeles basin from a proposed Colorado River dam. To many residents of the American Southwest, it was beginning to look as if the insatiable beast known as Los Angeles intended to commandeer the scarce water resources of an entire region of the United States.

Any prospect of bringing Colorado River water to L.A., however, was still years into the future. In the meantime, Mulholland had to find more water elsewhere, and he had to find it fast. So he turned again to the one source available to him at short notice: the Owens Valley.

The aqueduct was already siphoning off as much surface water in the southern part of the valley as that area could provide. But the northern part of the valley, above the aqueduct intake near Independence, still had water to spare. Mulholland's problem was that taking that water—while ensuring that the remaining Owens Valley farmers and ranchers had enough—would involve building that long-delayed storage dam at the site of the old Rickey Ranch at Long Valley. The owner of that ranch was still asking an exorbitant price for the land and rights that Mulholland needed. The problem, in other words, was the Chief's old friend and current nemesis, Frederick Eaton.

⁓

In the first few years after the completion of the aqueduct in 1913, relations between Los Angeles and the people of the Owens Valley had been relatively amicable. Valley locals did still feel that the city had been high-handed and deceptive in procuring its water rights. But Mulholland's subsequent arrangements had allowed enough Owens River water to remain in the valley to permit farming and ranching activities to continue—at least in that area north of the aqueduct intake, where several private "ditch companies" provided locals with irrigation water without infringing on the city's contractual supply. In fact, the late 1910s had been rather prosperous years for the Owens Valley. The absence of drought combined with the new railroad line from Mojave had allowed local agriculturalists both to produce more and to get their products to market more cheaply than ever before. Yes, the southern part of the valley had more or less been sacrificed to the water needs of the great city to the south, but the areas around Big Pine and Bishop in the north were still at least as productive as they'd ever been.

To ensure that there would continue to be enough water for everyone, Mulholland had hoped to build a 140-foot dam at Long Valley, which would create a large reservoir with a capacity of some 260,000 acre-feet. As part of the original agreement with Eaton, however, the city held an easement for a much smaller dam: just 100 feet high, to impound only 68,000 acre-feet. At the time, Eaton had set the price for the larger reservoir at a million dollars—far too rich a price for Mulholland's blood. But since Mulholland didn't yet need that reservoir to meet current water demand, nothing at all was built.

Now, a dozen years later, the situation was very different. L.A.'s explosive growth, combined with the onset of drought, was already straining the capacity of an aqueduct-and-reservoir system that was supposed to meet everyone's needs for a half-century. Mulholland, in other words, really needed that big dam. Fred Eaton still wouldn't budge on the million-dollar price tag, so Mulholland moved without him. After much negotiation with representatives from the Owens Valley, the two sides came to an agreement: Los Angeles would build a 100-foot dam on the site, but with a base large enough to eventually support a 150-foot dam, if and when the city could settle with Eaton for the rights to build it. Unfortunately, the former L.A. mayor, breaking with the pro-dam contingent of his fellow Owens Valley landowners, wouldn't allow it. Hoping to force the city to meet his price, Eaton filed suit to stop construction of even this compromise structure—after the city had already spent about $200,000 on the project.

This was when the real trouble began in the Owens Valley. Mulholland, disgusted with his former friend, had no choice but to explore other options. Desperate to increase the harvest of water, the Chief launched an aggressive new program to purchase upstream water rights and begin intensive pumping of the valley's groundwater reserves. To spite Eaton, moreover, he had city crews tear out some of the Eaton Ranch irrigation dams that were allegedly keeping water from reaching the aqueduct system via the Owens River. In one incident, Eaton's nephew Harold, who served as the manager of his uncle's cattle business, came across a crew of Mulholland's men cutting irrigation ditches on Eaton ranch land. "What the hell you doin' here?" Harold Eaton asked.

"We're going to turn the water back into the river," the crew leader responded.

When Eaton threatened to go get his shotgun, the crew ceded the field, ending the confrontation. But they were back a few days later, cutting more ditches to release water they claimed legally belonged to the city. The elder Eaton finally hired armed guards to patrol his land and stop any further depredations.

"They say I am no longer a friend of the city," he told an interviewer. "I deny that. But if they try to take something of mine away from me, I'll fight."

This was a sentiment now being voiced by Eaton's neighbors up and down the Owens Valley. They had been cheated by the city once before—back in 1905. They weren't going to allow that to happen again.

～

At the same time that the L.A. Water Department was newly plundering the Owens Valley, that other arm of the city's insatiable ambitions, the movie industry, also found a desirable resource in the valley: its rugged scenery. Sometime in late 1919, producers at Famous Players/Lasky (i.e., Paramount) realized that the new road and rail connections created for the aqueduct project had made the Owens Valley easily accessible from Hollywood. They also noted that the section of the valley known as the Alabama Hills (an area of distinctive rock formations, backed by the dramatic cordillera of the high Sierra Nevada) would make ideal scenery for movie westerns. So in early January 1920, they packed up a film crew to make a star vehicle for one of their hottest talents. Roscoe "Fatty" Arbuckle—that corpulent but amazingly agile comedian—had come a long way from his days at Keystone, when he was making one- and two-reelers opposite a young Charlie Chaplin. By now he was one of the most popular and highly paid actors in the industry, commanding a salary of five thousand dollars a week and swarmed by fans wherever he went. As the new decade began, he was making the leap to feature-length films with *The Round-Up*, a semicomic western about an endomorphic small-town sheriff named Slim Hoover, who proves to be unlucky at both love and crime-fighting. ("Nobody Loves a Fat Man" was the film's advertising catchphrase.) Featuring Wallace Beery as the villain and an uncredited cameo by Arbuckle's protégé and friend, the soon-to-be-famous Buster Keaton, the movie was a departure for Arbuckle, who was best known for his roles as an urban buffoon or a country rube. But it would prove to be one of the biggest critical successes of his career.

As bad as relations were at this time between the Owens Valley and the city of Los Angeles, Lone Pine welcomed the arrival of Hollywood with open arms. With only one real hotel in town (a second would be built in 1923), many of the extras and crew had to stay in lodging houses and even tents. But locals somehow managed to keep the whole company housed and fed. Horses and cattle for the scenes in the Alabama Hills were provided by a nearby rancher named Al Gallaher, while the streets of Lone Pine served admirably as a dusty Old West town (as it still was in many respects). During the filming, the movie's cast paid back the town's hospitality by putting on what the local paper called "a classy, up-to-date vaudeville show," featuring Arbuckle himself and other stars of the company. No review of the show is extant, but one can assume it made for a Monday evening unlike any other in the history of Lone Pine.

*The Round-Up* also helped spread the word about the Alabama Hills as a film location, and soon other studios were sending crews north from Hollywood into the Owens Valley. The scenery was varied enough to double at various times as India, the Gobi Desert, parts of Arabia, and even (for two Tarzan movies) the African savannah, so a wide range of movies could be made there. Later in 1920, Mary Pickford came north to film parts of *Pollyanna*. Goldwyn Pictures made a romantic comedy here—*For Those We Love*—starring Betty Compson and a young Lon Chaney. Erich von Stroheim, now coming into his own as a director, shot scenes from his massive epic *Greed* in the valley (though the famous culminating scene of two obsessed men dying of thirst in the desert was shot on location in nearby Death Valley).

It was as a setting for westerns, however, that the Alabama Hills became most famous. Virtually every cowboy star of the silent era came to the Owens Valley at some point. Tom Mix, Harry Carey, Buck Jones, Will Rogers, Jack Hoxie, Hoot Gibson, and Dustin Farnham (who had made his film debut in Cecil B. DeMille's *The Squaw Man* a decade earlier) all made multiple films here, riding off toward numerous sunsets over the towering snow-capped Sierra. The trend continued into the sound era. An estimated three hundred films were shot—wholly or partially—in the Alabama Hills from the 1920s to the 1950s.

But although this role as a kind of northern annex of Hollywood brought welcome money into the local economy, movies alone could not compensate for the losses created by the continuing diversions of the

valley's scarce water resources. Soon Mulholland's pumping of groundwater was lowering everyone's water table, making agriculture more
difficult and stirring heavy resentment throughout Inyo County. The
Chief, now in his mid-sixties, was at the height of his fame and popularity everywhere else: In April 1921 the American Association of Engineers named Mulholland (who never went to college, let alone graduate
school) one of the top engineers of the world, alongside George Washington Goethals and Orville Wright. A scenic highway along the crest
of the Santa Monica Mountains was created in 1923 in his honor, and
he was being written up adoringly in magazine profiles and engineering
journal articles nationwide. But in the Owens Valley, Mulholland was
rapidly becoming the most hated figure in local history.

Residents at first tried to fight back legally. Farmers from the Independence area filed an injunction against the city to halt the ground-
water-pumping program. In late 1922 two local bankers—the Watterson
brothers, Mark and Wilfred—helped organize an association called the
Owens Valley Irrigation District to consolidate local opposition and create a unified front to bargain with the city. Mulholland, increasingly desperate as the drought continued and city reservoirs reached alarmingly
low levels, refused even to recognize the organization. He responded to
its creation with newly aggressive measures to secure more water, in-
structing his crews to start breaking unauthorized canal heads and dams
(including another one on Fred Eaton's property) and buying north valley water rights from whoever would sell out to him.

In 1923 Mulholland bought out one of the largest of the valley's
private canal companies, the McNally Ditch, and commandeered over
80 percent of its water rights. When news of this deal became public, the
residents of nearby Bishop became outraged. Some farmers responded
by illegally diverting the McNally water into their own ditches, rendering the city's new canal all but dry. Mulholland retaliated by having one
of his crews dig its own new ditch near Big Pine, intending to take the
water right back. In August 1923 several Big Pine residents stumbled on
the city's construction site. They discovered grading and digging equipment and the beginnings of a ditch that would divert water from their
own canal. Incensed, they drove back to town, located one of the irriga-

tion district's directors, and asked him to get an injunction against the city's actions. The director, George Warren, told them not to bother with the court document. "We're not able to fight the city in court," he said. "What we want is a shotgun injunction!"

Warren proceeded to round up a posse of some twenty men armed with rifles and shotguns and rode with them back out to the canal head. After stationing them around the city's construction site, he went off with another rancher and found the camp of the construction crew.

Recalling any number of classic Old West movies, Warren presented an ultimatum: "Are you hired to fight for the city?" he asked the crew leader, known as One-eyed Dodson.

Dodson told him that they weren't.

"Well," Warren said, "we've got our men over there on the river. We don't want any shootin', but we're not going to let you make that cut."

Dodson apparently found this argument persuasive and agreed not to resume work on the project.

Satisfied, Warren returned to the construction site, where he and his men celebrated their victory by unceremoniously dumping the city's heavy equipment into the river.

At a public meeting that very evening in Bishop, cooler heads attempted to come to some kind of compromise with the city. Delegations from the Owens Valley Irrigation District and other local groups met with representatives of the city's water department, most notably lawyer William B. Mathews and Mulholland's deputy, Harvey Van Norman. The valley contingents presented a host of complaints, not least of which was the city's increasingly hard-line attempts to pressure individual landowners to sell their land and water rights. These efforts, they said, turned neighbor against neighbor, disrupting the valley's ability to bargain as a unit. The locals also accused the city of deliberately "checkerboarding" their purchases—that is, buying alternating properties along the waterway so that the holdouts in between found their farms cut off from their neighbors by idle city-owned lots. All of this was creating dissension in the valley. Gangs of diehards (some wearing hoods like Ku Klux Klansmen) were intimidating landowners desperate enough to consider selling to the city. Meanwhile, thanks to the city's groundwater pumping, real estate values (those not associated with water rights) were in decline, ranching and farming were stagnating, and schools and businesses were closing throughout the valley.

Attempting to break the cycle of reciprocal water stealing and canal breaking, Mathews and Van Norman, in consultation with a few members of the Irrigation District, floated a sweeping proposal. In exchange for a guarantee of one-third of the water from the Owens River, the city would agree to abandon any further land and water rights purchases in the valley. The city would also agree to construct water wells on Bishop-area properties, which the farmers could use in times of drought. Meanwhile Fred Eaton, who now led a group called the Owens Valley Protective Association (separate from the Wattersons' irrigation district association), would agree to lift the lawsuit against the dam at Long Valley.

This was, on balance, a reasonable compromise, and the city and the two associations seemed willing to sign on to it. But when there was a call for comments, George Warren, fresh from his confrontation with the city ditch-digging crew, stood up and said, "I have some criticism to make."

He proceeded to tear into the proposed agreement, objecting to it point by point and insinuating that the Wattersons might have ulterior motives for being so accommodating to the city's desires. Other Big Pine ranchers brought up the disputed cut they had just discovered near the Big Pine Ditch that day. They asked the city officials whether the city intended to continue work on it. When Mathews and Van Norman refused to commit one way or the other, negotiations quickly broke down.

"I think we'd better have a recess and talk this thing over," Wilfred Watterson said.

But the plainspoken Warren, who seemed to represent the majority of Owens Valley locals, refused to budge. "We don't need a recess," he announced. "That agreement is dead as hell."

And so it was. The meeting broke up noisily with nothing decided. Warren returned to Big Pine and set up a twenty-four-hour schedule of armed guards to ensure that no more ditch-digging occurred on the disputed site. After a two-day standoff, the city crew packed up their camp and departed.

Round one of what would soon be known as the California Water

War was finished, and apparently the Owens Valley locals had won. But William Mulholland, furious at being cheated out of water the city had bought and paid for, would not let things stand. David might have defeated Goliath in the old Bible story, but that wasn't the ending Mulholland had in mind here.

For the moment, at least, the Owens Valleyites were confident that they had turned back the city's recent depredations. In an editorial in the *Big Pine Citizen*, the editor was not shy about taunting the Goliath to the south. "Los Angeles, it's your move now," he wrote. "We're ready for you."

# CHAPTER ELEVEN
# Scandals in Bohemia

*The founders of United Artists: D. W. Griffith, Mary Pickford, Charles Chaplin, and Douglas Fairbanks (front row)*

**B**abylon was crumbling. The huge set left over from the filming of *Intolerance* stood in the empty lot at Sunset and Hollywood Boulevards, its ornamented facades and imposing plaster elephants warping and cracking in the hot California sun. The L.A. Fire Department had already issued several warnings that the set posed a fire hazard and should be dismantled immediately. But even now, long after the commercial failure of his great epic, Griffith could not muster the will to destroy what he had built. Instead, he was shooting another film within the ruins of the ancient city. Having constructed the interior of a rustic French farmhouse inside Belshazzar's weather-worn court, he was now finishing scenes from his war story *Hearts of the World* that he wasn't able to shoot in Europe.

The experience abroad had been good for the director's somewhat bruised ego. "Perhaps I was dreaming too big a dream when I conceived *Intolerance*," he had told Gish while they were touring Napoleon's Tomb in Paris. Yet when *Intolerance* opened in London on April 7, 1917—one day after the United States joined the Allied effort in the Great War—the film had met with near-universal acclaim. Griffith had been feted by the likes of Prime Minister David Lloyd George, Winston Churchill, George Bernard Shaw, and the Dowager Queen Alexandra. (Churchill and Shaw had both tried to sell the director a few movie ideas.) Afterward the prime minister had broached the topic of a film financed in part by the War Office Committee and the British Ministry of Information that could serve to unite the Allied peoples and cement their resolve to defeat the dreaded Hun.

As the creator of two of the greatest antiwar epics in cinema history, Griffith at first blanched at this prospect. But he soon came around. In May he summoned the Gish sisters and their mother, along with Bobby Harron and Billy Bitzer (whose Teutonic surname created great difficulties in that time of extreme anti-German paranoia), and proceeded to film the agreed-upon story—called *Hearts of the World*, about a group of ordinary people who must endure the horrors of war as their small French village changes hands among the clashing armies. Griffith shot a few scenes in Worcestershire and Surrey, with English villages standing in for the French originals, and then he and Lillian Gish proceeded to France to try to capture a few sequences in the war zone. Just how much real action Griffith witnessed remains unclear, given the director's growing tendency to bend the truth in support of his own private mythology. He at least claimed to have been "within fifty yards of the Boches" (the German army) at Ypres and to have witnessed the death of two members of his military escort under enemy fire. But he shot very little if any footage at the front, using instead battle scenes provided afterward by the British government. When he and his skeleton crew returned to the United States in the fall of 1917, what he had on film was just enough European footage to provide the illusion of verisimilitude. Two-thirds of the final film was shot in Hollywood after their return, despite what the publicity materials implied to the contrary.

Not that Griffith's reputation needed much bolstering at this time. Yes, the financial debacle of *Intolerance* had done some damage—leaving debts that would hamper him for years to come—but he was still being called "the supreme creator of the motion picture industry," his name the first to spring to anyone's mind when discussing the world's great directors. When he hired Erich von Stroheim, who had worked with him as an extra on *Birth* and *Intolerance*, the future epitome of Hollywood arrogance still felt it necessary to be obsequious to the master. "For you, Mr. Griffith," von Stroheim famously oozed when discussing his salary, "I would work for a ham sandwich a day."

*Hearts of the World*, when it opened in the spring of 1918, proved another success. After the New York premiere in April, according to the *New York Times*, "the spectators stood and shouted for Mr. Griffith until he appeared on the stage." Audiences flocked to see the film, at least until the Spanish flu epidemic closed many theaters and the signing of the Armistice in November cooled their ardor for war films. If not for Griffith's massively expensive traveling road show of premieres (featuring a full orchestra and lavish opening-night gala in every city it traveled to), the film would have been a major financial blockbuster. Clearly, the director was still at the top of his game. "Griffith was like a champion who had once been floored and who was now fighting his way out of a corner," Karl Brown insisted. "He was using nothing but his best blows, delivered with all the power he could put behind them."

Of course, the industry's moneymen had their own perspective on the matter. The demise of Harry Aitken's Triangle, due at least in part to the losses from *Intolerance*, was changing the whole landscape of the industry, as rival companies rushed to fill the vacuum. Adolph Zukor had moved most forcefully, picking up Triangle assets as they fell—including Griffith himself, whom he signed to do six new films for a Paramount subsidiary called Artcraft. (Zukor also nabbed Triangle escapees Thomas Ince and Mack Sennett, leading Hollywood wags to dub the mogul "Anaconda Adolph.") Zukor continued the vertical integration of the industry by aggressively buying and building new theaters—a move also being made by the studio of his rising rival William Fox. In response, a group of theater owners pulled off their own vertical integration, creating a new production company to make movies for their theaters to exhibit. First National, as the company was called, immediately became one of the major players in Hollywood, signing its two biggest stars—Mary Pickford and Charlie Chaplin—for astronomical figures. The ink was barely dry on these contracts when, in early 1919, rumors began circulating of a Paramount/First National merger. Fearing dominance of the industry by such a mega-studio, the four powerhouse talents of the day—Pickford, Chaplin, Douglas Fairbanks, and D. W. Griffith—joined with two former Zukor executives to engineer a new corporate entity, United Artists, which would distribute their independently produced pictures. As the 1910s ended, then, the roiling of the industry was in full swing, as the chaotic rush to industry expansion left in its wake a detritus of hurt feelings, broken contracts, and dangerously overextended artists and executives.

One of the most overextended of these artists was Griffith himself. Attempting to take advantage of the frenzied deal-making going on (he had debts to pay, after all), he signed up to make more movies than he could ever possibly do justice to. By 1919, after directing several bread-and-butter films under his contract with Zukor's Artcraft, he entered his agreement with United Artists, promising them four movies, and shortly thereafter closed a three-movie deal with First National. Since he still owed two more films to Zukor, this meant that he was committed to directing no fewer than ten projects over the next year or two. Naturally, this schedule was not conducive to quality production, and the resulting movies were largely forgettable (despite ambitious-sounding titles like *The Great Love*, *The Greatest Thing in Life*, and *The Greatest Question*). A couple of them, *A Romance of Happy Valley* and *True Heart Susie*, were charming if old-fashioned pastoral romances. Featuring his by-now favorite pairing of Lillian Gish and Bobby Harron, these films did decent business at the box office. But Griffith's commercial instincts were haphazard at best. For *Scarlet Days*, his last western, he briefly considered giving the lead role to a young Spanish dancer recommended by Dorothy Gish, but ultimately decided against it. "Women," he told the younger Gish sister, "are apt to find him too foreign-looking." Thus did Griffith miss the opportunity to launch an actor who would rise to unprecedented heights of adoration under the name of Rudolph Valentino.

Amid all these halfhearted projects designed to bolster Griffith's bottom line, however, there was one film for which the director was able to muster the creative brilliance he had displayed, however problematically, in his earlier epics. In the fall of 1918, Mary Pickford and Douglas Fairbanks came to Griffith with a slender volume of short stories called *Limehouse Nights* by the popular British writer Thomas Burke. "There's a great story in it," Fairbanks told the director. "You could make a wonderful picture of it."

The story in question, unfortunately titled "The Chink and the Child," was something of a chamber piece, featuring just three major characters—Battling Burrows, a cruel and abusive prizefighter; his twelve-year-old daughter, Lucy; and an immigrant Chinese poet-philosopher named Cheng Huan, who owns a small shop in the poverty-stricken Limehouse district of London's East End. Nothing about the narrative suggested the raw material of a hit film. The interracial attraction between Cheng Huan and Lucy—as innocuous as it was—seemed certain to be controversial. And rarely, if ever, had a film been made in which all its principal characters died in the end.

But the story's theme of innocence menaced by brutish malevolence was by now a signature Griffith obsession, and something about the setting seemed to pique the director's deepest poetic instincts. Working for the first time with a real production designer—English artist George Baker, who created gorgeous, atmospheric watercolors as a design blueprint for every scene—and using a soft-focus technique pioneered by photographer Hendrick Sartov, Griffith managed to create an uncharacteristically dark, moody film, projecting a visual intimacy unlike anything he had ever done before.

Like all of Griffith's masterpieces, the film, *Broken Blossoms* (though his irreverent crew sometimes called it *Busted Posies* behind his back), has major flaws. The delicate, simpering imitation of an Asian character as performed by white actor Richard Barthelmess can be hard for modern audiences to watch, and the malicious bully played by longtime Griffith troupe member Donald Crisp is almost comically exaggerated. But Lillian Gish, portraying a fragile girl half the actress's real age, gives an astonishing performance. In one late scene, she locks herself in a closet to escape her irate, raving father, who wants to punish her for consorting with the Chinese merchant. As he begins to break down the door to get at her, the trapped and terrified child flies into a fit of hysteria. "I played the scene with complete lack of restraint," Gish later recalled, "turning around and around like a tortured animal. When I finished, there was a hush in the studio. Mr. Griffith finally whispered, 'My God, why didn't you warn me you were going to do that?'"

The scene, which Griffith refused to reshoot, is arguably one of the most wrenching and horrifying three minutes in all of silent cinema.

Zukor, ever the businessman, hated the movie. "You bring me a picture like this and want money for it?" he exploded after seeing the first cut. "You may as well put your hand in my pocket and steal it. Everybody in it dies! It isn't commercial."

Furious, Griffith stormed out of the room. A few days later, he came back with $250,000 (God knows how he raised it) and slammed it down on Zukor's desk: "Here is the money," he said. "And here is the contract signing it [the movie] over to me. Now you give me my negative and print."

It was the kind of scene that Griffith had been playing out since the beginning of his career—bridling against the interference of cautious executives and insensitive financiers, and then putting himself out on a financial limb to wrest control of his work from those lacking the vision to understand what he had made.

This time, his instincts were right. *Broken Blossoms*—now regarded as the first true "art-house film"—opened to ecstatic reviews and, thanks to its modest cost, the healthiest profits of any Griffith film since *The Birth of a Nation*.

~

While Adolph Zukor may have been dead wrong about the prospects of Griffith's eccentric experiment in bleak lyricism, he had reasons for being cautious. The movie industry was just then facing the first pronounced downturn in its history. For one thing, the Spanish influenza epidemic had severely depressed box office receipts, as theaters in many cities were closed by government fiat and frightened moviegoers stayed home to avoid exposure to crowds. By 1919, the epidemic was tapering off, but the paranoia lingered. (Lillian Gish, who just barely survived a terrifying bout of flu before the filming of *Broken Blossoms*, claimed that Griffith refused to come within ten feet of her during rehearsals.) And as the 1920s began, the country was facing a postwar recession that would further complicate the economics of an industry heavily dependent on the free flow of disposable income among consumers nationwide.

What's more, movies were now extremely expensive to make. Film budgets had exploded in just a few short years, as audiences demanded higher production values and those who created them demanded more and more money for their services. Star salaries had continued their meteoric rise. (For instance, actress Gloria Swanson, who started with Essanay and then Keystone in the mid-1910s and now was working with Cecil B. DeMille at Paramount, had seen her salary go from $85 a week in 1917 to $6,500 a week in 1923.) But now every other element in motion pictures had also become tremendously expensive. Story properties, which in the early 1910s could be picked up for the equivalent of pocket change, were now a major expense, as studios increasingly went after the rights to bestselling novels and blockbuster plays. Sets and costumes, which used to be recycled from production to production, now had to be purchased or built anew for each movie, lest audiences recognize a Thomas Ince street scene or a Theda Bara gown in someone else's picture. Even the relatively minor crew members were demanding, and receiving, salaries that would boggle the mind of most people outside Hollywood. Ralph Spence, a title writer who specialized in perking up lackluster scenes with cleverly worded intertitles, could now command up to ten thousand dollars per film.

All of this had made filmmaking an extremely expensive endeavor. The head-turning budget of a huge epic in 1915 would, in 1920, barely pay the studio overhead on a second-tier serial western—witnessed by the fact that *Broken Blossoms*, a cheap film by the standards of its day, actually cost more to make than *The Birth of a Nation*. And now that the big money for many of these productions was coming from corporate shareholders (established firms like J.P. Morgan had begun listing studio stocks on Wall Street in 1919), the movies had to perform financially—or else. Gone was the seat-of-the-pants financing that Griffith and other pioneers had practiced in the early 1910s. Now directors had to run the gauntlet of itemized budgets, complex cost accounting, and minutely detailed profit-and-loss statements to get their visions onto the screen.

The industry had grown out of its chaotic adolescence and into a full-flowered adulthood, in other words. And Angelenos could see the difference on their own city streets. The studios scattered around town used to look a little like the summer camps of childhood, with clusters of jerrybuilt cabins tucked away among the orange orchards. Now they were beginning to resemble actual modern factories, their compounds divided into task-specific areas to maximize the efficiency of putting out product. Repeated expansions into adjacent lots, purchased from longtime residents who suddenly found their bucolic flower-draped cottages overshadowed by machine shops and costume warehouses, had made some of these studios very large indeed. By the early 1920s, some film companies realized that their in-town properties had become more valuable as potential residential subdivisions than as film factories, and as a result studios began moving out to less densely populated areas like Burbank and the aptly named Studio City in the San Fernando Valley.

But the center of the film industry was still very much in Hollywood. Far from the little country town it had been just a decade or two earlier—when, as film comedian Harold Lloyd famously pointed out, a law was passed prohibiting the driving of sheep through the streets in flocks of more than two thousand animals—Hollywood was now a bustling and, in parts, even elegant burg. Yes, given the proximity of those oil derricks, the air did smell "of eucalyptus or petrol according to the direction of the wind," as one observer put it, but the trappings of newfound motion picture prosperity were everywhere to be seen. The arid mountains north and west of town were now dotted with the lavish homes of overpaid stars and, increasingly, of overpaid studio executives, since by now many of them—Laemmle, Lasky, Mayer, Sam Warner— had followed their production companies to the West Coast from the East.

Down on Hollywood Boulevard, the main part of town started with the now-venerable Hollywood Hotel at the corner of Highland and Hollywood. Going east on the boulevard, one soon passed the only really decent eatery in town: Francois, a New York–style bar and restaurant. Francois was founded in 1919, but it is much better known by its post-1923 name, Musso & Frank (immortalized in classic Hollywood novels like Nathanael West's *The Day of the Locust* and Budd Schulberg's *What Makes Sammy Run?*). Beyond Francois the area was mainly residential, lined with stately residences set back from the road amid towering palms and curving driveways. Commercial development was still clustered around the boulevard's intersections with Cahuenga and Vine, where grocery stores, drugstores, banks, and, as the 1920s progressed, movie theaters brought people onto the streets. This was also where the city's growing cadre of would-be extras congregated, dressed conspicuously to attract the attention of casting directors. "I had never seen such weird costumes," Gloria Swanson recalled. "Loud suits, ruffled dresses, fur jackets, cowboy boots, and crazy hats. On every finger and ear, it seemed, jewelry flashed in the afternoon sun."

According to writer Lenore Coffee, Hollywood in the early 1920s "was like a carnival; or the way one feels when the circus is coming to town, only the circus was always there. Actors walked about in heavy grease-paint make-up, and out-of-work actors did precisely the same thing, hoping to create the impression that they, too, were employed."

~

Although the postwar recession was doing its part to make studio executives nervous in the early 1920s, there was another, potentially worse threat to the industry's health. For while moviemaking may have become the nation's fourth-*largest* industry, it was absolutely the single most *visible* one, its products consumed by an estimated 35 million Americans every week. Many of these viewers, especially the young ones, didn't just watch movies; they studied them—for fashion tips, home decorating ideas, and even behavioral role models. "There has never been anything like this before in the history of the human race," a *New York Times* writer mused in 1925. "The motion picture is the school, the diversion, perhaps even the church of the future."

The fact that so many people were now turning to Hollywood for cues on how to dress, act, and even think meant that movies were coming under increasing scrutiny by self-styled arbiters of public morals throughout the country. Needless to say, many did not like what they saw. Divorce, adultery, sexual romance, drinking, immodest dancing— all were now common elements in the stories being shown on neighborhood movie screens. Whether these movies were more a reflection of, rather than an inducement to, the new and looser 1920s morality didn't matter. For the clergymen, government officials, and other watchdogs of public morality, too many films seemed to celebrate sin and decadence, and the only appropriate response was censorship.

The specter of censorship had been looming over the industry for several years already. Many states and municipalities had passed strict censorship laws in the 1910s, causing much consternation among film directors in particular, who often had to recut a film for one or two markets. (D. W. Griffith once complained that a single police captain in Chicago "can tell two million American people what they shall and shall not see.") These censorship efforts were redoubled in the early 1920s—as the movies got racier and community puritans no longer had a world war to distract them from the task of domestic moral uplift. Some reformers were now saying that the federal government should inspect movies for the presence of dangerous or unwholesome ideas, just as it inspected stockyards and meatpacking plants for the presence of dangerous or unwholesome meats.

Of course, this kind of heavy-handed interference in the industry was something the big studio heads wanted to avoid at all costs. Leading the opposition was Adolph Zukor, now the biggest studio head of all. As the chief of the Famous Players/Lasky/Paramount/Artcraft combine, he was unquestionably the most powerful figure in Hollywood in the early 1920s, seeing himself as the guardian not just of his own companies but of the entire industry. Now taking in close to $750 million a year—with some films posting a return on investment of 500 to 700 percent—the movie industry had become a vast moneymaking machine, and Zukor was determined to protect his investments (and those of the industry's new Wall Street backers) by exercising strict control over the machine and all of its constituent parts. Nothing—not even the federal government—could be allowed to threaten or disrupt the assembly line of product that was generating so much wealth.

Like most of the moguls who rose to prominence after the fall of Edison's original trust, Zukor had been born poor. Orphaned at a young age in his native Hungary, he was raised by an inattentive uncle until he successfully petitioned the Orphan's Board to pay his passage to the United States. "I arrived from Hungary with a few dollars sewn into my vest," he would later recount. "No sooner did I put my foot on American soil than I was a newborn person." In New York, he attended night school and became an accomplished boxer and baseball catcher, earning a cauliflower ear and a permanently stiff finger in the process. In 1903, after achieving significant success as a novelty furrier, he and a partner opened a penny arcade called Automatic Vaudeville on Fourteenth Street. Taking note of the success of the new nickelodeons, he converted the upper floor of the arcade into a theater—accessible via a glitzy, glass-covered staircase—and started showing movies there. "We called it Crystal Hall," he later wrote, "and people paid their five cents mainly on account of the staircase, not the movies. It was a big success."

And it was only the beginning for Zukor. Unlike most industries in the United States in the early 1900s, the motion picture business presented few social barriers to Jewish entrepreneurs; it was still too new and too disreputable an enterprise for the Gentile establishment to bother with. So Zukor was able to build a formidable business, moving from exhibition into distribution and then to production, with breakneck speed. Admittedly, like the other so-called Hollywood Jews (Laemmle,

Fox, Mayer, the Warners), he was still barred from certain exclusive clubs and business associations. But that didn't stop him from achieving dominance in a game that had grown up so fast that the establishment barely noticed it until it was already an economic powerhouse.

Zukor's dominance by the early 1920s was unquestionable. At the start of the decade, Paramount and its associated businesses generated an estimated 35 percent of all motion picture revenues in the country. That made Zukor the de facto head of the industry—a role he took very seriously. So when the specter of government censorship reared its head, he and his partner Jesse Lasky decided to take matters into their own hands. Hoping to forestall any movement toward government-imposed censorship, they instituted a system of *self*-censorship to ensure that the reformers had nothing to complain about. At a February 1921 meeting of Hollywood VIPs—including Laemmle, Sam Goldwyn, William Fox, Louis Selznick, and D. W. Griffith—Zukor and Lasky outlined a voluntary fourteen-point production code to be followed by all moviemakers from that moment forward: No more pictures showing sexual attraction "in a suggestive or improper manner." No prostitutes. No lewd comedy. No nudity or lascivious dancing ("All close-ups of stomach dancing must be cut absolutely"). No disrespect to religion. No gratuitous bloodshed. And so on. By the end of the meeting, all those in attendance pledged— reluctantly—to sign the agreement.

Zukor knew that policing the content of motion pictures was only half the job; it would also be necessary to police the conduct of the content producers. Hollywood had in recent years developed a rather unfortunate reputation for scandal and misbehavior. As scenario writer Anita Loos observed, this was hardly surprising. "To place in the limelight a great number of people who ordinarily would be chambermaids and chauffeurs, [and] give them unlimited power and instant wealth, is bound to produce a lively and diverting result." And the film community's indiscretions—like the secret but widely acknowledged extramarital affair between Mary Pickford and Douglas Fairbanks—could very easily find their way into the pages of the voracious Hollywood press, whence it would be broadcast into schools and living rooms nationwide.

Beginning in 1920, however, the loose-moraled Hollywood community began generating a series of truly notorious scandals that would take a serious toll on the industry's already-fragile reputation. It started in September, when Griffith protégé Bobby Harron shot himself in the chest in a New York hotel room. Harron survived long enough to insist that the deed had been an accident—the loaded pistol had fallen out of his luggage, he claimed—but since the weapon was unregistered, the stricken actor was taken to the prison ward at Bellevue Hospital. When he died of his wound a few days later, the rumors began to swirl: that Harron, distraught over losing the lead role in *Broken Blossoms* to Richard Barthelmess, had intentionally shot himself with an ill-gotten revolver. Griffith tried to contradict these rumblings, claiming that Harron was a devout Catholic who would never have committed suicide, and that the illegal pistol was something he had kindly bought from a homeless man who needed the money. This version of events seemed to satisfy some fans, but the taint of the unsavory death lingered.

On the day after Harron's funeral, news broke of another actor's death—and this one would be harder to explain away. Selznick Pictures star Olive Thomas and her actor-husband Jack Pickford (younger brother of Mary) were on a troubled second honeymoon in Paris when the intoxicated actress drank a solution of mercury bichloride, prescribed as a topical treatment for her husband's syphilis lesions. She died a horrible death in a hospital five days later, and although her death was ultimately ruled accidental, rumors of suicide, drug addiction, and "champagne and cocaine orgies" were soon roiling. One lurid story had Pickford tricking his wife into drinking the poison in order to collect on her life insurance policies. Needless to say, none of this helped Zukor's ongoing efforts to depict Hollywood as a sober and hardworking community dedicated to the production of wholesome entertainment for the masses.

But the worst blows came in late 1921 and early 1922. On September 5, 1921, Fatty Arbuckle was celebrating his new three-million-dollar Paramount contract by hosting an alcohol-soaked marathon of a party in a San Francisco hotel suite. During the course of the debauch, the young actress Virginia Rappe, who had disappeared into a bedroom with Arbuckle, fell suddenly ill under mysterious circumstances; four days later, she died of peritonitis, caused by a ruptured bladder—the result, according to her friend, of being brutally raped by the obese comedian. Arbuckle vehemently denied this accusation, but he was arrested and charged with manslaughter. Three separate trials ensued over the next seven months, creating a tawdry media circus like none ever seen before and causing spewings of disgust and moral outrage nationwide. Numerous theaters canceled their showings of Arbuckle movies, while censorship boards demanded that the comedian's entire opus be pulled from distribution. Many of Hollywood's biggest names—Mack Sennett, Buster Keaton, Charlie Chaplin—testified to Arbuckle's good character, but they were no match for apoplectic reform organizations like the Anti-Saloon League and the Women's Vigilant Committee, not to mention the sensationalistic scandal-mongering of the Hearst newspapers. After two hung juries, Arbuckle was acquitted at the end of the third trial (with an unprecedented apology from the jurors and a complete exoneration), but the great comedian's career was finished.

In February 1922—while Arbuckle was still being tried—a second major scandal erupted when prominent film director William Desmond Taylor was found murdered at his home in the Westlake neighborhood of Los Angeles. Damaging enough was the rumored list of possible suspects, which included comedy superstar Mabel Normand and a lovesick young actress named Mary Miles Minter (supposed to be "the next Mary Pickford"). But the stories that emerged during the police investigation were even worse. Taylor, it turned out, had had a previous identity before coming to California, including an abandoned wife and child. He was also carrying on a surreptitious liaison with another man. And there were other rumors—of opium addiction, blackmail, and even a sinister "Oriental love cult" that met regularly in a downtown L.A. brothel. The press, of course, amplified and speculated freely on every sordid detail, arousing the public to even greater heights of fury.

For studio executives, this parade of dirty linen was a disaster of major proportions. Zukor in particular was tireless (some would say ruthless) in his efforts to contain the damage. He canceled Arbuckle's three-million-dollar contract and mothballed all of his films, even after the acquittal; in the Taylor case, he allegedly sent Paramount officials to the Westlake bungalow to spirit away any evidence that might hurt the industry—including a rumored cache of love letters from the dangerously underage Mary Miles Minter. But there was only so much he could do to contain the firestorm of public indignation. The scandals "exposed the debaucheries, the looseness, the rottenness of Hollywood," fumed one columnist in the *New York Daily News*. Outrage was even being voiced in the chambers of the U.S. Capitol in Washington. "At Hollywood, Calif., is a colony," Montana senator Henry Lee Myers informed his congressional colleagues, ". . . where debauchery, riotous living, drunkenness, ribaldry, dissipation, and free love seem to be conspicuous." Calls for national censorship of movies were intensifying, aided by the publication of polemical exposés like Ed Roberts's 1922 pamphlet "The Sins of Hollywood" and a book by Chicago's Archbishop Mundelein called *The Danger of Hollywood: A Warning to Young Girls*.

In another effort to sidestep outside interference, Zukor and his colleagues came up with a plan to create an organization, the Motion Picture Producers and Distributors of America (MPPDA), whose express purpose would be to self-police the industry and "clean up the pictures." Just as major-league baseball had installed a commissioner after the Black Sox Scandal of 1919, the movies would now have their own all-powerful moral watchdog: one Will H. Hays, then postmaster general in Warren Harding's administration, who would serve as the head of the MPPDA. A man of impeccable reputation himself, Hays vowed to bring to the movie industry "the sanity and conservatism of the banking world." He would do this by putting in place standards of production and rules of behavior, essentially formalizing Zukor's voluntary fourteen-point production code and extending it to cover the entire industry. Eventually all contracts for Hollywood stars would contain a morals clause, allowing for the abrupt termination of any studio employee caught engaging in unwholesome behavior. Such measures, Hays (and Zukor) hoped, would satisfy the industry's critics without ushering in government censorship. Hailed as a savior in Hollywood, Hays soon became one of the most influential figures in American cultural life—the "Little Napoleon of the Movies"—respected by almost everyone for his cool head and firm but flexible hand.

～

Hollywood thus earned a reprieve from the wrath of its enemies, at least temporarily. Of course, misbehavior in the movie colony didn't end; the scandalous 1923 death of drug-addicted actor Wallace Reid didn't help matters, nor did the suspicious death the next year of no less a figure than Thomas Ince, believed by some to have been murdered during a star-studded cruise on William Randolph Hearst's yacht. And the movies themselves did not instantly become chaste and respectable, as the transgressive films of sex symbols like Pola Negri, Theda Bara, and Rudolph Valentino continued to push the boundaries of acceptable lovemaking on celluloid. The studios soon learned, as cinema historian Arthur Knight has put it, that "they could present six reels of ticket-selling sinfulness if, in the seventh reel, all the sinners came to a bad end." Yes, the occasional overly titillating scene could still be nixed by some local censorship board in Peoria or Sioux City, but for the moment L.A.'s signature industry could flourish with minimal interference from small-town preachers and government bureaucrats.

Free from that interference, the immensely lucrative assembly line of motion pictures churned on. In the shadow of the new Hollywoodland sign, which went up in the summer of 1923 to advertise a new Harry Chandler–owned housing development (the "land" part would come down in 1949), filmmakers were now creating a product far more technically refined and narratively sophisticated than even the landmark films of the 1910s. But the increasing heavy-handedness of studio executives in policing content—both for decency and for commercial viability—created new tensions between the front offices and the creators out on the studio sets. Some directors, like Cecil B. DeMille and Allan Dwan, seemed to work well within these constraints, having little trouble aligning their creative visions with the dictates of the marketplace. But others—like the four principals of United Artists—chafed at the pressure to produce safe, reliable entertainments that would ensure Wall Street an adequate return on investment. "[Our] common object . . . is to give the world good pictures, and to develop the highest artistic forms possible, whether we make great fortunes or not," Mary Pickford told the *Times* in early 1921. "We don't any of us believe that pictures can be made like matches." For this reason, her colleague Charlie Chaplin declared himself "opposed to Wall Street having anything to do with my work."

And then, of course, there was D. W. Griffith, who had been battling corporate conservatism since the beginning of his career. "It is too expensive to experiment with the picture of today," he complained to an interviewer from *Motion Picture Magazine*. "A feature production [now] costs from $40,000 to $200,000, and very few firms can afford to try new paths at that price. The consequence has been that pictures continue to be produced according to the pattern of proven popularity." Encouraged by the unexpected success of his idiosyncratic *Broken Blossoms*, he had decided to leave Hollywood in 1920 and make movies independently in his own studio in Mamaroneck, New York.

The irony was stark. Los Angeles, the place that just ten years earlier had been the wild frontier of the new art—where pictures could be made free of corporate interference from New York offices—had become a hotbed of the kind of bottom-line industrialized moviemaking he hated. Now, it would seem, a director had to go *east* to achieve the freedom and autonomy required for really fine work.

And so Griffith bade a temporary farewell to the city he had helped build into the movie capital of the world. In his own little fiefdom, three thousand miles from the ever-growing movie mills of Hollywood, he could throw off the yoke of the Zukors and Aitkens of the industry and start making masterpieces again. It had been only five years since *The Birth of a Nation* made cinema history. Since then he had created a couple of fine films, along with an awful lot of bread-and-butter program features to satisfy his bosses. But he was still D. W. Griffith after all. Once in full control, the Father of Hollywood could focus his energies and engineer a return to his rightful place as the premier visionary of the motion picture pantheon.

Or that, at least, was the plan.

# CHAPTER TWELVE
# "Jesus, Jesus All the Day Long"

*The Angelus Temple advertising Sister McPherson's "Continuous Revival"*

The crowds started arriving in Echo Park before dawn. By noon, police were turning cars away from the neighborhood, and the streets were so overrun with people that the Red Cars couldn't move on their tracks. People from all parts of the world milled about the walkways of the beautifully landscaped park, picnicking on the banks of the lotus-filled lake and raising their voices in hymns as they waited. Some had come from as far away as Australia, where Sister McPherson had led a revival tour some months earlier. Others had arrived on a train from San Francisco chartered expressly to carry the faithful of northern California to the event. A contingent of gypsies—from New York, Florida, Colorado, Kansas, and elsewhere—had appeared in flower-strewn cars to pay homage to the woman who had once cured their ailing king and his mother. And as morning became afternoon, they just kept coming. By the time Aimee Semple McPherson mounted to a platform in front of the glittering Angelus Temple at 2:30 p.m. on that New Year's Day 1923, many thousands of believers filled the park and the surrounding streets, all hoping to witness the dedication of Sister's brand-new house of God.

After a prayer offered by Dr. Gale of the Oakland Temple Baptist Church, Sister stepped forward and led the multitudes in the hymn that had become one of her trademarks: "All Hail the Power of Jesus' Name." This was followed by a reading from 1 Kings, describing the dedication of another holy building—Solomon's temple in ancient Jerusalem. Whether many in the crowd could hear the words she spoke is doubtful, but all could see her as she stepped down off the platform and, trowel in hand, laid the dedicatory tablets at the building's foundation. One bore her own name and the name of the temple; the other cited its purpose: DEDICATED TO THE CAUSE OF INTER-DENOMINATIONAL AND WORLDWIDE EVANGELISM. Finally, after yet another prayer, the doors of the temple were flung wide, and the crowd, erupting again into a joyful hymn, streamed inside, moving as steadily and inexorably as a river flowing into a desert land.

The building they entered was a wonder unto itself: an expansive wedge-shaped auditorium, loosely modeled on the Royal Albert Hall in London. With a seating capacity of 5,300, it was, to hear Sister tell it, the largest class-A church building in the country. Its curved and colonnaded facade, centered on a modern theater marquee, gave it the look of a classical odeon updated for the movie age—"half like a Roman Coliseum, half like a Parisian Opera House," as one observer put it. Rising above this facade was a huge sun-bleached dome, sparkling with crushed seashells mixed into its cement. Inside, the furnishings were opulent, with two ornate balconies overlooking a broad stage on which stood an altar and a pulpit fitted out in "oriental velvets and brocades." The interior walls were hung with heavy burgundy curtains—a gift of the gypsies, it was said. One of these curtains could be pulled back to reveal the baptismal pool, fed by a small gurgling stream and framed by a painted backdrop depicting a scene from the banks of the river Jordan. The pipes of a soon-to-be-installed Kimball organ rose imposingly from the choir loft. And at the center of it all, beneath the dome painted with azure skies and fleecy clouds, stood the motto of the church and of Sister McPherson's entire ministry, in tall golden letters: JESUS CHRIST, THE SAME YESTERDAY, TODAY, AND FOREVER.

It was, in short, the most magnificent ecclesiastical building ever constructed in L.A. But perhaps most impressive of all was the fact that this lavish monument, which the newspapers estimated had cost close to a million dollars, had been built exclusively from donations, large and small, without (according to Minnie Kennedy, at least) incurring a single penny of debt.

Sister had worked hard for that money. In the years since she arrived virtually penniless in Los Angeles, she had preached countless sermons, prayed countless prayers, and healed countless ailing penitents. At revivals in the city and—more exhaustingly—out on her multicity tours, she had energized the religious multitudes, who responded by showering her with their nickels, dimes, and dollars. As one of her biographers described it: "The thirty revivals Sister Aimee conducted from mid-1919 until mid-1922 had a mass appeal unequaled by any touring phenomenon of theater or politics in American history. Neither Houdini nor Theodore Roosevelt had such an audience, nor P.T. Barnum. Lasting from one to four weeks, these meetings invariably overflowed the armories, opera houses, and convention halls rented to hold them. Aimee's voice created an excitement in the crowd bordering on hysteria."

The numbers she attracted were staggering—100,000 in Dallas, 200,000 in Oakland, 300,000 in San Diego. Unlike Billy Sunday and other evangelists of the day, her preaching was not all fire and brimstone, repent or be damned. "Who cares about old Hell, friends?" she once told an audience. "I think the less we hear about Hell the better, don't you? Let's forget about Hell." Instead, she insisted that her followers keep their eyes on an image of that other, better place: "Lift up your hearts. What *we* are interested in, yes Lord, is *Heaven* and how to get *there*!"

Not that she didn't condemn vice and sinful ways. Once she claimed that she would "rather see my children dead than in a public dancehall." But sin, she felt, was not something to be dwelt upon. Rather, it was to be rejected for the greater joys of piety: "Burn up the novels, the jazz music, the poker chips and playing cards, the theater tickets for next Thursday night, the dance program for Saturday, and the tobacco and snuff from your pockets." To replace those distractions, she urged her listeners to "wipe the dust from the family Bible and learn to read and pray." She used her own life story—or a carefully curated version of it—to bring this message home, recalling her own early flirtations with worldliness and how they were swept away by the overwhelming urgency of religious fervor. Her audiences were rapt. "Never did I hear such language from a human being as flowed from the lips of . . . Aimee Semple McPherson," a journalist reported in 1920 after witnessing one of her revivals. "Without one moment's intermission, she would talk from an hour to an hour and a half, holding her audience spellbound."

Wherever she traveled, she preached about her vision of "a center of evangelism in the west," situated in the young, growing city she had chosen as her home, where believers of all creeds could come together for the greater glory of God. To raise money to build that center, she sold one-dollar photos of herself and little talismanic bags of cement for five dollars apiece. Twenty-five dollars got the donor a miniature chair, representing a seat in the temple perpetually and permanently reserved just for that person. ("Chairholders," they were called—a play on the word *shareholders*, much used in that Wall Street–obsessed decade.) Eventually she sold thousands of the little chairs. God only knew what would happen if all of the chairholders showed up at the temple at once.

At first, her plans for this evangelical center in Los Angeles were modest. Her initial idea had been to build a plain wooden tabernacle. It was to be a simple but permanent structure dedicated to religious services—a place of her own, in other words, that would not have to be given up "on Monday night for a boxing tournament, Thursday night for a grand ball, [and] Saturday night for some prima donna." But as the months of revivals went on and her following grew ever larger, she had expanded on that original conception. Sometime in mid-1922, thanks to the donations that just kept rolling in, the simple wooden tabernacle in her mind evolved into a much grander temple. Although this larger structure would have to be built "by faith as the Lord provided the money," Sister was willing to take the chance.

"How much money do you have to start with?" contractor Brook Hawkins asked her when she first consulted him.

"About five thousand dollars," she replied.

Hawkins seemed dubious. "That should be enough to dig a good hole for a foundation."

But Sister reassured him. "By the time you dig the hole," she said confidently, "I expect to have money for the foundation."

Even the choice of building site seemed Heaven-ordained. Sometime in the summer of 1920, McPherson and her mother were driving around Echo Park, probably to see the damage from a recent minor earthquake epicentered there. Sister was impressed by the neighborhood. "Oh, this is heaven!" she exclaimed. "The most beautiful spot for a house of the Lord I have ever seen. It's right in the city, yet so restful!"

One location in the neighborhood was especially appealing to her—a large, fan-shaped lot on Glendale Boulevard, overlooking Echo Lake and its surrounding park. "The moment I saw it," Sister recalled, "I felt it should be the site of the Angelus Temple."

The only problem was that the lot was not for sale; the elderly owner had already refused numerous previous offers. But Sister had her own interpretation of this news: "The Lord must have been saving it for us all the time."

And sure enough, the next time McPherson and her mother inquired about the property, it was for sale. "I suddenly decided that I am land poor," the owner allegedly said. "This is the first piece of property I will sell." And she offered it to Sister at a "splendid price."

After the groundbreaking in February 1921, Sister redoubled her efforts out on the revival circuit, determined to keep paying the construction bills as they arose. Thanks to the growing readership of the *Bridal Call* magazine and increased coverage of her events by newspapers nationwide, she no longer had to drum up audiences once she arrived at a revival location; the resident believers would hear that she was coming and turn up by the thousands as soon as she arrived in town. Sister McPherson, they knew, would not harangue them with their own sinfulness and unworthiness. She would offer them a bright vision of the Kingdom of God that was due to arrive any moment now, and she'd serve it up with charm, charisma, and entertainment. There would be parody popular songs recast with religious lyrics, and plenty of other wholesome fun. ("My opponent in these bouts will be Satan," she once announced at San Diego's Dreamland Arena, a well-known boxing venue, "and I shall certainly thump him hard!") And there would be a message—cleverly turned and easily grasped—that would bring the all-encompassing immediacy of religious belief vividly to life:

> When I was a little girl [at] a Canadian school, we used to dare each other to see who could look at the sun the longest. When we would look back at the earth, there was sun everywhere, on the schoolhouse, on the woodpile, on the pump. . . . It is something like that when we have really been looking at Jesus, the Sun of Righteousness. We have seen his glory, his face, our blessed Redeemer, and when we look back, we see Jesus everywhere. It is just Jesus, Jesus all the day long.

But what really drew the multitudes to her revivals—at least at this stage in her ministry—were the astounding reports of Sister's faith healing. The evangelist would later try to downplay this aspect, claiming that her meetings were "99 percent salvation and one percent healing." She also tried to minimize her own role in these latter-day miracles. "Jesus is the healer," she would often say. "I am only the office girl who opens the door and says, 'Come in.'"

Even so, the power of these acts to move her audiences was undeniable. Ailing people by the hundreds swarmed her revivals, eager for the evangelist's healing touch. Accounts of these sessions—even those from hard-nosed, cynical journalists—sound miraculous: Sister rubs a deaf woman's ears with oiled hands, whispering prayers into each ear, louder and louder, until the woman flinches and cries out that she can hear. Sister massages the twisted limbs of a crippled ten-year-old boy, who then rises to his feet for the first time in his life. "Look, mama, look," he shouts, "see how I can run! Oh, mama, see! You're crying. . . . But look, mama, I can run and it doesn't hurt me either!"

Naturally, many outsiders were skeptical. Some claimed that the sick and disabled at these sessions were outright fakes, or else victims of hysterical illnesses "cured" by the emotional jolt of McPherson's charismatic personality. Others pointed to healings that turned out to be temporary, lasting only as long as the sufferers were under the influence of her "religious hypnosis." But many more were legitimately convinced, despite their initial suspicions. As one Presbyterian minister professed, "I cannot blame anyone for not believing things that can and will be told of these meetings, for I probably would not believe them myself had I not seen them, but I have seen them." In August 1921 the San Francisco chapter of the American Medical Association secretly sent representatives to the healing sessions at one of Sister McPherson's Oakland revivals. After witnessing several sessions and examining the beneficiaries of her ministrations, they issued a report approving of the evangelist's work and declaring her healings "genuine, beneficial, and wonderful."

Whatever was truly happening to those people throwing away their crutches and wheelchairs, Sister's acts of healing were effective as a recruiting device—as she herself was the first to admit. "Quite apart from their wonderful success in the relief of suffering," she wrote in one of her autobiographies, the healings "are immensely valuable as attractions to bring the throngs within sound of the Word. Obviously, when people hear of these things, it is impossible for the curious to refrain from coming themselves to see them, and when they see them, the curious become converts." And so the numbers of her followers multiplied. As one contractor responsible for organizing her revivals told her, "The crowds you are drawing to your meetings almost scare us."

Now, thanks to the largesse of these crowds, Sister McPherson finally had a magnificent temple of her own to serve as a home base—a place where, so to speak, the mountain could be brought to Mohammed. Her traveling revival tours would go on, but in the years to come, she would be spending months at a time right here in Los Angeles, preaching to Angelenos and their visitors, day in and day out. Her challenge, then, was clear. As Hollywood had discovered by now, no single production—not even *The Birth of a Nation*—could run forever. Audiences were always on the lookout for the next new thing. Now that Sister McPherson had her million-dollar temple, would she be able to keep those 5,300 seats full?

In the weeks and months after its opening, the Angelus Temple quickly established itself as a Los Angeles institution, as much a part of the city's civic and cultural life as the Hollywood Bowl, Exposition Park, and the University of Southern California. Sister initially intended the temple to serve mainly as a hub for her worldwide ministry, devoted to the conversion of souls and the training of future evangelists. The idea was not to become a neighborhood church with a static congregation and a predictable weekly schedule of weddings, funerals, Sunday school classes, and weekly church services. But Angelus soon became that and much more. The original plan to open the temple only four days per week went by the wayside. People would come on the off-days and camp out on the sidewalks and in the neighboring park, waiting eagerly to gain admission regardless of the official schedule. Sister responded by opening the temple every day of the week. But even services every weeknight and three times on Sunday did not satisfy the yearning throngs. Every seat in the main theater and every standing space in the aisles and hallways was regularly filled—for services, prayer meetings, and healing sessions. Sometimes hundreds, even thousands, had to be turned away.

Sister therefore began conducting additional services elsewhere in the city, with regular noon sessions at the county jail, the general hospital, the local Ford plant, and other places of business and industry.

And still the people kept coming. Like many in her adopted hometown, Sister McPherson had a genius for publicity, and soon her every move was being reported in the newspapers—even in the distant *New York Times*. She convinced newsstands all over L.A. to begin carrying *Bridal Call*, and whenever she drove through town, she would call out to passersby on the sidewalks, inviting them to come to the temple to see what she was doing there. She even set up a telephone service that people could call at any hour of the day or night to be told the correct standard time.

Soon the Angelus Temple was offering a full smorgasbord of services and activities to serve the community and keep the people coming through the doors. A month after the building's inauguration, Sister opened the prayer tower—a room where volunteers would come to pray around the clock. Working in two-hour shifts (women during the daytime, men at night), they would take telephone calls from anyone with a sick relative or other loved one needing divine intervention and pray for them, even at four a.m. That same month Angelus added a training institute for fledgling evangelists in a small building next door to the main temple. More than fifty students enrolled initially, but more kept joining, until the school had to be moved into a larger space within the temple called the 500 Room. Eventually an entirely new structure—called the L.I.F.E. Bible School—would be built to accommodate the overwhelming demand. There were also youth group meetings, special services for children, orchestral and choir performances, a sisterhood that sewed layettes for poor local mothers, and a brotherhood that helped recently released prisoners find jobs. The Angelus Temple became the focus of a congregant's entire existence, the anchor for a comprehensive lifestyle devoted to health, service, and spiritual realization. And it was this lifestyle—combined with the enduring appeal of southern California's sunshine and natural beauty—that Sister was advertising on every revival tour she took and in every issue of *Bridal Call* she published.

When broadcast radio got its start in the early 1920s, Sister McPherson recognized it as an opportunity to spread the word even more efficiently. According to her research, there were by 1923 more than 200,000 radio sets within a hundred-mile radius of Los Angeles, but only two full-time radio stations to serve them. So she raised the $25,000 necessary to start a 500-watt station and hired a man named Kenneth Ormiston to build it. In February 1924—just a few years after the first federally licensed commercial station in the United States began broadcasting in Pittsburgh—Aimee Semple McPherson's own KFSG went on the air, featuring hymns, testimonials from converts, organ recitals, readings of the classics, and live broadcasts of Sunday services. One of the most popular shows was the "Sunshine Hour," a seven a.m. live broadcast that Sister hosted every morning when she was in town. Her warm, enthusiastic persona proved perfect for the new medium, and soon, thanks to the long-range broadcast reach of the station in those days of sparsely populated airwaves, her voice was a welcome and familiar presence in living rooms throughout California, the West, and even the distant cities of the East. She was not—as legend sometimes has it—the first woman in the country to own a broadcast radio license, but she was an important pioneer in the medium, having recognized it as "a most unheard-of opportunity for converting the world."

Perhaps the most beloved and well attended of the Angelus Temple offerings were Sister's Sunday-night "illustrated sermons." Never one to underestimate the value of spectacle and stage imagery in winning souls for Jesus, she borrowed heavily in these productions from the techniques being perfected by the Hollywood studios a few miles up the road. (She often competed with local movie productions for rentals of costumes, lighting equipment, and animal extras.) Created in partnership with the temple's own set designer and stage manager, her illustrated sermons were heavy on costumes and pageantry, often featuring tableaux of biblical scenes with a cast of dozens. Once she showed up as a USC football player to dramatize a sermon about "carrying the ball for Christ"; on another Sunday, she donned a policeman's uniform and posed with a highway patrolman's motorcycle to "put sin under arrest." Even the biggest Hollywood stars were impressed by her showmanship. "You give your drama-starved people . . . a theater which they can reconcile with their narrow beliefs," Charlie Chaplin once rather condescendingly told her. "Whether you like it or not, you're an actress."

She was an actress, moreover, with a rich and spontaneous sense of humor. Once, when she borrowed a macaw from a local circus to help populate that Sunday's tableau of the Garden of Eden, she ran into some unexpected trouble. The impressive green-feathered bird proved capable of saying just one thing: "Oh, go to Hell!" The first time he said it, a horrified silence fell over the audience. But Sister did not rush the animal offstage. Instead, she worked his scandalous refrain into her sermon as a running gag—treating it like the voice of Satan that leads Adam and Eve to be expelled from paradise. Characteristically, too, she absolved the macaw at the end of the evening, promising it a perch in Heaven despite its foul mouth.

Some critics said that McPherson's performances, like Cecil B. DeMille's biblical epics, exuded a sexual undercurrent at odds with their pious subject matter. Admittedly, McPherson was hardly a Hollywood-style bombshell, but she was a vibrant, attractive, and charismatic young woman, and there are many contemporary reports of men in her congregations swooning with something other than religious fervor. This was especially true after 1925, when, against her mother's wishes, she cut her hair short after the current fashion and began to wear more stylish clothing. "Supernatural whoopee" was what one critic called her offerings, "sensuous debauch served up in the name of religion." And there was evidence in her history—confirmed by both her mother and her ex-husband, who allegedly complained about her "wildcat habits" in private—of an impulsive excitability in her makeup, a trace of rash imprudence that would often cause friction with those closest to her. (According to one former neighbor, "She had a fiery temper and . . . could throw herself into a fit at any time.") It was a trait that arguably would contribute to her eventual undoing.

Again like her Hollywood counterparts, Sister rarely lost sight of the bottom line. She was never shy in her appeals for contributions, the bigger the better. "Sister has a headache tonight," she might say before the offering, so "just quiet money please" (i.e., bills, not coins). That said, there's little evidence that those contributions made their way unduly into her own pockets. She and her mother (who handled all of the finances) seem instead to have used most of the money for its intended purpose: to further the temple's mission in the community.

And that mission grew accordingly. By the mid-1920s, Angelus could claim a regular congregation of some ten thousand members, making it allegedly the largest single Christian congregation in the world. The Red Car line had to build a special siding at Echo Park so that extra cars could be put on to carry temple-goers to and from the Sunday and larger weeknight meetings. The temple was even having a beneficial economic effect on the surrounding area. According to one journalist, "A territory little known has become the center of considerable developmental activity. Thousands of people now visit the district every week, and in recent months many new homes, apartment-houses, and duplexes have been built in the vicinity of Echo Park." One businessman writing to the *Times* noted that McPherson's activities were having an encouraging influence on the city's moral fiber as well. "The Temple is bringing thousands of people to Los Angeles," he wrote, "and scores and scores of radicals and all kinds of criminals are converted."

Certainly a large part of her church's explosive growth was attributable to the uniquely inclusive quality of Sister's message. People of all backgrounds and all denominations were responding to what she now called the Foursquare Gospel—a fourfold vision of Christ as Savior, Healer, Sanctifier, and Coming King. Her Jesus Christ was an active, living, twenty-four-hour presence in life rather than a God to be reckoned with only on Sunday mornings and the occasional religious holiday. And unlike the leaders of many other Christian denominations in this racist age, Sister McPherson made a special effort to reach out to Latino and African-American communities. Although she shied away from challenging racial patterns in the city (her regular congregations were almost exclusively white), she encouraged the formation of black and Mexican Foursquare branch churches in the region and used her radio broadcasts to bring her message into these communities. Occasionally, when contingents of KKK members would appear at her services in full hooded regalia, she would (very cautiously) urge them to live lives "that would stand the full light of day," promising them prayers as long as they "stood for righteousness" and "defended the defenseless." According to one story told by her daughter, Roberta Semple Salter, when hundreds of Klan members appeared at one of Sister's evening services in 1924, she told them a parable about Jesus appearing to an aged black man who had just been refused admittance to an all-white church. "Don't feel sad, my brother," Jesus said to him. "I, too, have been trying to get into that church for many, many years." To hear Salter tell it, Sister then stared at them in silence until, one by one, they rose from their seats and exited the temple. After a time, they all returned—minus their white robes, which park attendants allegedly found the next morning stuffed into the bushes all around Echo Lake.

～

Despite—or perhaps because of—her extraordinary success in winning souls to Jesus, Sister McPherson soon faced staunch opposition, both from competing religious organizations and from other elements in the L.A. community. The earliest complaints came from Pentecostalist groups suspicious of Sister's mainstream success and critical of what they considered her watered-down version of Pentecostal fire. Ever since coming to Los Angeles and taking her place on a national stage, McPherson had discouraged the more extreme manifestations of religious ecstasy among her followers—what one of her biographers called the "barbaric yawps and wild automatisms, rolling and babbling and twitching" that had characterized her early rural tent revivals. Reluctant to scare off the more traditional Christian believers she now attracted, Sister increasingly silenced those who interrupted her services with tongue-speaking or other flamboyant outbursts. While this suppression of what she called "frenzied fanaticism" and "boasting manifestations" proved far more palatable to the Methodists, Episcopalians, and Lutherans in her congregation, it alienated the Pentecostalist establishment. In 1922, after reporting on her activities with approval for several years, the *Pentecostal Evangel*, an official publication of the Assemblies of God, turned against her. An unsigned article entitled "Is Mrs. McPherson Pentecostal?" accused Sister of compromising her teachings in a quest for mainstream respectability. She disagreed and responded to the criticism with a pamphlet suggestively titled "The Narrow Line." But from that point onward her relationship with organized Pentecostalism remained contentious at best.

She did not fare much better with some leaders of the mainstream Christian denominations. Practices too tame for the Pentecostalists were still too outré for the traditional churches, especially after these churches began to lose congregation members to the Foursquare Gospel. The establishment clergy, which had been warmly supportive of her work when her emphasis was on itinerant evangelism, became rather more critical when she settled down as resident pastor at Angelus, drawing worshippers by the thousands week in and week out. Fundamentalist organizations like the Moody Bible Institute and the Bible Institute of Los Angeles began raising objections to practices like divine healing and tongue-speech, while other members of the L.A. Ministerial Association accused her of using the Gospel mainly to draw attention to herself. Claiming that her visions "must come from the devil," one prominent clergyman—Clifton L. Fowler, dean of the Denver Bible Institute— wrote that, with the possible exception of Mary Baker Eddy (the founder of Christian Science), "there has not been so dangerous a religious teacher in the United States in the past two hundred years."

Perhaps her most vocal critic was her main competitor in the religious life of the city: the Reverend Robert Shuler, pastor of the Trinity Methodist Church in downtown Los Angeles. A folksy but viper-tongued rabble-rouser from a coal-mining area of western Virginia, Shuler had arrived in L.A. a year or two after McPherson, and his rise to prominence had been almost as meteoric. Like his rival, he had quickly established a sizable local following while also achieving a nationwide audience by publishing his own magazine (aptly titled *Bob Shuler's Magazine*) and starting a radio station (KGEF, which began broadcasting in December 1926, some two years after Sister's KFSG). But there the similarities ended, for while McPherson's message was always upbeat and inclusive, Shuler's was unrelentingly negative and confrontational, his sermons bristling with attacks on Jews, Catholics, African-Americans, Hollywood moguls, newspaper publishers, public school officials, and politicians of every stripe. Known to supporters as "Fighting Bob," Shuler was eventually condemned by the *L.A. Times* as a "mischievous and troublemaking public gossip" who "threatens the good name of the city of Los Angeles and the safety of its citizens."

Fighting Bob saved some of his choicest barbs for Aimee Semple McPherson. Complaining that most of her converts were stolen from traditional Protestant churches, he regarded her as an "Isadora Duncan in the pulpit" whose flamboyant persona trivialized the gospel ministry. "Whatever the lips of Mrs. McPherson may say," he claimed, "the fact remains that thousands of people sit in Angelus Temple and worship Aimee McPherson, even as we are supposed to worship Jesus Christ. . . . Her answer to all is the story of herself." Gathering his critiques into a series of sermons entitled "McPhersonism," he accused her of commercializing religion, playing fast and loose with the proceeds from the collection plate, and engaging in all manner of falsehoods, dishonesty, and scandal. (Her characteristic response was to invite Shuler to come and speak at the Angelus Temple anniversary celebration one year, an invitation he chose to ignore.)

All of this criticism notwithstanding, it was someone much closer to home who posed perhaps the greatest threat to Sister McPherson's ministry: namely, Minnie Kennedy, her opinionated and strong-willed mother. As the temple's business manager, Kennedy received and paid out thousands of dollars every week, with minimal oversight. Within months of the temple's inauguration, staff members were already complaining about her ruthless economies and dictatorial ways. She forbade them to use the temple switchboard, for instance, and instead made them spend their own nickels in the pay phone in the lobby, even for business-related calls.

Noting that Kennedy and her daughter held title to the temple in their own names, some members wondered where all of the money from the overflowing collection plates was going. Kennedy also took it upon herself to be the temple's unofficial sergeant-at-arms. She made no secret of the fact that she regarded many of Sister's followers as "nuts," and she ruthlessly tried to weed them out of the congregation. In August 1923, eight months after the consecration of the temple, a faction of the congregation (calling itself the Committee) staged a revolt. They lodged a formal complaint against Kennedy, questioning the older woman's lack of accountability in the temple's financial matters and even threatening to take their complaint to the district attorney. Kennedy responded by excommunicating the entire Committee, tearing up their church membership cards without consultation.

Two years later, the Santa Ana branch of the Foursquare Church faced a similar situation. When Kennedy's high-handed behavior led the church to break away from the main congregation, she secretly sent in a moving crew to strip the Santa Ana temple of all of its furnishings while no one was present. That conflict eventually grew so ugly that Sister began traveling at all times with a volunteer bodyguard. "I've never asked [for] protection," she told a reporter from the *Times* in September 1925, "but my friends never let me pass from the Temple to the house alone, especially since this little trouble with the branch church in Santa Ana."

In this and other disputes, McPherson tended to back her mother, at least at this point in their relationship. Sister was in any case more concerned with spiritual matters than with the practical details of temple operations. And someone, after all, had to keep people from taking advantage of the evangelist's overly trusting nature. Nor was Minnie Kennedy wrong about the increasing number of "nuts" drawn to Sister McPherson as her celebrity grew. In that same month of September 1925, two separate women had to be incarcerated for threatening to do harm to the evangelist—a Mrs. Marion Evans Ray, for plotting to kidnap Sister for ransom, and a Mrs. Mercie Stannard, for coming to the temple with a revolver to kill her, claiming that McPherson had set up a radio broadcasting set in Stannard's home in order to reveal her family's secrets to the world.

Not all of Sister's most personal ill-wishers could be dismissed as crackpots, either. She was also making enemies among the city's increasingly powerful underworld of bootleggers, drug dealers, and illegal gambling-hall operators. In the pulpit Sister was vocal in her opposition to them, and she was active in municipal anticrime initiatives, appearing in the city's antinarcotics parade in July 1923. More to the point, she used her radio station to undermine their criminal activities, brazenly announcing the addresses of speakeasies and gambling halls over the air. She would even occasionally put repentant criminals on her show to broadcast the names of their associates still involved in prostitution, drug running, and other illegal rackets. This, of course, was a dangerous game, and she was often warned that her boldness could lead her into some serious trouble. But Sister was fearless—perhaps to a fault. "Threats and commands to 'lay off' were delivered," she would later claim, "but we went right ahead, like a child playing with a sizzling bomb or teetering on the edge of a volcano."

# CHAPTER THIRTEEN
# Thunder in the Valley

*A portion of the L.A. Aqueduct damaged after bombings*

At one-thirty on the morning of May 21, 1924, a thunderous explosion rocked the Owens Valley near the town of Lone Pine, echoing against the stark rampart of snowcapped Sierra to the west. Centered on a lonely stretch of the Los Angeles Aqueduct north of town, the explosion—caused by the detonation of five hundred pounds of dynamite—shattered one wall of the carefully engineered conduit channeling water to the distant city. By the time investigators arrived on the scene the next morning, millions of gallons of the precious stuff had been wasted, and more was running out of the aqueduct with each passing minute.

News of the explosion came as a shock to most Angelenos. True, tensions had been simmering in the Owens Valley for some time, but until now the trouble hadn't advanced beyond threats, bluster, and inconclusive standoffs. But the May 21 bombing signaled an escalation of the conflict to a new, more violent plane. As William Mulholland, who heard about the bombing in an early-morning telephone call, told an emergency session of the L.A. City Council: "We had heard of threats from disgruntled persons, but going on the theory that barking dogs do not bite, we did not pay any attention to them. Last night they bit."

In response to the bombing, the city sent a team of law enforcement officials north to assist the local sheriff's office in the investigation, followed by a gaggle of newspaper reporters and photographers. Over the next few days, as water department workers moved to repair the damage, it became clear what had happened in that remote stretch of the valley. Fresh footprints and tire tracks around the blast site indicated that a caravan of some forty people had been involved in this act of domestic terrorism. And although the L.A. papers at first speculated wildly about the source of the conspiracy—attributing the bombing to anarchists, Wobblies (members of the radical Industrial Workers of the World union), or even private power companies seeking to disrupt the city's attempts to develop hydroelectric capacity—the perpetrators were soon revealed to be local residents. Detectives traced the dynamite to a nearby warehouse that just happened to be owned by the Watterson brothers, leaders of the Owens Valley Irrigation District. Mulholland dispatched several private investigators to Lone Pine and offered a ten-thousand-dollar reward for information, but the guilty parties could not be found. As detective Jack Dymond later remarked, "Every resident of the Owens Valley knows who did the dynamiting, but no one will tell."

The cause of this lurch toward violence was not difficult to determine. Some ten days before the blast, Mulholland, frustrated with the persistent stalemate, had persuaded the city to file suit against the Owens Valley interests to recover the water from the McNally and Big Pine canals. As the Chief saw it, the water department had legally purchased those two properties back in 1923. The continuing diversion of those waters away from the L.A. Aqueduct—by armed vigilante groups like George Warren's—constituted an outrageous affront to the city's legal rights, especially as the drought continued to worsen in the entire region. The Owens Valley farmers and ranchers were incensed by the city's lawsuit, especially since some of them were named individually as defendants. According to *Owens Valley Herald* editor Harry Glasscock, who was emerging as one of the most vocal leaders of the resistance movement, the city's action was brought "mainly for the purpose of demoralizing this county, frightening the people, and depressing land values. . . . The defendants in this case, the water owners and users of this section, are the men who helped build the west."

This familiar trope of heroic western pioneers divided and undermined by conniving city slickers was played up in a series of articles written for the *San Francisco Call* by staff writer Court E. Kunze (who just happened to be a brother-in-law of Wilfred Watterson). Under the title "Valley of Broken Hearts," the series was hardly a paragon of dispassionate reporting. "Fear, suspicion, and bitter hatreds have pitched their black tents in every crossroad" ran a typical passage. "Neighbor no longer trusts neighbor. Rumors of sellouts or suspected betrayals are the chief topic of conversations," and so on. Second in vehemence only to Glasscock's intemperate diatribes in the *Owens Valley Herald*, Kunze's series did much to embolden the perpetrators of the May 21 bombing.

And this "western standoff" narrative was soon generating real-life plot twists worthy of one of the Hollywood westerns being shot in the Alabama Hills. In one incident, a local resident named L. C. Hall, perceived by his neighbors as sympathetic to the city's cause, was literally run out of town—kidnapped one night by a group of vigilantes and nearly lynched on a cottonwood tree before being told to leave the valley and never come back. (He was saved from hanging, according to one account, when he flashed a secret Masonic distress signal, which convinced some Masons in the mob to reconsider their plans.) Aqueduct employees and other city representatives received threats and intimidations of their own; Glasscock himself promised to shoot a reporter from an L.A. newspaper if he didn't stop asking questions. But when Mulholland received an explicit death threat—a letter that claimed he would be killed if he set foot in Bishop—the Chief responded in classic movie-western fashion: "They wouldn't have the nerve," he snarled. "I'd just as soon walk the whole length of Owens Valley unarmed."

Now that the bombing had earned them the city's undivided attention, the Wattersons and other valleyites did some hard bargaining. In a proposal presented to the L.A. Chamber of Commerce, an entity perceived as more sympathetic to their situation than Mulholland and his water department, the valley interests gave the city of Los Angeles a choice: either restore the valley's agricultural potential to what it was before Mulholland started pumping groundwater and secretly buying water rights in its upper reaches, or else buy out the entire valley, "not at your price, not at our price, but at a reasonable price fixed by a competent board of appraisers." This latter idea seemed reasonable to the chamber, which wrote a report suggesting the creation of an independent board of arbitration to set binding prices for property in the Owens Valley. But Mulholland and the water board ignored the report, claiming that the Wattersons and their contingent did not represent the majority of valley people. The chamber chose not to argue with this logic and left the matter there. "The president of the Chamber of Commerce is an old friend and former business associate of mine," an increasingly rigid and imperious Mulholland explained. "The chamber will never do anything to hurt me."

Frustrated by the failure of their proposal—and after rejecting a subsequent counterproposal by the public service commissioners as "the same old bunk"—the Owens Valley activists decided to take more dramatic action again. Shortly before dawn on Sunday, November 16, a contingent of between seventy and a hundred men set out from Bishop in a caravan of Ford Model Ts and drove south to the Alabama Gatehouse, on a stretch of the aqueduct about six miles north of Lone Pine. Led by banker Mark Watterson, Karl Keough, and other members of the Owens Valley Irrigation District, the vigilantes forcefully removed the two watchmen on duty and proceeded to occupy the surrounding waterworks. Once in control of the gatehouse, they turned the great wheels inside that opened the metal floodgates, releasing the aqueduct's flow of water down a concrete spillway, where it streamed out onto the valley floor. Then, in a show of defiance perhaps more symbolic than practical, they laid barbed wire at the foot of the hill on which the gatehouse stood—as if in preparation for a lengthy siege.

Inyo County sheriff Charles Collins arrived on the scene sometime after daybreak, but his sympathies were clearly with his fellow valley residents; after issuing pro forma demands that the crowd disperse— demands that were cheerfully ignored—he merely took down the names of all of the men involved. Eager to be publicly associated with this act of defiance, they gathered around the lawman, shouting out their names and making sure he spelled them right.

More meaningful opposition came a few hours later, when Edward Leahey, the local representative of Los Angeles in the valley, drove up to the gatehouse and parked his car at the foot of the hill. As he climbed the slope beside the roaring spillway, a noose allegedly dropped from one of the windows of the gatehouse and dangled in front of him. Leahey wasn't intimidated; he was angry. He was met at the gatehouse door by Mark Watterson and several others. After satisfying themselves that Leahey wasn't armed (and, curiously, after offering him coffee), they delivered their ultimatum: "You can tell [water department attorney] Mathews and Mulholland that we're going to stay here till they settle with us." And when Leahey expressed his determination to stop the wanton waste of city water they were perpetrating, Watterson warned him, "If you try to close these gates, we'll make our own gates"—a not-so-subtle threat to dynamite another hole in the aqueduct somewhere else.

Needless to say, when Mulholland heard about the takeover, he was apoplectic. Thanks to a reservoir he had built at Haiwee, lower in the valley, the vigilantes' actions did not threaten L.A.'s immediate water supply. But the diversion would cost the city upward of fifteen thousand dollars a day until it was stopped. Determined to end the siege immediately, he and Mathews dispatched two carloads of detectives and investigators from the city. When news of the approaching posse reached the Owens Valley, a crowd of local men gathered outside the Watterson hardware store in Bishop, demanding weapons to hold off the intruders. Sheriff Collins, fearing bloodshed, jumped into his car and sped south to intercept the oncoming detectives. He met them somewhere south of Lone Pine and warned of the brewing resistance. "If you go up there and start any trouble," he allegedly told them, "not one of you will get back to tell the tale." The detectives, perhaps wisely, decided to postpone the confrontation until tempers in the valley cooled off.

Meanwhile the scene at the Alabama Gates had taken on a festive aura, as more and more people gathered to show solidarity or merely to see what was going on. First came the inevitable corps of news reporters and photographers from the city—welcomed with open arms by the protesters, since one of the principal goals of the takeover was publicity. The press was followed by family members and sympathetic neighbors of the men holding the gatehouse. At noon on November 17, the day after the incident began, a group of some twenty women arrived from Bishop with hot dogs, potato salad, and other picnic supplies, and soon the siege resembled nothing so much as an outdoor community supper. By Tuesday the eighteenth, the crowd at the remote spot had grown to more than seven hundred people—most of them from in and around Bishop, where a hastily painted billboard at the town's main intersection now read "IF I AM NOT ON THE JOB, YOU CAN FIND ME AT THE AQUEDUCT." Cowboy film star Tom Mix, who was at the time filming a western in the Alabama Hills nearby, visited with a mariachi band that was part of his cast, and soon there was singing, dancing, and a barbecue under way—all while the precious lifeblood of aqueduct water drained unused into the ground.

City officials, of course, were not idle during this scofflaw carnival.

S. B. Robinson, Mathews's assistant in the water department's legal office, came north and demanded an injunction from Inyo County superior
judge William Dehy. The judge did issue a temporary restraining order,
but when Sheriff Collins attempted to serve it, the insurgents merely
tossed the documents into the still-raging spillway. "No, Sheriff," one of
them said, "we won't leave here until the state troops come in and put us
out." A group of them calmly lifted the sheriff up onto their shoulders
and carried him back to his vehicle.

Not to be discouraged, Robinson insisted that Judge Dehy issue arrest warrants for the men known to be the main instigators of the siege.
But here again he got no satisfaction. Dehy recused himself from the
matter, claiming to be disqualified "by personal interest." Since there
was no other judge to be found in this remote jurisdiction, Robinson had
no choice but to give up his legal challenge.

But as the occupation went on, it became clear that something had
to be done. Sheriff Collins appealed to California governor Friend Richardson to send in the state militia. This was exactly what the insurgents
wanted, since the resulting news stories would give their cause worldwide visibility. Even absent a confrontation with armed troops, the story
of their rebellion was making headlines nationwide (and even in one Parisian newspaper), and public support for the local militants was high.
Through reporters, the people of the Owens Valley were finally making
their plight known to the wider world, and their demands were clearly
articulated: Los Angeles must make amends to *all* of the people harmed
by its depredations in the valley. For the farmers and ranchers, the terms
were the same—either restore the agricultural viability of the properties remaining in valley hands, or else buy them all out at once, at a fair
price to be determined by an independent authority. But now the insurgents also sought reparations for valley town-dwellers whose businesses
had been hurt by the city's actions. According to the Wattersons, local
merchants, professionals, and members of the service trades had seen
drastic declines in their livelihoods as the city bought up properties and
their former occupants left the area, depressing the local economy. According to one calculation, merchants in Bishop had seen drops of over
50 percent in their volume of business. To compensate for these losses,

the valleyites were now demanding a total of $12 million, a figure that included $5.5 million in reparations and another $6.5 million for the purchase of all town properties by the city.

It was an extravagant sum, and yet the general public outside Los Angeles—moved by news stories about closing schools, unemployed laborers, and struggling general stores in the valley—was proving sympathetic. Even some of the L.A. newspapers were expressing solidarity with what they called "a depressed pioneer community." According to the *Los Angeles Daily News*, "the city can afford to be liberal in a settlement with these pioneers, whose work of half a century it will undo."

Unfortunately for the occupiers of the Alabama Gates, Governor Richardson ultimately refused to send the militia to Lone Pine, denying them the publicity coup they wanted. But he did agree to dispatch State Engineer W. F. McClure to the valley to conduct a special investigation into the valleyites' claims. Meanwhile an organization of L.A. bankers (known unmemorably as the Los Angeles Clearing House Association) rushed in where the Chamber of Commerce feared to tread. Worried that the standoff would go on indefinitely unless the city made some goodwill gesture, the bankers' association offered to mediate the dispute between valley residents and the city water department—but only if the unlawful occupation of the Alabama Gates ended immediately. It was a well-timed offer. Now in its fourth day, the valley's act of civil disobedience was losing momentum. And so, after a final barbecue to which all residents of the Owens Valley (even employees of the city water department) were invited, the insurgents set the machinery in motion to close the gates once again, stopping the roaring cascade down the spillway and restoring the full flow of water to the aqueduct. Then they peacefully dispersed, ending the four-day crisis. But they left with a caveat. "If the Clearing House [Association] fails to keep faith," Sheriff Collins warned, "I look for hell to pop."

For Mulholland, the important thing was that "his" water (minus the ongoing illegal diversions perpetrated by certain groups in the valley) was once again flowing toward Los Angeles. The proposed figure for reparations struck the Chief as both unjustified and ridiculously high, but ultimately the decision on whether to pay would belong to the public service commissioners, not to him. His job was to make sure the city had enough water to continue growing, which he did by resuming his unpublicized purchases of properties and water rights while the negotiations dragged on. Hoping to relieve the "hysteria" that had gripped the water department during the Alabama Gates incident, he also set out to build enough reservoir capacity around L.A. to ensure that any future aggressions by the Owens Valley extremists would not significantly threaten the city's supply.

His immediate goal was to build reservoirs enough to hold a full one-year supply of water for the city at its current size, and to do it as quickly as possible. A small reservoir in the Hollywood Hills was completed in 1925, and two more were planned for Tinemaha and San Gabriel. But the key element in his plan was a dam in the San Francisquito Canyon northwest of the city, where the terrain and lack of settled population would allow a much larger reservoir to exist. Mulholland had originally intended to build a small hydroelectric dam at this location, but that was before the events at the Alabama Gatehouse. Now he moved to build a 175-foot-high concrete dam in the remote canyon above Santa Clarita. In his haste, and with a characteristic confidence in his own abilities to match any challenge, he broke ground without extensive consultation with geological experts. While already pouring concrete at the site, he decided to make the dam twenty feet higher than originally planned, so that the reservoir behind it could hold as much as 38,000 acre-feet of water. That way, by his calculations, the city's needs could be supplied for months if necessary, no matter what disruptions the Owens Valley vigilantes might cook up.

Mulholland's concerns proved to be well founded, because matters in the valley did not improve. The L.A. bankers association, after some half-hearted attempts to negotiate a solution, abandoned their efforts, leading many to conclude that their promise to intervene had been merely a ploy to end the Alabama Gates occupation. In the spring of 1925, the valley got at least some good news when the California legislature—after an intense lobbying effort by valley interests—passed a bill making cities legally responsible for damages to business or property values caused by water diversions. Valley landowners quickly put together claims for several million dollars in damages—but the water board would not budge. *So sue us,* they essentially responded; any claims that held up in court would be paid. But since any such effort would involve a too-long, too-expensive legal challenge, the frustrating stalemate continued.

As more individual landowners succumbed to financial pressures and sold their properties to the city, their diehard neighbors felt only more bitter and betrayed. Some resorted again to dynamite. In April 1926, a city well near Bishop was blown up; in May, a ten-foot hole was blasted in the aqueduct wall near the Alabama Gates. The city hired a corps of Pinkerton private detectives to move into the valley to spy on possible conspirators. Then, in response to a rumored plan to attack the Hai-wee Reservoir, city representative Ed Leahey fortified the entire area. "It would be a terrible situation if you sent men with rifles to Haiwee," he told the alleged attackers through an intermediary, "because I've got three machine guns here."

By early 1927, the city's patience had run out. In a March advertisement placed in the Bishop newspapers, the water board set a May 1 deadline for purchases of valley properties. Until that day, the city would buy any land offered at appraised prices (considered far too low by the landowners); after that day, the deal would be off the table. Ed Leahey, who knew that ongoing negotiations were the only thing preventing all-out rebellion in the valley, disapproved of this ultimatum. "If you do that," he told the board, "they'll start dynamiting again."

But the board was adamant. So, too, were the valley diehards, who proceeded to ignore the deadline. Five days after it passed, the city added fuel to their fury by formally denying any claims for reparations. For many in the valley this was the final indignity. In the *Owens Valley Herald*, editor Harry Glasscock made no effort to hide his anger: The aqueduct "would run red with human blood," he predicted, "before this trouble was settled."

~

When the 1926 "Municipal Progress Edition" of the *Los Angeles Chronicle* appeared on newsstands in late 1925, its mainstream, mostly white, mostly middle-class readers could perhaps be excused for thinking that all was right in the great metropolis they called home. Like most documents that the city's establishment boosters had been putting out for over a half-century, the special edition presented an overwhelmingly positive vision of the city's present and future, emphasizing the twin gospels of growth and economic prosperity that would continue to propel Los Angeles along the road to greatness. Under headlines like "FOREIGN TRADE GAIN SURPASSES ALL HOPE," "LOS ANGELES TO BE MILLION BALE PORT," and "NOTHING THE MATTER WITH LOS ANGELES," reports of the city's rapid progress were glowing. Statistics about building permits, local bank deposits, and of course population growth were shattering records left and right; in article after article, sundry experts extolled the L.A. miracle and predicted more wondrous things ahead.

"Los Angeles is, in more ways than one, reminiscent of the Arabian Nights and Aladdin's Lamp," wrote one financial journalist. "The desert has been rubbed and, presto!, a great city has sprung up. Gleaming in its whiteness. Utterly new. Reared so swiftly that one wonders at the substantiability [*sic*] of its masonry." Another expert, an easterner identified as "one of the biggest bankers and utility operators in America," had nothing but praise for the city's potential: "The East doesn't question for a moment the great future of Los Angeles. There are undeveloped riches right under your nose [that] you don't even suspect today."

Of course, the city's riches to date also got their fair share of attention. An article about Hollywood ("HUNDRED MILLION SPENT BY PICTURE INDUSTRY IN L.A.") outlined the contribution of the film business. "It gives employment to thousands of persons, most of whom are good spenders, and the money finds its way quickly into general circulation," the article reported. What's more, "the business has become more stabilized as it has reached higher levels and has expressed more noble ideas. . . . Southern California is appreciative of the motion picture industry not only because of the payrolls it maintains and the other lines of business which it encourages by its extensive patronage, but [also] because of the great advertising value which attends the showing of California scenes all over the world." As for the future of this lucrative business, "Further expansion of the film industry is as certain as the further growth of the United States."

Elsewhere in the special edition, the *Chronicle* celebrated the role of religion and spirituality in the city's growth, with a full-page profile of Aimee Semple McPherson under the title "THE HOUSE THAT GOD BUILT." "People from all parts of the world come to the beautiful Angelus Temple at Echo Park to hear this inspired young Evangelist," the piece read. "The weekly average attendance is 40,000 to 50,000. . . . As the sunshine and beauty of Los Angeles attracts to itself people from all over the world, so does the charm and magnetism of Aimee Semple McPherson draw to herself throngs which are phenomenal." Special praise was heaped on the church's charitable work in the city, and on the evangelist's efforts to spread the word far beyond the borders of Los Angeles through her magazine publications and radio broadcasts. "Mrs. McPherson," the article claimed, "has spoken by pulpit, radio, and pen to more people than any living woman." Her message amounted to an "endeavor to spread the Gospel by the sunshine route"—a route that fortunately brought her tens of thousands of followers to the doorstep of Los Angeles, California.

Prime real estate in the Municipal Progress Edition was devoted to water, for, as *Chronicle* publisher R. S. Sparks rather superfluously pointed out in his editor's note, "No city can grow bigger than its water supply." To elucidate this topic the newspaper turned to Chief Engineer William Mulholland himself. In a piece entitled "HOW BIG WILL LOS ANGELES GROW?" Mulholland laid out the situation in simple terms: "Southern California and Los Angeles have just started to grow," he predicted. "In every section of the world, people are turning their attention to this section of the country. They are coming to our city in ever-increasing numbers—and will continue to come as long as there is water enough to go 'round."

How much water *was* there to "go 'round"? Mulholland had done the math: "With our Owens River aqueduct, Los Angeles now possesses a water supply sufficient to meet the needs of 2,000,000 people—no more. Already this city's population has passed the 1,000,000 mark and is marching steadily toward the second million at a rate of about 100,000 new residents a year." At that pace, he pointed out, the limit of population growth would be reached within a decade—dire news indeed, "unless we set about immediately the development of additional water supplies."

What followed was a full-throated pitch for Mulholland's latest cause célèbre: a brand-new aqueduct that would carry water from the distant Colorado River. A project that would dwarf the one he had undertaken a generation earlier, the new aqueduct could potentially supply the city with five times the water it was currently receiving via the Owens River conduit. "A fraction of the water that each year is wasted by [the Colorado] river into the Gulf of California," he wrote, "would be enough to meet the requirements of 10,000,000 people in Los Angeles and neighboring cities." The project would require construction by the U.S. government of an enormous dam at Boulder Canyon, but according to Mulholland's surveys, building the aqueduct to bring that water to L.A. "would be no more difficult, from an engineering standpoint, than was the construction of the Owens River aqueduct." All that would be required to ensure the city's future was the civic will to undertake the project. Work for the Boulder Canyon dam, he concluded, "and you will be working for the day when a great new supply of water will come tumbling into our city to support prosperity and unlimited growth."

For readers of the *Los Angeles Chronicle*, then—and for all of those who likewise embraced the boosters' gospel of unlimited urban growth—there were few shadows on the image of their city's bright future. "It has not been necessary to draw upon the imagination in any degree," publisher Sparks averred in this overview, "to support the claim that Los Angeles must continue to be considered the 'White Spot' on the map of America's prosperity." No reference was made in the Municipal Progress Edition to any of the problems endemic to all large cities—crime, municipal corruption, urban sprawl, poverty, homelessness, or unemployment. Nor was attention paid to any of the social complexities that arise with a rapidly diversifying population. There were no barrios in this version of Los Angeles, no Chinatown, no black metropolis like the one that was just beginning to thrive around Central Avenue on the city's south side. Here, still, was the wealthy white man's version of the ideal city, where upward mobility was the only social goal and where technology could solve all problems. It was a city without losers—at least among those the establishment cared about. A city that never was, in other words, and—as would soon become all too clear—a city that never would be.

~

On May 27, 1927—three weeks after the L.A. City Council voted unanimously to deny all reparations claims in the Owens Valley—the California Water War entered its decisive final stage. Early that quiet Friday morning, ten armed men drove up to the repair house near the so-called No Name Siphon, where a piped stretch of the aqueduct passed through a deep canyon in a remote corner of the Mojave Desert. After subduing the two watchmen on duty, the saboteurs proceeded to string a line of explosives on top of the massive steel tube at its lowest point in the canyon. They then climbed the canyon wall to the place where an open conduit channeled the rushing water into the end of the sag pipe. Into the flow of water, they dropped a waterproof device containing a small explosive with a lit fuse. They waited as the container sped down the pipe toward the much larger cache of dynamite below.

After a few moments, a massive explosion shook the canyon, sending up a geyser of rock, water, and twisted steel. The enormous pipe ruptured catastrophically, imploding like a flattened straw and spewing the entire flow of aqueduct water across the arid canyon floor. Having accomplished their task, the men returned to their cars and sped off, leaving the two watchmen looking on helplessly as four hundred second-feet of water turned the canyon into, as one observer put it, "a young Mississippi flowing out over the desert."

By the end of the day, Mulholland and Harvey Van Norman had arrived on the scene and were overseeing a crew of some 150 men clearing up the damage. Because 450 feet of new pipe would have to be special-ordered, repairs of this most damaging assault on the aqueduct so far would take almost three weeks to complete (at a cost of over fifty thousand dollars). But Mulholland assured Angelenos that, thanks to the recent completion of the St. Francis Dam, the city would suffer no shortage of water in the interim. When asked by the press to comment on the dynamiters, he growled that he could not do so "without using unprintable words."

Within hours, the saboteurs struck again. The night after the No Name Siphon bombing, a second explosion took out another sixty feet of pipe near the city's power plant at Big Pine Creek. A week later, near

Cottonwood Creek twelve miles south of Lone Pine, yet another bomb destroyed 150 feet of concrete conduit near another city powerhouse. Incensed, Mulholland and other city officials assembled a small army of six hundred reservists at city police headquarters to be sent north, followed by a contingent of detectives armed with tommy guns and orders to "shoot to kill" anyone posing a threat to the aqueduct. Another hundred armed troops, mostly World War I veterans, were dispatched a few days later, while the city offered a reward for information leading to the conviction of any of the culprits. But the bombings continued—another on June 19, yet another on June 25.

"A condition of civil war exists between Los Angeles, as represented by its officials, and the people of the Owens Valley," a story in the *Owens Valley Herald* reported in early June. Members of both sides armed themselves for battle. Some fifty sawed-off shotguns and rifles were issued to aqueduct employees, while valley locals ordered sixty Winchester carbines from the Watterson brothers' hardware store in Bishop. Something like martial law prevailed in the valley near the aqueduct, as searchlights swept the access roads at night looking for suspicious activity and guards stopped all unknown vehicles on the main road to search them for weapons.

Meanwhile the war for public attention raged on as well. The new bombing campaign received newspaper coverage nationwide, while Owens Valley publications like the *Herald*, the *Inyo Register*, and the *Inyo Independent* (along with the always-anti-Mulholland *Los Angeles Record*) inundated readers with stories of farmers committing suicide, ranchers going bankrupt, and townspeople forced to relocate. According to these reports, all of this was happening because of the "unscrupulous officials" of the L.A. Water Board and its "evil serpent, bringing ruin"—that is, the aqueduct. The city fired back with propaganda of its own, publishing a pamphlet called "The Dynamite Holdup," condemning attempts by "the lawless element of the valley" to extort money from the city of Los Angeles through violent blackmail. Just who was winning this war of words was hard to say. Sympathy for the valleyites waned as the spree of domestic terrorism went on, but many observers were also souring on the water czar they had lionized for so many years. The *L.A. Times* had harsh criticism for Mulholland's handling of the bombing crisis, which had already cost the city some $250,000 in damage; the *L.A. Record* even called on him to resign.

The campaign of "shooting the duck" (as the jeering bombers called their attacks on "Old Bill's Aqua-Duck") went on. By mid-July 1927, the aqueduct had been bombed no fewer than ten times. At this point, California's newly elected governor, Clement C. Young, decided to step in. Declaring the bombings a matter to be handled by the U.S. government, he made an official request to President Calvin Coolidge to intervene. The president dispatched a force of uniformed federal officers to guard the aqueduct, supported by another team of investigators from the Pinkerton Agency. The Owens Valley extremists had at last turned their complaints—quite literally—into a federal issue.

But what brought the end of the California Water War was neither the presence of federal agents, nor the outright militarization of the valley, nor any triumph in the propaganda campaign by either side. What lost the war was financial scandal, and the valleyites had no one to blame but themselves. In late July 1927 city representative Ed Leahey, hoping to find some evidence that the Watterson brothers were financing the bombings, managed to obtain a financial statement of the brothers' bank in Independence. The statement proved incriminating enough to generate an investigation by the California State bank superintendent, Will C. Wood. On August 3, Wood's investigator arrived at the doorstep of the Inyo County Bank for a surprise audit. What he discovered was stunning. Not only had the Wattersons been channeling funds to the bombers; they had obtained those funds through financial fraud of the very worst kind. According to the investigators' findings, the brothers had been selling securities owned by depositors without authorization. They had also failed to cancel loans and mortgages that had been paid off months earlier, instead diverting the proceeds into their own financially strapped commercial endeavors and falsifying state banking reports to cover their tracks. In short, the Wattersons had defrauded their friends and neighbors in the valley, at least in part, in order to keep their own businesses afloat.

Of course, the brothers claimed that they had been acting for the good of the people of the Owens Valley, to protect local landowners' interests against the city's depredations. But the fact of their misdeeds—

and the total of some $2.3 million in missing funds—could not be denied. At noon on August 4, the doors of the five Watterson bank branches in the valley were closed. The brothers were arrested and charged with thirty-six counts of embezzlement and fraud.

The failure of the Wattersons' bank proved to be the undoing of all organized resistance to the city in the Owens Valley. Virtually every remaining landowner in the valley had had a mortgage and other accounts with the Wattersons, and many lost their life savings when the institutions closed. "The people of the valley are left in the worst possible condition," declared one attorney working on the brothers' bankruptcy case. "They have absolutely nothing on which to live. Their every penny, in one form or another, went into the Watterson coffers, and the collapse of the Wattersons has left them penniless." None were more disillusioned than the other leaders of the Owens Valley resistance—in particular, Harry Glasscock, editor of the *Owens Valley Herald*. After writing a bitter editorial disavowing the Wattersons and apologizing for his long-term support of them, the ruined newsman removed himself from valley affairs. Several months later, he killed himself in an L.A. hotel room.

The denouement of the Owens Valley conflict occurred quickly. In November, after a brief trial, the Watterson brothers were found guilty on all charges and sentenced to ten years each in the state penitentiary in San Quentin (they would be paroled in 1933 but never returned to the valley). Later that month a valley resident named Perry Sexton, one of seven people arrested in the bombing investigation, confessed to actively participating in the sabotage campaign. His judge—a local justice of the peace based in Bishop—rejected his confession, however, and ended up releasing Sexton and the six other suspects. No one else was ever arrested for the bombings.

So the California Water War was over, and the ever-more-powerful city of Los Angeles had won. By the beginning of the 1930s, the city would own over 90 percent of the water rights in the valley and almost as much of the real estate. William Mulholland, the aging but triumphant general, was trying to be gracious in victory. During the conflict he had taken a hard line against the bombers. ("Justice?" he barked to a reporter when asked what justice he thought was due the Owens Valley ranchers. "Why, there are not enough trees in the valley to give the bastards justice!") But by early 1928 he was feeling conciliatory. "Now, perhaps," he announced, "the time has arrived when the city and the valley will be permitted to join hands in peace and mutual helpfulness." Given that the local Owens Valley economy had all but collapsed by this point, the comment seems more than a little disingenuous. And Mulholland's optimism would in any case prove to be misplaced. Within a few short weeks, in fact, L.A.'s water system—and Mulholland personally—would be facing the biggest debacle in its history.

# CHAPTER FOURTEEN
# A Sound Proposition

*Gloria Swanson in the 1920s*

The everyday business of Los Angeles all but ground to a halt on the morning of April 20, 1925, to mark the equivalent of a citywide holiday: the return of Gloria Swanson to Hollywood. Not that the actress had been gone for so long; it was only two years since she'd left town to make pictures in New York and Europe. But whereas she'd departed the city as a regular Hollywood star, she was returning as an American icon. She was now, in short, the single most popular female celebrity in the world ("with the possible exception of my friend Mary Pickford," as Swanson modestly admitted).

The difference had been two years of sensational headlines worldwide. After shooting a few Paramount films with director Allan Dwan in New York (including the classic *Manhandled*, a huge box office success), she'd sailed to Europe to make a film version of Victorien Sardou's play *Madame Sans-Gêne*. While on the set in Paris, she'd fallen in love with her translator, a handsome but impoverished nobleman named Henri, the Marquis de la Falaise de la Coudraye. A storybook wedding ensued (Swanson having quickly finalized a divorce from her estranged second husband), after which the brand-new marquise fell deathly ill. That her indisposition was caused by a botched abortion (necessitated by a premarital dalliance with Henri that would have violated the morals clause of her Paramount contract and quite likely ruined her career) was known to virtually no one, not even the marquis himself. The world knew only the Hollywood version of the story: a midwestern army brat grows up to be a movie star and ultimately a French marquise, only to have her charmed life nearly snatched away by a mysterious illness. It made for a powerful fantasy. As Swanson herself put it, "Suddenly I was not only Cinderella who had married the prince, but also Lazarus who had risen from the dead."

She was therefore welcomed back to the city that had created her with unprecedented fanfare. Her specially chartered Paramount train was met at the Los Angeles station by a teeming horde of her fans, along with a welcoming committee that included, besides Mayor George Cryer and a contingent of city officials, scores of the biggest names in Hollywood—Mary Pickford, Douglas Fairbanks, Charlie Chaplin, D. W. Griffith, Cecil B. DeMille, Rudolph Valentino, William S. Hart, Bebe Daniels, Mack Sennett, Francis X. Bushman, Hoot Gibson, Ford Sterling, Chester Conklin, and many more. "Two bands were playing," she recalled in her autobiography, "and we could see troops of policemen on horseback, Sid Grauman's theater usherettes on white ponies, a red carpet ten yards wide, and a huge platform decorated with flowers and bunting and signs of welcome."

After a few speeches from the dignitaries on hand, the marquis and marquise were led down the red carpet to an open white Rolls-Royce waiting at the curb. A platoon of motorcycle patrolmen cleared traffic as the white Rolls led a parade of similar automobiles through the spectator-choked streets—first to the Paramount studio at Sunset and Vine (where studio employees had been given the morning off to cheer and throw flowers at Swanson's feet), and then on to her luxurious mansion in Beverly Hills. There the newlyweds were given some time to unpack and prepare for that evening's premiere of *Madame Sans-Gêne* at Sid Grauman's Million Dollar Theater in downtown Los Angeles.

The madness only worsened at the premiere that night. "We caused a tremendous traffic jam near the tunnel on Third Street," Swanson recalled. "The motorcycle cops told us the streets were filled with people for ten blocks in every direction. There was no way around them."

When they finally arrived at the theater, the house was already full to bursting. As Swanson entered—dressed in a clinging silver lamé gown—the orchestra struck up a rendition of "Home, Sweet Home." "People were standing and yelling like Indians," she wrote. "Women were throwing orchids in the aisle. I couldn't move." By the time the film started, after a welcoming speech by Jesse Lasky and more cheers and thrown flora, the crowds inside and outside the theater had become unmanageable. An usher pushed through the throngs to tell her that the police had requested that she and Henri leave immediately, for their own safety. They were rushed backstage to the rear door, where their limousine was waiting to take them home. Just as they were leaving, Cecil B. DeMille pulled her aside. DeMille—the director who more than any other had been responsible for making her what she was that night— summed up the phenomenon she had just experienced. Every star, he told her, every director, and the president of every studio in Los Angeles had come out to honor her. "Hollywood has paid you a tribute tonight," he said, "that has never been equaled."

And it was almost true. This was the new Hollywood, and Swanson was its new ideal. The kind of woman she portrayed—both on and off the screen—represented the evolving sensibility of the 1920s. She was independent, fun-loving, knowing about sex (though hardly immune to romance), consistently fashionable, not afraid to drink and smoke with the boys, and game for just about anything. Gone were the innocent, pinafore-clad Pollyannas and Sunnybrook Farm Rebeccas of the early Hollywood era. As *Photoplay* had recently put it, "Mary Pickford now acknowledges that the crown has passed to Gloria Swanson. It's the popular decree written in the indisputable letters of the box-office." The new female icon in Hollywood was a more glamorous and sophisticated woman of the world—someone whom men could desire and women could envy and emulate, while at the same time considering her "the absolutely last word in chic."

That Swanson had become a marquise was particularly felicitous, for the sophistication of the new Hollywood had a definite Continental flavor to it—not least because the town was full of Europeans in the 1920s. The world war had left the film industries of many countries in a shambles, and even those that had remained healthy (most notably Germany's, which experienced something of a golden age in the Weimar years) could not match the salaries and production budgets on offer in the United States. As a result, Hollywood could poach European talent with impunity. Soon the movie capital was swarming with foreign actors, directors, and technicians, some of them even aristocrats. "We had counts and princes sousing film in the labs," cameraman Karl Brown recalled. Actors like Pola Negri, Greta Garbo, Emil Jannings, Lars Hanson, and Conrad Veidt; directors like Ernst Lubitsch, Victor

Sjöström (a.k.a. Seastrom), Jacques Feyder, Alexander Korda, and F. W. Murnau—these were the sensibilities giving movies a new cosmopolitan veneer. Lubitsch in particular revolutionized the depiction of life and love on the screen, creating a series of worldly-wise sex comedies (like *The Marriage Circle* and *Kiss Me Again*) that displayed what came to be known as the "Lubitsch touch"—"that naughty twinkle of Continental wit," as one writer has called it. These were an altogether more sophisticated product than even the risqué Hollywood comedies of the early 1920s, with a new emphasis on sex as a pastime rather than an earnest endeavor between a woman and a man destined to become her husband.

Even the genre films put out by Hollywood in the 1920s demonstrated new sophistication and complexity. Westerns were no longer simple horse operas in which the bad guys met their comeuppance in two, four, or six reels. Now the big studios were making sweeping cowboy epics like James Cruze's *The Covered Wagon* and John Ford's *The Iron Horse*—with big stars, big stories, and big budgets to match. Similarly, comedies had grown up from the days of slapdash, improvised productions consisting largely of pratfalls and other chaotic hijinks. Hollywood comedies were now more likely to be character-driven and carefully planned, with the rise of comedians like Harold Lloyd, Buster Keaton, and Harry Langdon (not to mention the mature Charlie Chaplin, who was so compulsively painstaking that he was now spending two or three years to make a single picture). Adventure movies, too, had come of age. Douglas Fairbanks productions like *Robin Hood* and *The Thief of Baghdad* were huge cinematic events, with million-dollar price tags and state-of-the-art special effects that left even jaded audiences gaping in wonder.

But the dominant figure in 1920s Hollywood was someone now known more for spectacle and soap opera than for European sophistication or a subtle grasp of character and story: Cecil B. DeMille. While he did direct a number of proto-Lubitsch-style sex comedies in the immediate postwar years (*Male and Female*, *Why Change Your Wife?*, *The Affairs of Anatol*), he had since turned to a genre that had been out of fashion more or less since *Intolerance*. DeMille (whom the astute screenwriter Adela Rogers St. Johns later described as "one hundred percent cynical") realized that American audiences liked their sex and sin with a patina of high-minded morality, especially in the wake of the epidemic of

Hollywood scandal in the early 1920s. So in 1923, he made a manner of biblical epic called *The Ten Commandments*. Unlike his later sound film of the same title, which was a straightforward dramatization of the life of Moses, this *Ten Commandments* used an elaborate fifty-minute biblical prologue to frame a modern story about a building contractor who manages to violate all ten shalt-nots over the course of the film. It was a brilliant ploy, since it allowed DeMille to purvey his usual cinematic titillation ("See your favorite stars committing your favorite sins" was the ad line for one of his earlier films) under the guise of Bible-beating rectitude. Audiences responded with enthusiasm. *The Ten Commandments* grossed over $4.1 million (against a negative cost of $1.5 million), solidifying DeMille's position at the very top of the industry.

It was a role DeMille played in grand style. His office at Paramount was more like a baronial residence than a business place, decorated with heavy old English furniture, Gothic stained-glass windows, and lavish rugs made from the skins of polar bears, buffalo, and Siberian wolves. (His brother William once claimed that he never knew whether he was entering "Westminster Abbey or the sitting room of Eric the Red.") On the set or on location, DeMille acted like an autocratic general leading a military campaign, always fitted out in his trademark jodhpurs, helmet, and riding crop, keeping himself well insulated from the hoi polloi of his cast and crew. Once, when the actors playing Moses and Aaron in *The Ten Commandments* couldn't get in to see the director, one of them buttonholed a passing assistant director and pleaded, "Just say that Moses and Aaron are waiting to see God!"

With their million-dollar salaries and twenty-four-hour publicity machines, celebrity directors like DeMille and megastars like Swanson were now the most visible faces of the movie industry. And yet there was never any doubt who were the real bosses in this new Hollywood: the executive producers, representing the studio heads and the moneymen behind them. Under the leadership of Will Hays, who, according to the *Wall Street Journal* in 1922, "want[ed] to do for the workers in the motion picture industry what Henry Ford has done for his automobile workers," the MPPDA finally turned the movie business into a traditional industry. Hays innovations like Central Casting (which eliminated the swarm of would-be extras gathering daily at every studio's gates) and the Studio Basic Agreement (regulating relations between producers and the trade unions) reorganized Hollywood along sound business lines. The result was a smoother-running, more reliable moneymaking machine. What cars were for Detroit, movies had become for Los Angeles, employing some 35,000 of the city's residents and pumping paychecks totaling some $65 million into its local economy. L.A., in turn, showed its appreciation. The city that had once scorned its early movie factories now regarded them as a source of pride, turning the opening of each new studio compound into a civic celebration not unlike the opening of Mulholland's aqueduct back in 1913. For many people both in and beyond the city, "Hollywood" and "Los Angeles" had become virtually synonymous.

~

D. W. Griffith's "Mamaroneck Interlude"—his four-year experiment in independent movie production on the East Coast, far from the pressures of this new Hollywood—had turned out to be a mixed success. Yes, there had been a few big winners. *Way Down East*, perhaps the best film of his post-*Intolerance* years, proved to be hugely popular with audiences, not least because of an intensely suspenseful climax in which Lillian Gish is rescued from swirling ice floes just before tumbling over a roaring waterfall. That Griffith had turned what even Gish called "a horse-and-buggy melodrama" into his biggest moneymaker since *The Birth of a Nation* was something of a miracle, and a propitious start to his new endeavor as an independent producer. Then came *Orphans of the Storm*, an elaborate costume epic of the French Revolution, for which Griffith had re-created much of the grandeur and pageantry of his best work of the 1910s. But although *Orphans*, like *Way Down East*, was well received by the critics and did excellent box office, it simply cost too much to be very profitable in the long term. And even the favorable reviews of these movies took note of the old master's "dated conventions" (especially his obsession with virtuous damsels in distress) and Victorian-tinged sentimentality.

Then there were the misfires—the smaller films Griffith churned out between major projects to make money to run the studio. Reviewing 1923's *The White Rose*, the story of a young Southern seminarian who impregnates a poor orphan girl in Louisiana, James Quirk of *Photoplay* expressed the impatience felt by many in the industry. "Isn't it about time that Mr. Griffith made a picture that would go far toward maintaining his title of the Master?" Quirk wrote. "That reputation, which is not so secure as formerly, may slip further unless he comes back into the ring and upholds his championship."

As if in response to this challenge, Griffith's next movie attempted to recapture some of the old American history magic of his most famous film. In the summer of 1923, Will Hays had come to him with a proposal. The Arbuckle, Taylor, and other scandals of recent years had taken a toll on Hollywood's reputation. Still fearing a move toward censorship and formal regulation of the industry by outsiders, Hays figured that a high-minded historical film about the American Revolution might be just what Hollywood needed to assert its clean, all-American bona fides. And who better to take it on than the creator of *The Birth of a Nation*? Working together with novelist Robert Chambers, Griffith settled on a story that would dramatize such iconic events as Paul Revere's ride, Nathan Hale's "One life to give for my country" speech, and George Washington's ordeal at Valley Forge. If such a production didn't redeem Hollywood (and Griffith) in the eyes of the public, nothing would.

Financing the film proved to be the typical Griffith nightmare. The director exceeded his budget constraints several times over, shooting an ambitious extravaganza that ultimately ran fourteen reels—as long as *Intolerance*—before substantial last-minute cutting down to twelve. To make the film he wanted, he had to improvise a Rube Goldberg contraption of loans and liens with a bevy of investors. It eventually became clear to him that unless the resulting film (which appeared under the title *America*) was a massive hit, his entire independent production company would be in jeopardy.

*America* was not a massive hit. Reviews were mixed, and receipts at the box office turned out to be anemic. With all of his assets under liens from various banks, Griffith was forced to sell his Mamaroneck studio. No one faulted the picture for lack of patriotism or high feeling—and in this respect it served Will Hays's purposes well—but for Griffith the project was a financial disaster. His salary for years to come would be garnished to pay back his company's investors.

Never one to let an opportunity pass him by, Adolph Zukor stepped in to pick up the distressed property that was David Wark Griffith. Zukor needed another big-name director in the Paramount stable to serve as leverage in his dealings with Cecil B. DeMille, whose spending habits were getting out of control. Zukor reasoned that whenever DeMille's demands for a particular project became unreasonable, he could threaten to turn the project over to the other legendary director in his employ. To entice Griffith aboard, Zukor first arranged secretly to guarantee a loan that would allow the director to make the last film he owed United Artists under his existing distribution contract (*Isn't Life Wonderful*, which turned out to be one of his best pictures, though hardly a commercial blockbuster). Then, in July 1924, Zukor contracted with Griffith to make four new films for Paramount at their Astoria studio. In full-page ads that appeared in all of the trade newspapers, Zukor announced his coup to the world. "There is a point in the life of every great artist," the ad copy ran, "when, if he is free from cares, he can produce his greatest works. . . . So it is with that master director David Wark Griffith, who is at work on a series of Paramount Pictures. In freedom from all worry and with the resources of the world's foremost film organization at his disposal, D. W. Griffith is now in the golden age of his art."

These were fine words indeed, but as Lillian Gish later remarked, "Behind the headlines and publicity releases I sensed the real story: D. W. had lost his gamble for independence."

The projects Zukor gave him were indeed not ones he'd likely have chosen on his own. Designed to be modest commercial films, they turned out forgettable, despite the fact that two of them featured a talented vaudeville and Broadway actor, new to film, named W. C. Fields. The first, a circus tale called *Sally of the Sawdust*, was pleasant enough, though hobbled by conventions (the poor orphan girl who discovers her wealthy parentage) that seemed fusty in the fast and irreverent 1920s. Reviewing the second—*That Royle Girl*, a Chicago-set gangster film (which, perhaps fortunately, is one of the few Griffith films lost to posterity)—a new publication called *The New Yorker* could barely conceal its disdain: "Mr. David Wark Griffith, saintly showman . . . is indisputably the grandmaster of moralistic-melodramatic balderdash. He has the corner on trickle, mush, and trash and automatically is out of our set."

Even the director's gentlemanly offscreen persona was wearing thin. More than one friend noted that the suits he wore were at least a decade out of fashion, and his comments to the press about the scanty attire of modern women reeked of Victorian starchiness. And though he retained a talented and fanatically loyal troupe of actors (including Mae Marsh and Lionel Barrymore), he lost his favorite leading lady. Lillian Gish, who could infuse even Griffith's most moth-eaten female characters with gravitas and vitality, was making movies for other directors now—at Griffith's suggestion, after he rather gallantly told her he could no longer afford to pay her what she was worth. She had been replaced in lead roles by a young woman named Carol Dempster (also reputedly Griffith's lover), a competent actress but nobody's idea of a box office draw.

Zukor came to regret his decision to employ the Father of Hollywood. For Griffith's third contracted film, he gave the director *The Sorrows of Satan*, based on a popular title by the bestselling Victorian novelist Marie Corelli. The story of a struggling writer tempted by Satan to abandon his lofty ideals in exchange for worldly success, *Sorrows* was given a generous budget (which Griffith, of course, exceeded) and the gift of Adolphe Menjou playing the title demon with his trademark urbane style. But Zukor was unhappy with the first cut; he took the film out of Griffith's hands to be recut by another director—producing a version Zukor liked even less than the original and for which he still somehow blamed Griffith. The movie that ultimately reached the public was not terrible (its dark, brooding look clearly influenced by German expressionism), but audiences failed to respond, and it became a notable bomb at the box office. Fed up with the "great artist" he had signed up just two years before, Zukor negotiated a premature end to Griffith's Paramount contract and cut the director loose.

Understandably bitter, Griffith did what he could to repair his damaged reputation. Hoping to remind Hollywood of his former glories, he gave interviews to the press lamenting the crass industrialization of the film industry and claiming credit for innovations (including the fade-out, which was actually cameraman Billy Bitzer's idea, and soft-focus photography, generally attributed to Hendrik Sartov) that he insisted would have been earning him millions had he patented them. Finally, he entered into an agreement to make films for Universal back in Los Angeles—a rather dramatic comedown, given Universal's reputation at this time as a hack factory. ("In those days," film historian Kevin Brownlow has written, "Universal compared to Paramount about as favorably as the YMCA compares to the Waldorf.")

In May 1927 Griffith returned west to the site of his greatest triumphs, checking in to a suite at the Biltmore Hotel in downtown L.A. Perhaps fortunately, the contract with Universal didn't pan out, and Griffith ended up signing again with United Artists, to work as a hireling for the company he had helped found some eight years earlier. This relieved his immediate anxieties, but he still had a formidable challenge ahead of him. As Lillian Gish observed, "To D.W., the new Hollywood [of 1927] was a strange land." Bigger, more regimented, and even more bottom-line-oriented than it had been when he left eight years earlier, the industry increasingly prioritized showcasing big stars—something Griffith never liked to do—and delivering a kind of reliable, ironic, sexually sophisticated entertainment that had never been the director's forte. "I believe deep down in their hearts every man and woman is clean [and] wants to see clean things," he once told a reporter. "I refuse to produce an underwear ad and label it a motion picture."

So Hollywood had changed, while D. W. Griffith had not. And the fact that Hollywood was about to change again—in a way that would rock the industry to its foundations—would not make the director's attempt at rehabilitation any easier.

~

The idea of talking motion pictures had existed long before the new technology's watershed year of 1926–27. As far back as 1891, Thomas Edison had considered trying to synchronize sound and moving image by combining his 1877 invention, the phonograph, with his brand-new invention, the Kinetoscope. But he quickly abandoned the idea as impractical. Others were more persistent. A series of inventions over the next two decades—going by names like Chronophone, Synchroscope, and Cameraphone—attempted to achieve at least the illusion of synchronicity by playing phonograph records and movies simultaneously. But these efforts were invariably doomed by exhibition problems; audiences laughed derisively when the sound (which had to be played at the front of the theater) and images (which had to be projected from the back) failed to match up perfectly. In 1913 Edison picked up the idea again, introducing the Kinetophone, which linked a movie projector to a phonograph with a silk cord running from the front to the back of the theater via a series of pulleys. This was an improvement—allowing for better image-and-sound synchronization during exhibition—but poor-quality recorded sound and inadequate amplification proved insurmountable problems. "The talking, instead of enhancing the picture, simply annoys," *Variety* wrote after one demonstration in Chicago. "The general verdict was that the Edison pictures are an out-and-out flop."

In the wake of these failures, it became conventional industry wisdom to say that sound movies were an idea whose time would probably never arrive. Griffith himself, who had experimented with sound sequences in his 1921 film *Dream Street*, certainly thought so. "It will never be possible to synchronize the voice with the pictures," he wrote in 1924. "I am quite positive that when a century has passed, all thought of our so-called speaking pictures will have been abandoned."

But engineers kept trying—in particular, one unsung inventor from Iowa named Lee de Forest. De Forest realized that problems of synchronization would disappear if the sounds and images could be recorded on the same medium. He decided to bypass the phonograph disk and work on a method of recording sound directly onto celluloid, using a "needle of light" instead of the physical needle employed in phonograph recordings. By 1924, he had developed a viable sound-on-film system, and produced a series of so-called Phonofilm shorts. These films—of vaudeville stars doing comedy routines and politicians reading speeches—were played at theaters all around the country as extras to accompany traditional silent features. Audiences seemed to enjoy them, but since the sound quality was variable at best, most people regarded them as an amusing novelty.

Other engineers improved on the original sound-on-disk technology. Most notable were the engineers at Western Electric, who developed something they called the Vitaphone, for which sound was recorded on a circular, two-inch-thick waxlike platter made of metallic soap. Vitaphone established an early lead in sound technology, but there was no shortage of competition; by the mid-1920s, no fewer than five different sound systems were vying for primacy. Still, few in the movie industry seemed interested. When in 1925 Western Electric organized Vitaphone demonstrations for the heads of the major studios, the moguls were decidedly unimpressed. Zukor at Paramount called the technology "a gimmick," while at MGM Louis B. Mayer dismissed it as "a toy."

Two of the smaller studios, however—reasoning that they had little to lose and much to gain by an industry shake-up—were more receptive. Fox (a midrange studio at this time) and Warner Bros. (near the bottom and financially precarious) pursued sound technology while their more powerful competitors sat on the sidelines. Sam Warner was a particularly fervent believer, embracing Western Electric's Vitaphone system despite rabid opposition within his own company. He had to trick his brother Harry into even attending a Vitaphone demonstration—"I would never have gone," Harry later confessed, "because [talking pictures] had been made up to that time several times, and each was a failure." But Harry left the demonstration a convert. He agreed to let Sam have the money to create some Vitaphone musical shorts as well as a synchronized score (recorded by the New York Philharmonic) for an upcoming silent film version of *Don Juan*. When that program opened at the Warner Theatre in New York on August 6, 1926—with a sound introduction by none other than Will Hays—audiences loved it. "No single word," enthused the *New York Times*, "is quite adequate to suggest the amazing trial which man has at last achieved in making pictures talk naturally, sing enthrallingly, and play all manner of instruments as skillfully as if living beings were present instead of their shadows. . . . Uncanny!"

When the same program played in Los Angeles on October 27, at Grauman's Egyptian Theater on Hollywood Boulevard, the response was equally tumultuous. The premiere was a by-now-familiar gala event, with the biggest names in the industry (Chaplin, Pickford, Fairbanks, Garbo, Negri, Goldwyn, Keaton, and Lloyd, though not, interestingly, D. W. Griffith) in attendance. "The house applauded, cheered, and stamped with its feet," *Variety* reported. "Every claim made by [the Vitaphone's] promoters was substantiated." An ecstatic Sam Warner wired his brother in New York: "WE ARE SPELLBOUND. ALL OTHER OPENINGS LIKE KINDERGARTEN IN COMPARISON WITH TONIGHT. . . . MULTIPLY YOUR WILDEST IMAGINATION BY ONE THOUSAND—THAT'S IT."

Meanwhile William Fox was pursuing a sound-on-film system, a Vitaphone rival called Movietone, with equal vigor. A few months behind the Warner brothers in his plans, he hoped to use sound to bring successful stage plays to the screen. Until then, his crews made sound shorts to put before invited audiences in major cities. (One of them, a film of Charles Lindbergh taking off for Paris in the *Spirit of St. Louis*, started a craze for Movietone newsreels that would persist for decades.) Fox also pulled a silent feature, *What Price Glory*, from exhibition and reissued it with a synchronized score and limited sound sequences, to glowing reviews. The *Motion Picture Herald* was so impressed that it devoted a two-page spread to the Fox programs, complete with a careful explanation of the Movietone technology set out in layman's terms.

The success of these sound experiments felt threatening to many in the industry, and they expounded in the press on why talkies would never replace silents. "Instead of making the movies more real," sound dialogue "makes them less real," the old Hollywood journalist Henry Carr insisted. "The voice accentuates a fact that we sometimes forget— that movie characters are flat shadows on the wall." Carr also predicted that many "lovely girls" and "handsome sheiks" of the screen would never make the transition to talkies. "In real life," he wrote, "some of them talk like sick peacocks."

Many industry executives also worried that the language barrier created by sound would kill the foreign market for American films. Silent movies, after all, could easily be shown abroad by simply replacing the English-language intertitles, at very little additional cost to the studio. And switching to sound would require an enormous capital investment in new equipment by both the studios and the exhibitors; according to one estimate, the cost of installing the Vitaphone system in a single theater could run from $16,000 to $25,000. These obstacles, combined with the fact that Hollywood was making plenty of money with the status quo of making silent films, led many executives to insist that, as MGM's Irving Thalberg said to his wife one evening in 1927, "sound is a passing fancy. It won't last."

Yet the enthusiasm of the press and especially the public could not be ignored. Acting behind closed doors, representatives from Paramount, MGM, Universal, First National, and Producers Distributing Corporation agreed to test the competing systems for a year before mutually deciding on one version that all would then adopt, creating an industry standard. Even so, many executives were secretly hoping that talkies would indeed prove to be a fad, and that after the year of testing they could all go back to doing business as usual—silently.

Warner Bros., on the other hand, was moving full speed ahead with sound. The studio had long been planning a screen adaptation of Samson Raphaelson's play *The Jazz Singer*, now running on Broadway with star performer George Jessel playing the lead. Jessel had signed on to do the movie as well, but his contract had been written for a silent film. Now Warners, buoyed by the success of *Don Juan*, wanted to make *The Jazz Singer* as a talkie—the first full-length feature with extensive sound sequences, including both songs and dialogue. When Jessel heard this news, he demurred. He worried that a sound film would steal business from his touring version of the stage play. After a bitter argument with Jack Warner, the executive pulled Jessel off the picture and offered the part to another popular stage performer, one whose earlier Vitaphone musical short had proven a big hit. Al Jolson, though leery about taking on a project everyone agreed would constitute a big risk, signed up to do the picture.

Jolson walked into the Warner Bros. studio to start work in May 1927—the same month D. W. Griffith returned to Los Angeles from New York. Jolson would thus step into Hollywood history just as Griffith, wounded by his recent failures, would make his play to avoid stepping out of it.

# CHAPTER FIFTEEN

# The Missing Saint

*Sister McPherson and Kenneth Ormiston at KFSG*

Sister was doing it again—talking on the telephone during the Sunday service, in full view of the Angelus Temple congregation. Her mother had already spoken to her about this behavior. It was unseemly, Minnie Kennedy felt, for the spiritual leader of the Church of the Foursquare Gospel to be seen chatting away during choir performances and Bible readings, giggling like a schoolgirl. Especially since everyone in the congregation knew exactly whom she was talking to. The telephone beside her pulpit connected to the temple's radio booth, high up under the building's dome, where engineer Kenneth Ormiston oversaw the broadcast of services on radio station KFSG. During their frequent sound checks, Ormiston—a decidedly worldly, undevout man—was given to making droll observations about the goings-on in the temple, while Sister bantered back in a way that could be, and was, interpreted as coquettish. A group of church members had even written Kennedy a note of complaint about these exchanges. Given the excellent acoustics in the temple, every word Sister said to Ormiston, who was married with a small child at home, could be heard in parts of the balcony.

But this was what Aimee was like nowadays. Her extraordinary success over the past few years had apparently given her leave to be as headstrong and imprudent as she wished. Whereas she used to heed her mother's counsel, even when she didn't like it, now she pouted like a willful child when Minnie tried to warn her off some choice or behavior—and then went ahead and did whatever she liked.

The Ormiston connection was a particular point of contention between mother and daughter. Ormiston was an attractive and witty man; he treated Sister not as a prophet but as a woman to be teased and flirted with, and Aimee responded in kind. Ormiston's wife had already made her displeasure known, even hinting that her husband's relations with the evangelist might go beyond flirting. Any such suggestion would of course be disastrous if made public, especially in the current climate, after the L.A. press had turned against the Angelus Temple following the defection of the Santa Ana branch church in the summer of 1925. Mother, daughter, and church were all vulnerable, and an adultery scandal would do more damage than any of them could afford.

Minnie Kennedy therefore began working behind the scenes, making things as uncomfortable as possible for Ormiston in the hopes that he'd quit (since she knew that Aimee would never consent to his firing). In December 1925 she succeeded—the engineer tendered his resignation. Afterward Sister demonstrated her unhappiness in countless small ways, clashing with her mother about everything from her new haircut to the amount of money she was spending on her wardrobe.

Noticing Sister's new moodiness and distraction from the cause, one of her most ardent adherents—Rudolf Dunbar, the temple's choir chaplain—suggested that she take a break from preaching. He knew a Chicago-based evangelist, Paul Rader, who might be willing to come to Los Angeles and stand in for her for a few months as she vacationed. Sister liked this idea and began planning a trip to Europe and the Holy Land with her fifteen-year-old daughter, Roberta. On January 11, 1926, the two of them—financed by special collections from the Angelus Temple congregation—set out from the railroad station in L.A., where Rader and thousands of Sister's followers gathered to bid her a lively, rose-strewn farewell. The travelers' first destination would be England and Ireland, where they would visit with members of Robert Semple's family in the old country. From there they'd move on to continental Europe before heading to the Middle East.

Even thousands of miles from L.A., however, Sister could not avoid trouble. Soon after the evangelist's departure, Mrs. Ormiston contacted Minnie Kennedy to report that her husband was missing; she hinted that she intended to divorce him, naming Sister McPherson as co-respondent. Then a temple staff member came to Kennedy with rumors that a Hollywood scandal sheet was preparing a report claiming that Kenneth Ormiston was traveling with Sister in Europe. Frantic, Kennedy cabled Thomas Cook Sons (the travel agent for the tour) and instructed them to assign a guard to keep an eye on Aimee twenty-four hours a day. She also sent a telegram to her daughter, informing her of the rumors and urging her to behave herself.

The telegram caught up with Sister in Italy, where she had moved on after leaving Roberta with relatives in Ireland. Whether the evangelist was traveling with a companion or not, Kennedy's warning had the desired effect. Sister returned to Ireland to collect her daughter, and the two of them embarked for the Holy Land without further ado. They made visits to Nazareth, Jericho, and Cairo before returning to London so that Sister could preach in the Royal Albert Hall. Finally, rested or not, Sister McPherson made her way back home.

When she and Roberta arrived in L.A. on April 24—again to a reception of admirers numbering in the thousands—the immediate crisis had passed. Some weeks earlier Kenneth Ormiston had called radio station KFSG as if unaware that anyone had been looking for him. Minnie Kennedy persuaded him to come to the temple and speak on that Sunday's radio broadcast, to prove that he was in Los Angeles while Sister was still one-third of the way around the globe. But Kennedy's suspicions lingered. And Aimee seemed even more willful after her Holy Land tour. She was wont to adopt a new strain of sarcasm with her mother, and allegedly began using the pronoun *I* instead of *we* when speaking of church matters. One day Sister asked her mother to increase her allowance from temple collections but refused to say why. Kennedy resisted, but then, realizing that she was in danger of completely alienating her daughter, she relented. She agreed to turn over the cash collected during the first Sunday service of every month, uncounted. This mollified Sister, though she never revealed why she needed the money.

McPherson threw herself back into her usual whirlwind of activity at the temple, directing prayer meetings, delivering radio sermons, hosting Bible study classes, and conducting daily worship services. Last-minute details for the opening of the new L.I.F.E. Bible School building behind the temple, which had been completed while she was away, consumed hours of her day. She was also occupied by a political issue: the beach resort of Venice, renowned for its plentiful assortment of speakeasies, dance halls, and gambling dens, had petitioned the city to create a special "amusement zone," exempting the resort from the Sabbath-day blue laws that prohibited dancing on Sundays. The issue was to come to a vote in the upcoming citywide elections, and Sister McPherson campaigned among her congregation and radio listeners to vote the issue down. (This was when she made her famous claim that's she'd rather see her children dead than in a public dance hall.) Although she ultimately lost this crusade, her strident opposition was still enough to earn her some powerful enemies among the Venetian underworld operators, a few of whom allegedly threatened to take unspecified measures to silence her moralistic interference. But Sister wasn't worried. "We had dealt telling blows at the underworld, to be sure," she later wrote, "but the thought of anybody striking back with a blow at the church didn't impress me as worthy of serious consideration."

On May 18, 1926, Sister set out for a relaxing day at the beach, and as if tempting fate, she chose a resort close to Venice: Ocean Park, just a mile or two up the coast. The three and a half weeks since her return from the Holy Land had been exhausting, and Minnie Kennedy, noting that Aimee looked drawn and pale, suggested she take an afternoon swim before her scheduled evening activities. Aimee agreed and took along her secretary, Emma Schaffer, for company. The two women drove out to Ocean Park, grabbed a quick bite (waffles and popcorn) at a beachside food stall, and rented an umbrella tent from the Ocean View Hotel to set up near the water.

For the next few hours Sister McPherson, clad in a pea-green bathing suit, worked on notes for that Sunday's sermon, stopping occasionally for a dip in the brisk Pacific as a fully dressed Emma Schaffer looked on. At some point, Sister began thinking about a lanternslide talk she was slated to give at the temple that evening. She had presented the show—featuring images from her recent Holy Land trip—the night before, to capacity audiences and great acclaim. But tonight's version was to be tailored to the children in her congregation. She wrote up a few changes to be made to the music program and then asked Schaffer to go to a nearby drugstore and telephone the temple with her last-minute instructions. "I guess I'll have another swim while you are gone," she told the secretary as she left.

When Schaffer returned to the beach tent sometime later, carrying a glass of orange juice she had bought for the evangelist, she saw—or thought she saw—Sister McPherson swimming far out in the water. She watched the figure anxiously until she realized it wasn't Sister after all. Schaffer scanned the other bathers in the water but saw no one who resembled her. Frantic, she ran up and down the shoreline, squinting into the surf, looking for the pea-green bathing suit. After about an hour of fruitless searching, she summoned the lifeguards.

It was nearly five o'clock when Frank Langon, manager of the Ocean View Hotel, called Minnie Kennedy with the news that Aimee Semple McPherson was missing. Kennedy seemed instantly certain of her daughter's fate. That night she stood before the packed audience that had come to see the lanternslide show and made a shocking announcement. "Sister is gone," she said. "We know she is with Jesus."

By noon the next day, one of the most extensive maritime searches in the history of California was under way. Lifeguards crisscrossed the waters off Ocean Park in glass-bottom boats, fishermen dragged their nets along the shore, and airplanes scoured the coastline from Venice to Santa Monica. Some ten thousand congregants from the Angelus Temple and Foursquare branch churches gathered on the Ocean Park beach, weeping, praying, and singing hymns while deep-sea divers searched offshore. One diver stayed down so long, he died of exposure, and one of Sister's more devoted followers became so distraught that she threw herself off the pier and drowned. But no trace of the evangelist could be discovered.

More than fifty newspaper reporters and photographers swarmed the beach and the Angelus Temple and Parsonage, hoping to dig up details on what was clearly the biggest story of the year. News of the disappearance—which had knocked coverage of the L.A. premiere of Cecil B. DeMille's *The Volga Boatmen* off the front pages, much to the director's annoyance—was filling miles of column inches, not just in Los Angeles but nationwide. Speculation was rampant. Most newspapers and their readers first assumed that Sister McPherson had drowned, either by exhausting herself in the surf or by getting caught in a riptide. But as the days passed without any trace of a body, more arcane explanations emerged. Some suspected foul play; others, that the overworked and overwrought evangelist had committed suicide. One self-described naturopath thought she might be wandering the Santa Monica Mountains with a case of amnesia. A former mayor of Venice suggested that she might have fallen prey to a six-finned sea monster sighted in recent days off Lick Pier, an amusement pier at Venice Beach.

*L.A. Times* columnist Alma Whitaker proposed the most poetic theory. Having interviewed McPherson and knowing the kind of pressure she was under at all times, Whitaker thought Sister might have just surrendered to the welcome liberation of being alone and free of obligation. "To swim back to shore was to swim back to endless burdens, endless responsibilities," Whitaker wrote. "I think perhaps she just swam on and on—to the Holy Land."

The theories turned uglier when, one week after the disappearance, the *L.A. Times* broke the story that Kenneth Ormiston had also gone missing, and that his estranged wife had taken their child and returned to her native Australia. The rumors of an affair between the evangelist and her radio engineer were now rekindled, given extra force by alleged "Aimee sightings" pouring into the temple and the DA's office from places as far-flung as Mexico, Denver, and Pismo Beach. Given these numerous reports—on one particularly busy day, Sister was "seen" in no fewer than sixteen different places—plus the absence of any corpse identifiable as McPherson's, the L.A. coroner refused to issue a death certificate. Minnie Kennedy offered a $25,000 reward to "the person or persons who will bring my daughter, Aimee Semple McPherson, to the Angelus Temple unharmed and as well as she left us," though she personally was convinced that her daughter had drowned. (The Lord had taken Sister, she told the temple congregation, which explains why no body had been found.)

Matters grew more complicated when a ransom note arrived at the temple, demanding $500,000 for the evangelist's safe return. Signed "the Revengers," the note, dated May 24, insisted that a temple representative wearing a Foursquare ribbon deliver the money to the lobby of the Palace Hotel in San Francisco on Saturday, May 29, at eleven o'clock, when he would be contacted and given further instructions. Minnie Kennedy dismissed the note as a hoax and turned it over to L.A. police captain Herman Cline, who was in charge of investigating the case. Cline, likewise convinced the letter was a fake, nonetheless contacted the San Francisco police, who sent two beribboned plainclothes policemen to the Palace Hotel for the rendezvous. When no one made contact with the disguised officers, the matter was dropped, and the original ransom note mysteriously disappeared from police files—the first of many strange irregularities that would plague the investigation for months to come.

The case took an interesting turn when Kenneth Ormiston turned up in the flesh at the ongoing temple vigil on Ocean Park beach on May 27. Confronted by police, he acknowledged that he had intentionally dropped out of sight earlier that spring, traveling around under a series of pseudonyms. He implied that an extramarital affair was the reason for this subterfuge, but categorically denied any knowledge of Sister McPherson's disappearance. He offered to help the investigation in any way he could, but since he appeared to have no relevant information, he was released. He then vanished again, for reasons known only to himself.

But the kidnapping story would not die. On the morning of Monday, May 31, a blind Long Beach attorney, R. A. McKinley, telephoned police to report that he had just been visited by two men claiming to be the kidnappers of Aimee Semple McPherson. According to McKinley, the men, who called themselves "Miller" and "Wilson," told him that they wanted his help in claiming the twenty-five-thousand-dollar reward for the evangelist's return, and that they had chosen him to act as go-between because he was blind and could therefore never identify them in court. They instructed McKinley to contact the temple, explain the situation, and take possession of the reward money. "You will hear from us on Wednesday," Miller said, "[and] if you assure us that you have the $25,000 . . . we will liberate Mrs. McPherson on the street at eight o'clock Wednesday night." For his role in this transaction, McKinley would receive a fee of five thousand dollars. "[But] if you try to trick us or double-cross us or catch us," Miller warned him, "your life isn't worth a damn."

The Long Beach police were skeptical, but they agreed to take McKinley to a meeting the next day with District Attorney Asa Keyes (pronounced "kize") and Captain Cline. Keyes and Cline were also doubtful about a kidnapping; they were still inclined to believe that McPherson had merely drowned (or, given the swirling rumors, that she was in hiding for reasons yet to be determined). But they did agree to ask Minnie Kennedy to provide a list of questions that only her daughter could answer. These questions would be conveyed to the alleged kidnappers when they made contact with the lawyer on Wednesday. If Miller and Wilson came back with accurate answers, everyone would at least know the evangelist was alive.

Kennedy found the whole idea ridiculous, but she did supply McKinley with four questions: "1. Describe hammock at home in Canada and where it was. 2. Describe my dog at home on farm and give name. 3. Describe dining room stove at home. 4. Who was Wallace at our house?" McKinley said he gave the list to Miller and Wilson, who agreed to return the answers from their captive by the following Monday. But when that deadline came and went without any further contact from the alleged kidnappers, the investigation was wide open again—much to the delight of the local newspapers, which were reportedly selling 25,000 to 50,000 extra copies of each daily edition to satisfy the public's craving for every unfolding rumor and innuendo associated with the case.

For her part, Minnie Kennedy—despite the reported sightings and bizarre kidnapping talk—remained convinced that her daughter was dead, and set about planning a grand memorial service at the Angelus Temple. Such an event, she hoped, would quiet the rampant speculation and allow Sister's followers to experience some sense of closure as to her fate. When the service took place on June 20, Kennedy tried her best. "We do not believe Sister's body will ever be recovered," she told the overflow crowd of some twenty thousand mourners. "Her young body was too precious to Jesus." The response from the congregation was overwhelming. A collection taken at the service raised nearly $35,000— $5,000 in cash and almost $30,000 more in pledges. This money would be used to support the ongoing mission of the new Bible school and, perhaps, to build a monument to the lost evangelist.

But any hopes that the memorial service would put an end to the uproar were dashed when, two days later, Minnie Kennedy opened a letter that had been buried under a pile of other mail at the temple for several days. It was another ransom note, presumably from the same source as the earlier one, though this one was signed "the Avengers" while the first had come from "the *Re*vengers." This letter went to greater lengths to be convincing: it enclosed a lock of hair purportedly snipped from Sister McPherson's head, and more significantly, it contained accurate answers to two of the four questions on Kennedy's list. The hammock at the old Canadian farmstead was "a woven wire one between two apple trees," and the family dog "was black and named Gyp."

In all other ways, however, the document lacked credibility. Its page and a half of densely typed prose needlessly revealed details about the abduction, describing how the kidnappers convinced McPherson to leave the beach with them to pray over a dying baby in their parked car. The note also outlined their reasons for taking her in the first place, "First To wreck that damned Temple and second to collect a tidy half million." The tone and diction of the letter, moreover, were oddly inconsistent; parts were written in polished, seemingly educated prose ("But though we've treated her respectfully in fairness to her position and value to us, what the future holds for her is entirely up to you"), while other lines seemed to come straight out of a Damon Runyon potboiler ("We realize you got to use [this letter] to raise the dough" and "Its plain no ordinary methods will work with you, so weve sure doped out a corker"). And what genuine criminals would reveal the particulars of their modus operandi for police to investigate? "It may interest you to know just what happened on the beach a month ago," the kidnappers had written. "Well we had inside workers who kept us informed about her whereabouts," and so on. The note even contained some rueful humor: "We are sick and tired of her infernal preaching, she spouts scripture in answer to everything."

Yet there *were* those answers to Kennedy's questions about the hammock and the dog—answers that only Aimee could know. Preposterous as it seemed, maybe her daughter had indeed been kidnapped by the authors of the letter.

As it turned out, Minnie Kennedy didn't have to decide what, if anything, to do about the ransom note. The very next day—June 23, almost six weeks after the disappearance—she received a long-distance telephone call from a hospital in Douglas, Arizona. She immediately recognized Aimee's voice on the line, gabbling on about her escape from some kidnappers in a shack somewhere in Mexico. Kennedy, aware that Police Captain Cline was listening in on the call, interrupted her with a barked order: "Don't talk!"

This was good advice. Her daughter was clearly alive, but that didn't mean she wasn't in trouble.

~

Aimee Semple McPherson, as usual, did not heed her mother's counsel. By the time Kennedy, Captain Cline, Deputy DA Joseph Ryan, and a swarm of L.A. newspaper reporters and photographers finally appeared in her hospital room in Douglas—having raced there overnight in a special Pullman car—Sister had already been telling her story to anyone who would listen. And now she told it again. Sitting up in her hospital bed, she held forth for the next three hours to a room full of witnesses, her every word recorded by a stenographer commandeered from a local army post. And the story she recounted was remarkable—a crime-adventure tale worthy of Hollywood's most imaginative screen-writers.

She began with the day she had vanished from the Ocean Park beach. After Emma Schaffer had left her to telephone the temple, Sister reported, a man and a woman had called her out of the water and begged her to go with them to pray for their dying baby. Sister was reluctant at first, but they persuaded her that the situation was grave and there wasn't a moment to lose. They then led her to a nearby parked car, in which another man sat with the engine running. Before Sister could wonder at this, the first man pushed her into the car's backseat and held a chloroformed cloth to her face. As she lost consciousness, she was aware of the car speeding away from the curb.

When she woke up sometime later, she was dressed in a white nightgown, lying in bed in a room with flowery wallpaper. Her three captors—a heavy-set man named Steve; a second, taller man whose name she never heard; and the woman, a former nurse named Rose—informed her that she was being held for a half-million-dollar ransom. Sister scoffed at this idea. Such a huge sum, she insisted, would be impossible to raise without bankrupting the church. But the kidnappers were confident that the ransom could be paid, assuming they could convince her mother that she was indeed still alive and that their first ransom note was not a hoax.

Some days or weeks later, Sister became suspicious when Rose—who had become friendly to her, always addressing her as "dearie"—began casually questioning her about her childhood, asking whether there was a hammock on her old farm and whether she had ever owned a dog. Aimee answered a few of the questions but then realized she was being pumped for information that could be used to prove she was their prisoner. "I won't answer any more questions," Sister said. "I'm not going to let them raise the money." Steve pressured her to cooperate; when she refused, he grabbed her arm and burned her finger with a lit cigar. Rose then cut off some of her hair. "If the locks of hair don't convince her people," Steve growled, "we can send that finger next."

The standoff continued until one night, weeks later, she was awakened in the middle of the night by Rose and the unnamed man, who blindfolded her and forced her back into the car. The three of them drove all that night and the next day until they arrived at a two-room shack somewhere in the desert, where Steve was waiting for them. Here they remained—"where nobody can find you," as Steve said—for several days, sleeping on army cots and eating simple meals from cans. This place was much hotter than the room with flowery wallpaper, and McPherson complained bitterly of the heat. Rose assured her that her confinement wouldn't last much longer. "Now, dearie," Rose said, "if your mother behaves, you will be out of here perhaps by Friday."

One morning shortly thereafter, the two men drove away in one of the cars. A little while later, Rose said she had to go into town for supplies. She carefully tied Aimee's wrists and ankles and pushed her onto the bed before leaving in the other car.

When Sister heard Rose pull away, she wasted no time. "Praise the Lord!" she thought. "Here is an opportunity to get away." After pausing a moment to pray, she rolled off the bed and wriggled across the floor to an open syrup can. The top of the can had been cut with a primitive opener, leaving a sharp, ragged edge. Maneuvering her hands behind her back, she used the edge to cut through the cloth tying her wrists together, then did the same for her ankles. Once free of her bonds, she climbed through a window, lowered herself to the ground, and ran away from the shack without looking back.

For the next seventeen hours, Sister wandered half-dazed through the desert. Well after nightfall, she saw the distant lights of a town that later proved to be Agua Prieta, Mexico. She had just entered the gate of the first respectable-looking house on the edge of town when she collapsed onto the walkway. The homeowners, a Sr. and Sra. Gonzalez, found her and nursed her back to consciousness, after which they found a taxi driver to take her across the border—first to the police station in Douglas, then on to the Douglas hospital. There she was tested for alcohol on her breath, and when it was clear that she wasn't intoxicated, she was put to bed. She had been there ever since, eager to get the entire ordeal behind her and finally go home.

When Sister McPherson had finished this remarkable recitation, Cline and Ryan professed to be satisfied for the moment, but they clearly found her story difficult to credit. Aside from its sheer preposterousness, there were certain incongruities that shed doubt on McPherson's account. Captain Cline noted that the evangelist's shoes were barely scuffed or worn; she wasn't dehydrated or sunburned; and there was little sign of perspiration on her clothing. Other witnesses would later dispute these perceptions, claiming that McPherson bore signs of wear and tear consistent with a lengthy desert hike, but doubts remained. Was it possible that this not exceptionally athletic woman had really enacted a daring and dramatic escape from a remote prison? Could she then have spent hours, without water, trudging across a desert landscape that by her own calculations was baking in ninety-plus-degree heat? Sister did point to some scarring on her fingers, the result of the cigar burn, as corroboration of her story. But on the wrist of that same hand, according to one report, she wore a watch that she had apparently not taken with her to the beach back on May 18. What's more, despite an exhaustive search of the surrounding area sometime later, McPherson could not locate the shack in which she'd supposedly been held.

True or not, McPherson's story made for some decidedly juicy newspaper fodder, and the national press responded with one of the biggest media frenzies of the decade. The always-competitive *L.A. Times* and

*L.A. Examiner* each hired an airplane to rush down to Douglas and bring back the first photographs of the kidnapped evangelist. Meanwhile Western Union had to put eight extra keymen on duty in Douglas to handle the flood of journalists' telegrams dissecting every detail of McPherson's story. Millions of people nationwide who had never heard of Aimee Semple McPherson before her disappearance were now eager to read every word that was printed about her. And in Los Angeles, where she had already been a household name, coverage of her ordeal would be front-page news for weeks and months to come. Not until Charles Lindbergh made his celebrated transatlantic flight the following spring would there be a story to compete with it.

While the newspapers and many of their readers responded to the kidnapping scenario with incredulity, Sister's most devoted followers accepted her account unconditionally. According to one church spokesman, the story was simply too unbelievable to have been made up. On June 26, some fifty thousand people showed up at the railroad station to greet her when she returned to Los Angeles on a special train guarded by a squad of L.A. police. A hired airplane showered the train with flowers as Sister was carried from the Pullman car on a wicker throne festooned with roses. Her automobile ride back to the temple took on the air of a grand parade, as bands played, fireworks crisscrossed the skies, and an estimated one hundred thousand additional Angelenos packed the streets to get a look at her. According to one observer, "Many presidents have visited Los Angeles, but no other man or woman was ever given such an ovation in the history of this city."

Official Los Angeles, however, was less welcoming. Much of the coverage of the kidnapping story had been openly skeptical, even derisive, of the evangelist's story. Upton Sinclair went so far as to compose a little poem in which Sister McPherson asks God to forgive her "one little lie." Worried that she was turning the city into a national laughingstock, the Chamber of Commerce put pressure on District Attorney Keyes to get to the bottom of the alleged kidnapping. Kenneth Ormiston was still missing; a report published in the *Sacramento Union* in late May cited several witnesses who claimed to have seen Ormiston and a woman resembling McPherson at a holiday cottage in Carmel, several hundred miles up the coast. Suspicions grew that the abduction had been a ruse to cover up a liaison between the married radioman and the divorced evangelist. Finally, Keyes convinced the grand jury to order an investigation, ostensibly to find and indict the kidnappers. Sister McPherson, of course, was subpoenaed; her mother and her lawyer both begged her to ignore the summons and let the matter drop, but she agreed to testify, claiming that she had nothing to hide.

At the grand jury hearing, McPherson, the supposed victim of the crime, was instead questioned as if she were a defendant. DA Keyes grilled her mercilessly, implying that she had invented the whole abduction tale as publicity for her ministry or for some other nefarious reason. McPherson—who had come to the hearing surrounded by a "purity brigade" of seven female attendants dressed in white uniforms and navy capes—stood firm under his questioning, repeating her story again and again with remarkable consistency. At the end of her testimony, she made a lengthy statement to the grand jury, during which she urged them to look at her past deeds and accomplishments when evaluating her story. "I have never put my money in oil wells or ranches or even clothes and luxuries," she said. "My great thought has always been—and this can be absolutely proven—for the service of the Lord and my dear people." She described her building of the Angelus Temple, the many services it provided to the city of Los Angeles, and the tireless Gospel preaching that had grown her congregation to what it was today. She didn't need more publicity. And would she really risk everything she had built for the kind of sinful activity being suggested by gossips and newspaper skeptics? "I would not work with one hand for seventeen years," she exclaimed, "and, just as I saw my dearest dreams coming true, sweep it over."

This was, in some respects, the most effective defense she could have given. It was Aimee Semple McPherson at her best—straightforward, earnest, vulnerable, and human. *You must believe me,* she said simply, *for why would I lie?* And certainly much of the gossip and rumor mongering about her disappearance was demonstrably nonsense (like the rumor that she had disappeared in order to get an abortion, an assertion handily disproved by the fact of her hysterectomy in Providence many years earlier). But her earnest appeal wasn't enough. After hearing other witnesses over the next week, including Minnie Kennedy, the grand jury voted on July 20 that there was insufficient evidence to issue indictments for any kidnappers, named or unnamed. Fourteen of the seventeen jurors, in other words, simply did not believe that a kidnapping had occurred.

But the investigation went on, since Keyes thought he now had evidence for a different set of charges: perjury and fraud, with Sister McPherson and her mother as the major defendants. Responding to pressure from the grand jury, the Chamber of Commerce, and local clergymen like the Reverend Robert Shuler (who seemed determined to use the scandal to destroy his rival), the district attorney aggressively pursued the Kenneth Ormiston angle, sending his deputy Joseph Ryan north to interview the witnesses who claimed to have seen Ormiston with a mysterious "Miss X" at a cottage in Carmel-by-the-Sea. Within days, Ryan turned up what he believed was irrefutable evidence that the evangelist and the radio engineer had spent ten days together there in late May, shortly after her disappearance—evidence that included several identifying eyewitnesses and a telltale grocery list found at the cottage written in what one expert claimed was undoubtedly McPherson's handwriting. Stories of an alleged "love nest by the sea" soon filled untold acres of newsprint, and over the next weeks, an estimated 75,000 rubberneckers flocked to Carmel to see the notorious bungalow. Robert Shuler, meanwhile, continued to pound away at Sister McPherson from the Trinity Church pulpit, over the radio waves, and in a Sunday afternoon rally that drew several thousand people—attacking her character and railing against city officials for the lethargic pace of their investigation. ("A dog may bark at a queen," Sister coolly responded to these broadsides, "but the queen doesn't necessarily have to bark back.")

The case hit a snag when a woman named Lorraine Wiseman-Sielaff appeared in late August, claiming that she, not McPherson, was the shadowy "Miss X" who was with Kenneth Ormiston in Carmel in late May. Naturally, this earned her intense scrutiny—both from a skeptical Keyes and from the newspapers, heavily invested in the circulation-boosting story of the McPherson-Ormiston affair. They needn't have worried. The *L.A. Times* soon unearthed evidence that Wiseman-Sielaff was wanted on charges of check fraud, and the would-be exculpatory witness was arrested. She applied to McPherson and her mother for bail money, and when they refused to supply it, she turned on them in revenge, changing her story entirely. She had been lying before, Wiseman-Sielaff said, because McPherson and Kennedy had paid her five thousand dollars to do so, in order to deflect attention from McPherson as the now-infamous Miss X. This revelation, true or not, sold more L.A. newspapers than even the most optimistic city editor could have hoped.

With this new evidence of fraud in hand, Asa Keyes felt he finally had enough of a case to file charges. On September 16 he had arrest warrants issued for McPherson, Kennedy, the already-incarcerated Wiseman-Sielaff, and the still-unlocatable Kenneth Ormiston, on charges of obstruction of justice, perjury, and conspiracy to manufacture false evidence. Sister suffered a nervous breakdown before her warrant could be executed, which delayed matters for a few days, but she was sufficiently recovered to come to court on the first day of the preliminary hearing on September 27, before Judge Samuel R. Blake.

This hearing alone lasted six weeks—reportedly the longest legal procedure of its kind in California history. The proceedings generated over 3,500 pages of transcript, as witnesses and defendants testified before a municipal courtroom that had been fitted with grandstands to accommodate the flood of eager spectators. DA Keyes had built his case on what McPherson herself called "a three-legged legal stool"—first, the evidence that she was cavorting with Ormiston when she was supposedly kidnapped; second, the sheer improbability of her abduction story, especially of her escape through the desert from the Mexican shack; and third, the testimony of Wiseman-Sielaff that McPherson and Kennedy had hired her to falsely confess to being Ormiston's companion in Carmel. The sheer volume of evidence to be presented promised a prosecution of unprecedented length and expense—though many of the costs, it later emerged, were helpfully paid by the two major Los Angeles newspapers.

As the weeks of testimony went on, however, it became clear that the district attorney's case was hardly airtight. Key witnesses who had encountered Ormiston's companion at the Carmel bungalow, for instance, flatly denied that the woman they saw was the Aimee Semple McPherson sitting in the courtroom. Others admitted that they had never previously seen the evangelist in person and had made the connection only when deputy district attorney Ryan showed them her picture—a notoriously unreliable kind of identification. One witness insisted that it was McPherson he had seen, but that she had had short hair then, meaning that she must now be wearing a wig or hair extensions; to evaluate this claim, the judge asked the evangelist to let down her hair—which she did before a rapt courtroom, unpinning her auburn tresses and allowing them to tumble, abundantly and provocatively, over her shoulders and nearly down to her waist. As one of her biographers described the scene: "The effect was almost as stunning as it would have been if she had taken off her clothes."

Nor were the second and third legs of the prosecution's stool much sturdier. The defense produced affidavits from numerous people in Douglas indicating that McPherson had been much more disheveled and debilitated from her alleged desert trek than Ryan and others had claimed. Several Douglas locals, moreover, insisted that they had traced a woman's footprints miles out into the desert, to the vicinity of a remote structure that could plausibly have been the adobe shack in which she was held captive. And Lorraine Wiseman-Sielaff's allegations of suborned perjury could hardly be considered rock solid, given that she had already changed her story several times and had once—according to a certified document from a so-called insane asylum in Utah—been incarcerated for "ungovernable lying."

But the evidence was strong enough, in the end, for Judge Blake to deem it sufficient for the case to go forward. On November 3, 1926, Sister McPherson and Minnie Kennedy were officially charged with three counts of criminal conspiracy and obstruction of justice, carrying a maximum sentence of forty-two years in prison. They were bound over for trial in the Superior Court, the proceedings to commence sometime after the new year. Free on bail until then, McPherson decided to make the most of the time. For the six weeks of the preliminary hearing, she'd taken to the radio every night, parodying the day's court proceedings and making a case for her innocence. Now she intensified these efforts, recasting the entire controversy as a struggle between true believers and "those who are opposed to the old-time religion." One week she staged an elaborate illustrated sermon called "The March of the Martyrs." The performance, which attracted some twelve thousand spectators, cast Sister McPherson as the latest in a long line of persecuted Christians extending from Jesus to Joan of Arc to William Jennings Bryan (ridiculed in the press for his recent role in the so-called Scopes Monkey Trial). Another Sunday she promised a sermon on the topic: "The Biggest Liar in Los Angeles." Congregants were left to wonder who it might be— Asa Keyes? Judge Blake? The Reverend Robert Shuler?—until Sister revealed him to be (rather disappointingly) the Devil, Satan himself, father of lies.

She had plenty of scorn for her more earthly enemies as well. "It isn't me that my detractors hurt," she wrote in a widely distributed newspaper column at this time. "They do not realize that they are striking at God in their attempt to pull down his temple."

But Sister McPherson was, in fact, being hurt. True, she didn't lack for adherents—temple membership was booming, and many secular people in L.A. were rooting for her simply out of sympathy for how she was being treated by the prosecution, who made no bones about calling her a liar, a hypocrite, and a fake in open court. Even a cynic like H. L. Mencken, in town to cover the trial for the *Baltimore Evening Sun*, was on her side. He seemed not to give much credence to the kidnapping story, but he did believe that a woman "guilty of unchastity" should in all decency be allowed to lie about it. "It is unheard of in any civilized community," he fumed, "for a woman to be tried for perjury uttered in defense of her honor."

Even so, with the Los Angeles city establishment ("the town Babbitts," as Mencken called them) lined up against her—and rivals like Shuler and the L.A. Church Federation piling on for good measure— she was losing much of the goodwill she had built up over the seven years of her ministry in the city. For many in L.A., the famous evangelist was now an embarrassment, a scandal, or—perhaps worst of all—a joke. The image she was projecting to the world was, for many people, a poor advertisement for the kind of serious, up-to-date city they were building to compete with the older cities of the East.

Right around the turn of the new year, Asa Keyes's case began to fall apart. His star witness, Lorraine Wiseman-Sielaff, suddenly recanted her testimony, claiming that she lied when she said that McPherson and Kennedy had paid her to pretend to be Miss X at Carmel. Without this leg of his three-legged stool, Keyes decided that any attempt to convict the defendants would be futile. On January 10, 1927, he announced that the trial would not go forward and that he was dropping all charges against mother and daughter. Keyes insisted that he still believed McPherson guilty, but the confused and contradictory evidence that had emerged would make a successful prosecution impossible. "Let her be judged in the only court of her jurisdiction," he told reporters, "the court of public opinion."

That unruly court was, to say the least, shocked at this development. According to one newspaper, McPherson's coup was "a 1926 Miracle: Hollywood style"—a feat of creative storytelling born of the age of cinema. Official Los Angeles was appalled. Rumors began swirling that the temple had paid Keyes a bribe of thirty thousand dollars to drop the case. Robert Shuler claimed that it was William Randolph Hearst who had pressured the DA to abort his prosecution, after McPherson threatened to use her radio program to expose the newspaper publisher's adulterous relationship with actress Marion Davies (though this was hardly a well-kept secret). Of course, Keyes was not above the sins of graft and undue influence (he would later go to prison for bribe-taking in an unrelated case), but although a grand jury did eventually look into the rumors, nothing ever came of the investigation.

So Aimee Semple McPherson and Minnie Kennedy were free. Sister, at least, was jubilant. "It has been so hard, all these months," she told reporters, "for two defenseless women to fight this tower of lies. But all through the trouble, the Lord prepared a table before me in the presence of mine enemies. His work will now go on bigger than ever." Her mother had a different perspective. Kennedy insisted that the lack of resolution in the case was hardly something to celebrate; it had left her daughter "in a dirty hole," as she put it, where suspicion about her guilt would never go away.

But Sister would not accept this interpretation. Flouting the advice of her mother and many members of her church, McPherson refused to adopt a low profile after the trial ("Get off the front pages," Minnie allegedly told her), instead announcing a nationwide "vindication tour" to celebrate her triumph. Taking along her new publicity manager—Ralph Jordan, a reporter from Hearst's *L.A. Examiner*, interestingly enough— she departed the very next day for Denver, the first stop on an itinerary that would include more than a dozen other cities ranging from Topeka and Des Moines to New York and Washington, D.C.. This would not be one of her usual revival tours; it would be a traveling one-woman show called "The Story of My Life"—a theatrical extravaganza climaxing in an account of her kidnapping and prayers for the defeat of all enemies of old-time religion. Her message: "The so-called 'case' had passed into the annals of yesterday. But the glorious revival goes on!"

All of this bravado notwithstanding, what Aimee Semple McPherson represented for Los Angeles would never be the same. For one thing, she herself was not the same. In the months after her court ordeal—while under the influence of Ralph Jordan and her other "worldly" handlers— she radically changed her persona, bobbing and marcelling her hair, wearing heavier makeup, and dressing in newly stylish and expensive clothing. Many of the more conservative members of her church objected. "The God of the Gospels is being replaced at Angelus Temple by the god of materialism," choir director Gladwyn Nichols complained, before breaking his association with the temple and taking about three hundred other members with him. Other defections would follow, as church members began to wonder whether Sister had really triumphed over the Devil in the trial, or vice versa.

In any case, Los Angeles—the city that had nurtured her and had in turn been nurtured *by* her—would never again embrace its warm and irrepressible celebrity evangelist with the same old enthusiasm. "McPhersonism," as Reverend Shuler called it, was now a compromised phenomenon for some. Thousands would continue to believe, and her church would grow even larger in the years ahead. But for many Angelenos, the spiritual paradise Sister McPherson had conjured up had proven to be a bust—just another ephemeral desert mirage.

# CHAPTER SIXTEEN
## A Silent Twilight

*The premiere of Cecil B. DeMille's* King of Kings *opens
Grauman's Chinese Theater*

On the evening of May 18, 1927, cars were backed up for a mile each way on Hollywood Boulevard for the L.A. premiere of *King of Kings*, the new blockbuster epic directed by Cecil B. DeMille. Held at Grauman's Chinese Theater, the showman's latest extravagant movie palace in the heart of the film capital, the opening was to be *the* occasion of the spring season—a "$5,000,000 event," according to the ads, to be attended by "every world-famous celebrity" in the business. The result was a mob scene by now familiar in this movie-crazed city. An estimated fifty thousand people jammed the boulevard in front of the theater, hoping to catch sight of some of the giants who, in just over two decades, had transformed "the flickers" from a primitive inner-city amusement into a worldwide cultural phenomenon.

One such giant, David Wark Griffith, was to serve as master of ceremonies for the night's extravaganza. After being introduced by fellow director Fred Niblo (whose own biblical epic, 1925's *Ben-Hur*, had been the most expensive film made in the silent era), Griffith would say a few ceremonial words before introducing Mary Pickford and Will H. Hays, who together would press the solid-jade button that would launch the film. There were no worries about how the movie would be received. DeMille's account of the life and death of Jesus had already opened in New York to universally stellar reviews. The *New York Times* had called it "the most impressive of all motion pictures," while *Life* magazine had described it as "moving, absorbing, inspiring, and everything else that DeMille intended it should be. . . . It is a masterpiece." More important (in an industry that existed first to make money and only second to make art), the film was poised to be a commercial triumph. DeMille, with his uncanny knack for knowing just how much titillation and visceral drama audiences wanted in their high-toned art, had created a rare thing: a pious and heartfelt expression of religious sentiment that also happened to be damned entertaining. Granted, the film's version of Mary Magdalen—depicted early in the film as a haughty courtesan and later as the motivation for a lustful Judas's betrayal of Christ—had caused some consternation among clergymen. And there had been protests from rabbis and the Jewish press about DeMille's portrayal of Jews. But for the most part, critics were entranced, and New York audiences had lined up to see it in huge numbers.

Just how painful all of this must have been for the evening's emcee can only be imagined. Griffith was still working in an office at the United Artists studio on North Formosa Avenue, casting around for ideas after the *Sorrows of Satan* debacle; 1927 would in fact be the first year in over a decade in which no Griffith film appeared. Joseph Schenck at UA had kept him busy in the meantime, asking him to rework an ill-conceived comic movie—*Topsy and Eva,* loosely based on characters from *Uncle Tom's Cabin*—that had already been picked up and abandoned by a series of UA writers and directors. But there was only so much recutting and reshooting he could do to salvage the awful material he was given.

Finding a new movie he could be proud to put his name on was a bigger problem. Griffith still had scruples. "I'll never use the Bible as a chance to undress a woman!" he had once told Lillian Gish, clearly thinking of the man whose film premiere he was currently hosting. Griffith and Schenck agreed that his first film under his UA contract should be a prestige project, so it had to be chosen carefully. They would eventually settle on *Drums of Love,* a reworking of the Paolo and Francesca story from Dante's *Inferno* (transposed to nineteenth-century Brazil). The movie would star Lionel Barrymore and reunite Griffith with his longtime cameraman Billy Bitzer, whom he hadn't worked with since 1924's *America.* But although the classic Italian story had a certain snob appeal, its commercial prospects were anybody's guess. This made it an odd choice, since at this point Griffith was less interested in making a work of great art than in making a film like DeMille's—that is, one that actually made money.

Complicating that task for Griffith—and for DeMille and Niblo and everyone else present at Grauman's Chinese Theater on that warm Wednesday evening—was the growing popularity of the talkies. In mid-1927 there were still many doubters about the long-term appeal of the new technology, but true believers William Fox and the Warner brothers were forging ahead. Filming on *The Jazz Singer* started in the summer of 1927, and although most of the movie was shot by director Alan Crossland as a traditional silent with written intertitles, Jolson improvised some sound dialogue in two of the recorded song sequences. These unplanned scenes were allowed to stay in the final cut, and when *The Jazz Singer* opened in New York on October 6 (a day after the untimely death of the film's champion, Sam Warner, who succumbed to a freak brain infection), the results confirmed every hope, and every dread, in the industry. The audience loved Jolson, loved the songs, and loved the dialogue—not least one bit of Jolson patter, "You ain't heard nothing yet!" which has provided easy fodder for every writer of Hollywood history ever since. Very few theaters were yet wired for sound, but the film ended up grossing some $2.6 million against a relatively modest cost of $422,000. By the new year, audiences were abandoning silents and clamoring to see any kind of movie that talked, no matter what the quality.

Nothing would ever be the same in Hollywood again. "I, for one," wrote Robert Sherwood in *Life* after seeing *The Jazz Singer*, "realized that the end of the silent era was in sight." Some in the industry remained skeptical, attributing the film's success to Jolson's charisma as a singer. "The big producers," wrote one *Fortune* magazine journalist, "said *The Jazz Singer* merely proved that songs by Jolson could carry one whole picture." But this was wishful thinking on the part of those wedded to the status quo. Sam Goldwyn's wife, looking around the celebrity-studded theater after the talkie's L.A. premiere, saw "terror in all their faces," as if they knew that "the game they had been playing for years was finally over."

Tragically, all of this was happening just when the silent film was reaching a stunning climax of achievement. By the mid- to late 1920s, Hollywood was producing one silent masterpiece after another, starting with Chaplin's *The Gold Rush* in 1925 and continuing with F. W. Murnau's *Sunrise*, Victor Seastrom's *The Wind*, King Vidor's *The Crowd*, Buster Keaton's *The General*, Josef von Sternberg's *Docks of New York*, and Raoul Walsh's *Sadie Thompson*. These were fully mature examples of an art form, lifting the silent film to unprecedented levels of expressiveness and technical mastery.

Meanwhile the early talkies, rushed out to meet the sudden demand, were almost without exception awkward and visually unsophisticated—to modern eyes, almost unwatchable. As one actress of the day complained, "To compare *The Jazz Singer* with *Sunrise* or with King Vidor's *The Crowd* was sheer blasphemy." Dialogue was hopelessly banal or stilted, and because of the requirements of early sound technology, camerawork was static and unimaginative. Actors couldn't move around since they had to position themselves near hidden stationary microphones to ensure that their dialogue would be audible. Nor could the camera move much, since it had to be encased in a soundproof booth to dampen its mechanical whirring. Set lighting had to be flat and uniform, in order to accommodate the extra camera angles required to compensate for this lack of movement. Filmmakers, producing movies with few of the techniques they had developed over two decades to bring stories to life on the screen, felt frustrated and coerced. As DeMille put it, "Everything that the silent screen had done to bring entertainment and the beauty of action . . . was gone." Douglas Fairbanks was even gloomier. While visiting a soundstage with set designer Lawrence Irving, Fairbanks, perhaps the most agile and athletic performer of the silent era, took a look at the wires and cables and microphones and sound dampeners cluttering up the set. "Lawrence," he said, "the romance of motion picture-making ends here."

But the marketplace had spoken, and the studio heads felt that they could no longer ignore its verdict. When the popularity of sound was confirmed by the tremendous success of an appallingly bad Warner Bros. film called *The Lights of New York* (released in July 1928 and regarded as the first true all-talkie), the studios went into high gear. As one Western Electric engineer remarked, "Producers now realized that it was a case of sound or sink." Warner Bros. decided to include Vitaphone footage in all of its future films. Adolph Zukor, berating Paramount executives for his own underestimation of the new technology, ordered that already-wrapped silent films be pulled from the schedule so that sound sequences could be added. Fox did likewise with Murnau's *Four Devils*, even after it had opened in some markets as a silent. The result was a flood of so-called goat gland movies, named after a bizarre surgical procedure of the day, in which a goat's testicles were transplanted into a man as a cure for impotence; the "goat glands" in the metaphor were short and often gratuitous sound sequences crudely inserted into otherwise silent films.

As terrible as these hybrids were, audiences came to see them in droves. People started calling theaters not to find out what movie was playing but whether whatever was playing was a talkie. The studios responded accordingly. Silent films remaining on their schedules that couldn't be goosed up with sound sequences were released with minimal promotion and advertising; at the same time, since anything with sound made money, shoddily filmed stage musicals and variety shows were rushed into production. (Even Aimee Semple McPherson produced a sound short around this time, speaking to the camera about her Angelus Temple and how her ministry soldiered on, despite the recent "times of trouble and test.") This change happened very quickly. In 1928 Paramount released seventy-eight films, all of them silent; in 1929 the studio released sixty-seven movies, only twenty of them silent.

This virtually overnight transition created instant winners and losers at all levels and in all areas of moviemaking. According to a 1929 article in *Variety*, "Sound didn't do any more to the industry than turn it upside down, shake the entire bag of tricks from its pocket, and advance Warner Brothers from the last place to first in the league." Warners' asset base, which in 1925 had been a mere $5 million, grew to $230 million by 1930—mainly because of the studio's early embrace of sound.

The talkies revolution had an even greater effect on individuals. "One half [of Hollywood's] occupants were contemplating vistas of a brave new world," vaudevillian Leonard Sillman quipped, "the other half—suicide." Even the biggest and most established stars in town now had to submit to sound tests before getting the go-ahead to make new films. Contrary to hoary Hollywood legend, few stars lost their jobs on the basis of these tests alone, but many simply did not take well to sound films. Romantic screen idol John Gilbert, the most notorious loser in the changeover, did not really have such a bad voice and actually did make several successful talkies. But audiences could not accept his rather thin, reedy voice as belonging to the suave and virile movie persona he had developed over the years, and he soon lost favor. Ronald Colman, on the other hand, got a massive career boost once producers heard how well his mellifluous baritone recorded. Foreign actors with heavy accents, of course, were generally losers in the sound sweepstakes. Garbo, whose deep Swedish purr enhanced her exotic allure, made the transition with no problem. But other big stars like Emil Jannings, Vilma Banky, and Conrad Veidt were eventually shown the door.

Other professions experienced similar upheaval. Sound engineers were the new gods on the set—everyone, even directors, had to submit to their requirements. Cameramen had to learn to shoot around microphones. Set designers were forced to create interiors with acceptable acoustics. Perhaps hardest hit were studio musicians, who had played on silent film sets to create the proper atmosphere. Their jobs were newly obsolete, as were those of theater orchestras and organists, since all sound films would henceforth have a prerecorded score.

Then there were the directors. Silent and sound films proved to be entirely different art forms, with different paces, different means of expression, and different ways of propelling narrative. Some of the greatest silent directors—Fred Niblo, Herbert Brenon, James Cruze, Clarence Badger—failed to adapt well to the new regimen, despite rapid improvements in technology that reduced the early awkwardness of filming in sound. Even Cecil B. DeMille, now under contract to MGM, was having trouble. His last silent film, *The Godless Girl*, made immediately after his *King of Kings* triumph, was a first-rate piece of entertainment but a financial disaster, since audiences were clamoring for sound and sound alone. He dutifully, if reluctantly, turned to talkies with his next two projects, *Dynamite* and *Madam Satan* (a blimp disaster musical!). They were, by all accounts, awful, but both made money—a fact that allowed DeMille to survive into the sound era with his reputation intact.

The man whom DeMille still cited as his major rival, whether true or not, was experiencing deeper difficulties. The first three films Griffith made for Joseph Schenck as part of his five-movie contract with United Artists had all been disappointments. *Drums of Love*, despite a dominating performance by Lionel Barrymore as the hunchbacked Duke Cathos de Avila, was a dull and slow-moving affair. Sensing its lack of commercial appeal, Griffith even apologized for it at the New York premiere on January 24, 1928. "I haven't got any brains, I guess, as far as that part of the business is concerned," he told the audience at the Liberty

Theatre—the site of his greatest triumph thirteen years earlier, with the premiere of *The Birth of a Nation*. "Although I really intended to try and hit public approval with this piece, I went ahead and did something different again. I am glad if you like it."

They did not like it—or at least most of the critics didn't. A writer from the *Telegram* spoke for many in Hollywood when he wrote, "Reviewing a Griffith picture is like nothing else in the experience of an American picture fan. For, after all, D.W. has been our first and foremost, our best beloved, our pet genius whom we could always count [on] when the great lords from overseas—the Murnaus, the Lubitsches, and the Stillers—arrived with their great bags of tricks to show us how it's done. And that's why it's so tarnation sad when the grand old man turns out a *Drums of Love*."

Griffith's next film was a remake of one of his earliest feature-length films—*The Battle of the Sexes*, the first motion picture he had made after leaving Biograph in 1913 (and unfortunately no longer extant except for a few fragments). Based on the same Daniel Carson Goodman novel as the earlier film, the 1928 remake was twice as long. Griffith tried to update the original's rather creaky moral lesson about infidelity and the sanctity of marriage, but his attempt at a breezy Jazz Age tragicomedy fell flat. The reviews were almost universally savage, with one critic in the *Herald Tribune* dismissing it as "a badly acted, unimaginatively directed, and thoroughly third-rate sex drama."

Perhaps the worst humiliation for Griffith came in the reception of his next (and actually much better) movie, *Lady of the Pavements*, a stylish melodrama featuring the up-and-coming young star Lupe Velez, dubbed "The Mexican Spitfire" by the industry press. Joseph Schenck, having little confidence by now in Griffith's ability to develop his own projects, had given him an already-completed shooting script to work from, just as he would with any B-list contract director. The Father of Film had obliged, swallowing his pride (and his creative instincts) to produce the movie precisely as ordered. Somehow everyone seeing the film sensed this demotion. In their reviews, the critics focused their attention almost exclusively on the actress, treating Griffith as a mere star vehicle director, mentioned only in passing. After the premiere, during which much was made of Velez while Griffith was largely ignored, the director took his guest—stage producer Jacob Kalich—by the arm. "Come," Griffith said as they exited the theater, "let's go back to your world; people are kinder there."

After this indignity, Griffith took some time off to regroup. Fortunately, he could afford the break. Whatever knocks his reputation had taken of late, he was in better financial shape than he had been in for some time. Thanks to the garnishing of his UA salary, his company, D. W. Griffith Inc., had paid off almost all the debt incurred during the Mamaroneck experiment. The company had also received an unexpected refund of $38,000 in overpaid taxes from as far back as 1921. Griffith's financial officer, Raymond Klune, put the windfall into stocks—which in retrospect sounds like a poor idea, given that the year was 1929, but these investments continued to pay dividends even after the market crash in October of that year.

And then Griffith pulled off something of a miracle. After a six-month hiatus (during which he drank heavily), he got an idea for his next project: a sound film about the life of Abraham Lincoln. No longer pessimistic about the long-term prospects of sound technology, as he had been earlier, Griffith now saw the advent of talkies as an opportunity rather than a disaster. ("We must preserve all the speed, action, swirl, life, and tempo of the motion picture today," he told an industry publication in January 1929. "Add dialogue to that and, boy, you will have people standing in their seats cheering.") Bringing sound to a movie about the most masterful orator in American history seemed especially propitious. Lincoln Talks!—how could that concept fail?

Even the lately skeptical Joseph Schenck could see the potential in this matchup of story and director. The Civil War was, after all, the subject Griffith had once turned into the highest-grossing movie of all time. Schenck gave the project a green light and even agreed to earmark it as a prestige (i.e., high-budget) production, though he insisted Griffith take a cut in his own salary to do it—a stipulation Griffith was in no position to argue with.

The logical first choice to script the film was poet Carl Sandburg. By 1929, Sandburg had been reviewing movies for the *Chicago Daily News* for almost a decade, so he presumably knew enough about the business to write a usable script. More important, he had published the first part of a multivolume biography of Lincoln three years earlier (*The Prairie Years*) to substantial critical acclaim. Sandburg did end up contributing a few suggestions for the project, but his proposed thirty-thousand-dollar script fee was too high for the newly cautious director. Eventually Griffith settled on another poet—Stephen Vincent Benét, whose book-length poem *John Brown's Body* had just won the Pulitzer Prize.

The collaboration with Benét, however, proved frustrating for everyone involved. The poet conscientiously produced draft after draft of a script, only to watch as most of his material was jettisoned or substantially rewritten, either by Griffith himself or by Schenck's factotum, John W. Considine, Jr., whose job appeared to be keeping the project from becoming too highbrow. ("I'll probably have to wheel in a Pulmoter after [Lincoln's] been assassinated and revive him," Griffith ruefully told Lillian Gish while working on the screenplay, "so we can have a happy ending.") It was perhaps the earliest example of what was to become a consistent pattern in sound-era Hollywood: hire a big-name author to write a screenplay, then proceed to ignore it. Benét eventually wanted to wash his hands of the whole mess. "If I don't get out of here soon I'm going to go crazy," he wrote in a letter to his agent. "Perhaps I am crazy now. I wouldn't be surprised." After delivering his final rewrite around the end of the year, he left Hollywood for New York, knowing that what ended up on the screen would bear little resemblance to what he had written.

The eight weeks it took to shoot the film were, by Griffith's own description, "a nightmare of mind and nerves." The director was blessed with a first-rate cast that included Walter Huston in the title role, old stalwart Henry B. Walthall as a Confederate colonel, and film pioneer Hobart Bosworth as General Robert E. Lee. But the challenges of sound production and the constant meddling of John Considine literally drove Griffith to drink. In the end, the director was forced to retreat (not for the first time) to a Texas health spa called the Crazy Ranch to dry out, while Considine oversaw the final cut of the picture. Griffith didn't see the finished version until August, two months before the premiere, at which point he wouldn't have been able to make many changes even if

Schenck and Considine had allowed him to. The whole endeavor looked like another Griffith disaster in the making.

To everyone's surprise, however, *Abraham Lincoln* turned out to be a significant success. For modern audiences, the finished film seems a bit stagy and wooden, but in the context of the appalling quality of early talkies, it amounted to a much-needed coup for Griffith. Unlike the static and lifeless first efforts of many directors making the transition to sound, Griffith's freshman effort was lyrical, often dynamic (employing a number of surprisingly fluid tracking shots), and as pictorially engaging as much of his early work. The *New York Times* ended up citing it as one of the ten best films of the year, while Griffith was named the year's best director by both *Film Daily* and *New Movie Magazine*. And the reviews were for once ungrudgingly enthusiastic: "Reverting after all these years to his beloved Civil War theme," the *New York Evening World* told its readers, "David Wark Griffith . . . takes his place in the van[guard] of present-day leaders." Richard Watts of the *Herald-Tribune* called the film "a handsome, dignified, and frequently moving photoplay . . . genuinely distinguished." The *Morning World* was even more effusive: "Mr. Griffith is in every way at his best." Box office, hurt by an economy veering toward Depression, was admittedly spotty, but the film did make money, particularly in major urban markets. More important, it reestablished Griffith, at least temporarily, as a film pioneer. *Abraham Lincoln* was, as Griffith biographer Richard Schickel puts it, "the first major historical film of the sound era, a beginning of an attempt to reclaim the past for the movies."

Encouraged by this unexpected victory, Griffith became convinced that he could engineer his much-desired comeback if only he could retain full artistic control of his next project. Though Schenck had liked the Lincoln movie, he agreed to release Griffith from his obligation to make the fifth film in his contract. This release, combined with the director's improved financial position, allowed Griffith to take a final stab at independent production. But the film he decided to make under his own aegis, *The Struggle*, seemed to everyone an odd choice—the story of an everyman's pathetic descent into alcoholism, based on Emile Zola's novel *The Drunkard*. To write the script, he turned to one of his best and earliest collaborators, Anita Loos, now a big name after the phenomenal success of her 1925 novel *Gentlemen Prefer Blondes* (later remade numerous times on film and on the Broadway stage). Loos instantly recognized Griffith's idea as unpromising. "I knew how bad it was," she would later say, "[but] I was the only writer he had any connection with." She and her writing partner, John Emerson (also her husband at this time), agreed to take it on anyway. At the very least, they hoped to inject some humor into the lugubrious story.

Griffith had other ideas. He wanted to make a straightforward tragic melodrama about the evils of drink—a huge gamble on his part, especially since the script seemed to waver on whether Prohibition helped or hurt the situation. What's more, for a man looking to recapture his past glory as king of the epic film, *The Struggle* seemed simply too small, too downbeat, too unremarkable to serve.

Sure enough, the film's reception was a disaster. Audiences at the previews laughed aloud at many points, and the reviews were brutal. One trade publication refused even to report on the film—presumably to spare the great man embarrassment. Others were less kind. Even *Film Daily*, a publication that had championed Griffith through thick and thin, had nothing good to say about it. "This is poor entertainment," its critic wrote. "It is old-fashioned domestic drama with little box-office appeal." Some latter-day scholars have attempted to rehabilitate the film's reputation (one even called it "a true Griffith masterpiece"), but the verdict of Griffith's contemporaries was clear. The movie closed after one sparsely attended week at the Rivoli Theater in New York, and didn't do much better elsewhere. "I passed [Griffith] on the street the other afternoon," one columnist reported a few days after the opening, "and I didn't stop to talk because, somehow, there's nothing one can say these days to D. W. Griffith, while big electric signs flash the title of his new ignominious effort."

From this humiliation, he would never recover. By his own report, Griffith was drunk from the night of *The Struggle*'s opening on December 10, 1931, until the end of the following January. And although he would continue trying to mount various new projects for years to come (he was still only fifty-six years old), he would never make another film. Lillian Gish summed up his predicament: "He could not make movies the Hollywood way, which meant that he could not make movies at all anymore."

The Father of Film thus joined the growing list of casualties created by the changing culture of Hollywood at the end of the 1920s. The talkies revolution was only part of the story. Many pioneers of the silent era—Pickford, Fairbanks, Sennett—probably could have adapted to the new culture if their hearts had been in the effort. Some, like Chaplin and Swanson, did continue to work, if sporadically, well into the new era. But for them and many others, Hollywood just wasn't the same place it had been in the early years of the century. Given the enormous capital investment required to make the transition, the advent of sound had brought the industry under the thumb of banks, large communications corporations, and Big Money with new finality, and the whole ethos of moviemaking had changed accordingly. That old, enticing image of Los Angeles as a place of independence and openness—where artists could experiment freely, far from the corporate pooh-bahs in New York—was gone, replaced by a world of budgets, scientific management, and ideas approved by committee. Even a survivor like Cecil B. DeMille didn't like it. "When banks came into pictures, trouble came in with them," he would later write. "When we operated on picture money, there was joy in the industry; when we operated on Wall Street money, there was grief in the industry."

But perhaps his brother William, a successful director and screenwriter himself by now, described the situation best: "Our old Hollywood was gone and in its place stood a fair, new city, talking a new language, having different manners and customs, a more terrifying city full of strange faces, less friendly, more businesslike, twice as populous—and much more cruel."

# CHAPTER SEVENTEEN

# A Perfect Disaster

*At the remains of the St. Francis Dam*

**S**hortly before midnight on March 12, 1928, a solitary motorcyclist wound his way up the tortuous curves of San Francisquito Canyon Road, in the rough Sierra Pelona Mountains about fifty miles north-west of Los Angeles. The rider was Ace Hopewell, a carpenter for the L.A. Bureau of Power and Light. On this crisp and still-moonless Monday night, Hopewell was on his way to a construction camp adjacent to the Bureau's Powerhouse No. 1, a hydroelectric plant located a couple of miles above the vast six-hundred-acre reservoir created by William Mulholland's new St. Francis Dam. Given the winding road and rugged terrain, the twenty-eight-year-old motorcyclist was moving rather carefully up the canyon. "I can make sixty miles an hour in the open," he would later say, "but a car can beat me on that road." He maneuvered slowly around its many sharp turns, his headlight sweeping across the sere hillsides like a spotlight in a darkened theater.

Not that he had to worry much about encountering other vehicles. San Francisquito Canyon was a lonely, sparsely populated place, and the road he was on was not heavily traveled even in the daytime. This had been part of its appeal to Mulholland as a site for his dam. The Chief's original idea had been to locate his dam in Big Tujunga Canyon, closer to the city, but he realized that landholders there would want too much money for their properties. Rather than pay inflated prices or initiate lengthy condemnation proceedings, he'd instead opted for the more re-mote San Francisquito location. Geologically it was not an ideal spot for dam construction, but the Bureau of Power and Light already had two hydroelectric plants in the canyon, and the location would create efficiencies that appealed to the ever-frugal Mulholland. So the land was purchased and, in August 1924, construction of the dam was begun.

The St. Francis was to be the largest of seven dams and storage basins that the Chief wanted to have completed by the end of 1926. The aqueduct bombing campaigns had convinced him of the need to have enough reservoirs near Los Angeles to supply the city's needs for a full year—in case the bombings continued and ended up putting the aqueduct out of commission for an extended period. To avoid trouble at the site from would-be saboteurs, he kept construction of the dam as secret as possible, making no public announcement of the project until January 1925, six months after work had begun. Of course, those living in the immediate area knew what was going on and even filed suit against the city, worried that Mulholland was trying to "steal their water" just as he had allegedly done to the residents of the Owens Valley. After a series of percolation tests and other studies, the city assured locals that the dam would not detract from the flow of the San Francisquito Creek that they relied on for their ranching and farming activities. All of the water confined by the dam, in other words, would be Owens Valley water that the city had legally acquired farther north.

Work on the dam—which was to be made of concrete, still a relatively new material for dam construction in the mid-1920s—went on for the better part of two years, during which time the rising concrete palisade served as a dramatic backdrop for at least one Hollywood movie (*The Temptress*, directed by Fred Niblo and starring Greta Garbo and Lionel Barrymore). According to some reports, workers on the site did not like the looks of the rock they were building on; the red conglomerate on the canyon's west wall didn't seem entirely solid, and the bluer mica schist directly under the dam and up the canyon's east wall struck them as "kind of greasy." Their concerns were not eased when Mulholland, hoping to increase the storage capacity of the reservoir-to-come, changed his plans midway through construction, increasing the original height of the structure without changing the thickness of its base. He even had to add a long wing dike to the design to capture the amount of water he deemed desirable.

When the project was completed, in May 1926, the dam stood at an imposing height of 208 feet, sufficient for a reservoir of 12.4 billion gallons of water. This prodigious amount—combined with the capacity of the other, smaller reservoirs he built around the region—meant that 60 percent of the entire system's water storage would now be located in and around the Los Angeles area. This, Mulholland reasoned, would be enough water to tide the city over no matter how long the ongoing drought continued and no matter what disruptions might be created farther up the line. Los Angeles was by now an immensely sprawling city; thanks to various annexations over the years, it covered more than four hundred square miles by the late 1920s. Keeping all that real estate adequately watered was a responsibility—some would call it an obsession—that required the Chief's constant attention.

Once the dam was finished, it took many months for the canyon behind it to fill with surplus water from the aqueduct. In January 1928, just as the reservoir was nearing its capacity, two sizable cracks appeared on the exposed (downstream) face of the dam, indicating that the abutments on both sides of the structure were becoming saturated with water and swelling upward. Perfectly normal, Mulholland assured everyone. He ordered that the cracks simply be filled with oakum and then caulked. "When concrete dries, it contracts, creating cracks," he would later explain. It was a phenomenon you could see "in curbs on the street any place."

Even so, many of the people living in the canyon downstream of the reservoir—including the sixty-seven city employees and family members living at the bureau's Powerhouse No. 2, a mile south of the dam—were made nervous by the cracks and by the seepages of water under the dam's abutments that had appeared as the reservoir filled. A few jokers indulged in gallows humor about the situation: "Well, goodbye, Ed," one worker reportedly said to a friend one day. "I will see you again if the dam don't break." Assistant dam-keeper Jack Ely even tried to put a scare into Chester Smith, a local rancher, as the two stood on the hillside above the leaky west abutment. "Ely, what are you sons-of-guns going to do here," the rancher asked in a lighthearted way, "going to flood us out down below?"

Ely responded in kind: "We expect this dam to break any minute!"

The head dam-keeper Tony Harnischfeger was less amused. Harnischfeger had grown increasingly worried about the leaks around the dam and had made no secret of this among friends and co-workers—so much so that his superiors in Los Angeles allegedly warned him that he could lose his position if he continued airing his misgivings. His concerns grew only worse when, on the morning of March 12, 1928, he noticed a new leak on the dam's western abutment. The water seeping out in this area appeared muddy rather than clear, an indication that the flow of water might be eroding the dam's foundational material. A disturbed Harnischfeger telephoned headquarters on South Broadway in downtown L.A. and asked that Mulholland come to have a look at it. The Chief and his deputy, Harvey Van Norman, immediately headed up to the canyon in Mulholland's chauffeur-driven Marmon sedan.

When they arrived at ten-thirty a.m., the two engineers inspected the leak and determined that the water seeping through was actually clear where it first emerged from the stone; the muddiness came from the water's subsequent passage through dirt piles left from recent road construction in the area. There was no cause for concern, in other words. After about two hours on-site, during which time they also examined some of the other leaks on both the western and the eastern sides of the dam, Mulholland declared the seepage normal for a dam of that size. Before they left the canyon, however, Mulholland had his deputy give orders to lower the level of the reservoir—first, by having workers block the adit diverting water into the reservoir from the aqueduct, and then by having them open three large gates to release excess water from behind the dam into a channel that ran along the bottom of the canyon. By twelve-thirty p.m., the Chief and Van Norman were on their way back to Los Angeles for a late lunch.

That evening Dave Mathews, one of the three workers who had blocked the adit, was driving back to his home in Newhall. As he traveled down the winding canyon road, he encountered his brother Carl coming in the opposite direction. Carl lived with his family at Powerhouse No. 2 and was driving two of his children home from Saugus, another town not far from Newhall. The cars stopped opposite each other on the road, and the two men got out. Dave pulled his brother aside, out of the children's hearing, and told him of his deep concerns about the condition of the dam, urging Carl to move his family out of the canyon as soon as possible.

"Dave," Carl said, "I will move them to Newhall tomorrow."

He would never get a chance to act on this resolution. That night Dave would be safely asleep at his home in Newhall; Carl and his family—his wife, four children, and a visiting cousin—would still be in their little cottage near Powerhouse No. 2, directly in the path of an oncoming disaster.

~

Later that same night motorcyclist Ace Hopewell passed the very spot where the two brothers had met on the canyon road. Like Carl Mathews, Hopewell was a carpenter for the Bureau of Power and Light, but he worked at the other powerhouse, located some four or five miles farther up the road, beyond the dam and its reservoir. Together these two hydroelectric plants, each located at a point where the aqueduct took a steep drop, generated 90 percent of the electricity used in the city of Los Angeles. Cheap, municipally produced electricity was one thing that had allowed the city to grow as fast as it had—an important side benefit of Mulholland's fifteen-year-old aqueduct.

A couple of miles up the road, Hopewell passed Powerhouse No. 2, its lights casting a ghostly sheen over the steep arid hillsides, its twin turbines humming in the quiet night. After a few more minutes of switchbacking, he passed the dam itself, barely visible in the glow of the just-rising moon. Then, about a mile past the dam, Hopewell thought he heard a deep, ominous rumble, over the sound of his motorcycle's engine. He stopped the bike by the side of the road and dismounted. After lighting a cigarette, he listened while scanning the hillsides around him. He heard more rumbling in the distance, but it seemed to come from far behind him. Probably a landslide somewhere, he concluded—not an uncommon occurrence in these hills. Thinking little more of it, he finished his cigarette, climbed back onto his bike, and continued up the road.

At that very moment, fifty miles south, the lights of Los Angeles flickered momentarily in the night. Operators at the bureau's Receiving Stations A and B in the city noted a sharp drop in line voltage lasting for approximately two seconds. Somewhere along the transmission lines, something was wrong.

Up at Powerhouse No. 1, operator Ray Silvey had just gotten off the phone with Lou Burns, his counterpart at the lower plant, when—at precisely 11:47 and thirty seconds—he noticed "a nibble or fish bite" (bureau parlance for a momentary voltage fluctuation) on his control board. Confused, he picked up the phone to call Burns again but found the line dead. He recorded the fluctuation in his logbook but kept an eye on the board. Nothing else seemed amiss, until at 12:02 and thirty seconds—exactly five minutes after the nibble—all power suddenly dropped out. "It went down in a heap," Silvey would later recall. "Everything went black."

In his cottage near Powerhouse No. 2 in the lower part of the canyon, Ray Rising (another of the workers who had closed the aqueduct adit earlier that day) woke with a start. He heard a rumbling in the distance—a deep reverberation that shook his bed and rattled all of the windows in their frames. Thinking it might be an earthquake or even a tornado, he jumped out of bed and ran to his front door. He opened it and gazed in disbelief at what he saw before him: a seething wall of water as high as a ten-story building. It was barreling down the narrow canyon straight toward him, its surface roiling with uprooted trees, electrical wires, and huge chunks of debris as big as school buses. Rising barely had enough time to call a warning back to his wife and children before the first rush of water hit him. As his cottage shattered around him, he was thrown head over heels in the turbulent blackness, the wildly churning waters tearing the clothes from his body and battering his head and limbs with stone and wood. Suffocating in the moiling mud, he was suddenly disgorged to the surface of the flood. A partially intact rooftop pinwheeled in an eddy beside him; without thinking, he grabbed the edge and hauled himself on top of it. And there he lay, spread-eagled over the shingles, as the roof careened at eighteen miles per hour down the narrow twisting canyon. At a sharp turn in its course, the rooftop slammed into the canyon wall, catapulting him onto the dry hillside above the rushing waters. Rising lay there in a state of semiconsciousness—naked and battered but alive—as the contents of an entire reservoir, 12.5 billion gallons' worth, flowed past him just a few feet away.

Lillian Curtis lived with her husband and three children in one of the other cottages near Powerhouse No. 2. She also was awakened by the approaching roar but thought it was a thunderstorm on the way. Worried about the laundry she'd left on the clothesline, she hurried outside, only to be stopped by the sight of an eerie mist hanging over the narrow canyon. Instantly, she knew what was coming. "The dam has broke!" she called back to her husband, Lyman. Acting quickly, he told her to grab their young son, Danny, from his crib and make for higher ground while he roused their two daughters. Waist-deep water was already churning around the cottage when she got back outside, but she managed to push through it and scramble with her son up the hillside behind the house. She turned around just in time to see a "great black wall" of water roll down the canyon, taking the cottage—and her husband and daughters—with it.

Ray Rising and Lillian and Danny Curtis were among the very few survivors sleeping at Powerhouse No. 2 that night. One or two of those whose homes stood higher—including E. H. Thomas and his mother, who lived in a cabin on top of the east canyon wall—also came through unscathed. Wakened by the enormous roar of the passing flood, Thomas dressed and hiked down the slope with a flashlight about fifteen minutes after midnight. What he saw astonished him. The powerhouse, a concrete and steel-reinforced building standing sixty-one feet high, had been completely swept away, leaving only the two metal turbines and their penstocks behind, caked with mud and debris. The rest of the settlement—cottages, toolsheds, vehicles—was gone. "Everything went with the first rush of water," he would later testify.

This was only the beginning of the destruction. As the unstoppable torrent of water surged down the canyon, it smashed and carried away everything in its path. The Raggio family's ranch, with its sizable home, barns, vineyard, and gardens, was wiped out in an instant—though fortunately Frank Raggio, his wife, and their seven children were staying in their other home in Los Angeles that night; three of their ranch hands on-site were battered by the flood but somehow survived. The neighboring Ruiz family were less lucky. Eight family members were staying at the homestead when the wall of water hit; none survived.

Cattleman Chester Smith, the man whom Jack Ely had teased earlier about the dam breaking, lived in this part of the canyon. Spooked by the assistant dam-keeper's grim joke, Smith had decided to sleep in his barn that night, with the sliding doors wide open to facilitate a quick escape if necessary. Sometime after midnight, a dog's barking roused him from sleep. Another sound drew him out of bed. "I could hear it coming," he would later report. "[I] could hear the trees breaking, and could hear a big pole snapping, could hear the wires on the electric poles going.

I knew what was coming." He ran from the barn to the ranch house, where his brother-in-law and his wife were staying, and shouted a warning. They, too, had heard the oncoming flood and evacuated with him, scrambling up a steep hillside in their nightclothes. They escaped just ahead of the leading edge of raging water, as severed power lines flashed like lightning in its path.

Up at Powerhouse No. 1, Ray Silvey was still frantically trying to figure out what had happened to all of the power in the canyon. He reported the situation to his superior, Chief Operator Oscar Spainhower, then tried to raise headquarters in Los Angeles on a backup radio communication system. At twelve-thirty a.m., a repair crew including engineer C. Clarke Keely was dispatched to find out what had happened down-canyon. The crew set out in three cars along the high road south, but when they got to where the reservoir should have been, it wasn't there. "It was just a mud flat out there," Keely recalled. The extent of the catastrophe was instantly and glaringly obvious to everyone on the crew. One of them—lineman Martin Lindstrum—climbed a utility pole and hooked into a telephone line to reach Ray Silvey back at the plant. "Ray," he said simply, "your lake is gone."

When radio communication was finally established between Powerhouse No. 1 and headquarters in Los Angeles, word and warning of the disaster-in-progress could finally be spread. Harvey Van Norman was roused from his bed by a phone call at 12:45 a.m.; the Los Angeles County Sheriff received word fifteen minutes later. From there notification of the police departments in all of the towns on the flood's route should have been automatic, but word seems to have spread erratically. Not until 1:09 a.m.—more than a full hour after the break—were evacuation orders relayed to communities in the flood's inevitable path.

Back in Los Angeles (where automatic power switching with Southern California Edison was, for a time, keeping most of the city's lights on), Harvey Van Norman made the phone call that he knew would be the most difficult of his life—to the man responsible for building the dam that had failed. When the upstairs telephone in the Mulholland household rang, it was the Chief's daughter Rose who answered. Van Norman quickly explained what had happened, and she rushed to her father's bedroom to wake him. Years later, she would remember how he pulled himself out of bed and staggered to the telephone, muttering, over and over again, "Please, God. Don't let people be killed." Mulholland must have known this prayer would not be answered.

~

At about 12:40 a.m.—shortly after razing the mostly deserted Harry Carey Indian Trading Post, a tourist attraction owned by the Hollywood western star—the leading edge of the flood, still over seventy-five feet high, emerged from the narrow confines of San Francisquito Canyon. Here, in the much broader Santa Clara Valley, the flood would spread out and make a hard right turn as it found its main artery west to the ocean. This would lower the height of the leading wave and slow its speed, but there would in all likelihood be more death and destruction than in the canyon. The Santa Clara Valley, an attractive, mostly agricultural area of farms and citrus orchards, had seen substantial population growth in the 1920s, particularly in the number of Mexican laborers. Many of these newcomers lived in vulnerable, low-lying places near the banks of the Santa Clara River, particularly in and around Santa Paula, the largest town in the flood's path.

But it would be two hours before the flood reached Santa Paula, which was about two-thirds of the way down the valley; there were many people in its more immediate pathway, still oblivious to the juggernaut coming their way. At the Edison Company's Saugus electrical substation, not far from the entrance to San Francisquito Canyon, workers had known that something was wrong for some time now. A transmission line had shorted out, probably at the moment the distant dam gave way, blowing up an oil switch and starting a small fire. But now they could hear what had caused that mishap: "We heard a roaring noise which at first we thought was a train on the tracks near the highway," Edison worker Frank Thees recalled. But then the sudden flash of another transmission line shorting out revealed the truth: "that a large volume of water was running down the Santa Clara River." The men ran for their pickup trucks, but the water came too fast for some to escape, and they were swept to their deaths.

A little farther down the valley, at a café/service station located near a small cluster of tourist cabins, seventeen-year-old George McIntyre and his father were looking east in confusion as flashes of light and a "ball of fire" streaked along the Southern Pacific railroad tracks in the distance. Their confusion deepened when the tourist cabins over toward the tracks seemed to rise up, turn toward them, and begin racing in their direction. Then the realization came. Just as George's father grabbed the boy's hand to run, they were hit by a massive wall of water. They were thrown about in the chaos of churning mud and water until they managed to grab a stationary utility pole and hold on. But the incessant pummeling of water, barbed-wire fencing, dead animals, and other debris proved too much for them. "Oh, my God! I'm hurt!" George's father cried as his grip failed and he was washed away. Then George himself was ripped from the pole. Again he was thrown about and battered, until finally becoming entangled in the branches of a cottonwood tree. Eventually the water receded, leaving the teenager beaten up and exhausted, still snarled in the sturdy tree, dangling above a landscape "swept as bare as a pool table."

The stories were similarly appalling all the way down the valley. At an Edison construction tent camp near a place called Kemp, well over a hundred men were sucked into a gigantic whirlpool created when the flood hit an outcropping of hillside in its path. Many were trapped in their closed tents, which bobbed on the swirling eddy as the men inside tore at the canvas with their fingernails to escape. (Of some 150 workers at the camp that night, 84 died.) At the town of Fillmore—after the flood passed near Rancho Camulos, where D. W. Griffith had filmed his two-reel version of *Ramona* back in 1910—a worker named Juan Carrillo received a warning call in time to evacuate his large family from their home in the willow bottoms near the river. Carrillo was rushing them toward higher ground when he parked the car momentarily to go and warn another neighbor. When he got back, the car—with his wife and seven children inside—was gone, carried away by the roiling waters now streaming over the road below him.

By now warnings about the coming flood were reaching the lower Santa Clara Valley, as female emergency switchboard operators, often remaining on duty at substantial risk to their own safety, relayed calls to police stations, businesses, and private homes in its path. Sirens, fire alarms, and factory whistles began blowing all up and down the valley.

In Santa Paula, patrolman Thornton Edwards received a call at his home at about one-thirty a.m. Like many people in the valley, he had never even heard of the distant St. Francis Dam, let alone known that it presented a danger to his community. But the thirty-three-year-old, who occasionally moonlighted as an actor and a motorcycle stuntman for low-budget movie studios, responded quickly. After getting his own family to safety, he set out on his motorcycle for what would be his most famous role—as the "Paul Revere of the St. Francis Flood." Racing through the lower-lying streets of Santa Paula, he spread word of the oncoming water. Joined eventually by another patrolman, Stanley Baker, Edwards was able to give many people the better part of an hour's notice—until, at around three a.m., he turned a corner and ran headlong into the now twenty-foot-high wall of water he was warning others about. Somehow, perhaps because of his training as a stuntman, he was able to turn his tumbling bike around and get out ahead of the water again—mud-caked and drenched but relatively uninjured.

The flood was now moving more slowly, though it was far wider—almost two miles across. Its menace was compounded by the twisted metal remains of several bridges and by uprooted utility poles acting like battering rams as the wave surged through the remaining towns. But most people this far down the valley had received warnings in time to make for higher ground. For another two and a half hours, the destructive surge moved inexorably seaward, still preceded by the ghostly flashing of the switches and power lines it ruptured as it advanced. At about 5:25 a.m., residents of Ventura on the coast watched from a hillside at the edge of town as the flood finally reached the sea. "At daybreak," one witness later wrote, "we saw the stream, filled with trees, houses, and debris, pour in a great arc over the Montalvo bridge. In the ocean, it formed a wide gray stripe stretching out to the channel islands."

Mulholland and Van Norman had driven up to the dam site hours earlier, their driver taking an alternative route unaffected by the flood. What the two old friends said to each other on the long drive north can only be imagined, but when they arrived at approximately two-thirty a.m. and saw what had happened, the Chief could barely remain upright. As they looked down on the ruined dam from the western hill-side, Mulholland "stood there with a cane," one witness reported, "and he was just shaking." Through wisps of fog illuminated by the waning gibbous moon, they saw that the dam had failed catastrophically at both its eastern and western ends. All that remained upright was a monolithic central slab, standing midcanyon like "a monstrous tombstone"—an image that would be made much of in the newspapers over the coming days. Behind the slab lay the former reservoir, now just a vast mudflat; in front of it lay the ravaged canyon, littered with giant concrete chunks of the dam, some of which had been carried hundreds of yards down-stream. Overcome, Mulholland could only cling to Van Norman's arm as he took in the magnitude of the disaster—of *his* disaster.

As day broke over the Santa Clara Valley, miles away, the effects of the flood could at last be fully appreciated. The aftermath was horri-fying—a sixty-five-mile swath of death and destruction, running from the mountains to the sea. By now hundreds of local volunteers were on the scene to search for victims and feed the survivors. One mother and her children were found alive, clinging to a mattress snagged high in a leafless treetop. Another woman was seen stranded on top of a water tank, dressed, incongruously, in an evening gown. A thirteen-year-old girl named Thelma McCauley was discovered sleeping soundly in the branches of a tree, nine miles beyond the home from which she had been swept away hours earlier.

Many, many more victims had no such miraculous escape. Dead bodies—some animal, some human—were dragged out of the slime by mules and packhorses all up and down the valley. In makeshift morgues at schoolhouses and town recreation centers, mud-caked corpses were stacked like cordwood, while grim-faced survivors filed past, looking for missing loved ones. It was said that there was little work for the doc-tors and nurses who arrived on the scene: most of those in the path of the water either escaped entirely unscathed or else they died almost in-stantly.

By late afternoon, Mulholland was back at his office in downtown L.A., making emergency arrangements for communication and power lines to be restored and breaks in the aqueduct to be repaired. Hoping to get a better sense of the extent of the damage, he conscripted a group of airmail pilots to make a survey of the entire area. "It's a scene of horror," one pilot reported back by telephone. "Thousands of people and automobiles are slushing through the mud and debris looking for the dead. Bodies have been washed into the isolated canyons. I saw one [man] alive stuck in the mud to his neck."

Mulholland sat at his desk, listening with his head in his hand.

Over the next few days, as impromptu local rescue forces were augmented by state militia, Red Cross workers, L.A. police officers, and teams from the LADWP, the details of the toll began to emerge—more than four hundred dead, and millions of dollars of damage to private homes and public infrastructure. The *L.A. Evening Express* was the first newspaper to run photos of the gruesome aftermath, under the headline "CORPSES FLUNG IN MUDDY CHAOS BY TIDE OF DOOM." Paramount sent a movie crew to record the devastation, developing and screening the film in L.A. theaters within a day of shooting. Soon papers and newsreels nationwide were covering what was being called the second-deadliest disaster (after the San Francisco earthquake and fire of 1906) in California history.

In the absence of hard facts, theories as to the cause of the dam failure ran rampant. Some self-styled experts cited the effects of a minor earthquake in Santa Barbara three days before the disaster. Others pointed to nearby dynamite work being done by a road crew in the canyon. One rumor—not discouraged by the LADWP—suggested that the cause might be terrorism. The trial of the so-called Inyo Gang—the group allegedly responsible for the earlier aqueduct bombings—had just begun, and there had been at least one bombing threat to the dam in the last year from unknown parties in the Owens Valley.

But most of the blame was being pinned on one man: William Mulholland, the person entirely responsible for the dam and its location. "RESIGN—NOW!" read a headline in the *L.A. Record*. A handwritten sign on the side of a destroyed ranch house in the Santa Clara Valley was more blunt: "HANG MULHOLLAND." Death threats against the Chief became so common that an armed guard had to be placed on his family home in L.A. At a meeting of the board of water commissioners on March 18, a visibly distraught Mulholland offered his resignation as chief engineer, after which, according to one witness, he "slumped into his chair, buried his face in his folded arms, and sobbed like a broken-hearted child." The board then voted—unanimously—to reject Mulholland's offer.

There could be no doubt that, whatever the exact cause of the break, the city of Los Angeles was responsible (yet again, some said) for a disaster that affected mostly people living well beyond its boundaries. To the city's credit, it met this devastation of the hinterland (unlike that in the Owens Valley) with immediate offers of restitution. Acting with uncommon dispatch, the L.A. City Council passed an ordinance providing a million dollars in relief funds, promising complete restoration and compensation for everyone materially affected by the flood. The council also authorized the formation of a Joint Restoration Committee, consisting of both a delegation of city representatives and a Santa Clara Valley Citizens Committee. Fortunately, both sides were eager for a speedy settlement of all cases. The city delegation wanted to act quickly for the sake of L.A.'s reputation, while the Santa Clara Valley Citizens Committee was eager to get the valley back to something resembling normal life, without waiting for lengthy and expensive court trials to run their course. The inevitable influx of personal injury lawyers into the valley did tempt a few clients to sue (despite not-quite-legal efforts by local law enforcement to run the "ambulance chasers" out of town), but most victims ended up accepting—after a bit of negotiation—the Joint Restoration Committee's compensation offers. Only a few dozen lawsuits against the city were ever filed, and all except one were settled out of court. Although there were some complaints that Anglo victims and their surviving families received more generous settlements than their Mexican and Mexican-American counterparts, the overall sense—at least as it was conveyed to the outside world—was that Los Angeles had promptly and fairly compensated those hurt by its actions, thus avoiding the kind of bad publicity the Owens Valley controversy had created.

Other parts of the L.A. community were also rising to the occasion. By March 18, the *L.A. Times* had collected over $55,000 in relief funds from its readers. Stage companies in downtown theaters gave special benefit performances, the proceeds of which were donated to the cause. The Angelus Temple responded with characteristic generosity: Sister McPherson was on a train to Denver when word of the disaster reached her, and she reportedly wanted to turn around immediately, until a telegram from a temple group called City Sisters reassured her that the church was doing its part in her absence. The Sisters donated more than eleven thousand items of clothing and provided food, furniture, and blankets for hundreds of survivors in the valley. But as might be expected, the most high-profile relief came from L.A.'s moviemaking community. On March 21, a late-night benefit for flood victims was held at Grauman's Metropolitan Theater in downtown L.A.—a gala event attended by many of Hollywood's biggest stars, including Gloria Swanson, Charlie Chaplin, W. C. Fields, Tom Mix, and Laurel and Hardy. Adolph Zukor even donated sixteen searchlights for the occasion.

~

On March 21, 1928, amid reports that dead bodies and debris were washing up on beaches far down the coast, an inquest was convened by Los Angeles County coroner Frank E. Nance at the county courthouse downtown. This was to be only one of many investigations launched in the wake of the dam collapse. No fewer than nine separate inquiries and studies—sponsored by California governor Clement C. Young, the L.A. City Council, the L.A. Board of Supervisors, the LADWP, and the California Railroad Commission, among others—would look into what went wrong at the St. Francis Dam that night. Most of these would focus on engineering issues, however; only the L.A. coroner's inquest attempted to determine whether anyone was criminally liable for the deaths and damage. (Even the coroner's inquest in Ventura County, where the majority of deaths had occurred, was intended only to identify victims and establish their cause of death.) District Attorney Asa Keyes—conducting his most heavily publicized prosecution since the McPherson case—promised that if the inquest pointed to defective construction as the cause of the failure, he would be asking the grand jury for nothing less than indictments for murder.

The day before the opening of the inquest, Hearst's *L.A. Examiner* created a stir by reporting startling new evidence that dynamite had been responsible for the dam collapse. The paper wrote that, according to one investigating engineer, a large number of dead fish found just below the ruined dam showed signs of having been killed by an explosion. Even more shocking, an investigation by the Pyles Detective

Agency turned up evidence of a bombing plot, including overheard conversations about "drowning half the people of Los Angeles" and a note dropped on Hollywood Boulevard that seemed to give instructions for planting the explosives. ("Do a <u>DAM</u>good job," the note allegedly read. "DON'T USE flash MUCH.") This supposed evidence was ridiculed as nonsense by many, in particular the always anti-water-department *L.A. Record*, which claimed that the only dead fish involved in this matter was "the red herring [that] the Water Board would like to drag across the trail that leads to those responsible for the Saint Francis Dam disaster." Nonetheless, because of the rumors, security was beefed up at all dams, reservoirs, and other vulnerable points in the city's water system.

At ten o'clock on the morning of March 21, Coroner Nance finally brought to order the "Inquest over Victims of the St. Francis Dam Disaster." Technically, the nine-person jury of engineering experts would be hearing evidence related only to those sixty-nine victims who died in Los Angeles County—that is, the initial flood zone in San Francisquito Canyon and the upper Santa Clara Valley. But all the deaths, whether in L.A. or Ventura County, had come about as the result of the same dam collapse. It was the builder of that dam, the seventy-two-year-old chief engineer of the LADWP, who would be the main focus of the inquiry.

After showing the court grisly film footage of the aftermath of the flood, Coroner Nance disposed of a few witnesses and then moved to the main event, calling William Mulholland to the stand. "The white-haired engineer walked to the stand with feeble steps," one reporter wrote. That Mulholland was described in the same article as "nearly 80 years of age" suggests how much the disaster had aged him. Dressed somberly in a three-piece suit, with patterned tie and a somewhat old-fashioned winged-collar shirt, the Chief maintained a grave but steely dignity on the stand, obviously still despondent over the events of the past weeks. "On an occasion like this," he said at one point in the proceedings, "I envy the dead." Even so, he was adamant in his contentions that every reasonable precaution and safety measure had been taken at all stages in the location, design, and building of the dam.

Under aggressive questioning from DA Keyes, his assistant E. J. Dennison, Coroner Nance, and the jurors, Mulholland first described his choice of site for the dam, expressing confidence in both the schist of the eastern canyon wall and the conglomerate on the western wall. To make certain of the suitability of these substances as a base for the dam, he had conducted a battery of tests, all of which had confirmed that they were "quite solid and impervious" to undue water saturation. As for the concrete used in the construction of the dam, he defended it heatedly, pointing out that he had been making his own concrete since the early days of the aqueduct's construction, without previous mishap. At one point, Coroner Nance—appearing somewhat exasperated by Mulholland's self-assurance—asked him point-blank whether he had considered the dam absolutely safe as built. "I surely did," Mulholland replied. "I have built nineteen dams in my day, and they are all in use. . . . I certainly took all the care that prudence suggested."

When asked about the late Tony Harnischfeger's concerns (the dam-keeper's body had never been found), and about the inspection Mulholland and Van Norman had made on the morning before the break, Mulholland was almost dismissive. "Like all dams," he said, "there are little seeps here and there . . . [but] of all the dams I have built and all the dams I have ever seen, it was the driest dam of its size I ever saw in my life." When Dennison insisted that the seepage must have caused him at least some concern, Mulholland denied it. "It never occurred to me that it was in danger," he testified.

At several points, the Chief implied that the failure might have come about as a result of "human aggression"—an allusion to the dynamite rumors—and certainly such an explanation would have let him off the hook as far as responsibility for the break was concerned. But he also claimed that he was "willing to take my medicine like a man," were he himself proved negligent. "If there is an error of human judgment, I was the human," he admitted grimly. "I won't try to fasten it on anybody else."

The coroner's inquest went on for three weeks, during which time evidence was heard from dozens of engineers, geologists, dam construction workers, and other witnesses. The jury even made a field trip up to the San Francisquito Canyon to view the dam site. Their task was clearly a complex one, but they knew that they had to make a definitive assignment of blame for the disaster.

All of Los Angeles was watching when, on April 13, 1928, the inquest closed and the jury delivered its verdict. It was a long and complicated judgment, but its conclusion was couched in no uncertain terms: Responsibility for the St. Francis Dam disaster "rests upon the Bureau of Water Works and Supply, and the Chief Engineer thereof." Also responsible were "those to whom the Chief Engineer is subservient, including the Department of Water and Power Commissioners, the legislative bodies of city and state, and to the public at large." According to the jurors, the dam had failed mainly because of "the very poor quality of the underlying rock structure," and while the design and construction quality of the dam might have been adequate in a better location, the structure lacked up-to-date safety features that would have perhaps mitigated the poor choice of site. Unfortunately, Mulholland had not consulted with geologists and dam engineering experts who could have warned him about these issues. The water department had, in other words, relied too heavily and exclusively on Mulholland's "ability, experience, and infallibility in matters of engineering judgment"—a judgment that, in this case at least, had proved inadequate to the task. Though there was no indication of any criminal negligence in the case, the error was clear: "The construction and operation of a great dam should never be left to the sole judgment of one man, no matter how eminent."

For DA Keyes, the verdict was only a partial victory. Blame had been fixed on the man he was after, but without a ruling of criminal negligence, Keyes could not go forward with a criminal case against him for manslaughter. For Mulholland, this was the end nonetheless—the end of his reputation, and the end of his career. The man whose identity was entangled, more than that of any other figure, with the rise of Los Angeles had now fallen. In November 1928, after almost fifty-one years of service, the chief engineer of the L.A. Department of Water and Power resigned. But although he stayed on with the department as a consultant under his successor, Harvey Van Norman, the era of Mulholland was over.

The creator of that era claimed to have few regrets. "If I knew of anything that would afford me as much amusement and entertainment as the constructive work in this job," he had once told a reporter back in

1925, "I would retire and do it." Even in 1930, after his great debacle, he could still proudly write, at the close of a short unpublished autobiography: "Although never a soldier, I have devoted most of my life to the service of the city of Los Angeles, the county of Los Angeles, and the state of California."

# EPILOGUE
# World City

*Flying over the newly constructed Los Angeles City Hall*

On April 26, 1928, just two weeks after the verdict in the St. Francis Dam inquest, the largest-ever civic parade west of Chicago filled the streets of downtown Los Angeles to celebrate the opening of the magnificent new City Hall. Thirty-two stories high and designed in an ecumenical collection of Greek, Roman, and Renaissance styles, the Spring Street structure was, for many in the city, an emblem of how far they had come in the world, and how much farther they would go—"a sheer gleaming tower of white," as the *L.A. Times* called it, "symbolizing a new era of progress and accomplishment ahead." Having just passed the one million population mark (the L.A. County population, at 2.2 million, was already significantly larger), Los Angeles was now the fifth-largest city in the country, and it would not stop there. Already on the heels of Detroit and Philadelphia, Los Angeles would eventually surpass even Chicago to become, by 1960, the new second city of the United States.

That this megalopolis had grown up in such an unlikely place was, in retrospect, little short of miraculous—a bravura act of self-invention rooted in a culture of titanic engineering and cunning artifice. Beginning with its conjuring of an oasis in the desert, an achievement itself made possible only through a campaign of deception and elusive intentions, the city had attracted the population it needed by selling another mirage: a lifestyle image of leisure, health, easy prosperity, and spiritual fulfillment, all in a place where it never rains or turns cold. Oil strikes and real estate booms provided part of the economic foundation for explosive growth, but it was Hollywood, the city's homegrown industry (and one, of course, predicated on the creation of image and illusion), that brought Los Angeles worldwide visibility and the unique identity it is still known for today. By this idiosyncratic path, L.A. had grown from the country's thirty-sixth-largest city in 1900 to the powerhouse it was on that April afternoon in 1928.

But the establishment triumphalism embodied in that gleaming white tower masked the fact that Los Angeles had become something far more complex and polychromatic than the image being sold by its boosters. The Reverend Bob Shuler might still approvingly depict L.A. as "the only Anglo-Saxon city of a million population left in America" and "the only such city that is not dominated by foreigners," but the city's transition from "Iowa-on-the-Pacific" to a diverse, multicultural metropolis was, by the end of the 1920s, already well under way. The last decade had seen enormous growth in the city's ethnic and nonwhite populations, particularly Mexicans and African-Americans. Barrios were now springing up in places like East L.A. and the San Fernando Valley, as Los Angeles surpassed San Antonio as the city with the largest Mexican population in the country. Meanwhile the 1928 opening of the Hotel Somerville (later called the Dunbar Hotel) marked the coming-of-age of the thriving black metropolis on Central Avenue. Immigrant Jews and Russians flooded into Boyle Heights, and a not-so-little Little Tokyo spread out from First and San Pedro Streets downtown. Not until the 1930s and especially the 1940s—when World War II brought heavy industry to the city in a much bigger way—would the influx of immigrants, blacks, and various working-class groups bring Los Angeles fully into line with the diversity of other large American cities. But by 1930, it was already clear that groups heretofore marginalized by the city's wealthy white establishment would play a much more prominent role in the chapters of the city's history to come.

Many of those who had helped create the thriving L.A. of 1928 would not share in its bright prospects in the years ahead. The story of D. W. Griffith's last two decades, for instance, offers as much pathos as anything he ever put into his movies. After the debacle of *The Struggle*, Griffith floundered for years, splitting with United Artists in 1933 and then trying unsuccessfully to secure funding for independent projects that were increasingly out of touch with popular tastes, including talkie remakes of *The Birth of a Nation* and *Broken Blossoms*. Symbolic gestures of respect would be forthcoming from the film community—an honorary Oscar in 1936, an honorary membership in the Directors Guild in 1938, and retrospectives of his films at the Museum of Modern Art in 1936 and 1940—but no actual job offers. For a time, Griffith tried his hand at a few non-movie-related projects. He researched a book about his home state of Kentucky; he began writing a play, called *The Treadmill*, that featured caged monkeys commenting on human folly, and another that (bizarrely) included mosquitoes in its cast of characters. Perhaps unsurprisingly, nothing came of these efforts.

Some friends claimed that he was not entirely unhappy during these years. Thanks to the proceeds from the sale of his United Artists stock, plus an annuity purchased in the flush times right after *The Birth of a Nation*, he was hardly strapped for money. And he even found love late in life—with a much younger woman, Evelyn Baldwin, whom he married in March 1936, two days after finally getting an official divorce from Linda Arvidson. But what Griffith really wanted to do, despite de rigueur denials in interviews, was get back to work. His longtime rival, after all, had managed to pull off that trick. After a period in the 1930s when he couldn't get a job, Cecil B. DeMille took matters into his own hands, borrowing money to purchase the rights to a popular play called *The Sign of the Cross* and then offering it (and himself) to Paramount in a deal too attractive to turn down. True, the critics were split on the resulting movie, but it was a modest financial success, and more important, it got DeMille back onto the list of employable directors in Hollywood. The only similar opportunity Griffith got—a 1939 offer from Hal Roach to consult on the filming of his prehistoric fantasy, *One Million B.C.*—ended in the usual disagreements over artistic choices. Griffith eventually asked that his name be removed from the film and its publicity.

By the mid-1940s, Griffith was doing little besides imbibing heavily. After a drunken spat that landed him in jail overnight, Evelyn divorced him, at which point he took up residence at the Knickerbocker Hotel on Hollywood Boulevard. Four months before his death, journalist Ezra Goodman went to see him: "The father of the American film sat in an easy chair in a hotel room in the heart of Hollywood," Goodman wrote, "guzzling gin out of a water glass and periodically grabbing at the blonde sitting on the sofa opposite him. . . . It was Griffith all right, his lordly, arrogant, aquiline features surmounted by sparse white hair, attired in pajamas and a patterned maroon dressing gown, and, at the age of seventy-two, sitting alone, drunk and almost forgotten in a hotel room in the town he had been instrumental in putting on the map."

D. W. Griffith died of a cerebral hemorrhage on July 23, 1948.

~

Unlike Griffith, Aimee Semple McPherson still had plenty of drama ahead after her near self-destruction in the late 1920s. The 1926 kidnapping drama had turned her into something of a media superstar on the national stage, and movie offers began flooding in, with MGM and Universal competing for the honor of dramatizing the evangelist's life (to the chagrin of Will Hays, who worried that the story would be too sensational). After these deals failed to get off the ground, Sister incorporated her own movie company, Angelus Productions, to film and distribute her sermons and to produce a feature called *Clay in the Potter's Hands*, based on her own life. But this project, too, never materialized—despite the fact that McPherson lost forty pounds to prepare for the part and, by some accounts, even had a surreptitious facelift. Undeterred, Sister soldiered on, writing religious operas, planning her ever-more-elaborate illustrated sermons, and launching an evangelistic vaudeville act that ran for a week at the Capitol Theater on Broadway in the fall of 1933.

Her fame was at an apex in these years—one writer estimated that, between 1926 and 1937, McPherson's name was on the front pages of the L.A. newspapers an average of three times per week—but Sister faced increasing dissension in the church she had created. The evangelist's new worldliness unsettled many of her most devoted followers, especially after her surprise 1931 elopement with David Hutton, a singer performing in her opera *The Iron Furnace*, who happened to be eleven years her junior. Since her divorced husband, Harold McPherson, was still alive, many conservative believers regarded the new relationship as a violation of the Bible's stricture against adultery. McPherson met the resulting defections and threats of defection with defiance: "Let them walk out of the temple. I'll fill it up again."

Her worst troubles came via her mother, who never seemed to forgive Aimee for whatever betrayal her "kidnapping" represented. The strife between them, often involving disagreements over the disposition of Sunday collection receipts, became increasingly strident until the two split decisively in 1929. "The situation has become nearly intolerable," a tearful Minnie Kennedy told reporters, "when it has reached the point where I can talk to my daughter only through an attorney." Severing her connection with the temple, Kennedy moved to the Pacific Northwest and established her own ministry there. But given the peculiar codependency of daughter and mother—"Aimee and Ma," as the papers now called them—there would be other reconciliations and other stormy partings over the years. (One of the latter ended in Sister allegedly breaking her mother's nose!) There would also be many unfinished or aborted projects, including a Foursquare summer resort on Lake Tahoe and a Foursquare cemetery in Burbank ("Go up with Aimee" was the tagline); neither one ever came about, and each left a trail of lawsuits in its wake. Even Sister's marriage to David Hutton ultimately ended in an embarrassing divorce. "It's just a comic strip, this life of ours," lamented Minnie Kennedy when her own rushed marriage collapsed after a bigamy charge against her husband of several months. There were by now many in Los Angeles who would have agreed.

The controversies just kept erupting. McPherson, who was frequently ill during these years, eventually managed to fall out with virtually everyone close to her—her mother, her husband, her substitute preacher, her longtime lieutenant (Harriet Jordan), and even her daughter and heir apparent, Roberta Semple, who ended up suing her mother's lawyer for slander. The L.A. newspapers became fed up with these antics: "A news moratorium on the McPhersons *et al* is the crying need of the day," the *L.A. Times* declared, reporting on the latest family hubbub in 1937. "The first time it was a sensation. The second time it was still good. But now it is like the ninth life of a cat, about worn out."

None of this, however, could negate the legitimate good that McPherson continued to do, particularly in the city she had chosen as her home. When the Depression hit Los Angeles hard, the Angelus Temple created a commissary to feed any and all comers—an institution that evolved into a twenty-four-hours-a-day, seven-days-a-week combination soup kitchen, employment office, and first aid station. "She literally kept most of that Mexican community alive," actor Anthony Quinn (who played sax in the temple band and sometimes served as Sister's translator) once told an interviewer, "and for that I'm eternally grateful." Though her taste for dramatics never waned, she continued to do valuable work into the 1940s, selling bonds for the war effort in World War II.

When Aimee Semple McPherson died in 1944—of an accidental overdose of Seconal, amid rumors of suicide and a predictable family scuffle over her estate—the outpouring from the community was overwhelming. Over fifty thousand mourners came to the temple over the course of three days to pay their respects. In the end, she left the church in the far steadier, if less colorful, hands of her son, Rolf, who led it through a time of exponential growth over the next decades. Today, the International Church of the Foursquare Gospel has over six million members in more than fifty thousand branch congregations around the world.

~

William Mulholland, having experienced the mightiest fall from grace, had the most difficult time in the years to come. After weathering the coroner's inquest, as well as a civil trial brought by Ray Rising, the man who survived the flood by climbing aboard a floating rooftop, Mulholland largely retired from public life. He spent more and more time at his ranch in the San Fernando Valley, though he received anonymous death threats even in his isolation. Some say he was clinically depressed; certainly he was no longer the man who, on his first trip to L.A. in 1877, spoke of opening the oyster of the world. "I see things, but they don't interest me," he told his daughter one day in 1929. "The zest for living is gone." Even so, hard work was a balm to his psychic wounds. He remained active in the LADWP in an advisory capacity until the end.

Sometime in 1933, after years of not speaking, Mulholland went to visit his old friend and mentor, Fred Eaton. Facing bankruptcy after the collapse of the Wattersons' bank in the Owens Valley, Eaton had finally been forced to sell his long-contested Long Valley ranch to the city— for $650,000, after decades of stubbornly holding out for a million or more. Now, with the source of their feud finally gone, both men were eager for a reconciliation. Mulholland was summoned to Eaton's house and ushered into the bedroom, where Fred lay looking aged and feeble, his health failing rapidly after a recent stroke. The two men talked for just a few minutes about old times, but they parted as friends. Not long thereafter—on March 11, 1934—Eaton died. "For three nights in succession I dreamed of Fred," Mulholland told his daughter that night. "The two of us were walking along—young and virile like we used to be. Yet I knew we both were dead."

One day shortly before his own death, Mulholland took his successor as chief engineer, Harvey Van Norman, to a hillside overlooking the San Fernando Valley. "The fact that the valley has developed as it has is compensation enough for all of us," the old man said. It may even have been true. In any case, he lived just long enough to see the Boulder (now Hoover) Dam begun, and plans approved for an aqueduct to bring much of its water to L.A. (The Colorado River aqueduct, as well as the long-contested dam at Eaton's Long Valley ranch location, would be completed in 1941.) William Mulholland died on July 22, 1935. The official cause of death was arteriosclerosis and complications of a stroke, but his longtime driver had a different diagnosis: "It was that damned dam that killed him."

On July 24, as his body lay in state in the rotunda of that gleaming white City Hall, all flags in the city were lowered to half-staff. Later, at the moment of his interment at Forest Lawn cemetery, the flow of water down the Los Angeles Aqueduct from Haiwee Reservoir was halted, and all work on the Colorado River aqueduct was stopped, for a full sixty seconds of silence. It was an appropriate tribute, perhaps, but a minute of work time that Mulholland would have hated to waste.

⌁

By the mid-twentieth century, then, the Artist, the Evangelist, and the Engineer were all gone from the scene, but the marks they had left were evident everywhere. Los Angeles was now the city that boasted the greatest religious pluralism in the country, that served as the center of the world's most lucrative creative industry, and that was sustained by an ingenious water system not substantially different from what its creator first envisioned half a century before. Granted, the Depression hit southern California as hard as it hit elsewhere, stopping the city's rapid growth and turning the boomtown L.A. of the 1920s into the noir L.A. of the 1930s and '40s, rife with all of the urban anxieties, municipal corruption, and social conflicts immortalized in the literature of the period. But rapid industrialization during World War II gave the city the broader-based economic foundation it needed to become a true world-class city. Thus did one of the country's least industrial, least ethnically diverse cities become the opposite.

It was already obvious that it would never be like any other major American or European city. L.A. was, as one writer put it, a "polycentric conurbation"—widely dispersed, decentralized, and lacking monumental structures and foci like the Brooklyn Bridge, Trafalgar Square, or Chicago's Loop. These characteristics struck many critics as flaws. "Los Angeles, at first glance, is not quite real," observed the always-scornful *New York Times* in 1927. "The traveler from the East, after rolling over many leagues of picturesque but not especially fertile desert, has to pinch himself to be sure that this sudden congestion of buildings and humanity, multiplying and transforming themselves almost under his eyes, is not a mirage. What business have thirteen hundred thousand people . . . out here on the edge of things?" And certainly the jibes since then have been frequent and similarly condescending, from Dorothy Parker's description of L.A. as "seventy-two suburbs in search of a city" to Norman Mailer's knock on the place as "a constellation of plastic." As late as the 1980s, critics were still skeptical of its urban bona fides, with theorist Edward Soja calling it not so much a city as "a gigantic conglomeration of theme parks, a lifespace composed of Disneylands."

But even today, when the twenty-first-century city's downtown revival, its increasingly sophisticated cultural life, and its thriving, diverse populations have rendered most of these well-worn criticisms obsolete, the question remains: Should Los Angeles, given its geographical disadvantages, have been allowed to grow so large? With water becoming such a dire issue in southern California and throughout the American West, the temptation may be to say no. But it's worth noting that, thanks to more enlightened conservation policies in recent years, the city consumed less water in 2015 than it did in 1970, despite gaining more than one million additional residents. And short of some kind of disaster scenario recalling a Hollywood blockbuster, Los Angeles is not going to disappear anytime soon. Thanks to Mulholland, Griffith, and McPherson—and many others before and after them—the mirage in the desert has become indelibly real. It's up to a new generation of urban image-makers to ensure that it continues to flourish.

# BIBLIOGRAPHY

Adamic, Louis. *Laughing in the Jungle.* 1932; reprint: Arno Press and *New York Times*, 1969.

Aiken, Katherine G. "Sister Aimee Semple McPherson and the Interwar West, 1920 to 1940." In *Western Lives: A Biographical History of the American West*, edited by Richard W. Etulain. Albuquerque: University of New Mexico Press, 2004.

Aitken, Roy (as told to Al P. Nelson). *The Birth of a Nation Story.* Middleburg, Va.: Denlinger, 1965.

Alexander, Estrelda Y. *Black Fire: One Hundred Years of African American Pentecostalism.* Downers Grover, Ill.: InterVarsity Press, 2011.

Ansell, Martin R. *Oil Baron of the Southwest: Edward L. Doheny and the Development of the Petroleum Industry in California and Mexico.* Columbus: Ohio State University Press, 1998.

Arvidson, Linda. *When the Movies Were Young.* (See entry on page 309 under "Mrs. D. W. Griffith.")

Basinger, Jeanine. *Silent Stars.* New York: Knopf, 1999.

Bauer, Susan Wise. *The Art of the Public Grovel: Sexual Sin and Public Confession in America.* Princeton, N.J.: Princeton University Press, 2008.

Beauchamp, Cari, ed. *My First Time in Hollywood: Stories from the Pioneers, Dreamers, and Misfits Who Made the Movies.* Los Angeles: Asahina & Wallace, 2015.

Bernstein, Arnie, ed. *"The Movies Are": Carl Sandburg's Film Reviews and Essays, 1920–1928.* Chicago: Lake Clermont Press, 2000.

Bitzer, G. W. *Billy Bitzer: His Story.* New York: Farrar, Straus & Giroux, 1973.

Blumhofer, Edith L. *Aimee Semple McPherson: Everybody's Sister.* Grand Rapids, Mich.: Eerdsman, 1993.

Bosworth, Hobart. "Development of Motion Pictures in Los Angeles." Text of a lecture given at the University of Southern California, February 26, 1930. Private collection of Cari Beauchamp.

Brook, Vincent. *Land of Smoke and Mirrors: A Cultural History of Los Angeles.* New Brunswick, N.J.: Rutgers University Press, 2013.

Brown, Karl. *Adventures with D. W. Griffith.* New York: Farrar, Straus & Giroux, 1973.

Brownlow, Kevin. *The Parade's Gone By . . .* Berkeley: University of California Press, 1968.

Camarillo, Albert. *Chicanos in a Changing Society: From Mexican Pueblos to American Barrios in Santa Barbara and Southern California, 1848–1930.* Cambridge, Mass.: Harvard University Press, 1979.

Card, James. *Seductive Cinema: The Art of the Silent Film.* New York: Knopf, 1994.

Caughey, John, and LaRee Caughey, eds. *Los Angeles: Biography of a City.* Berkeley: University of California Press, 1977.

Chalfant, W. A. *The Story of Inyo.* Bishop, Calif.: Privately printed, 1922; ebook version.

Clark, David L. "Miracles for a Dime: From Chautauqua Tent to Radio Station with Sister Aimee." *California History* 57, no. 4 (Winter 1978–79): 355–63.

Cooper, Miriam, with Bonnie Herndon. *Dark Lady of the Silents: My Life in Early Hollywood.* Indianapolis: Bobbs-Merrill, 1973.

Cox, Raymond L. *The Verdict Is In.* Los Angeles: Research Publishers, 1983.

Cruikshank, Jeffrey L., and Arthur W. Schultz. *The Man Who Sold America: The Amazing (but True!) Story of Albert D. Lasker and the Creation of the Advertising Century.* Boston: Harvard Business School Press, 2010.

Davis, Margaret Leslie. *Rivers in the Desert: William Mulholland and the Inventing of Los Angeles.* New York: HarperCollins, 1993.

DeMille, Cecil B. *The Autobiography of Cecil B. DeMille.* Edited by Donald Hayne. Englewood Cliffs, N.J.: Prentice Hall, 1959.

Deverell, William. *Whitewashed Adobe: The Rise of Los Angeles and the Remaking of Its Mexican Past.* Berkeley: University of California Press, 2004.

Drew, William M. *D. W. Griffith's Intolerance: Its Genesis and Its Vision.* Jefferson, N.C.: McFarland, 1986.

Epstein, Daniel Mark. *Sister Aimee: The Life of Aimee Semple McPherson.* New York: Harcourt Brace Jovanovich, 1993.

Everson, William K. *American Silent Film*. New York: Da Capo Press, 1998.

Eyman, Scott. *Empire of Dreams: The Epic Life of Cecil B. DeMille*. New York: Simon & Schuster, 2010.

————. *The Speed of Sound: Hollywood and the Talkie Revolution, 1926–1930*. New York: Simon & Schuster, 1997.

Fenton, Charles. *Stephen Vincent Benét: The Life and Times of an American Man of Letters, 1898–1943*. New Haven, Conn.: Yale University Press, 1958.

Fenton, Charles, ed. *The Letters of Stephen Vincent Benét*. New Haven, Conn.: Yale University Press, 1960.

Fogelson, Robert M. *Fragmented Metropolis: Los Angeles, 1850–1930*. Cambridge, Mass.: Harvard University Press, 1967.

Fussell, Betty Harper. *Mabel: The Life of Mabel Normand*. New York: Limelight, 1992.

Gabler, Neal: *An Empire of Their Own: How the Jews Invented Hollywood*. New York: Crown Publishing, 1988.

Geduld, Harry M., ed. *Focus on D. W. Griffith*. Englewood Cliffs, N.J.: Prentice Hall, 1971.

Gish, Lillian, and Ann Pinchot. *The Movies, Mr. Griffith, and Me*. Englewood Cliffs, N.J.: Prentice Hall, 1969.

Griffith, D. W. *The Man Who Invented Hollywood: The Autobiography of D. W. Griffith*. Edited by James Hart. Louisville, Ky.: Touchstone, 1972.

Griffith, Mrs. D. W. (Linda Arvidson). *When the Movies Were Young*. New York: B. Blom, 1925.

Groff, Frances A. "Frank Wiggins." *American Magazine* 71, no. 1 (1910): 34–35.

Henabery, Joseph E. *Before, In, and After Hollywood: The Autobiography of Joseph E. Henabery*. Lanham, Md.: Scarecrow Press, 1997.

Henderson, Robert M. *D. W. Griffith: His Life and Work*. New York: Oxford University Press, 1972.

————. *D. W. Griffith: The Years at Biograph*. New York: Farrar, Straus & Giroux, 1970.

Henstell, Bruce. "How God and Rev. Shuler Took L.A. by the Airwaves." *Los Angeles*, December 1977, pp. 92–104.

————. *Sunshine and Wealth: Los Angeles in the Twenties and Thirties*. San Francisco: Chronicle Books, 1984.

Hine, Robert V. *California's Utopian Colonies*. Berkeley: University of California Press, 1983.

Hoar, Reverend Thomas F. X. "Religious Broadcasting 1920–1980: Four Religious Broadcast Pioneers and the Process of Evangelization." Ph.D. thesis, Salve Regina University, 2011.

Hoffman, Abraham. *Vision or Villainy: Origins of the Owens Valley–Los Angeles Water Controversy*. College Station: Texas A&M University Press, 1981.

Hundley, Norris, Jr., and Donald C. Jackson. *Heavy Ground: William Mulholland and the St. Francis Dam Disaster*. Berkeley: University of California Press, 2015.

Hunt, Darnell, and Ana-Christina Ramón, eds. *Black Los Angeles: American Dreams and Racial Realities*. New York: New York University Press, 2010.

Jackson, Donald C., and Norris Hudley, Jr. "Privilege and Responsibility: William Mulholland and the St. Francis Dam Disaster." *California History* 82, no. 3 (2004): 8–47.

Kahrl, William L. *Water and Power: The Conflict over Los Angeles' Water Supply in the Owens Valley*. Berkeley: University of California Press, 1982.

Kittell, Wade E. "A Visit to Aimee's Temple." *Branding Iron*, Winter 1994, pp. 4–9.

Knight, Arthur. *The Liveliest Art: A Panoramic History of the Movies*. Rev. ed. New York: Mentor, 1979.

Libecap, Gary D. "The Myth of the Owens Valley." *Regulation* 28, no. 2 (2005): 10–17.

Lippincott, J. B. "William Mulholland—Engineer, Pioneer, Raconteur." *Civil Engineering* 11 (1941): 105–7, 161–64.

Lombardi, Frederic. *Allan Dwan and the Rise and Decline of the Hollywood Studios*. Jefferson, N.C.: McFarland & Co., 2013.

Loos, Anita. *A Girl Like I*. New York: Viking, 1966.

Los Angeles County Coroner. "Transcript of Testimony and Verdict of the Coroner's Jury in the Inquest over Victims of the St. Francis Dam Disaster." April 1928.

Louvish, Simon. *Keystone: The Life and Clowns of Mack Sennett*. New York: Faber & Faber, 2003.

Mann, William J. *Tinseltown: Murder, Morphine, and Madness at the Dawn of Hollywood*. New York: HarperCollins, 2014.

Marsh, Mae. *Screen Acting*. Los Angeles: Photo-Star Publishing, 1921.

McGilligan, Patrick. *Oscar Micheaux: The Great and Only: The Life of America's First Black Filmmaker*. New York: HarperCollins, 2007.

McPherson, Aimee Semple. *In The Service of the King: The Story of My Life*. 1927; reprint: Foursquare Publications, 1988.

———. *The Story of My Life: Aimee Semple McPherson*. Waco, Tex.: Word, 1973.

———. *This Is That: Personal Experiences, Sermons and Writings*. 1919; Jawbone Digital, 2015.

McQuade, James S. "Public Works in Pictures: The Building of the Great Aqueduct of Los Angeles." *Moving Picture World* 15 (1913): 471.

McWilliams, Carey. *Southern California Country: An Island on the Land.* New York: Duell, Sloan & Pearce, 1946.

Mjagkij, Nikki. *Organizing Black America: An Encyclopedia of African American Associations.* Abingdon-on-Thames, U.K.: Routledge, 2001.

Modell, John. *The Economics and Politics of Racial Accommodation: The Japanese of Los Angeles, 1900–1942.* Urbana: University of Illinois Press, 1977.

Mulholland, Catherine. *William Mulholland and the Rise of Los Angeles.* Berkeley: University of California Press, 2000.

Mulholland, William. "Autobiography." Typescript. Los Angeles Public Library.

O'Dell, Paul. *Griffith and the Rise of Hollywood.* New York: A.S. Barnes, 1970.

Ostrom, Vincent. *Water and Politics: A Study of Water Policies and Administration in the Development of Los Angeles.* Los Angeles: Haynes Foundation, 1953.

Outland, Charles. *Man-Made Disaster: The Story of the St. Francis Dam.* Rev. ed. Glendale, Calif.: Arthur H. Clark Co., 1977.

Pickford, Mary. *Sunshine and Shadow.* New York: Doubleday, 1955.

Piper, Karen. "Turning on the Fantasy Fountain: How the Los Angeles Aqueduct Made 'Hollywood.'" *Places Journal*, October 2014. https://placesjournal.org/article/turning-on-the-fantasy-fountain/.

Pitt, Leonard, and Dale Pitt. *Los Angeles A to Z: An Encyclopedia of the City and County.* Los Angeles: University of California Press, 1997.

Ramsaye, Terry. *A Million and One Nights: A History of the Motion Picture.* Abington, U.K.: Routledge, 1964.

Rayner, Richard. *A Bright and Guilty Place: Murder, Corruption, and L.A.'s Scandalous Coming of Age.* New York: Doubleday, 2009.

Reisner, Marc. *Cadillac Desert: The American West and Its Disappearing Water.* New York: Viking Penguin, 1986.

Robeck, Cecil M., Jr. "The Azusa Street Mission and Historic Black Churches: Two Worlds in Conflict in Los Angeles' African American Community." In *Afro-Pentecostalism: Black Pentecostal and Charismatic Christianity in History and Culture*, edited by Amos Yong and Estrelda Y. Alexander. New York: New York University Press, 2011.

Robeck, Cecil M., Jr., and Amos Yong. *The Cambridge Companion to Pentecostalism.* New York: Cambridge University Press, 2014.

Robinson, David. *Hollywood in the Twenties.* New York: A.S. Barnes, 1968.

Romo, Ricardo. *East Los Angeles: History of a Barrio.* Austin: University of Texas Press, 1983.

Rudolph, Marci'a Lincoln. *My Father, Elmo Lincoln: The Original Tarzan*. Las Vegas: Empire Publishing, 1999.

Schickel, Richard. *D. W. Griffith: An American Life*. New York: Simon & Schuster, 1984.

Schiesl, Martin, and Mark M. Dodge, eds. *City of Promise: Race and Historical Change in Los Angeles*. Claremont, Calif.: Regina Books, 2006.

Sennett, Mack, as told to Cameron Shipp. *King of Comedy*. New York: Doubleday, 1954.

Shiel, Mark. *Hollywood Cinema and the Real Los Angeles*. London: Reaktion Books, 2012.

Silva, Fred, ed. *Focus on* The Birth of a Nation. Englewood Cliffs, N.J.: Prentice Hall, 1971.

Sitton, Tom, and William Deverell, eds. *Metropolis in the Making: Los Angeles in the 1920s*. Berkeley: University of California Press, 2001.

Sklar, Robert. *Movie-Made America: A Social History of American Movies*. New York: Random House, 1975.

Slide, Anthony. *Silent Players: A Biographical and Autobiographical Study of 100 Silent Film Actors and Actresses*. Lexington: University Press of Kentucky, 2002.

Slide, Anthony, ed. *D. W. Griffith: Interviews*. Jackson: University Press of Mississippi, 2012.

Spriggs, Elisabeth Mathieu. "The History of the Domestic Water Supply of Los Angeles." Master's thesis, University of Southern California, 1931.

Standiford, Les. *Water to the Angels: William Mulholland, His Monumental Aqueduct, and the Rise of Los Angeles*. New York: Ecco, 2015.

Starr, Kevin. *Inventing the Dream: California Through the Progressive Era*. New York: Oxford University Press, 1985.

———. *Material Dreams: Southern California Through the 1920s*. New York: Oxford University Press, 1990.

Sutton, Matthew Avery. *Aimee Semple McPherson and the Resurrection of Christian America*. Cambridge, Mass.: Harvard University Press, 2007.

Swanberg, W. A. *Citizen Hearst: A Biography of William Randolph Hearst*. New York: Collier Books, 1961.

Swanson, Gloria. *Swanson on Swanson: An Autobiography*. New York: Random House, 1980.

Talbot, Margaret. *The Entertainer: Movies, Magic, and My Father's Twentieth Century*. New York: Riverhead Books, 2012.

Taves, Brian. *Thomas Ince: Hollywood's Independent Pioneer*. Lexington: University Press of Kentucky, 2012.

Taylor, Raymond G. *Men, Medicine, and Water: The Building of the Los Angeles Aqueduct, 1908–1913, a Physician's Recollections.* Edited by Doyce B. Nunis, Jr. Los Angeles: Friends of the LACMA Library, 1982.

Thomas, Lately. *Storming Heaven: The Lives and Turmoils of Minnie Kennedy and Aimee Semple McPherson.* New York: William Morrow, 1970.

Torrence, Bruce T. *Hollywood: The First 100 Years.* New York: New York Zoetrope, 1982.

Troy, Austin. "Thirsty City." *Places Journal,* January 2012, https://placesjournal.org/article/thirsty-city/.

Tzeng, Timothy. "Eastern Promises: The Role of Eastern Capital in the Development of Los Angeles, 1900–1920." *California History* 88, no. 2 (2011): 34–63.

Ulin, David L. *Sidewalking: Coming to Terms with Los Angeles.* Oakland: University of California Press, 2015.

Usai, Paulo Cherchi, ed. *The Griffith Project.* 12 vols. London: British Film Institute, various dates.

Van Norman, H. A. "Memoirs: William Mulholland." *Transactions of the American Society of Civil Engineers* 101 (1936): 1604–8.

Wakida, Patricia, ed. *LAtitudes: An Angeleno's Atlas.* Berkeley: Heyday, 2015.

Waldinger, Roger, and Mehdi Bozorgmehr, eds. *Ethnic Los Angeles.* New York: Russell Sage Foundation, 1996.

Walton, John. "Picnic at Alabama Gates: The Owens Valley Rebellion, 1904–1927." *California History* 65, no. 3 (1986): 193–206.

———. *Western Times and Water Wars: State, Culture, and Rebellion in California.* Berkeley: University of California Press, 1992.

Wehrey, Jane. *Images of America: The Owens Valley.* Charleston, S.C.: Arcadia, 2013.

Widney, Erwin W. "We Build a Railroad." *Touring Topics* (March 1931), pp. 36–41, 52–53.

Wilkman, Jon. *Floodpath: The Deadliest Man-Made Disaster of 20th-Century America and the Making of Modern Los Angeles.* New York: Bloomsbury, 2016.

Williams, Gregory Paul. *The Story of Hollywood: An Illustrated History.* Los Angeles: BL Press, 2006.

Williams, Martin. *Griffith: First Artist of the Movies.* New York: Oxford University Press, 1980.

Williams, Robert Lewis, Jr. "The Negro's Migration to Los Angeles, 1900–1946." *Negro History Bulletin* 19 (February 1956).

Workman, Boyle. *The City That Grew.* Los Angeles: Southland, 1936.

Yallop, David. *The Day the Laughter Stopped: The True Story Behind the Fatty Arbuckle Scandal.* New York: St. Martin's Press, 1976.

Zukor, Adolph, with Dale Kramer. *The Public Is Never Wrong: The Autobiography of Adolph Zukor.* New York: G.P. Putnam's Sons, 1953.

## MANUSCRIPTS, PAPERS, ETC.

Aimee Semple McPherson Archives. The Parsonage, Angelus Temple, Los Angeles. (See also Pentecostalarchives.org.) Includes the comprehensive "Aimee Semple McPherson Chronology," "ASM Legends" (debunking McPherson apocrypha), as well as digitized versions of *Bridal Call* and other publications.

Catherine Mulholland Papers. Special Collections, Oviatt Library, California State University, Northridge, Calif. (incorporates the LADWP Office Files).

Charles G. Clarke Collection. Margaret Herrick Library, Academy of Motion Picture Arts and Sciences, Los Angeles.

D. W. Griffith Papers. Microfilm version, Library of Congress.

Early Film Collection. Neversink Valley Museum of History and Innovation, Cuddebackville, N.Y.

Foursquare Heritage Archives (see Aimee Semple McPherson Archives above).

Hobart Bosworth Papers. Margaret Herrick Library.

Joseph and Jeanne Henabery Papers. Margaret Herrick Library.

Los Angeles Aqueduct Digital Platform. Digital Collections, UCLA Library, digital.library.ucla.edu.

Los Angeles Department of Water and Power Archives. Eastern California Museum, Independence, Calif.

Mary Pickford Papers. Margaret Herrick Library.

Museum of Western Film History (Lone Pine, Calif.). Archives and Publications.

William Selig Papers. Margaret Herrick Library.

## HISTORICAL NEWSPAPERS

*Bridal Call, Inyo Register, Inyo Independent, Los Angeles Examiner* (LAE), *Los Angeles Express* (LAExp), *Los Angeles Herald* (LAH), *Los Angeles Herald-Examiner* (LAHE), *Los Angeles Record* (LAR), *Los Angeles Times* (LAT), *Los Angeles Tribune* (LATrib), *New York Times* (NYT), *The Moving Picture World.*

# NOTES

## PROLOGUE

3 **1976 Alabama Gatehouse bombing:** LAHE and LAT, September 15–17, 1976.

4 **"If I ever find out who bombed":** LAT, October 30, 2013. The *Times* reporter Louis Sahagun tracked down one of the two bombers thirty-seven years after their deed.

4 **tensions between Los Angeles and the Owens Valley:** The decades-long controversy has been written about extensively. For this book, I have relied most heavily on William Kahrl's *Water and Power*, Catherine Mulholland's *William Mulholland and the Rise of Los Angeles*, and Abraham Hoffman's *Vision or Villainy*. All three are exemplars of thorough and careful scholarship, though Kahrl is far more critical of Mulholland, Eaton, Lippincott, and the city of Los Angeles. Catherine Mulholland, as might be expected, gives a more sympathetic account of her grandfather and his associates. Hoffman's book may be the most objective source. For other important sources, see the notes for Chapter 1.

4 **"Land of Little Rain":** The title of a lyrical travel book written in 1903 by Mary Austin.

4 **forty Sierra streams:** For physical aspects of the valley, see Wehry, *Owens Valley*, pp. 7–10.

4 **L.A.'s intensive pumping in 1976:** LAHE and LAT, September 15–17, 1976.

5 **"We'd all thought about doing":** LAT, October 30, 2013.

5    **aftermath of the bombing:** LAT, October 30, 2013.

7    **"It struck me as an odd thing":** Fogelson, *Fragmented*, p. 3.

7    **L.A.'s disadvantages as a city site:** Ibid., pp. 1–5.

8    **L.A. population figures:** U.S. Census and Fogelson, *Fragmented*, p. 21.

8    **"no future":** For the National Irrigation Congress's assessment, see Brook, *Smoke*, p. 130.

9    **fastest-growing U.S. city west of the Mississippi:** Fogelson, *Fragmented*, p. 79.

10    **thirty-sixth-largest city in 1900:** U.S. Census.

## 1. A THIRSTY PLACE

12    **date of departure:** C. Mulholland, *Mulholland*, p. 104.

12    **a mule-pulled buckboard wagon:** Useful and reliable sources for the aqueduct and the Owens Valley controversy include (aside from the previously mentioned Hoffman, Kahrl, and Catherine Mulholland books) Kevin Starr's *Material Dreams*, Remy Nadeau's *Water-Seekers*, Vincent Ostrom's *Water and Politics*, and Les Standiford's *Water to the Angels*. Marc Reiser's *Cadillac Desert* is well-written and provocative, but contains some serious errors and, in my opinion, misjudgments.

12    **"a demijohn of whiskey":** Ibid., p. 348n13. C. Mulholland says he told his children that they took a demijohn on the trip, but the legend is that their trail was marked by (presumably smaller) whiskey bottles.

12    **bacon and canned baked beans:** Nadeau, *Water-Seekers*, p. 15.

12    **Mulholland laughing at Eaton's idea in 1892:** LAE, July 30, 1905.

12    **more than enough water for fifty thousand:** LAE, July 30, 1905.

12    **"on the face of it":** Kahrl, *Water*, p. 47.

13    **enough to support a city ten times:** Standiford, *Angels*, p. 42.

13    **No detailed records:** Mulholland and Eaton gave extremely brief accounts of the trip to the press, which hasn't stopped some authors from creating detailed accounts from their own imaginations. The far more reliable Standiford, *Angels*, p. 75, mentions Mulholland's taking notes and barometric readings.

14    **"a pair of Dublin jackeens":** For Mulholland's childhood and pre-L.A. years, I have relied most heavily on C. Mulholland, *Mulholland*, pp. 3–13.

14    **"would get me nowhere":** W. Mulholland, unpublished autobiographical sketch, p. 1.

14    **"it was doubtless the 'salt-horse'":** Ibid., p. 1.

14    **brink of suicide:** C. Mulholland, *Mulholland*, p. 11.

15    **"Damn a man who doesn't read":** C. Mulholland, *Mulholland*, p. 32.

15    **"all phases of experience except girls":** W. Mulholland autobiographical sketch, p. 2.

15    **Charles Nordhoff's book:** Starr, *Inventing*, pp. 40–41.

15    **"There's Cousin Hugh and Cousin Willie!":** For the stowaway incident and the crossing of the isthmus, see interview with Bill Bodine Mulholland (Hugh Mulholland's son) in Catherine Mulholland Papers, Box 39, Folder 5.

16    **"I was tremendously interested" and "Los Angeles was a place after my own heart":** W. Mulholland autobiographical sketch, p. 3.

16    **1877 population of L.A.:** Ibid., p. 6, and most other sources have it at nine thousand in 1877, but Hoffman, *Vision*, p. 26, puts it at only 5,700.

16    **1871 lynchings:** Starr, *Inventing*, p. 43, and McWilliams, *Southern California*, p. 91.

16    **forty-four Spanish settlers:** For early pueblo history, see Hunt and Ramón, *Black*, pp. 22–24, and Caughey and Caughey, *Biography*, p. 42.

16    **Southern Pacific Railroad:** Fogelson, *Fragmented*, p. 55.

17    **Frank Wiggins:** Starr, *Material*, p. 101.

17    **romanticized legend:** Brook, *Smoke*, pp. 35, 39–41, and McWilliams, *Southern California*, p. 70.

17    **"The American Italy," "a Mediterranean land," and "functional female disturbances":** Ibid., pp. 96–98. During this time the Mulholland brothers put in a short stint as prospectors in Arizona; they gave up after a few unsuccessful weeks and returned to Los Angeles.

17    **Compton well-drilling:** Standiford, *Angels*, p. 33.

17    **"constantly in motion":** Kahrl, *Water*, pp. 20–21.

17    **"These things fired my imagination":** C. Mulholland, *Mulholland*, p. 17.

18    **"Sometimes I had to jump":** W. Mulholland autobiographial sketch, p. 5.

18    **"The river was the greatest attraction":** Ibid., pp. 3–4.

18    **early *zanja* water system:** Hoffman, *Vision*, p. 28; Lippincott, "Mulholland," p. 107; and Van Norman, "Memoirs," p. 2.

18    **thirty-year lease:** C. Mulholland, *Mulholland*, p. 21, and Lippincott, "Mulholland," p. 166.

18    **reluctant to make expensive improvements:** W. Mulholland, speech to the Sunset Club, 1905, in Mulholland Collection WP04-22:24.

18    **little fish swimming:** C. Mulholland, *Mulholland*, p. 31.

18    **only a dozen employees:** Ibid., p. 26.

18   a second long-distance railroad line: McWilliams, *Southern California*, p. 118, and Brook, *Smoke*, p. 36. See also Caughey and Caughey, *Biography*, pp. 201ff.

18   fare war: McWilliams, *Southern California*, p. 118.

18   quintupled the population: Fogelson, *Fragmented*, pp. 21, 78.

19   "It's none of your goddamned": Standiford, *Angels*, pp. 38–39.

19   promoted him to foreman: For Mulholland's early years with the water company, see C. Mulholland, *Mulholland*, pp. 26–31.

19   contrast between Eaton and Mulholland: Kahrl, *Water*, p. 21.

20   "more of an office man": For the succession from Eaton to Kelley to Mulholland, see C. Mulholland, *Mulholland*, pp. 35–36.

20   "Just let me alone": paraphrase of a remark in Standiford, *Angels*, p. 127.

20   Christmas Eve: C. Mulholland, *Mulholland*, p. 42, and Standiford, *Angels*, p. 42.

20   "I never had my shoes off": W. Mulholland autobiographical sketch, p. 6.

20   marriage to Lillie Ferguson: C. Mulholland, *Mulholland*, p. 42.

20   sketch out the entire system from memory: Standiford, *Angels*, p. 52. This ubiquitously told story is probably apocryphal.

21   several years of arbitration: Spriggs, "History of the Domestic," pp. 47–58.

21   "When the city bought the works": Kahrl, *Water*, p. 23.

21   "at least ten years behind": C. Mulholland, *Mulholland*, p. 82.

21   a thorough renovation: Kahrl, *Water*, pp. 24–25.

21   tenth straight year of drought: Ostrom, *Politics*, p. 8.

21   flow of the Los Angeles River: C. Mulholland, *Mulholland*, p. 87.

21   sinking precipitously: Standiford, *Angels*, pp. 61–62.

21   "driest I have ever known": C. Mulholland, *Mulholland*, p. 99.

21   "CROP REPORTS NOT ENCOURAGING": LAH, January 27, 1904.

21   "It is because we are so wicked": LAH, January 17, 1904.

22   near crisis: Ostrom, *Politics*, p. 10.

22   Cattle were dying: Standiford, *Angels*, p. 62.

22   "The time has come": Kahrl, *Water*, p. 25.

## 2. ALTERNATE REALITIES

24 **Owens Valley description:** Wehrey, *Images*, pp. 7–10, and my own observations.

24 **"develop marginal land":** Hoffman, *Vision*, p. 47.

24 **Clausen was dispatched:** Chalfant, *Inyo*, loc. 3757, and Hoffman, *Vision*, p. 46.

25 **possible large-scale federal project:** Hoffman, *Vision*, p. 53.

25 **"high-line canals":** Chalfant, *Inyo*, loc. 3757–71.

25 **"Every detail of the undertaking":** Ibid., loc. 3771.

25 **Lippincott's history with Eaton:** Kahrl, *Water*, pp. 45–47.

25 **the town of Bishop:** Hoffman, *Vision*, p. 59.

25 **Eaton met with Mulholland:** Kahrl, *Water*, p. 49.

26 **board gave the plan its blessing:** Hoffman, *Vision*, p. 61.

26 **"the greatest good to":** Ibid., p. 48.

26 **backroom colloquy:** Kahrl, *Water*, p. 54, and Hoffman, *Vision*, pp. 61–64.

26 **he insisted that the project:** Hoffman, *Vision*, p. 64.

27 **"When my shirt got dirty":** Standiford, *Angels*, p. 84.

27 **"Los Angeles should grapple":** LAH, December 17, 1904.

27 **"the Chicago of the Southwest":** LAT editorial, December 17, 1904.

27 **He was obviously a prosperous type:** Kahrl, *Water*, pp. 58–63, and Standiford, *Angels*, p. 79.

27 **letter from Joseph Lippincott:** Hoffman, *Vision*, pp. 68–79, esp. n37. Hoffmann provides the most evenhanded assessment. C. Mulholland is too lenient, while Kahrl may be too harsh. Lippincott's behavior was, to my mind, patently unethical, though his intentions may have been honest.

28 **well, so be it:** It's also hard to characterize Eaton's activities as ethical, though it seems that he never explicitly told anyone that he represented the Reclamation Service, instead encouraging them to make that assumption on their own. Since he was arguably acting as an individual at this time (though as a de facto agent for the city of Los Angeles), he should perhaps be held to less stringent standards of private business.

28 **buying on his own private account:** Hoffman, *Vision*, pp. 69–70, 79–80, and Chalfont, *Inyo*, loc. 3771. Eaton explained his own behavior in a letter to the editor, *Inyo Independent*, July 31, 1905.

28 **Rickey Ranch:** Hoffman, *Vision*, p. 80.

29   L.A. officials' secret trip: Hoffman, *Vision*, p. 81, and C. Mulholland, *Mulholland*, p. 115.

29   quickly approved Mulholland's formal proposal: Hoffman, *Vision*, p. 81.

29   Eaton's deal for the Rickey Ranch: Kahrl, *Water*, p. 68, and Starr, *Material*, p. 53.

29   "WHERE IS MAYOR MCALEER HIDING?": LAT, May 3, 1905.

29   "prominent business man": Hoffman, *Vision*, p. 83.

29   "the last spike is driven": Kahrl, *Water*, p. 79.

30   "TITANIC PROJECT": LAT, July 29, 1905.

30   "WATER SUPPLY FOR 2,000,000": LAE, July 30, 1905.

30   "The scale of expansion": LAH, August 5, 1905.

30   "The work of constructing": LAH, August 3, 1905.

30   "Metropolis of the Great Southwest": LAR, July 29, 1905.

30   "Gardens instead of desert": Ibid.

30   Harrison Gray Otis: For a rather pointed description, see Reiser, *Cadillac*, p. 71.

31   Promised Land and "Great is Water!": LAT, July 29, 1905.

31   a separate state: McWilliams, *Southern California*, p. 15.

31   Mulholland's somewhat optimistic estimate: Hoffman, *Vision*, p. 19.

31   rivalry between San Diego and Los Angeles: Fogelson, *Fragmented*, pp. 43, 114.

32   meeting in Bishop: Walton, *Western Times*, p. 145.

32   "If the Government's reclamation project": Ibid., pp. 145–46.

32   "Judas B. Lippincott": Hoffman, *Vision*, p. 103.

32   Lippincott's private contract: Kahrl, *Water*, p. 58. He did this despite Newell's long-standing objections to Lippincott's taking on any private work. Lippincott was called away to see to the Salton Sea emergency of March 1905; see Hoffman, *Vision*, p. 74.

32   "After considering the whole matter": Hoffman, *Vision*, p. 119.

33   Caught by surprise: Kahrl, *Water*, p. 81, and Starr, *Material*, p. 53.

33   "I used to be the best fellow": C. Mulholland, *Mulholland*, p. 123.

33   "To the ranchers, Eaton": LAH, July 31, 1905.

33   "the deceptions that these simple folk": LAT, July 29, 1905.

33   "Los Angeles scoundrels": C. Mulholland, *Mulholland*, p. 124.

34 "PEOPLE WANT ALL THE FACTS": LAE, July 31, 1905.

34 "TAXPAYERS DEMAND MORE LIGHT": LAE, August 1, 1905.

34 "typhoid germs": For this and other objections, see LAE, August 2 and 3, 1905.

34 "If there are any people in Los Angeles": LAE, August 3, 1905.

34 opposed the aqueduct plan: Hoffman, *Vision*, p. 142, and Starr, *Material*, p. 56.

34 whether Mulholland had been exaggerating: Kahrl, *Water*, p. 85.

34 flushed through the sewer system: LAH, August 3, 1904; C. Mulholland, *Mulholland*, p. 104; and Standiford, *Angels*, p. 62.

34 a syndicate of prominent L.A. businessmen: Kahrl, *Water*, pp. 96, 101; Hoffman, *Vision*, p. 127; Standiford, *Angels*, p. 61; and C. Mulholland, *Mulholland*, p. 61. The latter two authors point out that the original option on the land was purchased in October 1903 (a sale that was publicly reported in LAT, October 23, 1903), long before the aqueduct plan was conceived. But Hoffman makes a convincing case for why this does not exonerate the syndicate of corrupt behavior.

35 the Porter Ranch: C. Mulholland, *Mulholland*, p. 98.

35 Mulholland and corruption: Ibid., pp. 206–7, does a good job of clearing Mulholland of accusations of corruption, explaining why the aqueduct had to end at the head of the San Fernando Valley.

35 first bond issue: Fogelson, *Fragmented*, p. 98, and Kahrl, *Water*, p. 101. The *Examiner* changed to support the aqueduct bond issues after Hearst became convinced of the project's value; see Hoffman, *Vision*, p. 128.

35 second bond vote: Kahrl, *Water*, p. 157.

35 Reclamation Service had officially abandoned its irrigation plans: Hoffman, *Vision*, p. 144.

35 "It is a hundred or a thousandfold more important": Walton, *Western Times*, p. 150. The quote is often incorrectly attributed to Roosevelt himself.

36 "The chance to acquire": C. Mulholland, *Mulholland*, p. 99.

36 "Everybody in the valley has money": LAT, July 29, 1905.

36 "The government held Owens Valley": Chalfont, *Inyo*, loc. 3853.

## 3. STORIES IN LIGHT AND SHADOW

38 Boggs, the director: For the filming of *Monte Cristo*, I rely heavily on Bosworth, "Development of Motion Pictures." Special thanks to Cari Beauchamp for generously providing me with a copy of this hard-to-find

manuscript. Also Hobart Bosworth, Scrapbook no. 5, in Hobart Bosworth Papers, and file 25f-533, in William Selig Papers. See also Caughey and Caughey, *Biography*, p. 254.

39   **Hobart Bosworth:** Bosworth, Scrapbook no. 5, p. 3, and Bosworth, Scrapbook no. 2, Hobart Bosworth Papers. Other details are derived from Brownlow, *Parade's Gone*, p. 31.

39   **"not a tremendous financial success":** Bosworth, Scrapbook no 5.

39   **"a quiet gentleman in fashionable clothes":** Bosworth, "Development of Motion Pictures," p. 3.

39   **"I was shocked":** Ibid.

39   **"Alas, my code of ethics fell":** Ibid., p. 4.

40   **"Never mind the floor":** Unidentified newspaper article in Bosworth, Scrapbook no. 5.

40   **"continuity notes" for *Sultan*:** File 25f-553a, Selig Papers. Some secondary sources refer to this film as *In the Power of the Sultan*, but the Selig publicity materials identify the film as I have. See the advertising booklet for the film containing a synopsis, ibid. Other details are in Bosworth, "Development," p. 5.

40   **"All was hurried":** Bosworth, "Development," pp. 6–7.

40   **laundry next door:** LAT, May 5, 1940, and May 9, 1949.

40   **"I watched the development":** Bosworth, "Development," p. 7.

41   **"All Saturday":** LAT, May 5, 1940. Some sources list Boggs's *The Heart of a Race Tout* as the first film made entirely in California (e.g., Torrence, *Hollywood*, p. 68), but although it may have been filmed earlier, it was released several weeks after *Sultan*. Brownlow, *Parade's Gone*, p. 31, claims that Biograph had a studio office in L.A. as early as 1906, though apparently no Biograph films were made in the city until later.

41   **It would not be the last:** There have been many, many good overviews of early film history. I have relied most heavily on Robert Sklar's excellent *Movie-Made America*, William K. Everson's *American Silent Film*, and Kevin Brownlow's *The Parade's Gone By . . .* Arthur Knight's *The Liveliest Art* contains some dated information, but it brilliantly synthesizes cinema history into a compact volume. Neal Gabler's *An Empire of Their Own* is superb on the major (mostly Jewish) studio heads. Many of the biographies and memoirs of individual directors, actors, cameramen, and producers discussed later in these notes also do a good job of laying out the early history of film.

41   **Thomas Edison:** For his exaggerated role in the development of film technology, see Sklar, *Movie-Made*, pp. 10–11.

41 **Kinetoscope:** Knight, *Liveliest*, p. 8, and Sklar, *Movie-Made*, p. 13.

41 **selling them to penny arcades:** Knight, *Liveliest*, pp. 7–8.

41 **Developments in film projection:** Ibid., p. 9.

42 ***The Execution of Mary, Queen of Scots*:** Sklar, *Movie-Made*, p. 21, and Knight, *Liveliest*, p. 13.

42 **George Méliès:** Brownlow, *Parade's Gone*, p. 9, and Knight, *Liveliest*, p. 14.

42 ***The Great Train Robbery*:** Everson, *Silent*, p. 36, and Knight, *Liveliest*, pp. 14–16. The film is twelve minutes long at a projection rate of eighteen frames per second.

42 **rise of nickelodeons:** Knight, *Liveliest*, p. 17.

43 **steal ideas and stories:** Sklar, *Movie-Made*, p. 22.

43 **a pastime of the inner-city working class:** Sklar, *Movie-Made*, pp. 4, 30, and Brownlow, *Parade's Gone*, pp. 2, 11.

43 **David Wark Griffith, a frustrated thespian:** The most readable and authoritative biography of Griffith is that by Richard Schickel. Griffith's own autobiography (assembled from a series of sit-down interviews with the director over several years, and published as *D. W. Griffith: The Man Who Invented Hollywood*) is not particularly enlightening and, like many memoirs, should be approached with caution. Special mention should go to Robert M. Henderson's careful, authoritative *D. W. Griffith: The Years at Biograph*, which was useful for this chapter. (Henderson's *D. W. Griffith: His Life and Work* is also very good.) An exhaustive, multivolume series of essays, analysis, and information called *The Griffith Project* is indispensable, published by the British Film Institute and edited by Paolo Cherchi Usai.

43 **Lofty Green:** For Griffith's Kentucky childhood, see Schickel, *Griffith*, pp. 16–35, and Griffith, *Man Who Invented*, pp. 24ff.

43 **Jacob Griffith:** He was known as both "Thundering" and "Roaring" Jake. See Schickel, *Griffith*, p. 15.

43 **a line of Welsh warrior kings:** Ibid.

43 **"Here was whelped":** Griffith, *Man Who Invented*, p. 19.

44 **"listening to whittling oldsters":** Ibid., p. 23.

44 **"variously assorted villainies":** Ibid., p. 49.

44 **"I was forced to beat my way":** Ibid., p. 50.

44 **a Sarah Bernhardt production:** Ibid., p. 52.

44 **Alessandro in the play *Ramona*:** Schickel, *Griffith*, p. 67.

44 **"Success was always just around":** Griffith, *Man Who Invented*, p. 63.

44 **Linda Arvidson:** Schickel, *Griffith*, pp. 64–65.

45   **they were married:** Ibid., p. 70.

45   **a producer had bought** *A Fool and a Girl*: Ibid., p. 82. Griffith, *Man Who Invented*, claims the selling price was $1,000, not $700.

45   **a period of success for the neophyte writer:** Schickel, *Griffith*, pp. 82–84, and Griffith, *Man Who Invented*, p. 69.

45   **closed after a short run:** Schickel, *Griffith*, p. 87.

45   **"pretentious":** Arvidson, *When*, 51/435.

46   **"I'll lose standing":** Schickel, *Griffith*, p. 91, and Griffith, *Man Who Invented*, p. 73.

46   **"I found it silly":** Schickel, *Griffith*, p. 51.

46   **Edison Studio in the Bronx:** Ibid., p. 92.

46   *Rescued from an Eagle's Nest*: Ibid., pp. 90–93.

46   **American Mutoscope and Biograph Company:** Henderson, *Biograph*, p. 30, and Schickel, *Griffith*, pp. 92–93.

47   **nine principal film studios:** Henderson, *Biograph*, p. 5, lists them as Edison, Biograph, Vitagraph, Kalem, Lubin, Selig, Essanay, Méliès, and Pathé.

47   **Dickson's Mutoscope, camera, projector:** Bitzer, *Bitzer*, p. xiv.

47   **"Edison licensees":** For the new combine, see Henderson, *Biograph*, pp. 7–8.

48   **McCutcheon's son Wallace:** Ibid., p. 9.

48   **Marvin was making inquiries:** Schickel, *Griffith*, p. 106, and Henderson, *Biograph*, pp. 16–17.

48   **responsibilities of director:** Henderson, *Biograph*, pp. 17–18.

48   **Griffith might be a good prospect:** Schickel, *Griffith*, p. 107.

48   **"It's not so bad, you know":** Arvidson, *When*, p. 31 (57/435), and Schickel, *Griffith*, p. 104.

48   **"I am working regularly":** Schickel, *Griffith*, p. 107. Arvidson, *When*, p. 84 (86/435), renders the scene slightly differently.

49   *Dollie* **synopsis as a "lemon":** Henderson, *Biograph*, p. 30.

49   **"Heart Interest, Drama":** Bitzer, *Bitzer*, pp. 65–66.

49   **Just promise him a bottle:** Ibid., p. 66.

49   **two days of photography:** Henderson, *Biograph*, p. 34. Some sources, such as Arvidson, say the film was made in New Jersey, not Connecticut.

49   **Arthur Johnson and sixty-five dollars:** Griffith, *Man Who Invented*, p. 74.

50    **Keith and Proctor's Theatre:** Henderson, *Biograph*, p. 35.

50    **"Not a snore was to be heard":** Arvidson, 92/435.

50    **audience demand for the film:** Schickel, *Griffith*, p. 110.

50    **his first one-year contract:** Henderson, *Biograph*, p. 43.

50    **a royalty:** Schickel, *Griffith*, p. 11, pegs it at one-twentieth of a cent per foot.

50    **"without parallel":** Knight, *Liveliest*, p. 23.

50    *For the Love of Gold:* Henderson, *Biograph*, p. 44.

51    *Fred Ott's Sneeze:* Bitzer, *Bitzer*, p. 10.

51    **"Now Griffith was able to express thought":** Henderson, *Biograph*, p. 45.

51    *The Fatal Hour:* Ibid., p. 54

51    *The Lonely Villa:* Ibid., pp. 67–68.

51    **Vignette shots, fade-outs:** For more on Griffith/Bitzer innovations, see Ibid., pp. 55–61, 63–64.

51    **"a coherent, basic screen grammar":** Schickel, *Griffith*, p. 112.

52    **Griffith was freeing the medium:** Everson, *Silent*, p. 55, is especially good.

52    **signing his real name:** Schickel, *Griffith*, p. 153.

52    **"How can you tell a story":** Ibid., p. 112.

52    **Film stock was too expensive:** Bitzer, *Bitzer*, p. 70.

52    **"the finish, the roundness" and "Even we children":** For Biograph days, see Henderson, *Biograph*, pp. 49, 52–53.

52    **identifying their favorites:** Sklar, *Movie-Made*, p. 40.

53    **Florence Lawrence:** Schickel, *Griffith*, p. 116.

53    **Henry Walthall:** Ibid., p. 129.

53    **"a big bear-like figure":** Ibid., p. 116.

53    **"my day school":** Ibid., p. 117.

53    **"In rapid fire":** Griffith, *Man Who Invented*, p. 77.

53    **"You're too little and too fat":** Henderson, *Biograph*, p. 66.

54    **look like Pancho Villa:** Basinger, *Silent*, p. 20.

54    **head was too big:** Griffith, *Man Who Invented*, p. 78.

54    **more than two hundred films:** Griffith made 57 pictures in 1908 and 151 pictures in 1909 according to Henderson, *Life*, pp. 58, 92.

54    **"highbrow effects":** NYT, October 10, 1909.

54   **"perhaps because he was a Southerner"**: Bitzer, *Bitzer*, p. 76.

54   **"he could guarantee"**: Ibid.

55   *The Newlyweds*: Henderson, *Biograph*, pp. 94–95.

55   **traveled in style**: Schickel, *Griffith*, p. 146, and Henderson, *Biograph*, p. 97.

## 4. ON LOCATION

58   Many Hollywood memoirs touch on Griffith's early years. Most relevant is Linda Arvidson's *When the Movies Were Young* (for which the author is sometimes listed as "Mrs. D. W. Griffith"), which is remarkably free of rancor, given that her marriage to the director didn't last. Bitzer's *Billy Bitzer: His Story* is indispensable, as is Karl Brown's *Adventures with D. W. Griffith*, written by Bitzer's assistant during the early L.A. years. Mary Pickford's *Sunshine and Shadow*, Lillian Gish's *The Movies, Mr. Griffith, and Me*, Miriam Cooper's *Dark Lady of the Silents*, and Anita Loos's *A Girl Like I* are also excellent. Mack Sennett's *King of Comedy* is fascinating but full of apocrypha. Cari Beauchamp has gathered excerpts from these and other memoirs in the superb anthology *My First Time in Hollywood*.

58   **January 20 arrival in L.A.**: Henderson, *Biograph*, p. 97.

58   **a permanent Selig studio**: Bosworth, "Development," pp. 7–8.

58   **the part of Virgilias**: LAT, May 5, 1909.

58   **Charles Baumann and Adam Kessel**: Henderson, *Biograph*, p. 96; Bosworth, "Development," p. 20; and Louvish, *Keystone*, p. 45.

58   **companies that arrived**: Bosworth, "Development," p. 21; Henderson, *Biograph*, p. 5; and Brownlow, *Parade's Gone*, p. 31.

58   **"We could make Westerns here"**: Bosworth, "Development," p. 14.

59   **Red and Yellow Cars**: Fogelson, *Fragmented*, pp. 85–92, and Schickel, *Griffith*, p. 148.

59   **Electric Theatre**: Schickel, *Griffith*, p. 96.

59   **"NO JEWS, ACTORS, OR DOGS" and Conscientious Citizens**: Beauchamp, *First Time*, p. 20.

59   **"a lazy little village"**: Eyman, *DeMille*, p. 67.

60   **William and David Horsely**: Brownlow, *Parade's Gone*, p. 31.

60   **downtown loft on Main Street**: For the first Biograph studio in L.A., see Henderson, *Biograph*, p. 97.

60   **"Our studio consisted of an acre"**: Beauchamp, *First Time*, p. 15.

60   **"watching the proceedings"**: Arvidson, *When*, p. 256 (60/435).

60 "a kitchen table": Beauchamp, *First Time*, pp. 15–16.

60 *The Thread of Destiny*: For the first three Griffith films shot in L.A., see Henderson, *Biograph*, pp. 98–99.

60 *In Old California*: Schickel, *Griffith*, pp. 149–50.

60 "They resented the love-making": Beauchamp, *First Time*, p. 13.

61 work on *The Two Brothers*: Schickel, *Griffith*, p. 151.

61 "California pictures": Ibid., p. 147.

61 "Anything on film made money": Louvish, *Keystone*, p. 52.

61 long-fought lawsuit against the Movie Trust: Schickel, *Griffith*, p. 198.

61 "Now the combine was broken": Griffith, *Man Who Invented*, p. 86.

61 a $40 million industry and weekly audience of 45 million: Louvish, *Keystone*, p. 39.

61 "The vast waves of nickels": Bosworth, "Development," p. 22.

62 "All was fish that came to our net": Ibid., p. 8.

62 more than forty different companies: Eyman, *DeMille*, p. 63.

62 "During the noon hour": Beauchamp, *First Time*, p. 21.

62 " 'D.W.' was the master": Ibid., p. 109.

62 "The Belasco of Motion Pictures": Schickel, *Griffith*, p. 154.

62 "I watched everything he did": Brownlow, *Parade's Gone*, pp. 97–98.

62 Boggs was shot and killed: LAT, LAH, and LAE, October 27, 1911, and days following.

62 "Every scene I made": Bosworth, "Development," p. 18.

63 without an art director: Brownlow, *Parade's Gone*, p. 56.

63 *The Lonedale Operator* and *A Girl and Her Trust*: I am indebted to Everson, *Silent*, pp. 43–46, for this illuminating comparison. Further details from Henderson, *Biograph*, pp. 115–16 and 132–33.

63 "from the lifting of an eyelid": Schickel, *Griffith*, p. 165.

63 "Mr. Griffith would move around us": Gish, *Movies*, pp. 84–85.

63 "Not so much": Ibid., p. 87.

64 he even told Miriam Cooper: Cooper, *Dark Lady*, p. 70.

64 Griffith chanced upon them: For the first Gish/Griffith encounter, see Henderson, *Biograph*, pp. 139–41.

64 "That will make a wonderful scene": Gish, *Movies*, pp. 37–38.

64 Pickford had quit: Brownlow, *Parade's Gone*, p. 126.

64 Mack Sennett left: Schickel, *Griffith*, p. 179.

64  Linda Arvidson, who found: Ibid., p. 163.

64  Griffith's ambitions had grown: Ibid., p. 179.

65  *His Trust* and *His Trust Fulfilled*: see Henderson, *Biograph*, p. 109.

65  *Enoch Arden*, a two-reel adaptation: Schickel, *Griffith*, p. 160, and Gish, *Movies*, p. 63. For Griffith's other two-reelers, including *The Mothering Heart* and *The Battle of Elderbush Gulch*, see Schickel, *Griffith*, pp. 186–89.

65  tried-and-true single-reel format: Henderson, *Biograph*, p. 126.

65  Griffith secured Biograph's permission: Ibid., p. 146.

65  *Judith of Bethulia*: Ibid., pp. 151–53.

65  the accountant was converted: Schickel, *Griffith*, p. 195.

65  six reels long: Henderson, *Biograph*, p. 154.

66  "If you stay with Biograph": Schickel, *Griffith*, pp. 197–98.

66  "I thought I knew an exit cue": Griffith, *Man Who Invented*, p. 87.

66  Adolph Zukor's offer: Henderson, *Biograph*, p. 156.

66  Harry Aitken's offer: Ibid., p. 155, and Schickel, *Griffith*, p. 202.

66  "We are just grinding out sausages": Bitzer, *Bitzer*, p. 89.

66  Griffith's break with Biograph: Henderson, *Biograph*, p. 156.

66  five years and some 457 films: They are listed in ibid., pp. 193–215.

66  "We were going [back] to California": Bitzer, *Bitzer*, p. 90.


### 5. "A RIVER NOW IS HERE"

70  some thirty to forty thousand people: For attendance estimates and dignitaries present, see LAT, LAE, and LAR, November 5 and 6, 1913. The population of L.A. in the 1910 U.S. Census was about 319,000.

70  "the biggest and most heartfelt": LAT, November 6, 1913.

70  "the Goethals of the West": Standiford, *Angels*, p. 208.

70  "I would rather give birth": C. Mulholland, *Mulholland*, p. 230.

70  his wife lay ailing: Ibid., p. 246.

70  a motion picture documentary: *The Building of the Great Aqueduct of Los Angeles*, produced by Aitken's American Film Manufacturing Company, was reviewed in *Moving Picture World* 15 (January–March 1913): 471.

70  Since 1906: Wehrey, *Images*, p. 41.

71  train line to Lone Pine: Kahrl, *Water*, p. 152.

71  hydroelectric power plants: Taylor, *Men*, p. 21.

71   **"I'm going into this as a man"**: C. Mulholland, *Mulholland*, p. 159.

71   **Adna R. Chaffee**: Ibid., p. 160.

71   **eleven divisions**: Ibid., p. 161.

71   **Over 500 miles**: The statistics in this paragraph are from LAT, September 12, 1909, and Nadeau, *Water-Seekers*, p. 35.

71   **"Well, we have spent about $3 million"**: Mulholland's Chamber of Commerce speech is in Nadeau, *Water-Seekers*, p. 36.

71   **commissary service**: For the three contracted services, see Taylor, *Men*, p. 22.

71   **Mulholland was convinced**: Ibid., p. 22.

72   **trusted and familiar lieutenants**: Hoffman, *Vision*, pp. 145–47.

72   **Working without extensive notes**: Kahrl, *Water*, p. 159.

72   **For years on end he traveled**: Starr, *Material*, p. 57.

72   **"could scrape barnacles"**: C. Mulholland, *Mulholland*, p. 354n11.

72   **inspired intense loyalty**: Kahrl, *Water*, p. 155.

72   **"I took a vacation once"**: Standiford, *Angels*, p. 266.

72   **camping trip to the Sierra**: C. Mulholland, *Mulholland*, p. 154.

72   **fourth-largest engineering project**: Kahrl, *Water*, p. 158.

72   **close to four thousand men**: Nadeau, *Water-Seekers*, p. 41.

72   **eight-to-ten-hour shifts**: Standiford, *Angels*, p. 136, and Nadeau, *Water-Seekers*, pp. 27–28.

72   **mostly Mexicans**: For the ethnic makeup of the workforce, see Widney, "We Build," p. 36, and Standiford, *Angels*, p. 135.

73   **occasional tension between**: Hoffman, *Vision*, p. 150.

73   **"one crew drunk"**: Nadeau, *Water-Seekers*, p. 40.

73   **"the wickedest town in the West"**: C. Mulholland, *Mulholland*, p. 172.

73   **"I saw lights on in every saloon"**: Widney, "We Build," p. 36.

73   **"At a rough estimate"**: Ibid., pp. 39–40.

73   **outlawing saloons**: Hoffman, *Vision*, p. 151, and Taylor, *Men*, p. 56.

73   **speed records**: Standiford, *Angels*, p. 143.

73   **bonus system**: Nadeau, *Water-Seekers*, p. 37, LAT, September 12, 1909. Hoffman, *Vision*, p. 147, says it was Lippincott's idea.

73   **450 days ahead**: For statistics about finishing the Elizabeth Tunnel, see Nadeau, *Water-Seekers*, p. 37.

74   **"That is very rough and difficult country"**: Nadeau, *Water-Seekers*, p. 38, and LAT, September 12, 1909.

74 Sag pipes: The mechanics were explained to me by Fred Barker, former engineer with the LADWP. See also *Los Angeles Magazine*, September 24, 2013.

74 caterpillars: Standiford, *Angels*, p. 130.

74 low-tech mules: C. Mulholland, *Mulholland*, p. 175.

74 combination of old and new technologies: Hoffman, *Vision*, p. 145.

74 hydraulic sluicing technique: Davis, *Rivers*, p. 106.

74 "as though it were his baby": C. Mulholland, *Mulholland*, p. 168.

75 "We'll pull her through on time": Standiford, *Angels*, p. 131.

75 expenditures were outpacing: C. Mulholland, *Mulholland*, p. 187.

75 fluctuations in the New York bond market: Nadeau, *Water-Seekers*, p. 41.

75 Mulholland and Mathews hurried east: C. Mulholland, *Mulholland*, p. 187.

75 massive layoffs: Nadeau, *Water-Seekers*, p. 41.

75 resumed buying bonds: C. Mulholland, *Mulholland*, p. 188.

75 difficulty rehiring laborers: Nadeau, *Water-Seekers*, p. 43, says Mulholland wasn't fully staffed again until May 1911.

75 quality of the food: C. Mulholland, *Mulholland*, p. 180.

75 San Francisco earthquake: Hoffman, *Vision*, p. 152.

75 spoiled quickly in the desert heat: Ibid., p. 153.

75 violent food riots: Taylor, *Men*, p. 56.

75 renegotiated his contract: Nadeau, *Water-Seekers*, p. 42, and C. Mulholland, *Mulholland*, p. 189.

76 WFM had been trying to organize: Taylor, *Men*, p. 152.

76 strike of tunnelers: Nadeau, *Water-Seekers*, p. 42.

76 "Preferring loafing to working": C. Mulholland, *Mulholland*, p. 190.

76 one of the least union-friendly places: Kahrl, *Water*, p. 170.

76 open shop as the only way to compete: McWilliams, *Southern California*, pp. 275–78.

76 "presented so able an array": Caughey and Caughey, *Biography*, p. 260.

76 antipicketing ordinance: McWilliams, *Southern California*, pp. 279–80.

76 an explosion ripped though: The *L.A. Times* building bombing has received book-length treatment in Lew Irwin's *Deadly Times* (Guilford, Conn.: Globe Pequot Press, 2013). Specifics here come from Caughey and Caughey, *Biography*, pp. 260–61.

77   who was responsible: For the blame game, see ibid., p. 262.

77   reputation for vindictiveness: McWilliams, *Southern California*, p. 275.

77   nationwide investigation: Caughey and Caughey, *Biography*, p. 264.

77   "As there seems to be no possible way": Nadeau, *Water-Seekers*, p. 43.

77   John and James McNamara: Caughey and Caughey, *Biography*, pp. 264–65.

77   "Saint Mulholland": C. Mulholland, *Mulholland*, p. 203.

77   Harriman rehashed: Hoffman, *Vision*, p. 158.

78   Mulholland answered every charge: C. Mulholland, *Mulholland*, p. 205.

78   In October Harriman won: Ibid., p. 202, describes the 1911 election as the first in which L.A. women could vote.

78   changed their plea: C. Mulholland, *Mulholland*, p. 204. Nadeau, *Water-Seekers*, p. 44, claims that Harriman assisted Darrow.

78   set back the labor movement: McWilliams, *Southern California*, p. 283.

78   the Chief requested: Nadeau, *Water-Seekers*, p. 44.

78   legal action against Fred Eaton: For the report's recommendation, see C. Mulholland, *Mulholland*, p. 225.

79   "a knowledge of human nature": Nadeau, *Water-Seekers*, p. 44.

79   poor judgment and engineering expediencies: For justified criticisms in the report, see Hoffman, *Vision*, p. 167.

79   Socialist-backed candidate Henry H. Rose: For the investigation as a factor in the 1913 election, see ibid., p. 169.

79   "criticism of the aqueduct is captious": C. Mulholland, *Mulholland*, p. 240.

79   "poison": The Socialist-leaning paper was the *L.A. Record*. Standiford, *Angels*, p. 183.

79   "an outstanding example of waste": J. Gregg Layne, official historian of the L.A. Department of Water and Power, quoted in Hoffman, *Vision*, p. 168.

79   last work on the Jawbone sag pipes: Nadeau, *Water-Seekers*, p. 47.

79   opening the gates: Ibid., p. 47, and C. Mulholland, *Mulholland*, p. 231.

79   released in May: Nadeau, *Water-Seekers*, pp. 47–48.

80   tunnel at Sand Canyon: C. Mulholland, *Mulholland*, p. 235.

80   "The big job is finished": Ibid., p. 242.

80   bright, sunny afternoon: Ibid., p. 244.

80   special trains: LAE, November 5, 1913.

80   **little drinking cups:** Hoffman, *Vision*, p. 171.

80   **well within its $23.5 million budget:** For the final statistics on costs and budget, see Standiford, *Angels*, pp. 208–9. According to the *Final Report of Construction* (1916), the actual under-budget figure, after accounting for things like the salvage value of leftover supplies, was close to $3 million.

80   **"The completion of the Owens River Aqueduct":** LAE, November 5, 1913.

80   **"A mighty river":** LAT, November 6, 1913.

80   **At 12:10:** Details of the ceremony were reported in the local papers of November 5 and 6, 1913.

81   **"Throughout the ceremony":** LAE, November 6.

81   **"rather skin dead dogs":** C. Mulholland, *Mulholland*, p. 150.

81   **uterine cancer:** Ibid., p. 243.

81   **"This is a great event":** LAT, November 6, 1913. Details of the ceremony are mostly from LAE and LAT, November 6, 1913.

81   **As the flag unfurled:** Details of Angelenos welcoming the water are from LAE, November 6, 1913.

81   **"The water came":** LAT, November 6, 1913.

82   **"There it is. Take it!":** Ubiquitously reported.

82   **Exposition Park:** The program for the celebration is in LAE, November 5, 1913.

82   **April 1915:** Standiford, *Angels*, p. 212.

82   **"magnificent heritage":** Nadeau, *Water-Seekers*, p. 45.

83   **"I am only sorry":** LAE, November 6, 1913.

83   **feuding for some years:** Hoffman, *Vision*, p. 172.

83   **"I'll buy Long Valley":** Nadeau, *Water-Seekers*, p. 52.

83   **the rights for a smaller dam:** Hoffman, *Vision*, p. 172.

83   **plenty of water for everyone:** On the improvement of city/valley relations, see Walton, *Western Times*, p. 152.

83   **adding an estimated 100,000 new residents:** LAE, June 19, 1912.

83   **smaller reservoirs:** On the future trouble caused by the lack of a large reservoir at Long Valley, see Starr, *Material*, p. 58.

84   **"Lift your voice in gratitude":** Hoffman, *Vision*, p. 171.

## 6. THE BIRTH OF AN INDUSTRY

86 **"After the others leave"**: On Griffith explaining his plans for *The Clansman*, see Gish, *Movies*, pp. 131–32.

87 **director Allan Dwan**: Lombardi, *Allan Dwan*, p. 20.

87 **Biograph had held the picture**: Gish, *Movies*, p. 109.

87 **several even longer productions**: Release dates for the Ince, DeMille, and Bosworth longer films are listed on IMDb.com.

87 **two Wisconsin farm boys**: Aitken, *Birth*, pp. 11–12.

87 **thirty-one different film exchanges**: Louvish, *Keystone*, p. 52.

87 **"People with capital"**: Aitken, *Birth*, p. 22.

88 **two films per week**: Ibid., pp. 25–26.

88 **in-between times**: Schickel, *Griffith*, p. 211.

88 **"This Clansman picture"**: Aitken, *Birth*, p. 26.

88 **cost $40,000 to produce, plus Dixon's additional $25,000**: Schickel, *Griffith*, p. 207. Although Aitken, *Birth*, p. 26, claims that no previous American film had cost more than $10,000 to make, there had been costlier films.

88 **"Gentlemen, $65,000 is a very big sum"**: Aitken, *Birth*, p. 26.

88 **directors rejected the project**: Schickel, *Griffith*, p. 208, and Aitken, *Birth*, p. 30.

88 **raise the money for Griffith**: Aitken, *Birth*, p. 34.

88 **Dixon received $2,000**: Schickel, *Griffith*, p. 222.

89 **"the story of the South"**: Geduld, *Focus*, p. 38.

89 **"changed D. W. Griffith's personality"**: Schickel, *Griffith*, p. 215.

89 **"You get that old camera of yours"**: Bitzer, *Bitzer*, p. 106.

89 **Thomas Ince, who had**: For Ince's early career, see Taves, *Ince*, pp. 29–36, and Sklar, *Movie-Made*, p. 40.

89 **"by the specter of the wolf"**: Taves, *Ince*, p. 24.

89 **one-quarter of all films produced**: Ibid., p. 32.

89 **Hart, Ince's old roommate**: Basinger, *Silent*, p. 181.

89 **lean, unsentimental**: Knight, *Liveliest*, p. 30.

89 **101 Ranch Wild West Show**: Taves, *Ince*, p. 33.

89 **"Ince Punch"**: Ibid., pp. 40–41.

90 **pioneer of studio specialization**: Schickel, *Griffith*, p. 307, and Taves, *Ince*, pp. 41–42.

90   "A director could no longer be": Ibid., p. 46.

90   Ince could give up directing: Taves, *Ince*, p. 46.

90   his personal stamp: Knight, *Liveliest*, p. 31.

90   Mack Sennett: For his early career, see Knight, *Liveliest*, pp. 33–34, and Louvish, *Keystone*, p. 49.

90   "It's got to move": Knight, *Liveliest*, p. 34.

90   parody a Griffith film: Louvish, *Keystone*, p. 72.

90   Sennett allowed his stars to direct: Ibid., p. 80.

90   meetings while bathing: Knight, *Liveliest*, p. 39.

91   Roscoe "Fatty" Arbuckle: Louvish, *Keystone*, p. 78, points out that Arbuckle made movies at Selig before coming to Keystone.

91   "like floating in the arms": Brownlow, *Parade's Gone*, p. 362.

91   Charles Chaplin: Louvish, *Keystone*, p. 88.

91   to give Ford Sterling a little: Knight, *Liveliest*, p. 40.

91   "IS THERE A MAN": Louvish, *Keystone*, p. 88.

91   salary of $150 per week: Knight, *Liveliest*, p. 37.

91   *Tillie's Punctured Romance*: Louvish, *Keystone*, p. 97.

91   Essanay at $1,250 a week: For Chaplin's rising salary, see Knight, *Liveliest*, p. 38.

91   Cecil B. DeMille: For his childhood and early education, see Eyman, *DeMille*, pp. 20, 27, 28, and 34.

92   "Let's go down to Mexico": Ibid., p. 52.

92   start of the Lasky Feature Play Company: Ibid., pp. 54–55. Lawyer Arthur Friend was a fourth partner, in addition to DeMille, Lasky, and Goldfish.

92   "galloping tintypes": Ibid., p. 48.

92   "After all, you do come of a cultured family": Ibid., p. 55.

92   shooting *The Squaw Man*: Beauchamp, *First Time*, pp. 67–69.

92   "It was a barn": Ibid., p. 67.

93   adopted the uniform: Brownlow, *Parade's Gone*, p. 180.

93   killing rattlesnakes: Beauchamp, *First Time*, p. 72.

93   "cock in a barnyard": Ibid., p. 102.

93   less than a month: Eyman, *DeMille*, p. 71.

93   *The Virginian*: Ibid., p. 78.

93   early merger interest: Ibid., p. 82.

93   **William signed up:** Ibid., p. 84.

93   **"Griffith has now been working":** Ibid., p. 84.

93   **Universal, under Carl Laemmle:** Lombardi, *Allan Dwan*, p. 27, among others.

94   **"on company time":** Schickel, *Griffith*, p. 209. Bitzer, *Bitzer*, p. 103, describes these pre-*Clansman* features as "quickies."

94   **son of a Confederate colonel:** Geduld, *Focus*, p. 40.

94   **his current mistress:** Beauchamp, *First Time*, p. 146.

94   **other major roles:** For cast details, see Usai, *Griffith Project*, p. 8:51. Henabery, among others, disputed von Stroheim's claim that he was in this film.

94   **as a health aide:** Taylor, *Men*, pp. 59–60.

94   **cinema's first Tarzan:** Silva, *Focus*, p. viii, and Rudolph, *Elmo Lincoln*, passim.

95   **Frank "Huck" Wortman:** Usai, *Griffith Project*, p. 8:50.

95   **locations all around:** Ibid.

95   **understandably nervous:** Schickel, *Griffith*, p. 223.

95   **"He receives $25,000 credit":** Aitken, *Birth*, p. 37.

95   **book by Thomas Dixon:** Usai, *Griffith Project*, p. 8:60. Some of the material in the film was adapted from another Dixon novel, *The Leopard's Spots*. My characterization of the story is based on the e-book of *The Clansman* available at www.gutenberg.org.

95   **"Personally, I did not share":** Bitzer, *Bitzer*, p. 106.

95   **"Terribly biased":** Brown, *Adventures*, p. 32.

96   **"I knew Griffith's thoroughness":** Ibid., p. 33.

96   **"This was not just another picture for Griffith":** Bitzer, *Bitzer*, p. 107. None of those around Griffith seem to have told him of their doubts about the *Clansman* story.

96   **"the man worked harder":** Blanche Sweet, oral history recording, Mary Pickford Papers.

96   **trademark tailored suit:** Gish, *Movies*, p. 123.

96   **"I had never seen so much delight":** Brown, *Adventures*, p. 65.

96   **battle tableaux, filmed:** Everson, *Silent*, p. 81.

96   **flags and mirror semaphores:** Schickel, *Griffith*, p. 226.

96   **exaggerated the number of extras:** Ibid., p. 145.

96   **Henabery described chasing:** Henabery, *Before*, p. 75. See also Brownlow, *Parade's Gone*, p. 49.

97   **"Look, Mr. Griffith":** Brown, *Adventures*, p. 55.

97   **a complaining telegram from the Aitkens:** Schickel, *Griffith*, p. 229.

97   **"I wake up nights dreaming":** Aitken, *Birth*, p. 37.

97   **Aitkens took a train:** Schickel, *Griffith*, p. 239.

97   **"Make the picture with the $40,000":** Aitken, *Birth*, p. 41.

97   **raise additional money:** Schickel, *Griffith*, p. 239, and Aitken, *Birth*, p. 44.

97   **"WE WILL SEND NO MORE MONEY":** Bitzer, *Bitzer*, p. 110.

98   **J. R. Clune:** Bitzer, *Bitzer*, p. 111, says Clune gave $15,000; Aitken, *Birth*, p. 45, puts the figure at only $5,000.

98   **"Mrs. Gish, I can't let you":** Gish, *Movies*, p. 143.

98   **shooting wrapped up:** Usai, *Griffith Project*, p. 8:61, says it was in October; Schickel says November.

98   **cast and crew were working on credit:** Brown, *Adventures*, p. 83.

98   **"until we start getting money":** Gish, *Movies*, pp. 144–45.

98   **edit the miles of footage:** Schickel, *Griffith*, p. 242.

98   **musical score:** Brown, *Adventures*, p. 87.

98   **overseeing a half-dozen other films:** Usai, *Griffith Project*, vols. 8 and 9.

98   **then-astronomical sum:** Estimates of the cost of the production vary. Everson, *Silent*, p. 78, gives the range of $65,000 to $112,000. Schickel, *Griffith*, p. 244, says it cost "a little more than $110,000."

99   **"Well, Roy":** Aitken, *Birth*, p. 52.

99   **Griffith had changed the title:** Although Aitken, *Birth*, p. 46, claims that Dixon requested the title change, Gish, *Movies*, p. 154, says it was Griffith's idea.

99   **preview for the press:** Schickel, *Griffith*, p. 275.

99   **"I did not fall asleep immediately":** Aitken, *Birth*, p. 52.

99   **two sneak previews:** Schickel, *Griffith*, pp. 244–45.

99   **Clune's Auditorium:** Ibid.

99   **forty-piece orchestra and large chorus:** Gish, *Movies*, p. 153, and Schickel, *Griffith*, p. 247.

99   **"leaping up, cheering":** Schickel, *Griffith*, p. 250.

99   **"They literally tore the place apart":** Brownlow, *Parade's Gone*, p. 49.

99   **spiritual conversion:** Brown, *Adventures*, pp. 86–88.

99   **"I was wrong":** Ibid., p. 92.

100   **at the White House:** Schickel, *Griffith*, pp. 268–70.

100  **"It is like writing history"**: The much-disputed Wilson quote is discussed in ibid., p. 270, and in many other sources.

100  **sought an injunction**: On the NAACP's work against the film, see Schickel, *Griffith*, p. 246, and Usai, *Griffith Project*, p. 8:93.

100  **heavy police presence**: LAT, February 9, 1915.

100  **National Board of Censorship**: Schickel, *Griffith*, pp. 271–72, and Usai, *Griffith Project*, p. 8:93.

100  **significant cuts**: Silva, *Focus*, p. 4.

100  **"stupid persecution"**: Geduld, *Focus*, p. 41.

100  **"balanced" them, in his own mind**: Knight, *Liveliest*, p. 29.

100  **few African-American actors**: Griffith's excuses for not casting black actors are in Gish, *Movies*, p. 163.

101  **reprehensible piece of propaganda**: The characterizations of the film here are based on my own repeated viewings of the 1931 reissue version.

101  **two dollars per ticket**: Schickel, *Griffith*, p. 267.

101  **standees three deep**: Ibid., p. 276

101  **"an impressive new illustration"**: For the reviews, see ibid., pp. 276–77.

102  **None of these reviews mentioned**: Ibid., p. 276.

102  **actual riots**: Usai, *Griffith Project*, p. 8:295.

102  **Thompson tried to ban exhibition**: Gary Krist, *City of Scoundrels* (New York: Crown, 2012), p. 72.

102  **"a pernicious caricature"**: Schickel, *Griffith*, pp. 282–83.

102  **"It is a rebel play"**: Ibid., p. 295.

102  **twenty different "road shows"**: Aitken, *Birth*, p. 59, and Usai, *Griffith Project*, p. 8:97.

102  **Other distribution rights**: Schickel, *Griffith*, p. 273.

102  **Louis B. Mayer**: Aitken, *Birth*, p. 55.

103  **his small share**: Bitzer, *Bitzer*, p. 113.

103  **"The worldwide success"**: Aitken, *Birth*, p. 64.

103  **earned out its substantial cost**: Gish, *Movies*, p. 156.

103  **reportedly for twelve years straight**: Ibid.

103  **"From the day this picture opened"**: Bitzer, *Bitzer*, p. 113.

103  **25 million people paying up to two dollars**: Schickel, *Griffith*, p. 281.

103  **suddenly convinced Wall Street**: Aitken, *Birth*, p. 75.

103  **"The once lowly movie"**: NYT, June 18, 1915.

103   speeches at road show openings: Aitken, *Birth*, p. 61.

103   wrote and published a pamphlet: Schickel, *Griffith*, p. 304.

103   Griffith's freedom to make whatever kind: Ibid., p. 300.

103   Aitken urged him to temper his ambitions: Aitken, *Birth*, p. 64.

104   "Moving pictures are still only": Slide, *Interviews*, pp. 23–24.

104   "I haven't dreamed an impossible thing": Ibid., p. 24.


## 7. WATER AND CELLULOID

106   "no local forests to burn": Henstell, *Sunshine*, p. 31.

106   Having outstripped Denver: Fogelson, *Fragmented*, p. 78.

106   Great War in Europe: McWilliams, *Southern California*, p. 130.

106   industrialization in other areas: Tzeng, "Eastern," pp. 52–53.

106   Goodyear Tire and Rubber: For the letter naming L.A.'s water as the key factor, see Ostrom, *Politics*, pp. 165–66.

107   still lagged: Fogelson, *Fragmented*, pp. 122–23.

107   Doheny sank his first well: McWilliams, *Southern California*, p. 130, and Ansell, *Oil Baron*, pp. 25, 36.

107   went on to drill many more: Ibid., pp. 33–34.

107   Derricks sprouted: For the ways oil was physically changing L.A., see McWilliams, *Southern California*, p. 130 ("oil-worker's shacktown"), and Caughey and Caughey, *Biography*, p. 248. Fogelson, *Fragmented*, p. 127, points out that the real growth came after the postwar oil strikes.

107   more intensive cultivation: Modell, *Economics*, p. 26.

107   under the single name Sunkist: Tzeng, "Eastern," p. 52. Standiford, *Angels*, p. 216, and Starr, *Inventing*, p. 162, put the date somewhat earlier.

107   their ad campaigns: Cruikshank and Schultz, *Man Who*, pp. 117–19.

108   Sun-Maid: Ibid., pp. 123–24.

108   Walnuts and almonds: Starr, *Inventing*, p. 160.

108   expansion came through annexation: Fogelson, *Fragmented*, pp. 226–27, table 24.

108   valley could now use the water: On the syndicate's ability to use aqueduct water after annexation, see ibid., p. 223, and Starr, *Material*, p. 60.

108   area of L.A. proper would increase: Fogelson, *Fragmented*, p. 223.

108   development of seaside resorts: McWilliams, *Southern California*, pp. 130–31.

108 **Venice**: Henstell, *Sunshine*, p. 104.

109 **"The visitor to the city can"**: LAT, April 15, 1911.

109 **five miles of new streets per month**: LAE, June 19, 1912.

109 **theoretical subdivisions**: McWilliams, *Southern California*, p. 134, and Caughey and Caughey, *Biography*, p. 247.

109 **erect "SOLD!" signs**: McWilliams, *Southern California*, p. 133.

109 **a certain cultural confusion**: McWilliams, *Southern California*, p. 351.

109 **"New England homes"**: Ibid., p. 356.

110 **California bungalow and the Spanish colonial architecture**: Caughey and Caughey, *Biography*, p. 247, and McWilliams, *Southern California*, pp. 357–58.

110 **romanticized re-creation**: Brook, *Smoke*, pp. 27–32.

110 **private zoos, jungle picture**: Piper, "Turning on the Fantasy Fountain," n.p.

110 **"The tepees sat cheek-by-jowl"**: Ibid.

110 **decidedly middle-class**: McWilliams, *Southern California*, p. 150.

111 **"the Iowa Coast"**: Ibid., p. 171.

111 **middle-American vibe**: Fogelson, *Fragmented*, p. 189.

111 **"The inhabitants of Los Angeles"**: McWilliams, *Southern California*, p. 158.

111 **"At heart, Los Angeles is a vast cross-section"**: Ibid., p. 171.

111 **city's lack of diversity**: Schiesl and Dodge, *City*, p. 50.

111 *The Land of Sunshine*: Starr, *Inventing*, p. 85.

111 **"The ignorant, hopelessly un-American type"**: Schiesl and Dodge, *City*, p. 50.

111 **distant enhancement of local color**: Starr, *Inventing*, pp. 86–89.

111 **90 percent of the population**: Starr, *Material*, p. 120.

111 **"Aryan city of the sun"**: Starr, *Inventing*, p. 91.

111 **about 7,600 in 1910**: Modell, *Economics*, p. 23.

111 **majority of the original *pobladores***: Hunt and Ramón, *Black*, p. 22.

112 **Bridget "Biddie" Mason**: Ibid., pp. 30–31.

112 **"safe haven" for African-Americans**: Schiesl and Dodge, *City*, pp. 59–62.

112 **well-off black families to town**: R. Williams, "Negro's Migration," pp. 102–3.

112 **Afro-American Council:** On the black associations, see ibid., p. 68, and Mjagkij, *Organizing*, p. 271.

112 **blacks could own land:** Robeck, "Azusa," p. 24.

112 **Shenk Rule:** Schiesl and Dodge, *City*, pp. 64–65.

112 **Copp Building judgment:** Ibid.

112 **first waves of the Great Migration:** McWilliams, *Southern California*, p. 160.

112 **Chinese Exclusion Act:** Schiesl and Dodge, *City*, pp. 40–41.

112 **sank from 7,500:** Starr, *Material*, p. 146.

112 **"a Chinaman's chance":** Schiesl and Dodge, *City*, p. 41.

112 **just 152 individuals:** Modell, *Economics*, p. 23, but he notes that that number is probably significantly too low.

113 **"Gentlemen's Agreement":** Schiesl and Dodge, *City*, p. 42, and Fogelson, *Fragmented*, p. 77.

113 **about 45 percent of the farm labor:** Starr, *Inventing*, p. 172.

113 **paucity of Mexicans:** Fogelson, *Fragmented*, p. 76.

113 **over 90 percent Spanish-speakers:** Schiesl and Dodge, *City*, p. 12.

113 **term wasn't typically used:** Romo, *East*, p. ix.

113 **"Sonoratown":** Ibid., p. vii.

113 **Mexican immigrants began returning:** McWilliams, *Southern California*, p. 315, and Schiesl and Dodge, *City*, pp. 11–12.

113 **institutions of the barrio:** Camarillo, *Chicanos*, pp. 119–20.

113 **Sonoratown's blocks were razed:** Ibid., p. 204, and Schiesl and Dodge, *City*, p. 16.

113 **"the most American city":** Romo, *East*, p. 10.

114 **a city dominated by newcomers:** "Other communities have also had to assimilate newcomers, but newcomers have been a 'continually perpetuated majority' in Los Angeles." McWilliams, *Southern California*, p. 238.

114 **"peculiarly susceptible":** Fogelson, *Fragmented*, p. 197.

114 **"faddists and mountebanks":** Starr, *Material*, pp. 135–36.

114 **"A vast amount of therapeutic lore":** McWilliams, *Southern California*, pp. 257–58.

114 **Llano del Rio colony:** Hine, *Utopian*, pp. 114–31, and Starr, *Inventing*, pp. 168–69.

115 **"If you have two loaves of bread":** McWilliams, *Southern California*, pp. 284–87.

115 Katherine Tingley: Hine, *Utopian*, pp. 33–54.

115 "OUTRAGES AT POINT LOMA": McWilliams, *Southern California*, pp. 252–54.

115 some $7,500 in damages: Hine, *Utopian*, p. 45.

115 southern California as a global center: Ibid., p. 254.

116 Albert Powell Warrington: Torrence, *Hollywood*, pp. 67–68, and McWilliams, *Southern California*, p. 254 ("magnetically impregnated," etc.).

116 mystic Phil Thompson: Ibid., p. 255.

116 Krotona and Hollywood: Torrence, *Hollywood*, p. 68.

116 Theater Arts Alliance: McWilliams, *Southern California*, p. 255.

116 "Christianity ranked": Starr, *Material*, p. 135.

116 Azusa Street Revival: Robeck, *Cambridge*, pp. 20–21

116 "Full of noisy manifestations": Robeck, "Azusa," pp. 29–30.

117 McPherson on the eastern seaboard: Aiken, "Sister," p. 307.

117 "gigantic improvisation": McWilliams, *Southern California*, p. 13.

## 8. EPIC TIMES

120 "Bigger and better": Brown, *Adventures*, p. 113 (italics mine).

120 "the sudden cascading of money": Ibid., pp. 98–99.

120 brought in from Broadway: Schickel, *Griffith*, p. 308.

120 "They were everywhere": Brown, *Adventures*, p. 101.

120 Aitken's creation of Triangle: Schickel, *Griffith*, p. 307; Henderson, *Life*, p. 159; Taves, *Ince*, p. 89; and Lombardi, *Allan Dwan*, p. 44. Some sources say the Wall Street investment was $5 million.

120 Triangle Film Company: Gish, *Movies*, p. 167.

121 "two-dollar pictures": Lombardi, *Allan Dwan*, p. 45.

121 to attract audiences who would never: Robinson, *Twenties*, p. 34.

121 renamed the Fine Arts Studio: Henderson, *Life*, p. 161.

121 the old Keystone compound: Louvish, *Keystone*, p. 114.

121 hindered by brush fires: Taves, *Ince*, pp. 92–93.

121 Each studio would operate: Taves, *Ince*, p. 91.

121 "We have decided": Louvish, *Keystone*, p. 115.

121 Triangle made overtures: For details of the intended talent grab, see Taves, *Ince*, p. 89.

121 "This is very important": Louvish, *Keystone*, p. 115.

122   distribute its own films nationwide: Everson, *Silent*, p. 106.

122   worldwide chain of movie theaters: Taves, *Ince*, p. 89.

122   Zukor engineered a merger: Zukor, *Public*, pp. 176–80, and Eyman, *DeMille*, pp. 120–25. Zukor forced out Goldfish, who went on to team up with Edgar Selwyn to found Goldwyn Pictures, a name Goldfish then adopted for himself as well. See Gabler, *Empire*, p. 109n.

122   Fox Film Corporation: Gabler, *Empire*, pp. 65–69.

122   Metro Pictures: Ibid., p. 89.

122   Zukor and Aitken: LAT, April 12, 1916, and Taves, *Ince*, p. 103.

122   *A Daughter of the Gods*: Ramsaye, *Million*, p. 705.

122   "the first cinematic spectacle": Eyman, *DeMille*, p. 125.

123   Ince's *Civilization*: Taves, *Ince*, pp. 95–97.

123   elaborate road shows: Usai, *Griffith Project*, p. 9:44

123   "temples of art": Knight, *Liveliest*, p. 47, and Gabler, *Empire*, pp. 95–98, 101.

123   "as insignificant as a four-reeler": Cooper, *Dark Lady*, p. 86, tells the story of the dinner.

123   "He was smarting": Bitzer, *Bitzer*, p. 131.

123   "We all agreed": Gish, *Movies*, p. 166. See also Schickel, *Griffith*, p. 306.

124   "I always said I would rebuild Babylon": Gish, *Movies*, p. 165.

124   renting an extensive tract: Bitzer, *Bitzer*, pp. 131–32.

124   "vestal virgins of Uplift": Film intertitle.

124   he reshot some scenes: Usai, *Griffith Project*, p. 9:39.

124   toured the city jail: Brown, *Adventures*, pp. 113–20.

124   Panama-Pacific International Exposition: Ibid., p. 120.

124   "vaguely Asiatic" buildings: Schickel, *Griffith*, p. 311.

125   painters and sculptors: Henabery, *Before*, p. 118.

125   shooting order and dates for four parts of the film: Ibid., p. 40.

125   St. Bartholomew Day massacre and Passion stories: Usai, *Griffith Project*, pp. 9:31 and 40; also Schickel, *Griffith*, p. 314.

125   "It was the same story": Brown, *Adventures*, p. 130.

125   they don't "believe as we do": Film intertitle.

125   referring to them as F2, F3, F4: Brown, *Adventures*, p. 130.

125   "So now if [Griffith]": Cooper, *Dark Lady*, p. 94.

125   Scenario writer Anita Loos: Loos, *Girl*, pp. 92, 100.

126 "There was so much about the film": Brown, *Adventures*, p. 171.

126 Griffith seemed totally at ease: Henabery, *Before*, pp. 79–80.

126 adding new scenes: Ibid., p. 120.

126 "shooting miles of film": Ibid., p. 145.

126 Oscar Wilde's *The Ballad*: Brown, *Adventures*, p. 121.

126 designer Walter L. Hall: Usai, *Griffith Project*, p. 9:32.

126 "Spec" was short for "Perspective": Ibid., p. 150.

126 absentmindedly play with coins: Henabery, *Before*, p. 68.

126 "Everybody on the crew": Brown, *Adventures*, p. 147.

126 "I don't see why everyone": Ibid., p. 148.

126 ways Griffith was being pulled: Gish, *Movies*, pp. 167–68.

126 Granville Warwick: Henderson, *Life*, p. 162.

127 "the dean of films": Ibid., p. 168.

127 somewhat pompous: Ardent admirers like Muriel Bowser and Martin Williams admitted to Griffith's growing pomposity in interviews.

127 "Of course, it hurts my sense of modesty": Slide, *Players*, p. 53.

127 "The public can not care": Ibid., p. 31.

127 "There seemed to be an invisible barrier": Brownlow, *Parade's Gone*, p. 91.

127 Erich von Stroheim's "von": Card, *Seductive*, pp. 232–33.

127 Theda Bara: Basinger, *Silent*, p. 204.

128 "raised in an atmosphere of roasts": Louvish, *Keystone*, pp. 105–6.

128 "It's the elephants, sir": Brown, *Adventures*, pp. 158–59.

129 he really did have thousands: Bitzer, *Bitzer*, p. 135.

129 fifteen directorial assistants: Usai, *Griffith Project*, p. 9:31.

129 benighted Monte Blue: Brown, *Adventures*, p. 158.

129 sixty-seven extras: Henabery, *Before*, p. 125.

129 "Let's try it again": Brown, *Adventures*, p. 161.

129 feast of Belshazzar: Ibid., pp. 167–68.

130 Dominguez Slough: Schickel, *Griffith*, p. 323.

130 "Nobody seemed to care": Brown, *Adventures*, p. 160.

130 "unlike anything": Gish, *Movies*, p. 169.

130 a mile deep: M. Williams, *First Artist*, p. 81.

130 "The court": Gish, *Movies*, pp. 169–70.

130 **"The trouble was that the basket"**: Bitzer, *Bitzer*, p. 135.

130 **a 150-foot elevator**: Schickel, *Griffith*, p. 327. For other details about the dolly shot, see Brown, *Adventures*, p. 170.

131 **"technically innovative, confident in manner"**: Schickel, *Griffith*, p. 327.

131 **Starting a quarter-mile back**: M. Williams, *First Artist*, p. 87.

131 **five thousand parading extras**: Bitzer, *Bitzer*, p. 135.

131 **"That was very fine"**: Brown, *Adventures*, p. 170.

131 **he accepted money**: Henderson, *Life*, p. 172. See also Gish, *Movies*, p. 176.

131 **"criminal folly"**: Loos, *Girl*, p. 157.

132 **film would surpass even *Birth***: Henderson, *Life*, p. 172.

132 **"[It] was what he had been doing"**: Brown, *Adventures*, p. 161.

132 **some late-addition scenes**: Usai, *Griffith Project*, p. 9:31.

132 **"Griffith shuffled all four versions"**: Brown, *Adventures*, p. 173.

132 **"Each story shows"**: Film intertitle.

132 **eight hours**: Gish, *Movies*, p. 179.

132 **twelve or thirteen reels long**: see Usai, *Griffith Project*, p. 9:31.

133 **some fifty times**: Drew, *Intolerance*, p. 20.

133 **"I sat a moment"**: Loos, *Girl*, pp. 102–3.

133 **"I was utterly confused"**: Brownlow, *Parade's Gone*, p. 62.

133 **"He had switched from period"**: Henabery, *Before*, p. 146.

133 ***The Downfall of All Nations***: Usai, *Griffith Project*, p. 9:31.

133 **footage of naked harem women**: Schickel, *Griffith*, p. 331, and Henabery, *Before*, p. 149.

133 **official premiere**: Usai, *Griffith Project*, p. 9:42, and Schickel, *Griffith*, p. 331.

134 **135 people were required**: Usai, *Griffith Project*, p. 9:42, and Slide, *Players*, p. 70.

134 **standing ovation**: Gish, *Movies*, p. 180.

134 **"Stupendous, tremendous"**: For positive reviews, see ibid., p. 180, Drew, *Intolerance*, pp. 120–21, and Schickel, *Griffith*, p. 332.

134 **"a real wizard of lens"**: For negative reviews, see Schickel, *Griffith*, p. 332, and Drew, *Intolerance*, p. 121.

134 **early road shows**: Ibid., p. 334.

135 ***Intolerance* actually outgrossed *Birth***: M. Williams, *First Artist*, p. 90.

135 **"something went wrong"**: Gish, *Movies*, p. 180.

135   **Attendance dwindled:** Drew, *Intolerance*, p. 118.

135   **no word-of-mouth:** Schickel, *Griffith*, p. 334.

135   **Many critics still regard it:** Drew, *Intolerance*, p. 119.

135   **huge success in Europe:** M. Williams, *First Artist*, p. 91.

135   **too "difficult":** Drew, *Intolerance*, p. 119.

135   **Gish's opinion:** Gish, *Movies*, p. 179.

135   **wrong message:** Brown, *Adventures*, p. 175.

135   **"barking his shins" and "I don't know where to go":** Gish, *Movies*,
      p. 180.

135   **"The picture business was booming":** Brown, *Adventures*, p. 176.

135   **the losses incurred:** Schickel, *Griffith*, p. 326.

136   **"He had been knocked flat":** Brown, *Adventures*, p. 176.

136   **success of *Civilization*:** Drew, *Intolerance*, p. 124.

136   **Zukor would swoop in:** Taves, *Ince*, p. 106, and Schickel, *Griffith*,
      pp. 338–41.

136   **the postwar mood turned:** Drew, *Intolerance*, p. 126, and Robinson,
      *Twenties*, p. 35.

## 9. ONE MILLION SOULS TO SAVE

138   **Oldsmobile sedan:** Details on McPherson's arrival in L.A. come from the
      "Aimee Semple McPherson Chronology," McPherson Archives (hereinafter
      Chronology). The most complete version in McPherson's own words is in
      McPherson, *Story*, pp. 103–4.

138   **"Here in the City of Angels":** Henstell, *Sunshine*, p. 95. This quote is
      phrased slightly differently in other sources.

138   **"ten dollars and a tambourine":** Thomas, *Storming*, p. 20.

138   **"The streets were not paved with gold":** McPherson, *Story*, p. 104.

139   **"As the great gate swung open":** Ibid.

139   **remote farmhouse in rural Ontario:** The existing biographies of
      McPherson run the gamut from adoringly uncritical to condescendingly
      hostile. Probably the most balanced is Edith L. Blumhofer's *Aimee Semple
      McPherson: Everybody's Sister*, which I have relied on most heavily for my
      account. Lately Thomas's *Storming Heaven*—a dual biography of Sister
      and Minnie Kennedy—emphasizes the psychodramas of the later years,
      relying heavily on newspaper rumors and innuendo, and is often critical of
      both women. Daniel Mark Epstein's *Sister Aimee* is a far more sympathetic

biography, but is regarded by Foursquare archivists as fictionalized. A more recent work that focuses on the larger issues around the McPherson phenomenon is Matthew Avery Sutton's *Aimee Semple McPherson and the Resurrection of Christian America*. Sister McPherson herself wrote several autobiographies—*This Is That, In the Service of the King*, and *The Story of My Life*—though she reports her life so as to support and amplify her teachings.

139  **October 9, 1890:** For Aimee's early life, see Blumhofer, *McPherson*, pp. 24, 44–49.

139  **practical, rather joyless marriage:** McPherson, *This Is That*, pp. 57, 68.

139  **ray of sunlight:** Ibid., 79/7476.

139  **three weeks old:** Blumhofer, *McPherson*, p. 44.

140  **"You'll kill that baby!":** McPherson, *This Is That*, 111–121/7476.

140  **rode the five miles:** McPherson, *Story*, pp. 9–10.

140  **"Salvation War":** Blumhofer, *McPherson*, p. 44.

140  **rather lackadaisical Methodist:** Ibid., p. 30.

140  **"soup and salvation":** Ibid., pp. 34, 43–44.

140  **ecclesiastical child prodigy:** Ibid., p. 45.

140  **none of the letters:** McPherson, in *Story*, p. 15, claims she didn't know the alphabet when she started school.

140  **Methodist church and Sunday school:** Chronology.

140  **won a gold medal:** Epstein, *Sister*, p. 28.

140  **"the oyster suppers":** McPherson, *This Is That*, 223/7476.

141  **"had a remarkable effect":** Ibid., 245–256/7476.

141  **questioning the existence of God:** McPherson, *Story*, pp. 18–19.

141  **Minnie wondered aloud:** McPherson, *This Is That*, 299/7476.

141  **keep an open mind:** Ibid., 310/7476.

141  **announcing a Pentecostal mission:** Chronology and McPherson, *This Is That*, 315/7476.

141  **"they jump and dance":** Ibid., 325/7476.

141  **Modern Pentecostalism:** Blumhofer, *McPherson*, pp. 69–70. See also Robeck and Yong, *Pentecostalism*.

142  **"the same yesterday, today, and forever":** Hebrews 13:8.

142  **"the cradle of American Pentecostalism":** Blumhofer, *McPherson*, p. 70.

142  **William Durham and Robert Semple:** Ibid., pp. 71, 76–77.

142 **"felt just a little bit above" and "I giggled foolishly"**: McPherson, *This Is That*, 325/7476.

143 **"I sobered suddenly"**: McPherson, *Story*, p. 23.

143 **road-to-Damascus experience**: Blumhofer, *McPherson*, p. 63, and McPherson, *This Is That*, 359/7476.

143 **quit the Christmas play**: On giving up worldly pleasures and skipping school, see McPherson, *Story*, pp. 24, 28.

143 **"rank fanatics"**: McPherson, *This Is That*, 420/7476; Blumhofer, *McPherson*, p. 65; and McPherson, *Story*, p. 28.

143 **"tarry for the baptism"**: McPherson, *This Is That*, 432/7476.

143 **"And then the glory fell"**: McPherson, *Story*, p. 30.

144 **corresponding with Robert Semple**: McPherson, *This Is That*, 617/7476, and McPherson, *King*, p. 15.

144 **"mighty millions"**: McPherson, *Story*, p. 33.

144 **"I rose and said yes to God"**: Ibid., p. 34.

144 **an outdoor ceremony**: Blumhofer, *McPherson*, p. 77.

144 **Robert worked in a boiler factory**: McPherson, *Story*, p. 36.

144 **Chicago and Aimee's becoming "ordained"**: Blumhofer, *McPherson*, p. 80.

144 **"was my theological seminary"**: McPherson, *Story*, p. 34.

144 **mission to China**: Blumhofer, *McPherson*, pp. 86–89.

145 **"Bringing in Chinese"**: McPherson, *This Is That*, 799/7476.

145 **living conditions in China**: McPherson, *Story*, p. 55.

145 **she was pregnant**: Blumhofer, *McPherson*, p. 87.

145 **he died at one a.m.**: Ibid., pp. 91–92.

145 **"[Then] came hours of terror"**: McPherson, *Story*, p. 66.

145 **she considered remaining in China**: Ibid., pp. 66–67.

145 **money for a return ticket**: Blumhofer, *McPherson*, p. 92.

145 **"My first duty"**: McPherson, *Story*, p. 67.

145 **Minnie's apartment on 14th Street**: Blumhofer, *McPherson*, p. 96.

145 **"I have a persistent feeling"**: McPherson, *Story*, pp. 69–70.

146 **she wandered from**: Blumhofer, *McPherson*, pp. 97–99.

146 **Harold McPherson**: Ibid., p. 99.

146 **Minnie Kennedy disapproved**: Ibid., p. 101.

146   **needed stability and protection**: McPherson, *Story*, p. 72, and McPherson, *This Is That*, 927/7476.

146   **"that if at any time in my life"**: McPherson, *Story*, p. 72.

146   **"backsliding"**: McPherson, *This Is That*, 927/7476.

146   **"Earthly things"**: Ibid., 938/7476.

146   **multiple surgeries**: Blumhofer, *McPherson*, p. 104, and Chronology.

146   **"hover[ing] between life and death"**: McPherson, *This Is That*, 993–1003/7476.

147   **pain was instantly gone**: McPherson, *Story*, p. 75.

147   **took a taxi to the train**: Blumhofer, *McPherson*, p. 106.

147   **sent money for her train**: McPherson, *This Is That*, 1061/7476.

147   **"wash the dishes"**: For Harold McPherson's telegrams to his wife, see Blumhofer, *McPherson*, p. 109, and McPherson, *This Is That*, 1113/7476.

147   **Pentecostal camp meeting**: Blumhofer, *McPherson*, p. 106.

147   **Mount Forest**: Ibid., p. 108.

147   **She grabbed a chair**: McPherson, *King*, p. 149, and Blumhofer, *McPherson*, pp. 108–9.

147   **"I mounted the tiny rostrum"**: McPherson, *Story*, p. 81.

148   **"People!" and "Lock that door!"**: Ibid.

148   **"From that August day"**: Blumhofer, *McPherson*, p. 109.

148   **a natural as an evangelist and Harold's conversion**: Blumhofer, *McPherson*, pp. 110–11.

148   **he was struck with the baptism**: McPherson, *This Is That*, 1135/7476.

149   **"a dress in the pulpit"**: For McPherson as female evangelist, see McPherson, *King*, p. 151.

149   **Pentecostal camps, revivals, and missions**: For her early travels as an evangelist, see Chronology.

149   **Harold quit his job and the "Gospel Car"**: Blumhofer, *McPherson*, pp. 110–12.

149   **Minnie would care for Roberta**: Ibid., p. 115.

149   **reversible front seats**: McPherson, *This Is That*, 1520/7476.

149   **"I don't believe"**: Ibid., 1257/7476.

150   **"we heard a great shout"**: Ibid., 1257/7476.

150   **"bind her scattered supporters"**: Blumhofer, *McPherson*, pp. 119–20.

150   **"So plainly the Lord spoke"**: Ibid., p. 120.

150   launching his own career as a traveling evangelist: Ibid., pp. 124–25.

151   quietly divorced: Ibid., p. 127.

151   Aimee soldiered on: Thomas, *Storming*, p. 16.

151   soak her night's bedding: *This Is That*, 1595/7476.

151   raging hurricane: Ibid., 1627/7476.

151   Minnie was free: Thomas, *Storming*, p. 17, and McPherson, *This Is That*, 1639/7476.

151   Spanish influenza: Ibid., 2085/7476.

151   despite violent chills: McPherson, *Story*, p. 100.

151   "Fear not": Ibid., p. 101.

152   clamoring for a house: McPherson, *Story*, p. 101.

152   roadworthy Oldsmobile: Thomas, *Storming*, p. 18.

152   departure from New York: McPherson, *This Is That*, 2131/7476.

152   handing out religious tracts: Blumhofer, *McPherson*, pp. 138–40.

152   revivals along the way: Chronology.

152   miraculously lifted: Blumhofer, *McPherson*, p. 140.

152   coal miners and Native Americans: Chronology.

152   travel mishaps: Chronology.

152   "angels [that] seemed to hold the car": McPherson, *This Is That*, 2153/7476.

153   finally rode through the gates: Ibid., 2352/7476.

153   "Shout, for the Lord hath given you": Chronology.

153   "the most celebrated of all incubators": McWilliams, *Southern California*, p. 249.

153   "Certainly Los Angeles was ripe for revival": McPherson, *Story*, p. 118.

154   Victoria Hall: Blumhofer, *McPherson*, p. 141.

154   Temple Auditorium: Epstein, *Sister*, p. 152.

154   drifting Pentecostal community: Blumhofer, *McPherson*, pp. 142–43.

154   "The Lord shows me that I am": McPherson, *Story*, p. 105, and McPherson, *King*, p. 210. The dialogue combines elements from both sources.

154   "popcorn meeting": a term used in McPherson, *King*, p. 210.

155   "the House that God Built": Blumhofer, *McPherson*, p. 142.

155   "the glorious One": McPherson, *This Is That*, 2438/7476.

155 **with a central headquarters:** Blumhofer, *McPherson*, p. 198.

155 **"to build a house unto the Lord":** For God's ratification of the decision, see McPherson, *Story*, p. 118.

## 10. A DRINKING PROBLEM

158 **"The only way to stop the growth":** Henstell, *Sunshine*, p. 20.

158 **a "smokeless success":** Kahrl, *Water*, p. 231.

158 **"It is no longer a question":** Henstell, *Sunshine*, p. 13.

158 **surpassing San Francisco in population:** Standiford, *Angels*, p. 217.

158 **tenth-largest city:** C. Mulholland, *Mulholland*, p. 266.

158 **poised to double:** Kahrl, *Water*, p. 259.

158 **350 new Angelenos:** Henstell, *Sunshine*, p. 13.

158 **volume of building permits:** Ibid., p. 14.

158 **"Where are the citrus and olive groves":** Ibid.

159 **lived outside downtown:** Sitton, *Metropolis*, p. 2.

159 **suburban, even antiurban, ethos:** Fogelson, *Fragmented*, p. 147.

159 **"a city without a center":** McWilliams, *Southern California*, p. 235.

159 **an estimated 160,000 automobiles:** Henstell, *Sunshine*, p. 25.

159 **ban parking on downtown streets:** Ibid., pp. 25–26.

159 **"Southern California throb[s]" and "The sooner [the authorities] realize":** Ibid., p. 26.

160 **lower middle class:** For trends in class migration, see McWilliams, *Southern California*, p. 150.

160 **local farmer named Alphonzo Bell:** Henstell, *Sunshine*, pp. 32–35.

160 **even bigger strikes:** Ibid., pp. 31–32.

160 **extensive irrigation:** Nadeau, *Water-Seekers*, p. 54. He claims that cultivation went from 3,000 to 75,000 acres in just three years.

160 **a demand for labor:** Fogelson, *Fragmented*, p. 127.

160 **Mexicans, African-Americans, and Japanese:** McWilliams, *Southern California*, p. 160; Wakida, *LAtitudes*, pp. 132–33; and Starr, *Material*, pp. 147–48.

161 **"had funds":** Henstell, *Sunshine*, p. 20.

161 **"the westernmost outpost of Nordic civilization":** Sitton, *Metropolis*, p. 116.

161 wealth created: Kahrl, *Water*, p. 259.

161 Los Angeles Philharmonic: Starr, *Material*, p. 163, and Henstell, *Sunshine*, p. 7.

161 Hollywood Bowl: Starr, *Material*, pp. 166–67.

161 higher education: Starr, *Material*, pp. 152–53. UCLA finally settled in its current location in Westwood in 1929.

162 blighted many residential neighborhoods: Sitton, *Metropolis*, pp. 125–29.

162 "It was like drilling for oil at Fifth Avenue": Rayner, *Bright*, p. 47.

162 isolated at the outskirts: Sitton, *Metropolis*, pp. 14, 80–85.

162 "a land of smokeless, sunlit factories": Ibid., p. 98.

162 crime, drug use: Rayner, *Bright*, pp. 80–83, is best.

162 "the L.A. System": Ibid., and Henstell, *Sunshine*, pp. 47–57.

162 "The surface was bright and pleasing": Sitton, *Metropolis*, p. 1.

163 how and where to get more: Ostrom, *Politics*, p. 14.

163 New conservation measures: C. Mulholland, *Mulholland*, p. 259.

163 "[Los Angeles] stole our water, gas, and power": Ibid., p. 276.

163 surveys for another long aqueduct: Kahrl, *Water*, p. 264, and Standiford, *Angels*, p. 217.

164 Mulholland's problem: Walton, *Western Times*, p. 152.

164 relatively amicable: Walton, "Picnic," p. 201, and Wehrey, *Images*, p. 50.

164 a 140-foot dam at Long Valley: Nadeau, *Water-Seekers*, p. 51.

165 Eaton still wouldn't budge: Kahrl, *Water*, p. 249, and Nadeau, *Water-Seekers*, p. 55.

165 a 100-foot dam: Kahrl, *Water*, p. 250, and Nadeau, *Water-Seekers*, p. 53, cite the start of such a dam with a base that would allow it to go higher, and Eaton's suit against it.

165 pumping of the valley's groundwater: Kahrl, *Water*, p. 271.

165 cutting irrigation ditches on Eaton's ranch: Nadeau, *Water-Seekers*, p. 54.

165 "What the hell you doin' here?": Ibid., pp. 53–54.

166 "Fatty" Arbuckle: For general information, see Yallop, *Day*, passim.

166 *The Round-Up*: "The Round-Up" (handout), published by the Museum of Western Film History Archives in Lone Pine, Calif.; and C. Langley, "The Museum of Western Film History."

167 **Alabama Hills as a film location:** A list of movies filmed there is available at http://www.lonepinefilmhistorymuseum.org/. See also "Movie Road: A Self-Guided Tour" (e-booklet), also on the museum's website.

168 **height of his fame:** Kahrl, *Water*, p. 230.

168 **American Association of Engineers:** C. Mulholland, *Mulholland*, p. 276.

168 **scenic highway:** Ibid., p. 280, and Sitton, *Metropolis*, pp. 45–76.

168 **magazine profiles:** C. Mulholland, *Mulholland*, p. 275, discusses this and other examples of the Chief's growing eminence.

168 **filed an injunction:** Hoffman, *Vision*, p. 178.

168 **Owens Valley Irrigation District:** Nadeau, *Water-Seekers*, pp. 55–56; Walton, *Western Times*, p. 202; and Hoffman, *Vision*, p. 178.

168 **newly aggressive measures:** Walton, *Western Times*, pp. 156–57.

168 **McNally Ditch:** Nadeau, *Water-Seekers*, pp. 57–58, and Hoffman, *Vision*, pp. 179–80.

169 **"We're not able to fight":** Nadeau, *Water-Seekers*, pp. 59–60.

169 **"Are you hired to fight for the city?":** Ibid., pp. 59–60, and Hoffman, *Vision*, p. 180.

169 **cooler heads:** Hoffman, *Vision*, p. 180, and Nadeau, *Water-Seekers*, p. 59.

169 **"checkerboarding":** Walton, "Picnic," p. 201.

169 **Gangs of diehards:** Kahrl, *Water*, p. 278, and Walton, "Picnic," p. 202.

169 **consequences of groundwater pumping:** Walton, *Western Times*, p. 155; Wehrey, *Images*, p. 53; and LADPW-5 1924, Los Angeles Department of Water and Power Archives.

170 **sweeping proposal:** Hoffman, *Vision*, p. 180, and Nadeau, *Water-Seekers*, p. 60.

170 **"I have some criticism to make":** All quotes by Warren and Watterson are from Nadeau, *Water-Seekers*, p. 60.

170 **twenty-four-hour schedule:** Ibid., p. 60, for this and the disbandment of the city's digging crew.

171 **"Los Angeles, it's your move now":** Ibid., p. 61.


## 11. SCANDALS IN BOHEMIA

174 **huge set:** O'Dell, *Griffith*, p. 39.

174 **inside Belshazzar's weather-worn court:** Schickel, *Griffith*, p. 352; Brown, *Adventures*, pp. 189–90; and Henderson, *Life*, p. 186.

174 **"Perhaps I was dreaming":** Gish, *Movies*, p. 187.

174  **opened in London:** Schickel, *Griffith*, pp. 344–45.

174  **Churchill and Shaw had both:** Henderson, *Life*, p. 183, and Schickel, *Griffith*, p. 345.

174  **financed in part:** Henderson, *Life*, p. 184.

174  **blanched at this prospect:** Gish, *Movies*, p. 188, speculates on the conflict in Griffith's mind about making a pro-war movie.

174  **summoned the Gish sisters:** Schickel, *Griffith*, p. 347.

174  **Teutonic surname:** Gish, *Movies*, p. 196, and Bitzer, *Bitzer*, p. 183. Some doubt exists as to who, besides Griffith, actually went to war-torn France.

175  **tendency to bend the truth:** Henderson, *Life*, p. 185.

175  **"within fifty yards":** Slide, *Players*, pp. 80–86.

175  **just enough European footage:** Schickel, *Griffith*, p. 350.

175  **Two-thirds of the final film:** Henderson, *Life*, p. 185.

175  **debts that would hamper him:** Brown, *Adventures*, p. 208.

175  **"the supreme creator":** Slide, *Players*, p. 104.

175  **his name the first to spring:** Schickel, *Griffith*, p. 378.

175  **"For you, Mr. Griffith":** Ibid., p. 352.

175  **proved another success:** Henderson, *Life*, p. 187.

175  **"the spectators stood and shouted":** Ibid., p. 188.

176  **"Griffith was like a champion":** Brown, *Adventures*, p. 192.

176  **he signed to do six new films:** Schickel, *Griffith*, p. 379.

176  **Zukor also nabbed Ince and Sennett:** Taves, *Ince*, p. 112, and Louvish, *Keystone*, p. 181.

176  **"Anaconda Adolph":** Lombardi, *Allan Dwan*, p. 102.

176  **rising rival William Fox:** Knight, *Liveliest*, p. 48.

176  **First National:** Schickel, *Griffith*, p. 396.

176  **Paramount/First National merger:** Lombardi, *Allan Dwan*, p. 103, and Everson, *Silent*, p. 111.

176  **United Artists:** Schickel, *Griffith*, pp. 399–400.

176  **several bread-and-butter films:** Henderson, *Life*, pp. 193, 196, and Schickel, *Griffith*, p. 404.

177  **"Women are apt to find him too foreign-looking":** For the near-miss on Valentino, see Gish, *Movies*, p. 211.

177  **"There's a great story in it":** Ibid., p. 217.

177  **three major characters:** Henderson, *Life*, p. 201.

178  **George Baker:** Ibid., p. 201.

178  **Hendrick Sartov:** Bitzer, *Bitzer*, p. 205.

178  *Busted Posies*: Brown, *Adventures*, p. 227.

178  **locks herself in a closet:** Schickel, *Griffith*, p. 392.

178  **"I played the scene":** Gish, *Movies*, p. 220.

178  **"You bring me a picture like this" and "Here is the money":** Ibid., p. 221.

179  **first true "art-house film":** Schickel, *Griffith*, pp. 394–95, though the "art-house" characterization is my own.

179  **ecstatic reviews and healthiest profits:** Brown, *Adventures*, p. 242, and Bitzer, *Bitzer*, p. 212.

179  **Spanish influenza epidemic:** Schickel, *Griffith*, p. 387.

179  **come within ten feet:** Gish, *Movies*, pp. 218–19.

179  **a postwar recession:** Sklar, *Movie-Made*, p. 82. The recession had a delayed effect on box office receipts.

179  **$85 a week:** For Swanson's salary escalation, see IMDb.com.

179  **every other element:** Knight, *Liveliest*, p. 108.

180  **Ralph Spence:** Brownlow, *Parade's Gone*, pp. 296–97.

180  **cost of *Blossoms* as compared with *Birth*:** Henderson, *Life*, p. 201.

180  **listing studio stocks on Wall Street:** Lombardi, *Allan Dwan*, p. 108.

180  **directors had to run the gauntlet:** Knight, *Liveliest*, p. 111.

180  **resemble actual modern factories:** Shiel, *Hollywood*, pp. 113, 121.

180  **Harold Lloyd's sheep story:** Beauchamp, *First Time*, p. 36.

181  **smell "of eucalyptus or petrol":** Ibid., p. 163.

181  **followed their production companies:** Shiel, *Hollywood*, p. 76.

181  **main part of town:** Brown, *Adventures*, p. 182.

181  **Francois was founded:** G. P. Williams, *Story*, p. 100.

181  **would-be extras congregated:** Henabery, *Before*, pp. 54–55.

181  **"I had never seen such weird costumes":** Beauchamp, *First Time*, p. 134.

181  **"was like a carnival":** Ibid., p. 175.

182  **35 million Americans:** Mann, *Tinseltown*, p. 20.

182  **"There has never been anything":** Ibid.

182  **increasing scrutiny:** Knight, *Liveliest*, p. 112.

182  **"can tell two million American people":** O'Dell, *Griffith*, p. 42.

182    **censorship efforts were redoubled:** Sklar, *Movie-Made*, p. 82.

182    **government should inspect movies:** Ibid., pp. 123–24.

183    **close to $750 million a year:** Figures on gross and return of investment are from Mann, *Tinseltown*, p. 13.

183    **Zukor had been born poor:** For Zukor's early history, see Gabler, *Empire*, pp. 13–14, and Zukor, *Public*, pp. 14–15.

183    **"No sooner did I put my foot on American soil":** Gabler, *Empire*, p. 15.

183    **cauliflower ear and stiff finger:** Zukor, *Public*, p. 8.

183    **Automatic Vaudeville:** Gabler, *Empire*, p. 17–18.

183    **"We called it Crystal Hall":** Ibid., p. 22.

183    **few social barriers to Jewish entrepreneurs:** Gabler, *Empire*, pp. 4–5.

183    **moving from exhibition into distribution:** Ibid., p. 94.

184    **an estimated 35 percent:** Mann, *Tinseltown*, p. 39.

184    **February 1921 meeting:** Ibid., pp. 111–12.

184    **"To place in the limelight":** Loos, *Girl*, p. 121.

184    **Pickford-Fairbanks affair:** Ibid., pp. 165–69. Lombardi, *Allan Dwan*, p. 86, says that rumors of the affair were already leaking by August 1918.

184    **truly notorious scandals:** Kenneth Anger's *Hollywood Babylon* is a well-known account of these scandals but is hobbled by unsubstantiated rumor and gossip. See Sklar, *Movie-Made*, pp. 78ff.

185    **Bobby Harron:** Mann, *Tinseltown*, pp. 12–17.

185    **Olive Thomas and Jack Pickford:** Ibid., pp. 18, 21–31.

185    **Virginia Rappe:** Yallop, *Day*, is a book-length treatment of the Arbuckle scandal. See also Louvish, *Keystone*, pp. 174–78.

186    **William Desmond Taylor:** Mann, *Tinseltown*, provides the most complete account.

186    **comedy superstar Mabel Normand:** The LAPD never seriously considered Normand a suspect, though the gossip magazines did.

186    **"Oriental love cult":** Louvish, *Keystone*, p. 182.

186    **cache of love letters:** Mann, *Tinseltown*, p. 213.

187    **"exposed the debaucheries":** Ibid., p. 250.

187    **"At Hollywood, Calif., is a colony":** Talbot, *Entertainer*, p. 156.

187    **polemical exposés:** Sklar, *Movie-Made*, p. 81.

187    **"clean up the pictures":** Ibid., p. 82.

187    **"the sanity and conservatism":** Mann, *Tinseltown*, p. 263.

187  "Little Napoleon of the Movies": Ibid., pp. 293–94.

187  misbehavior in the movie colony: Louvish, *Keystone*, pp. 206–10; Mann, *Tinseltown*, p. 283; Loos, *Girl*, p. 116; and Lombardi, *Allan Dwan*, p. 27.

188  "they could present six reels": Knight, *Liveliest*, p. 114.

188  new Hollywoodland sign: Brook, *Smoke*, pp. 7–11.

188  "[Our] common object": Lombardi, *Allan Dwan*, p. 115.

188  "opposed to Wall Street": Shiel, *Hollywood*, p. 76.

188  "It is too expensive to experiment": Slide, *Players*, p. 115.

189  bread-and-butter program: Ibid.

## 12. "JESUS, JESUS ALL THE DAY LONG"

192  The crowds started arriving: For the Angelus Temple opening, see LAT, January 2, 1923.

192  train from San Francisco: Blumhofer, *McPherson*, p. 238.

192  contingent of gypsies: Epstein, *Sister*, p. 239.

192  After a prayer: Blumhofer, *McPherson*, p. 235, is best on the program.

192  laid the dedicatory tablets: Epstein, *Sister*, p. 247.

193  The building they entered: Blumhofer, *McPherson*, pp. 5–6; Epstein, *Sister*, p. 247; and McPherson, *Story*, p. 123.

193  modern theater marquee: Aiken, "Sister," p. 311.

193  "half like a Roman Coliseum": Sutton, *McPherson*, p. 22.

193  "oriental velvets and brocades": Sutton, *McPherson*, p. 21.

193  baptismal pool: Thomas, *Storming*, p. 26.

193  JESUS CHRIST, THE SAME YESTERDAY: McPherson, *Story*, p. 124.

193  close to a million dollars: Thomas, *Storming*, p. 26.

194  "The thirty revivals": Epstein, *Sister*, p. 156.

194  staggering: For attendance at her revivals, see Blumhofer, *McPherson*, pp. 160, 168, 189.

194  "Who cares about old Hell": Clark, "Miracles," p. 357.

194  "rather see my children dead": Aiken, "Sister," p. 308.

194  "Burn up the novels": Blumhofer, *McPherson*, pp. 225–26.

194  "wipe the dust from the family Bible": Ibid., p. 173.

194  She used her own life story: Ibid., p. 156, is best.

194  "Never did I hear such language": Ibid., p. 153.

194  **"a center of evangelism in the west"**: For her fundraising on the road, see Sutton, *McPherson*, p. 15, and Blumhofer, *McPherson*, p. 167.

195  **"Chairholders"**: Thomas, *Storming*, p. 25.

195  **plain wooden tabernacle**: McPherson, *Story*, pp. 118, 123.

195  **"on Monday night for a boxing tournament"**: Ibid., p. 119.

195  **she had expanded on**: Ibid., p. 123.

195  **"by faith as the Lord provided the money"**: Ibid., p. 120.

195  **"How much money"**: Ibid.

195  **"Oh, this is heaven!"**: Ibid., p. 119. "ASM Legends," in McPherson Archives, speculates that they came to view earthquake damage.

195  **"The moment I saw it"**: McPherson, *King*, p. 246.

196  **"The Lord must have been saving it"**: McPherson, *Story*, p. 119.

196  **"I suddenly decided"**: Ibid., p. 120.

196  **1921 groundbreaking**: Epstein, *Sister*, p. 212.

196  **offer them a bright vision**: Blumhofer, *McPherson*, p. 228.

196  **"My opponent in these bouts"**: Sutton, *McPherson*, p. 16.

196  **"When I was a little girl"**: Blumhofer, *McPherson*, p. 216.

196  **"99 percent salvation"**: Ibid., p. 174.

197  **"Jesus is the healer"**: Thomas, *Storming*, p. 21.

197  **"Look, mama, look"**: Epstein, *Sister*, p. 183.

197  **outsiders were skeptical**: Sutton, *McPherson*, p. 18, and Epstein, *Sister*, p. 233.

197  **"religious hypnosis"**: Sutton, *McPherson*, p. 18.

197  **"I cannot blame anyone"**: Blumhofer, *McPherson*, p. 167.

197  **"genuine, beneficial"**: Epstein, p. 233, and "ASM Legends," McPherson Archives.

197  **"Quite apart from their wonderful"**: McPherson, *King*, p. 230.

198  **"The crowds you are drawing"**: McPherson, *Story*, p. 121.

198  **hub for her worldwide ministry**: Epstein, *Sister*, p. 247.

198  **camp out on the sidewalks**: Blumhofer, *McPherson*, p. 247.

198  **early temple services, both on-site and off**: Ibid., pp. 4–5, 247–48.

199  **her every move was being reported**: Epstein, *Sister*, p. 248.

199  **begin carrying *Bridal Call***: Blumhofer, *McPherson*, p. 248.

199  **call out to passersby**: Thomas, *Storming*, pp. 27–28.

199   telephone service: McPherson, *King*, p. 252, and Thomas, *Storming*, p. 27.

199   prayer tower: Blumhofer, *McPherson*, p. 249.

199   the 500 Room and L.I.F.E. Bible School: Blumhofer, *McPherson*, p. 253; Epstein, *Sister*, p. 275; and Thomas, *Storming*, pp. 26–28.

199   other groups active in the temple: Epstein, *Sister*, p. 272, and McPherson, *King*, p. 253.

199   broadcast radio: Blumhofer, *McPherson*, p. 182.

200   two full-time radio stations: McPherson, *Story*, p. 127.

200   a 500-watt station: LAT, February 5, 1924.

200   Kenneth Ormiston: Epstein, *Sister*, p. 264.

200   broadcasting in Pittsburgh: Hoar, "Religious Broadcasting," p. 3.

200   featuring hymns, testimonials: Blumhofer, *McPherson*, pp. 266–68.

200   not the first woman: "ASM Legends," McPherson Archives.

200   "a most unheard-of opportunity": Hoar, "Religious Broadcasting," p. 4.

200   "illustrated sermons": Blumhofer, *McPherson*, p. 259.

200   "carrying the ball for Christ": Starr, *Material*, p. 142.

200   "put sin under arrest": Blumhofer, *McPherson*, p. 261, and Epstein, *Sister*, p. 258.

200   "You give your drama-starved people": Blumhofer, *McPherson*, p. 230.

201   "Oh, go to Hell!": Epstein, *Sister*, pp. 256–57.

201   sexual undercurrent: Blumhofer, *McPherson*, pp. 198–99, and Kittell, "Visit," p. 8.

201   stylish haircut and clothing: Blumhofer, *McPherson*, p. 274.

201   "Supernatural whoopee" and "sensuous debauch": Aiken, "Sister," p. 312.

201   "wildcat habits": Thomas, *Storming*, p. 37.

201   "She had a fiery temper": Epstein, *Sister*, p. 218.

201   "Sister has a headache today": Starr, *Material*, p. 140; see also Kittell, "Visit," p. 7.

202   largest single Christian congregation: Thomas, *Storming*, p. 32.

202   special streetcar siding: McPherson, *King*, p. 256.

202   "A territory little known": Sutton, *McPherson*, p. 28.

202   "The Temple is bringing thousands": Ibid., p. 28.

202   Foursquare Gospel: Blumhofer, *McPherson*, p. 191.

202 **outreach to Latinos and African-Americans:** Sutton, *McPherson*, pp. 31–32.

202 **encouraged black and Mexican branch churches:** Hoar, "Religious Broadcasting," p. 88.

202 **"that would stand the full light of day":** Blumhofer, *McPherson*, p. 187.

203 **"Don't feel sad, my brother":** Blumhofer, *McPherson*, p. 277.

203 **their white robes:** Epstein, *Sister*, pp. 261–63.

203 **Pentecostalist groups suspicious:** Blumhofer, *McPherson*, p. 217.

203 **discouraged the more extreme manifestations:** Ibid., p. 172.

203 **"barbaric yawps":** Epstein, *Sister*, p. 161.

203 **"frenzied fanaticism" and "boasting manifestations":** McPherson, *Story*, p. 110.

203 **"Is Mrs. McPherson Pentecostal?":** Blumhofer, *McPherson*, pp. 185, 219.

203 **mainstream Christian denominations:** Thomas, *Storming*, p. 31, and Blumhofer, *McPherson*, p. 257.

204 **objections from Moody and Bible Institute:** Ibid., p. 163.

204 **L.A. Ministerial Association:** Epstein, *Sister*, p. 259.

204 **"must come from the devil":** Sutton, *McPherson*, p. 19.

204 **Reverend Robert Shuler:** Henstell, "Shuler," pp. 92–94.

204 *Bob Shuler's Magazine:* Ibid., p. 96.

204 **KGEF:** Clark, "Miracles," p. 357.

204 **unrelentingly negative:** LAT, June 1, 1930, and Blumhofer, *McPherson*, p. 257.

204 **"mischievous and troublemaking":** Henstell, "Shuler," p. 92.

204 **most of her converts:** Blumhofer, *McPherson*, p. 257.

204 **"Isadora Duncan in the pulpit":** Starr, *Material*, p. 139.

205 **"Whatever the lips of Mrs. McPherson may say":** Blumhofer, *McPherson*, p. 258.

205 **sermons entitled "McPhersonism":** LAT, June 1, 1930.

205 **all manner of falsehoods:** Sutton, *McPherson*, p. 36.

205 **response was to invite:** Blumhofer, *McPherson*, p. 258.

205 **perhaps the greatest threat:** Epstein, *Sister*, p. 273, and Blumhofer, *McPherson*, p. 271.

205 **followers as "nuts":** Epstein, *Sister*, p. 273.

205 **excommunicating the entire Committee:** Thomas, *Storming*, p. 274.

205 **Santa Ana branch incident:** Epstein, *Sister*, p. 284, and Blumhofer, *McPherson*, p. 272.

206 **"I've never asked [for] protection":** LAT, September 3, 1925.

206 **tended to back her mother:** Blumhofer, *McPherson*, p. 270.

206 **Mrs. Marion Evans Ray:** LAT, September 3, 1925.

206 **Mrs. Mercie Stannard:** LAT, September 15, 1925.

206 **antinarcotics parade:** Blumhofer, *McPherson*, p. 264.

206 **brazenly announcing:** McPherson, *King*, p. 258, and Blumhofer, *McPherson*, p. 268.

206 **"Threats and commands":** McPherson, *King*, p. 259.

## 13. THUNDER IN THE VALLEY

208 **a thunderous explosion:** For the May 21 bombing, see Hoffman, *Vision*, p. 181, and C. Mulholland, *Mulholland*, p. 287.

208 **escalation of the conflict:** Walton, *Western Times*, p. 158.

208 **"We had heard of threats":** C. Mulholland, *Mulholland*, p. 287.

208 **officials and press entourage:** Hoffman, *Vision*, p. 181.

208 **speculated wildly:** Walton, *Western Times*, p. 170.

209 **traced the dynamite:** Nadeau, *Water-Seekers*, p. 66.

209 **"Every resident":** Walton, *Western Times*, p. 170.

209 **persuaded the city to file suit:** Hoffman, *Vision*, p. 181, and Nadeau, *Water-Seekers*, pp. 65–66.

209 **"mainly for the purpose of demoralizing":** Walton, *Western Times*, p. 158.

209 **"Valley of Broken Hearts":** C. Mulholland, *Mulholland*, p. 286, and Hoffman, *Vision*, p. 183.

209 **"Fear, suspicion, and bitter hatreds":** C. Mulholland, *Mulholland*, p. 286.

210 **L. C. Hall kidnapping:** Standiford, *Angels*, p. 226, and Hoffman, *Vision*, p. 181.

210 **Glasscock himself promised:** Nadeau, *Water-Seekers*, p. 67.

210 **"They wouldn't have the nerve":** Ibid., p. 68.

210 **"not at your price, not at our price":** Walton, *Western Times*, p. 160.

210 **Chamber's recommendation of arbitration:** Hoffman, *Vision*, p. 182.

210  "The president of the Chamber": Ibid., p. 182.

211  "the same old bunk": Walton, *Western Times*, p. 160.

211  Alabama Gatehouse: Ibid., p. 160, and Hoffman, *Vision*, p. 160. Nadeau, *Water-Seekers*, p. 72, adds the detail about barbed wire.

211  Charles Collins arrived: Walton, *Western Times*, p. 164.

211  Edward Leahey: Hoffman, *Vision*, p. 195. Again, Nadeau, *Water-Seekers*, p. 71, adds a telling detail: the noose.

211  "You can tell Mathews and Mulholland" and "If you try to close these gates": Nadeau, *Water-Seekers*, p. 71.

212  fifteen thousand dollars a day: C. Mulholland, *Mulholland*, p. 296.

212  "If you go up there": Nadeau, *Water-Seekers*, p. 71.

212  scene at the Alabama Gates: Walton, *Western Times*, pp. 160–65. See also his "Picnic." Other details are from Nadeau, *Water-Seekers*, p. 72.

212  more than seven hundred people: Walton, *Western Times*, p. 164.

212  "IF I AM NOT ON THE JOB": Nadeau, *Water-Seekers*, p. 73.

213  "No, Sheriff, we won't leave": Ibid., p. 72.

213  "by personal interest": Walton, *Western Times*, p. 164.

213  no other judge to be found: Nadeau, *Water-Seekers*, p. 72.

213  appealed to California governor: Walton, *Western Times*, pp. 164–65.

213  depressing the local economy: Ostrom, *Politics*, p. 123.

214  now demanding a total of $12 million: Kahrl, *Water*, p. 293.

214  "a depressed pioneer community" and "the city can afford": Kahrl, *Water*, p. 293.

214  Governor Richardson ultimately refused: Walton, *Western Times*, p. 164.

214  Clearing House Association: Hoffman, *Vision*, p. 189, and Walton, *Western Times*, p. 165.

214  only if the unlawful occupation: Hoffman, *Vision*, p. 186.

214  final barbecue: Nadeau, *Water-Seekers*, pp. 75–76.

214  "If the Clearing House [Association] fails": Ibid., p. 76.

215  resuming his unpublicized purchases: Walton, *Western Times*, pp. 165–67.

215  build enough reservoir capacity: Kahrl, *Water*, pp. 311–12; C. Mulholland, *Mulholland*, p. 281.

215  a 175-foot-high concrete dam: Kahrl, *Water*, p. 312.

215  abandoned their efforts: Nadeau, *Water-Seekers*, p. 77.

215    a bill making cities legally responsible: Ibid., p. 80.

215    claims for several million dollars: Hoffman, *Vision*, pp. 190–91.

215    *So sue us*: Ibid., p. 192, though not in those terms.

216    resorted again to dynamite: Nadeau, *Water-Seekers*, pp. 80–81, and Walton, *Western Times*, p. 173.

216    Pinkerton private detectives: Nadeau, *Water-Seekers*, p. 80.

216    "It would be a terrible situation": Ibid., p. 81.

216    a May 1 deadline: Ibid., p. 87.

216    "If you do that": Ibid.

216    denying any claims: Walton, *Western Times*, p. 176.

216    "would run red with human blood": Nadeau, *Water-Seekers*, p. 87.

217    "FOREIGN TRADE GAIN SURPASSES": Headlines are from "Municipal Progress Edition of 1926," *Los Angeles Chronicle*, pp. 19, 29. A bound copy is in History Division, Los Angeles Public Library.

217    "Los Angeles is, in more ways than one" and "The East doesn't question": Ibid., p. 33.

217    "HUNDRED MILLION SPENT" and "It gives employment to thousands": Ibid., p. 29.

218    "THE HOUSE THAT GOD BUILT" and "People from all parts": Ibid., p. 8.

218    "No city can grow bigger than its water supply": Ibid., p. 33.

218    "HOW BIG WILL LOS ANGELES GROW?" and "Southern California and Los Angeles have just started to grow": Ibid., p. 19.

218    "With our Owens River aqueduct": Ibid.

219    "A fraction of the water that each year": Ibid.

219    "It has not been necessary to draw": Ibid., p. 33.

220    voted unanimously to deny: Hoffman, *Vision*, p. 176.

220    No Name Siphon attack: Nadeau, *Water-Seekers*, p. 88, and Walton, *Western Times*, p. 176.

220    "a young Mississippi": Davis, *Rivers*, p. 163.

220    repairs of this most damaging assault: Standiford, *Angels*, p. 233, and Walton, *Western Times*, p. 176.

220    Mulholland assured Angelenos: C. Mulholland, *Mulholland*, p. 313.

220    "without using unprintable words": Nadeau, *Water-Seekers*, p. 88.

220    power plant at Big Pine Creek: Hoffman, *Vision*, p. 196, and Walton, *Western Times*, p. 173.

220  **near Cottonwood Creek:** Nadeau, *Water-Seekers*, p. 89.

221  **six hundred reservists and contingent of detectives:** Kahrl, *Water*, p. 305.

221  **a reward for information leading:** Walton, *Western Times*, p. 173.

221  **bombings continued:** Ibid., pp. 176–77.

221  **"A condition of civil war exists":** Clipping in LADPW-9, May–June 1927, Los Angeles Department of Water and Power Archives.

221  **both sides armed themselves:** Nadeau, *Water-Seekers*, pp. 89–90.

221  **stories of farmers committing suicide:** Kahrl, *Water*, p. 303.

221  **"unscrupulous officials" and "evil serpent":** LAR, May 31, 1927.

221  **"the lawless element of the valley":** Hoffman, *Vision*, p. 197.

222  **$250,000 in damage:** C. Mulholland, *Mulholland*, p. 314.

222  **"shooting the duck":** Nadeau, *Water-Seekers*, p. 91.

222  **no fewer than ten times:** Hoffman, *Vision*, p. 196.

222  **official request to President Calvin Coolidge:** Davis, *Rivers*, p. 164.

222  **obtain a financial statement:** Hoffman, *Vision*, p. 199.

222  **Wood's investigator:** Ibid., p. 198, and Nadeau, *Water-Seekers*, p. 92.

222  **Wattersons had defrauded:** the most complete rundown is in Hoffman, *Vision*, p. 199.

223  **some $2.3 million in missing funds:** Nadeau, *Water-Seekers*, p. 94.

223  **thirty-six counts of embezzlement and fraud:** Hoffman, *Vision*, p. 199.

223  **"The people of the valley are left in the worst":** Ibid., p. 200.

223  **Glasscock's suicide:** Nadeau, *Water-Seekers*, p. 95, and C. Mulholland, *Mulholland*, p. 315.

223  **Watterson brothers were found guilty:** Hoffman, *Vision*, p. 201, and Walton, *Western Times*, p. 191.

223  **Sexton's confession:** Nadeau, *Water-Seekers*, p. 96.

223  **over 90 percent of the water rights:** Walton, *Western Times*, p. 189. Ostrom, *Politics*, p. 123, puts the figure at 80 percent.

223  **"Justice? Why, there are not enough trees":** Kahrl, *Water*, p. 304. The newspaper—and Kahrl—redacted the epithet, but it seems likely the word used was "bastards."

224  **"Now, perhaps, the time has arrived":** Kahrl, *Water*, p. 311.

224  **Owens Valley economy had all but collapsed:** *Owens Valley Herald*, November 2, 1927, LADPW-11, Los Angeles Department of Water and Power Archives.

## 14. A SOUND PROPOSITION

226 return of Gloria Swanson: Swanson, *Swanson*, pp. 1–11, and Lombardi, *Allan Dwan*, p. 142.

226 "with the possible exception of my friend Mary Pickford": Swanson, *Swanson*, p. 4.

226 the classic *Manhandled*: Ibid., p. 214.

226 handsome but impoverished: Basinger, *Silent*, p. 227.

226 finalized a divorce: Swanson, *Swanson*, pp. 4–5.

226 botched abortion: Ibid., pp. 4-5; Lombardi, *Allan Dwan*, pp. 139–40.

226 "Suddenly I was not only Cinderella": Swanson, *Swanson*, p. 5.

227 "Two bands were playing": Ibid., p. 8.

227 "We caused a tremendous traffic jam": Ibid., pp. 9–10.

227 "People were standing and yelling": Ibid., p. 10.

228 "Hollywood has paid you": Ibid., pp. 10–11.

228 Swanson was its new ideal: Eyman, *DeMille*, pp. 150–52.

228 "Mary Pickford now acknowledges": Lombardi, *Allan Dwan*, p. 143.

228 new female icon: Zukor, *Public*, p. 221.

228 "the absolutely last word in chic": Basinger, *Silent*, p. 216.

228 town was full of Europeans: Knight, *Liveliest*, pp. 85–88.

228 most notably Germany's: Ibid., p. 52.

228 "We had counts and princes sousing film": Brown, *Adventures*, p. 208.

228 Actors like: For individual foreign talents brought to Hollywood, see Knight, *Liveliest*, pp. 65 and 110, and Brownlow, *Parade's Gone*, pp. 510–11.

229 "Lubitsch touch": Everson, *Silent*, p. 268.

229 "that naughty twinkle of Continental": Knight, *Liveliest*, p. 132.

229 sweeping cowboy epics: Everson, *Silent*, pp. 253–55, and Knight, *Liveliest*, p. 123.

229 comedies were now: Knight *Liveliest*, p. 124, and Sklar, *Movie-Made*, p. 116.

229 Fairbanks productions: Brownlow, *Parade's Gone*, p. 251.

229 proto-Lubitsch-style sex comedies: Robinson, *Twenties*, p. 87.

229 out of fashion more or less since *Intolerance*: Ibid., p. 89.

229 "one hundred percent cynical": Brownlow, *Parade's Gone*, p. 85.

230 *The Ten Commandments*: Eyman, *DeMille*, p. 204.

230 **cinematic titillation**: Sklar, *Movie-Made*, p. 95.

230 **"See your favorite stars"**: Knight, *Liveliest*, p. 116.

230 **grossed over $4.1 million**: Eyman, *DeMille*, pp. 202, 205.

230 **"Westminster Abbey"**: Ibid., pp. 119–20.

230 **like an autocratic general**: Ibid., p. 198, and Beauchamp, *First Time*, p. 72.

230 **"Just say that Moses and Aaron"**: Eyman, *DeMille*, p. 198.

230 **"want[ed] to do for the workers"**: Shiel, *Hollywood*, p. 115.

230 **Hays innovations**: Sklar, *Movie-Made*, p. 84.

231 **35,000 workers and $65 million payroll**: Shiel, *Hollywood*, p. 132.

231 **opening of each new studio**: Ibid., p. 152.

231 *Way Down East*: Brownlow, *Parade's Gone*, p. 80.

231 **"a horse-and-buggy melodrama"**: Gish, *Movies*, p. 229.

231 **biggest moneymaker since Birth**: Henderson, *Life*, p. 215.

231 *Orphans*: Everson, *Silent*, pp. 175–76.

231 **"dated conventions"**: Schickel, *Griffith*, p. 508.

232 **"Isn't it about time"**: Brownlow, *Parade's Gone*, p. 81.

232 **a high-minded historical film**: Schickel, *Griffith*, p. 486, and Henderson, *Life*, p. 246.

232 **garnished to pay back**: Slide, *Players*, p. 162.

233 **to serve as leverage**: Eyman, *DeMille*, p. 208.

233 **guarantee a loan**: Schickel, *Griffith*, p. 498.

233 **"There is a point in the life"**: Brownlow, *Parade's Gone*, p. 81.

233 **"Behind the headlines"**: Gish, *Movies*, p. 262.

233 **new to film, named W. C. Fields**: Schickel, *Griffith*, pp. 511, 646.

234 **"Mr. David Wark Griffith, saintly showman"**: Ibid., p. 517.

234 **Victorian starchiness**: Ibid., pp. 526–28.

234 **Lillian Gish's firing**: Gish, *Movies*, p. 248.

234 *The Sorrows of Satan*: Schickel, *Griffith*, pp. 517–58.

234 **recut by another**: Ibid., p. 523, and Gish, *Movies*, p. 292.

234 **notable bomb**: Schickel, *Griffith*, p. 525.

235 **gave interviews to the press**: Slide, *Players*, pp. 163, 180, and Schickel, *Griffith*, pp. 527–28.

235 **"In those days"**: Brownlow, *Parade's Gone*, p. 82.

235 **a suite at the Biltmore**: Schickel, *Griffith*, p. 529.

235  hireling for the company: Henderson, *Life*, p. 266.

235  "To D.W., the new Hollywood": Gish, *Movies*, p. 297.

235  "I believe deep down": Schickel, *Griffith*, p. 461.

235  talking motion pictures: For the advent of the talkies, Eyman, *Sound*, is a superb account.

236  Chronophone, Synchroscope: For early sound experiments, see ibid., pp. 26–35.

236  "The talking, instead of enhancing the picture": Ibid., p. 35.

236  conventional industry wisdom: Ibid., p. 43.

236  *Dream Street*: Gish, *Movies*, p. 241.

236  "It will never be possible to synchronize": Schickel, *Griffith*, p. 497.

236  Lee de Forest: Eyman, *Sound*, p. 41.

237  Western Electric's Vitaphone system: Ibid., p. 55.

237  five different sound systems: Ibid., p. 46.

237  "a gimmick" and "a toy": Ibid., p. 68.

237  little to lose and much to gain: Gabler, *Empire*, p. 198, and *Liveliest*, p. 145.

237  "I would never have gone": Eyman, *Sound*, p. 69.

237  New York Philharmonic: Gabler, *Empire*, p. 138, and Eyman, *Sound*, pp. 87–89.

237  "No single word is quite adequate": Ibid., p. 93.

237  "The house applauded, cheered": Eyman, *Sound*, pp. 103–4.

238  Fox's Movietone advances: Ibid., pp. 111–14.

238  "Instead of making the movies more real": Ibid., p. 105.

238  kill the foreign market: Robinson, *Twenties*, p. 166.

238  cost of installing the Vitaphone: Eyman, *Sound*, p. 118.

239  "sound is a passing fancy": Ibid., p. 160.

239  secretly hoping: Gabler, *Empire*, p. 138, and Eyman, *Sound*, p. 115.

239  *The Jazz Singer*: Gabler, *Empire*, pp. 140–41, and Eyman, *Sound*, pp. 131–32.

## 15. THE MISSING SAINT

242  talking on the telephone: Thomas, *Storming*, p. 39, and Epstein, *Sister*, p. 287.

242   note of complaint: Thomas, *Storming*, pp. 38–40.

242   headstrong and imprudent: Ibid., p. 40.

242   Minnie tried to warn her: For the reactions of Kennedy and Mrs. Ormiston, see Blumhofer, *McPherson*, p. 275, and Thomas, *Storming*, p. 39.

243   in the hopes that he'd quit: Blumhofer, *McPherson*, p. 275.

243   Rudolf Dunbar: Ibid., and Thomas, *Storming*, pp. 40–41.

243   lively, rose-strewn farewell: Thomas, *Storming*, p. 41.

243   Ormiston was traveling with Sister rumors: Ibid., pp. 41–42, and Epstein, *Sister*, p. 289.

244   returned to Ireland: For the rest of McPherson's journey, see Thomas, *Storming*, p. 43, and Blumhofer, *McPherson*, p. 280.

244   Kenneth Ormiston had called: Thomas, *Storming*, p. 43.

244   even more willful: Ibid., p. 44.

244   new strain of sarcasm: Sutton, *McPherson*, p. 92.

244   turn over the cash collected: Epstein, *Sister*, p. 292.

244   whirlwind of activity: McPherson, *Story*, p. 144, and Chronology.

244   "amusement zone": Sutton, *McPherson*, p. 92.

245   "We had dealt telling blows": McPherson, *Story*, p. 144.

245   a day at the beach: Ibid., pp. 145–46.

245   lanternslide talk: Blumhofer, *McPherson*, p. 282.

245   "I guess I'll have another swim": McPherson, *Story*, p. 146.

246   Frantic, she ran up and down: Epstein, *Sister*, p. 292.

246   Frank Langon: Ibid., p. 293.

246   "Sister is gone": Blumhofer, *McPherson*, p. 282.

246   extensive maritime searches: Epstein, *Sister*, p. 294, and Blumhofer, *McPherson*, p. 283. Blumhofer says the number of congregants at the beach was five thousand, not ten.

246   newspaper reporters and photographers: Blumhofer, *McPherson*, p. 283.

246   coverage of DeMille's premiere: Cox, *Verdict*, p. 1.

246   Speculation was rampant: Ibid., pp. 22, 24–25.

247   sea monster: Sutton, *McPherson*, p. 95.

247   "To swim back to shore": Ibid., p. 99.

247   Ormiston had also gone missing: Cox, *Verdict*, pp. 36–37.

247   "Aimee sightings": Ibid., pp. 27–28, and Thomas, *Storming*, p. 46.

247   sixteen different places: Cox, *Verdict*, p. 33.

247 "the person or persons": Thomas, *Storming*, p. 48, and Cox, *Verdict*, p. 34.

247 a ransom note arrived: Chronology, and Cox, *Verdict*, p. 41.

248 turned the note over to Cline: Cox, *Verdict*, pp. 41–42.

248 no one made contact: McPherson, *Story*, p. 153.

248 ransom note mysteriously disappeared: Cox, *Verdict*, pp. 41–42.

248 Ormiston turned up: Thomas, *Storming*, pp. 47–48, and Blumhofer, *McPherson*, pp. 285–86.

248 R. A. McKinley: Cox, *Verdict*, pp. 42ff.

248 "You will hear from us on Wednesday": Ibid., pp. 43–44.

248 meeting the next day: Ibid., pp. 44–45.

249 swirling rumors: Blumhofer, *McPherson*, pp. 285–86.

249 list of questions: Cox, *Verdict*, p. 45.

249 "1. Describe hammock": Ibid., p. 46.

249 extra copies of each daily edition: *Angelus Temple Bulletin*, June 13, 1926.

249 "We do not believe Sister's body": Thomas, *Storming*, p. 48.

249 twenty thousand mourners: Epstein, *Sister*, p. 295.

249 money would be used: In her autobiographies, McPherson denies that any funds collected at her memorial were to support creation of a monument.

249 another ransom note: Cox, *Verdict*, p. 51.

250 "a woven wire": All quotes come from my photograph of the framed copy of the ransom note on the wall of the Temple Parsonage. The note is also in Cox, *Verdict*, pp. 54–56.

251 "Don't talk!": Thomas, *Storming*, p. 49.

251 special Pullman car: Ibid.

251 her every word recorded: Blumhofer, *McPherson*, p. 287.

251 She began with the day: McPherson gave her account of the alleged kidnapping in *Story*, pp. 148–64.

251 a second, taller man: Some later accounts identify the third kidnapper as "Jake."

252 "I won't answer any more questions" and "If the locks of hair": McPherson, *Story*, pp. 154–55.

252 "where nobody can find you": Ibid., pp. 155–57.

252 "Now, dearie": Ibid., p. 156.

252 "Praise the Lord!": Ibid., p. 157.

252 Once free of her bonds: Ibid., pp. 157–63.

253 **certain incongruities:** Cox, *Verdict*, p. 77.

253 **ninety-plus–degree heat:** McPherson, *Story*, p. 217.

253 **could not locate the shack:** McPherson claimed that a cabin that could have been her desert prison was later found by a third party, but Keyes refused to investigate it.

253 **biggest media frenzies:** Epstein, *Sister*, p. 298, and Thomas, *Storming*, p. 53.

254 **at the railroad station to greet her:** Epstein, *Sister*, p. 299, and Thomas, *Storming*, p. 51.

254 **Sister was carried from the Pullman car:** Blumhofer, *McPherson*, pp. 291–92.

254 **"Many presidents":** Epstein, *Sister*, p. 301.

254 **"one little lie":** Sutton, *McPherson*, p. 102.

254 **a national laughingstock:** Thomas, *Storming*, p. 60, and Epstein, *Sister*, p. 300.

254 **holiday cottage in Carmel:** Ibid., p. 298.

255 **ignore the summons:** Blumhofer, *McPherson*, p. 293, and Epstein, *Sister*, p. 303.

255 **"I have never put my money":** McPherson, *Story*, pp. 187–90.

255 **"I would not work with one hand":** Ibid., p. 189.

255 **get an abortion:** Cox, *Verdict*, p. 88.

255 **grand jury voted:** Sutton, *McPherson*, p. 107, and Blumhofer, *McPherson*, p. 293.

256 **perjury and fraud:** Blumhofer, *McPherson*, p. 294, and Sutton, *McPherson*, p. 108.

256 **"love nest by the sea":** Sutton, *McPherson*, p. 109.

256 **Shuler continued to pound:** Ibid., p. 108, and Cox, *Verdict*, p. 127.

256 **"A dog may bark at a queen":** Sutton, *McPherson*, p. 108.

256 **Lorraine Wiseman-Sielaff:** Cox, *Verdict*, pp. 176–80.

256 **sold more L.A. newspapers:** Sutton, *McPherson*, p. 117.

257 **arrest warrants issued:** Ibid., p. 118.

257 **longest legal procedure of its kind:** Epstein, *Sister*, p. 309.

257 **"a three-legged legal stool":** McPherson, *Story*, p. 214.

257 **paid by the two major Los Angeles newspapers:** Sutton, *McPherson*, p. 137.

257 **flatly denied that the woman:** Cox, *Verdict*, p. 194, and Sutton, *McPherson*, p. 124.

258  wig or hair extensions: Ibid., p. 126.

258  "The effect was almost as stunning": Epstein, *Sister*, p. 309.

258  more disheveled and debilitated: Cox, *Verdict*, pp. 202, 214. See also "It's Time That the Truth Be Told," unsigned typescript, McPherson biography file, History Division, Los Angeles Central Public Library.

258  "ungovernable lying": Cox, *Verdict*, p. 203.

258  deem it sufficient: Thomas, *Storming*, p. 57.

258  three counts of criminal conspiracy: Epstein, *Sister*, p. 312.

258  taken to the radio every night: Thomas, *Storming*, p. 57.

258  "those who are opposed to the old-time religion" and "March of the Martyrs": Sutton, *McPherson*, p. 124.

259  "The Biggest Liar in Los Angeles": Blumhofer, *McPherson*, p. 297.

259  "It isn't me that my detractors hurt": Epstein, *Sister*, p. 308.

259  temple membership was booming: Chronology.

259  out of sympathy for how: Epstein, *Sister*, p. 307, and Sutton, *McPherson*, p. 126.

259  "guilty of unchastity": Blumhofer, *McPherson*, p. 297, and Sutton, *McPherson*, pp. 119, 302.

259  "It is unheard of": Blumhofer, *McPherson*, p. 297.

259  "the town Babbitts": Sutton, *McPherson*, pp. 119–20.

259  Keyes's case began: Cox, *Verdict*, p. 228, and Sutton, *McPherson*, p. 136.

260  "Let her be judged": Thomas, *Storming*, p. 62.

260  "a 1926 Miracle: Hollywood style": Sutton, *McPherson*, p. 137.

260  had paid Keyes a bribe: Cox, *Verdict*, p. 228.

260  Hearst who had pressured: Sutton, *McPherson*, p. 139.

260  prison for bribe-taking: Cox, *Verdict*, p. 7, and Sutton, *McPherson*, p. 137.

260  "It has been so hard": Thomas, *Storming*, p. 62.

260  "in a dirty hole": Ibid., p. 63.

260  "Get off the front pages": Epstein, *Sister*, p. 316.

260  "vindication tour": Sutton, *McPherson*, p. 138, and Blumhofer, *McPherson*, p. 300.

261  dozen other cities: McPherson, *King*, p. 313.

261  "The Story of My Life": Epstein, *Sister*, p. 317.

261  "The so-called 'case' had passed": McPherson, *King*, p. 276.

261  **radically changed her persona:** Thomas, *Storming*, pp. 66, 75, and Epstein, *Sister*, pp. 317–18.

261  **"The God of the Gospels is being replaced":** Ibid., p. 76.

261  **breaking his association:** Blumhofer, *McPherson*, p. 307.

261  **whether Sister had really:** Epstein, *Sister*, p. 320.

261  **a compromised phenomenon:** The question remains, was McPherson really kidnapped? Some writers, like Cox, believe so implicitly; others, like Thomas, clearly do not think it happened. Blumhofer, Sutton, and Epstein, meanwhile, are more circumspect. I myself am extremely doubtful that it all happened as she described. For me, the deciding factor is the correlation between McPherson's story and the Avenger's ransom note. In my opinion, the ransom note is obviously a fake, not only because of the unlikelihood of the story it tells but, more critically, because its wavering tone and unmotivated offering of details (like the kidnappers' having operatives at the temple, and so on) clearly signal a literary composition rather than a real-life ransom note. Since McPherson's story so closely adheres to an obviously fake document, I can only conclude that her story is similarly inauthentic. Having said that, I do not necessarily believe that she concocted the kidnapping story in advance in order to spend time with Kenneth Ormiston or any other person (especially since the Carmel evidence is very weak and was clearly coerced by Deputy DA Ryan). It's possible that McPherson had a mental breakdown of some kind—perhaps from extreme overwork—or perhaps the disappearance was a spontaneous act of rebellion that she eventually came to regret. It may also be, as Keyes suspected, that the story was created for publicity purposes (in which case it was fabulously successful). We will never know for sure. However, the story as she told it—of a kidnapping and a daring desert escape—has to be regarded with extreme skepticism by anyone applying the kind of reasonableness standard one must always apply to the reported events of history.

## 16. A SILENT TWILIGHT

264  **L.A. premiere of *King of Kings*:** Eyman, *DeMille*, pp. 242–44.

264  **Niblo's *Ben-Hur*:** Brownlow, *Parade's Gone*, pp. 385–414.

264  **"the most impressive":** Review quotes are in Eyman, *DeMille*, pp. 242–43.

265  **film's version of Mary Magdalen:** Ibid., p. 230.

265  **rabbis and the Jewish press:** Ibid., pp. 244–46.

265  **Griffith was still working in an office:** Schickel, *Griffith*, p. 533. (For a year-by-year Griffith filmography, see ibid., pp. 637–47.)

265 *Topsy and Eva*: Ibid., p. 532, and Usai, *Griffith Project*, pp. 10:205–6.

265 "I'll never use the Bible": Gish, *Movies*, p. 316.

265 *Drums of Love*: Schickel, *Griffith*, p. 539; Henderson, *Life*, p. 268; and Usai, *Griffith Project*, pp. 10:207–10.

266 Filming on *The Jazz Singer*: Eyman, *Sound*, pp. 135–36.

266 Jolson improvised some sound: Gabler, *Empire*, p. 153, and Eyman, *Sound*, pp. 137–38.

266 results confirmed every hope: Eyman, *Sound*, p. 145.

266 "I, for one, realized": Ibid., p. 141.

266 "The big producers": Ibid., p. 144.

266 "terror in all their faces": Ibid., p. 160.

266 climax of achievement: Brownlow, *Parade's Gone*, p. 572, and Robinson, *Twenties*, pp. 71, 94–95, 130–36.

267 "To compare *The Jazz Singer* with *Sunrise*": Beauchamp, *First Time*, p. 267.

267 Dialogue was hopelessly banal: For problems on early talkie sets, see Eyman, *Sound*, pp. 166, 189, 220–25, and Brownlow, *Parade's Gone*, p. 572.

267 "Everything that the silent screen had done": Eyman, *Sound*, p. 261.

267 "Lawrence, the romance": Lombardi, *Allan Dwan*, p. 166.

267 *The Lights of New York*: Eyman, *Sound*, pp. 175–76.

267 "Producers now realized": Brownlow, *Parade's Gone*, p. 571.

267 silent films be pulled: Eyman, *Sound*, pp. 179–80.

267 Murnau's *Four Devils*: Ibid., p. 187.

267 goat gland movies: Ibid., p. 208.

268 People started calling theaters: Ibid., p. 268.

268 released with minimal promotion: Ibid., p. 260.

268 shoddily filmed stage musicals: Knight, *Liveliest*, p. 154.

268 "times of trouble and test": Eyman, *Sound*, p. 270. It's available on YouTube (at https://www.youtube.com/watch?v=2rCZVjyCiBg).

268 sixty-seven movies: Figures on Paramount releases come from ibid., p. 259.

268 "Sound didn't do any more": Knight, *Liveliest*, p. 153.

268 Warners' asset base: Eyman, *Sound*, p. 360.

268 "One half [of Hollywood's] occupants": Ibid., p. 229.

268 John Gilbert and Ronald Colman: Ibid., 264, 300.

269   **Foreign actors with heavy accents:** Ibid., pp. 260ff.

269   **Sound engineers:** For effects felt in other fields, see ibid., pp. 185, 286.

269   **the directors:** Ibid., p. 192.

269   **DeMille, now under contract:** Eyman, *DeMille*, pp. 255, 265, 273.

269   *Drums of Love:* Schickel, *Griffith*, p. 539; Henderson, *Life*, p. 268; and Usai, *Griffith Project*, pp. 10:207–10.

269   **"I haven't got any brains":** Gish, *Movies*, p. 298.

270   **"Reviewing a Griffith picture":** Schickel, *Griffith*, p. 539.

270   *The Battle of the Sexes:* Schickel, *Griffith*, p. 643, and Usai, *Griffith Project*, pp. 10:211–12.

270   **"a badly acted, unimaginatively directed":** Schickel, *Griffith*, p. 543.

270   *Lady of the Pavements:* Schickel, *Griffith*, p. 545, and Usai, *Griffith Project*, pp. 10:219–20.

270   **already-completed shooting script:** Henderson, *Life*, p. 270.

271   **"Come, let's go back to your world":** Schickel, *Griffith*, p. 545.

271   **better financial shape:** Schickel, *Griffith*, p. 546, and Henderson, *Life*, p. 275.

271   **drank heavily:** Usai, *Griffith Project*, p. 10:218.

271   **life of Abraham Lincoln:** Schickel, *Griffith*, pp. 549–50.

271   **"We must preserve all the speed, action":** Usai, *Griffith Project*, p. 10:228.

271   **prestige (i.e., high-budget) production:** Usai, *Griffith Project*, p. 10:229.

271   **poet Carl Sandburg:** Bernstein's excellent *"The Movies Are"* collects Sandburg's film criticism.

272   **Sandburg did end up:** Schickel, *Griffith*, pp. 551–52.

272   **script fee was too high:** Usai, *Griffith Project*, p. 10:229.

272   **Stephen Vincent Benét:** Schickel, *Griffith*, p. 554, and Usai, *Griffith Project*, pp. 10:229–30.

272   **"I'll probably have to wheel in a Pulmotor":** Gish, *Movies*, p. 304.

272   **"If I don't get out of here soon":** Fenton, *Benèt*, p. 236.

272   **"a nightmare of mind and nerves":** Schickel, *Griffith*, p. 555.

272   **first-rate cast:** Usai, *Griffith Project*, pp. 10:226, 230.

272   **Crazy Ranch:** Schickel, *Griffith*, p. 555.

272   **Considine oversaw the final cut:** Henderson, *Life*, p. 274.

273   **a much-needed coup:** For the film's virtues, see Usai, *Griffith Project*, p. 10:231.

273 **one of the ten best films:** Henderson, *Life*, p. 274.

273 **"Reverting after all these years":** Reviews are quoted in Schickel, *Griffith*, pp. 556–57.

273 **"the first major historical film":** Ibid., p. 558.

273 **agreed to release Griffith:** Henderson, *Life*, p. 274, and Usai, *Griffith Project*, p. 10:231.

273 *The Struggle*: Gish, *Movies*, p. 314, claims the film was based on *The Drunkard*.

274 **"I knew how bad it was":** Schickel, *Griffith*, p. 563.

274 **straightforward tragic melodrama:** Usai, *Griffith Project*, p. 10:241.

274 **reception was a disaster:** Schickel, *Griffith*, p. 560.

274 **reviews were brutal:** Usai, *Griffith Project*, p. 10:241.

274 **"This is poor entertainment":** Henderson, *Life*, p. 278.

274 **"a true Griffith masterpiece":** Anthony Slide, according to Schickel, *Griffith*, p. 566. Other pro-*Struggle* critics in Usai are more measured but still, in my opinion, dead wrong.

274 **closed after one sparsely attended week:** Henderson, *Life*, p. 277.

274 **"I passed [Griffith] on the street":** Schickel, *Griffith*, p. 560.

274 **drunk from the night:** Ibid., p. 594.

274 **"He could not make movies the Hollywood way":** Gish, *Movies*, p. 314.

275 **changing culture of Hollywood:** Knight, *Liveliest*, p. 157; Shiel, *Hollywood*, p. 136; and Sklar, *Movie-Made*, p. 157.

275 **"When banks came into pictures":** Eyman, *DeMille*, p. 259.

275 **"Our old Hollywood was gone":** Eyman, *Sound*, p. 378.

## 17. A PERFECT DISASTER

278 **a solitary motorcyclist:** The best sources on the St. Francis Dam disaster, aside from the transcript of the coroner's inquest, are Outland's *Man-Made Disaster*, Wilkman's *Floodpath*, and Hundley and Jackson's *Heavy Ground*.

278 **Ace Hopewell, a carpenter:** Outland, *Man-Made*, p. 76, and Wilkman, *Floodpath*, pp. 92–93.

278 **six-hundred-acre reservoir:** Wilkman, *Floodpath*, p. 17.

278 **"I can make sixty":** inquest testimony as quoted in ibid., p. 92.

278 **Big Tujunga Canyon:** C. Mulholland, *Mulholland*, p. 320, and Nadeau, *Water-Seekers*, p. 97.

278  Geologically it was not: Kahrl, *Water*, p. 312.

278  August 1924: Nadeau, *Water-Seekers*, p. 97.

278  largest of seven dams: Standiford, *Angels*, pp. 238–39.

278  wanted to have completed: Wilkman, *Floodpath*, p. 60.

279  supply the city's needs for a full year: Kahrl, *Water*, pp. 311–32.

279  public announcement: Wilkman, *Floodpath*, p. 69.

279  filed suit against the city: Ibid., p. 73.

279  residents of the Owens Valley: Outland, *Man-Made*, p. 25.

279  would be Owens Valley water: C. Mulholland, *Mulholland*, p. 320.

279  concrete, still a relatively new: Wilkman, *Floodpath*, pp. 63–64.

279  *The Temptress*: Ibid., p. 83.

279  "kind of greasy": For workers' distrust of the rock, seee Outland, *Man-Made*, p. 34, and Nadeau, *Water-Seekers*, p. 98.

279  increasing the planned height: Wilkman, *Floodpath*, pp. 67, 71, and Outland, *Man-Made*, pp. 29–30.

279  height of 208 feet: Wilkman, *Floodpath*, pp. 3, 11, 77. Two hundred eight feet is the distance from the deepest excavation to the dam top; it was 185 feet from the streambed to the top.

280  two sizable cracks: Nadeau, *Water-Seekers*, p. 98.

280  "When concrete dries": Wilkman, *Floodpath*, p. 17.

280  sixty-seven city employees: Ibid., p. 88.

280  by the seepages of water: Outland, *Man-Made*, p. 44.

280  "Well, good-bye, Ed": C. Mulholland, *Mulholland*, p. 321.

280  Harnischfeger had grown increasingly worried: Outland, *Man-Made*, pp. 53–57, 71.

280  allegedly warned him: Ibid., p. 55.

281  muddy rather than clear: Wilkman, *Floodpath*, p. 11, and Outland, *Man-Made*, pp. 63–64.

281  The Chief and his deputy: Wilkman, *Floodpath*, pp. 12–17.

281  inspected the leak: Ibid., pp. 86–87.

281  By twelve-thirty p.m.: Outland, *Man-Made*, p. 66.

281  "Dave, I will move them": Wilkman, *Floodpath*, p. 182, and Outland, *Man-Made*, p. 72.

282  generated 90 percent of L.A.'s electricity: Wilkman, *Floodpath*, p. 17.

282  he heard a deep, ominous rumble: Ibid., p. 92, and Outland, *Man-Made*, p. 76.

282 lights of Los Angeles flickered: Outland, *Man-Made*, p. 77.

282 "a nibble or fish bite": Outland, *Man-Made*, p. 79.

283 "It went down in a heap": Wilkman, *Floodpath*, pp. 93–94.

283 Ray Rising woke: Outland, *Man-Made*, p. 78, and Wilkman, *Floodpath*, pp. 94–95.

283 Lillian Curtis lived: Wilkman, *Floodpath*, p. 95, and Standiford, *Angels*, pp. 242–43.

283 "The dam has broke!": Wilkman, *Floodpath*, p. 95.

284 "Everything went": Ibid., pp. 90, 95.

284 Raggio and Ruiz ranches: Ibid., p. 96.

284 "I could hear it coming": Outland, *Man-Made*, p. 82, and Wilkman, *Floodpath*, p. 96.

285 Silvey was still frantically: Outland, *Man-Made*, pp. 79, 82, and Wilkman, *Floodpath*, p. 95.

285 "It was just a mud flat" and "Ray, your lake is gone": Wilkman, *Floodpath*, pp. 96–97.

285 Van Norman was roused: Outland, *Man-Made*, pp. 96–97.

285 notification of the police departments: Ibid., p. 99.

285 automatic power switching: Wilkman, *Floodpath*, p. 92, and Outland, *Man-Made*, p. 92.

286 "Please, God. Don't let people be killed": C. Mulholland, *Mulholland*, p. 319.

286 Harry Carey Indian Trading Post: Wilkman, *Floodpath*, p. 97.

286 emerged from the narrow confines: Ibid., p. 98, and Outland, *Man-Made*, p. 91.

286 Mexican laborers: Wilkman, *Floodpath*, p. 82.

286 vulnerable, low-lying places: Ibid., p. 106.

286 it would be two hours: Outland, *Man-Made*, p. 131.

286 blowing up an oil switch: Ibid., p. 77.

286 "We heard a roaring noise": Wilkman, *Floodpath*, p. 97.

287 "ball of fire": Ibid., p. 99.

287 gigantic whirlpool: Outland, *Man-Made*, pp. 86, 106, and Wilkman, *Floodpath*, p. 102.

287 Of some 150 workers: Outland, *Man-Made*, p. 106.

287 Juan Carillo: Wilkman, *Floodpath*, p. 106.

287  emergency switchboard operators: Ibid., pp. 104, 108.

288  "Paul Revere of the St. Francis Flood": Outland, *Man-Made*, pp. 108–10, 121, and Wilkman, *Floodpath*, pp. 105–8.

288  almost two miles across: Wilkman, *Floodpath*, pp. 109, 113.

288  "At daybreak": Outland, *Man-Made*, pp. 129–30.

288  at approximately two-thirty a.m.: Ibid., p. 96.

289  "stood there with a cane": Wilkman, *Floodpath*, p. 115.

289  "a monstrous tombstone": Ibid.

289  Survivors in trees; woman on a water tank: Davis, *Rivers*, p. 176.

289  Thelma McCauley: Wilkman, *Floodpath*, p. 121.

289  unscathed or else they died: Nadeau, *Water-Seekers*, p. 101.

290  "It's a scene of horror": Davis, *Rivers*, pp. 177–78.

290  details of the toll: Standiford, *Angels*, p. 245.

290  "CORPSES FLUNG": Davis, *Rivers*, p. 179.

290  Paramount sent a movie crew: Wilkman, *Floodpath*, p. 122.

290  theories as to the cause: Davis, *Rivers*, pp. 181, 199, 202.

290  "RESIGN—NOW!": Ibid., p. 183.

290  "HANG MULHOLLAND": Wilkman, *Floodpath*, p. 137. Sources disagree on whether the sign said "HANG" or "KILL."

290  Death threats against the Chief: C. Mulholland, *Mulholland*, p. 326.

290  "slumped into his chair": Wilkman, *Floodpath*, p. 164, and Standiford, *Angels*, p. 247.

291  L.A. City Council passed: Outland, *Man-Made*, pp. 157–58, and Wilkman, *Floodpath*, p. 143.

291  Joint Restoration Committee: C. Mulholland, *Mulholland*, p. 324; Outland, *Man-Made*, pp. 149–50; and Nadeau, *Water-Seekers*, p. 101.

291  eager for a speedy settlement: Outland, *Man-Made*, p. 149, and Wilkman, *Floodpath*, p. 149.

291  personal injury lawyers: Outland, *Man-Made*, pp. 152–53.

291  Only a few dozen lawsuits: Ibid., p. 167.

291  complaints that Anglo victims: Wilkman, *Floodpath*, p. 151.

291  bad publicity: Outland, *Man-Made*, p. 168.

291  over $55,000 in relief funds: Wilkman, *Floodpath*, p. 139.

292  temple group called City Sisters: *Foursquare Crusader*, March 21 and April 18, 1928.

292  **late-night benefit:** Davis, *Rivers*, p. 184, and Wilkman, *Floodpath*, p. 140.

292  **inquest was convened:** Wilkman, *Floodpath*, p. 163.

292  **nine separate inquiries:** Kahrl, *Water*, p. 312; Hoffman, *Vision*, p. 204; Wilkman, *Floodpath*, p. 165; and Outland, *Man-Made*, p. 171.

292  **coroner's inquest in Ventura County:** Wilkman, *Floodpath*, p. 176.

292  **indictments for murder:** Ibid., p. 166.

292  **dead fish found:** Kahrl, *Water*, p. 313, and Wilkman, *Floodpath*, p. 167.

293  **"drowning half the people of Los Angeles" and "Do a DAMgood job":** Wilkman, *Floodpath*, pp. 168–69, and LAT, March 22, 1928.

293  **"the red herring":** Kahrl, *Water*, p. 313.

293  **security was beefed up:** Wilkman, *Floodpath*, p. 167.

293  **"Inquest over Victims":** Ibid., p. 176.

293  **those sixty-nine victims:** C. Mulholland says there were sixty-five, rather than sixty-nine, victims in L.A. County.

293  **grisly film footage:** Wilkman, *Floodpath*, p. 178.

293  **"The white-haired engineer" and "nearly 80 years of age":** LAT, March 22, 1928.

293  **"On an occasion like this":** Standiford, *Angels*, p. 248.

294  **"quite solid and impervious":** Wilkman, *Floodpath*, p. 180.

294  **defense of the concrete:** Ibid., p. 181.

294  **"I surely did":** Ibid.

294  **"Like all dams":** Ibid., pp. 181–82.

294  **"It never occurred to me":** Ibid., p. 182.

294  **"human aggression":** C. Mulholland, *Mulholland*, p. 325.

294  **"willing to take my medicine" and "If there is an error":** Wilkman, *Floodpath*, p. 190, and LAT, March 28, 1928.

294  **jury even made a field trip:** Ibid., p. 184.

295  **"rests upon the Bureau of Water Works":** "Verdict of Coroner's Jury," Los Angeles County Coroner, R625.4 L871. I'm indebted to Fred Barker for a copy of this document. Other details reported in Wilkman, *Floodpath*, pp. 205–10, and Standiford, *Angels*, p. 250.

295  **resigned:** There is disagreement on whether Mulholland officially retired in November (Nadeau, *Water-Seekers*, p. 104) or December (Wilkman, *Floodpath*, p. 226).

295  **"If I knew of anything":** C. Mulholland, *Mulholland*, p. 304.

296  **"Although never a soldier":** W. Mulholland, "Autobiography," p. 8.

## EPILOGUE: WORLD CITY

298 **civic parade:** For the City Hall festivities, see Brook, *Smoke*, p. 132.

298 **"a sheer gleaming tower":** Ibid., p. 133.

298 **L.A. County population at 2.2 million:** Waldinger and Bozorgmehr, *Ethnic*, p. 45.

298 **Other population figures**—e.g. "thirty-sixth largest—are from the 1900 and 1930 U.S. Census.

299 **establishment triumphalism:** Starr, *Material*, p. 123.

299 **polychromatic:** Deverell, *Whitewashed*, pp. 5–6.

299 **"the only Anglo-Saxon city":** Starr, *Material*, p. 137, and Romo, *East*, p. 11.

299 **transition from "Iowa-on-the-Pacific":** Waldinger and Bozorgmehr, *Ethnic*, p. 24.

299 **growth in the city's ethnic and nonwhite populations:** Ibid., p. 53, and Sitton, *Metropolis*, p. 161.

299 **Barrios:** Wakida, *LAtitudes*, p. 133.

299 **surpassed San Antonio:** Starr, *Material*, pp. 146–47.

299 **opening of the Hotel Somerville:** Sitton, *Metropolis*, p. 156.

299 **coming-of-age of the thriving black metropolis:** Hunt and Ramón, *Black*, pp. 60–63.

299 **Jews in Boyle Heights and Japanese in Little Tokyo:** Waldinger and Bozorgmehr, *Ethnic*, p. 51, and Starr, *Material*, p. 146.

299 **World War II brought heavy industry:** McWilliams, *Southern California*, p. 160, and Waldinger and Bozorgmehr, *Ethnic*, p. 7.

299 **splitting with United Artists:** Schickel, *Griffith*, p. 571.

299 **talkie remakes:** Henderson, *Life*, p. 283.

299 **honorary Oscar and Directors Guild membership:** Schickel, *Griffith*, pp. 583, 589.

299 **MoMA retrospectives:** Henderson, *Life*, p. 288.

300 **two plays:** Gish, *Movies*, p. 329, and Schickel, *Griffith*, p. 585.

300 **hardly strapped for money:** Brownlow, *Parade's Gone*, p. 84.

300 **Evelyn Baldwin:** Henderson, *Life*, p. 284.

300 **DeMille took matters:** Eyman, *DeMille*, pp. 288–97.

300 *One Million B.C.*: Henderson, *Life*, p. 287.

300 **in jail overnight:** Schickel, *Griffith*, p. 600.

300 Knickerbocker Hotel: Henderson, *Life*, p. 290.

300 "The father of the American film": Brownlow, *Parade's Gone*, p. 79.

301 media superstar: Sutton, *McPherson*, pp. 153–54.

301 Angelus Productions and *Clay in the Potter's Hands*: Thomas, *Storming*, p. 150, and Sutton, *McPherson*, p. 155.

301 weight loss and alleged facelift: Sutton, *McPherson*, pp. 159–60, 164.

301 evangelistic vaudeville act: Blumhofer, *McPherson*, pp. 336–37, and Sutton, *McPherson*, p. 181.

301 three times per week: Thomas, *Storming*, p. 330.

301 worldliness unsettled many: Blumhofer, *McPherson*, pp. 322–23.

301 elopement with David Hutton: Ibid., pp. 319–21.

301 "Let them walk out": Thomas, *Storming*, p. 67.

302 "The situation has become nearly intolerable": Ibid., p. 55.

302 "Aimee and Ma": Ibid., p. 155.

302 reconciliations and partings; alleged nose-breaking: Ibid., pp. 127, 158–59.

302 "Go up with Aimee": Ibid., pp. 94–97.

302 "It's just a comic strip": Ibid., p. 248.

302 controversies just kept erupting: Blumhofer, *McPherson*, pp. 365, 366, 370, and Thomas, *Storming*, pp. 292, 299, 325.

302 Roberta Semple suing the lawyer: Blumhofer, *McPherson*, p. 365.

302 "A news moratorium": Ibid., p. 370, and Thomas, *Storming*, p. 329.

302 commissary: Sutton, *McPherson*, pp. 186–89, and Blumhofer, *McPherson*, pp. 343–44.

302 "She literally kept most of that Mexican community alive": Sutton, *McPherson*, p. 196.

303 accidental overdose of Seconal: Ibid., p. 267.

303 fifty thousand mourners: Thomas, *Storming*, p. 341.

303 over six million members: Sutton, *McPherson*, p. 276.

303 Rising's civil trial: Davis, *Rivers*, pp. 251–52.

303 time at his ranch: C. Mulholland, *Mulholland*, p. 328.

303 "I see things, but they don't interest me": Nadeau, *Water-Seekers*, p. 104.

303 Mulholland visited Eaton: Ibid., pp. 109–10; Wilkman, *Floodpath*, p. 238; and C. Mulholland, *Mulholland*, p. 330.

304 "For three nights": Nadeau, *Water-Seekers*, p. 110.

304  **"The fact that the valley has developed":** Kahrl, *Water*, p. 317.

304  **1941 completion of Long Valley Dam and Colorado River aqueduct:** Davis, *Rivers*, p. 260.

304  **William Mulholland died:** C. Mulholland, *Mulholland*, pp. 330–31.

304  **"It was that damned dam that killed him":** Standiford, *Angels*, p. 252.

304  **appropriate tribute:** C. Mulholland, *Mulholland*, p. 331.

304  **greatest religious pluralism:** Sitton, *Metropolis*, p. 212.

304  **most lucrative creative industry:** Ibid., p. 269.

305  **stopping the city's rapid growth:** Fogelson, *Fragmented*, p. 273.

305  **broader-based economic foundation:** Waldinger and Bozorgmehr, *Ethnic*, pp. 13–18.

305  **"polycentric conurbation":** Ibid., pp. 60, 70.

305  **lacking monumental structures:** Shiel, *Hollywood*, p. 82.

305  **"Los Angeles, at first glance, is not quite real":** NYT, May 8, 1927, in Shiel, *Hollywood*, p. 79.

305  **"seventy-two suburbs":** Brook, *Smoke*, p. 245.

305  **"a constellation of plastic":** *Miami and the Siege of Chicago*; NYT, October 3, 2009.

305  **"a gigantic conglomeration of theme parks":** Brook, *Smoke*, pp. 96–97.

305  **L.A.'s water consumption in 2015 compared to 1970:** Wilkman, *Floodpath*, p. 273.

# PHOTO CREDITS

# ACKNOWLEDGMENTS

Books, like cities, are never solo creations, and I'm extremely grateful to a number of people for helping me transform a wild, inchoate idea into something solid and tangible.

I owe a particularly heavy debt to Fred Barker, a retired engineer who worked for many years at the Los Angeles Department of Water and Power. Fred, who is widely regarded as the DWP's unofficial historian, graciously agreed to go over all of the water-related sections of the book, and he set me straight on numerous points of history and engineering (including the physics behind a sag pipe and why it is really not an "inverted siphon," despite being described as such in so much of the aqueduct literature). Thanks go as well to the chain of people who first led me to Fred—journalist Randy Dotinga, who connected me with blogger and L.A. tour guide Richard Schave, who put me in contact with Christine Mulholland (the Chief's great-grandniece), who in turn steered me to Fred.

For the early Hollywood material I had similar help from author and friend Arnie Bernstein, who has written extensively on silent film. I'm also indebted to the formidable Hollywood scholar Cari Beauchamp, who kindly gave me a copy of a very hard-to-find lecture by Hobart Bosworth that proved to be an indispensable source for chapter 3 in particular.

I owe thanks to numerous other librarians, experts, and archivists on both sides of the country, including Jenny Romero and Louise Hilton of the Academy of Motion Picture Arts and Sciences' Margaret Herrick Library; Jon Klusmire, director, and Roberta Harlan, curator of Collections & Exhibits, at the Eastern California Museum in Independence, California; Bob Sigman, director, and Catherine Kravitz, collections manager, at the Lone Pine Film History Museum in the Owens Valley (thanks, too, to museum volunteer Maria Carillo); Robert Vaughn of the American Film Institute's Louis B. Mayer Library in L.A.; David H. Lawrence and Seth Goldman of the Neversink Valley Museum in Cuddebackville, New York; Ashley Swinnerton of the Museum of Modern Art's Film Study Center in New York City; and the staffs of the History Department at the Los Angeles Central Library, the USC libraries, and the Special Collections Department of the Oviatt Library at Cal State Northridge. (Thanks are due as well to those who, for one reason or another, prefer to remain anonymous.) As always, the University of Maryland's library collections were a godsend to an unaffiliated scholar from the community; I want to particularly thank the staffs of the McKeldin Library and the Hornbake Library's Media Services Department (where I spent many happy hours watching DVDs, VideoDiscs, and even VHS tapes of countless silent films). A special thank-you also goes to Deborah Bull, for her excellent assistance on picture research for the book.

For helping me feel at home in the city when I wasn't rooting around in libraries and archives, I'd like to give a shout-out to the West Coast friends who were always willing to meet up for a meal: the Natas Pastries posse of Jill Baer, Ken Blackwell, and Denis de Boisblanc; Ellie Baer and Terry Barge (when they weren't on the other side of the Pond); David Dunbar and Alison Brower; Gerd Ludwig; Mark Wexler; and, in La Jolla, Lisa Lytton and Tony Shugaar. Special thanks go to Lynell George, who played the double role of welcoming friend *and* resident expert. Lynell, an L.A.-born and -raised writer with New Orleans family roots who just happened to review my last book for the *Chicago Tribune*, was someone I clearly had to meet, given that those three cities were the subjects of my three most recent books. This urban trifecta aside, Lynell turned out to be both a fount of local knowledge and a delightful tour guide and dinner companion. I don't make a habit of seeking out the people who review me (even the ones who say nice things), but I am very happy to now have Lynell as a friend.

Two East Coast compadres deserve thanks as well: Dennis Drabelle, who lent me a dozen or so volumes from his impressive collection of books on early Hollywood (you'll get them back soon, Denny!), and my longtime pal Lisa Zeidner, who once again agreed to read the entire manuscript with an eye to ironing out the assorted tics and idiosyncrasies of my prose.

This is my third book with Crown Publishers, but somehow—because of the vagaries of the publishing industry—I have yet to finish one with the same editor I started with. (As Lady Bracknell might say, "To lose one editor may be regarded as a misfortune; to lose three looks like carelessness.") And yet it has all worked out beautifully, probably because the editors I've inherited have invariably turned out to be as terrific as the ones I lost. So while I was heartbroken when the wonderful Domenica Alioto left the company two years into this project, I was delighted when the marvelous Meghan Houser stepped in to pick up where Domenica left off; Meghan has proven to be a superb editor and an insightful, hardworking collaborator. Thanks this time also go to Crown's deep marketing, production, and design bench of Becca Putnam, Robert Siek, Jessica Heim, Elina Nudelman, and Elena Giavaldi. Meanwhile, to provide continuity through all three books, I've had a staunchly supportive publisher in Molly Stern and a great and energetic publicist in Dyana Messina. I'm also incredibly lucky to have the best agent in the business—Eric Simonoff at William Morris Endeavor—as my representative and friend.

Finally, as always, I want to thank my wife, Elizabeth Cheng, and our daughter, Anna Krist—who are the *sine qua non* of my existence.

# INDEX

# ABOUT THE AUTHOR

GARY KRIST is the author of the bestselling *Empire of Sin* and *City of Scoundrels*, as well as the acclaimed *The White Cascade*. He has also written five works of fiction.

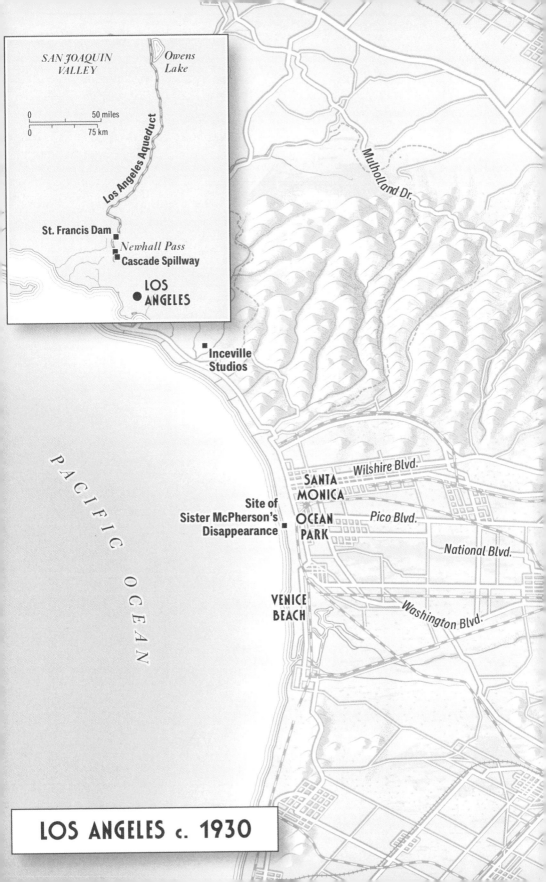

SAN JOAQUIN
VALLEY

Owens
Lake

0        50 miles
0        75 km

Los Angeles Aqueduct

St. Francis Dam

Newhall Pass
Cascade Spillway

LOS
ANGELES

Mulholland Dr.

Inceville
Studios

PACIFIC OCEAN

Wilshire Blvd.

SANTA
MONICA

Site of
Sister McPherson's
Disappearance

Pico Blvd.

OCEAN
PARK

National Blvd.

VENICE
BEACH

Washington Blvd.

LOS ANGELES c. 1930